the *Expositor's* WORD *for* EVERY DAY

Take up the Cross Daily
Luke 9:23-24

A DAILY DEVOTIONAL

BY JIMMY SWAGGART

ISBN 978-1-934655-66-5

09-139 • COPYRIGHT © 2015
15-054 15-055 15-056 15-057 15-058 15-059 15-060
Published by World Evangelism Press®
JIMMY SWAGGART MINISTRIES

366 Messages with the Cross of
Christ as the constant Theme

ISBN 978-1-934655-66-5
08-334
COPYRIGHT © 2005, 2011
15 16 17 18 19 20 21 22 23 24 / CNPC / 12 11 10 9 8 7 6 5 4 3
Published by, and the sole property of,
JIMMY SWAGGART MINISTRIES
P.O. BOX 262550
Baton Rouge, Louisiana 70826-2550
Website:www.jsm.org

INTRODUCTION

This Devotional is, I believe, the most unique Devotional of its kind in the world today. Every Message, for every day in the year, emphasizes the Cross of Christ in some way. Consequently, the help provided will be that which the Word of God always gives; the provision also will be, we think, extremely instructional.

As you read through this Daily Devotional, my prayer is that you will be brought in touch, hopefully, in a greater way than ever, with the price paid by our Saviour at the Cross of Calvary and with the Redemption we now possess. It did not come cheaply!

For each day of the year, you will find a Scripture dealing with the Cross, accompanied by a brief exegesis, that hopefully will guide you during your daily walk. I trust you will find comfort, encouragement, and inspiration in these pages.

This Daily Devotional is the product of a Revelation — a Revelation of the Cross — which has changed my life, even as the Cross has changed the lives of untold millions, and the Cross alone, I might quickly add. In fact, every life that has ever been changed, and without exception, has been through Christ as the <u>Source,</u> and the Cross as the <u>Means.</u>

Great effort has been made to bring you a book that I believe will truly bless your soul. I want you to see our concern for your spiritual life as the reason for bringing you this Daily Devotional.

May God bless you every day of your life, and may this Devotional play a part in that blessing, as hopefully the Word of God is opened up to you.

Jimmy Swaggart

Jimmy Swaggart

For information on *THE EXPOSITOR'S STUDY BIBLE* or *THE EXPOSITOR'S NEW TESTAMENT*, please call 1-800-288-8350 or visit our Website at www.jsm.org.

JANUARY
1

*i*n the beginning God created the heaven and the Earth (Gen. 1:1).

Beginnings are one thing, while endings are another!

On this first day of a brand-new year, which is a new beginning of sorts, the Lord offers to every person a brand-new beginning in their life, irrespective as to what the past has been. Millions this year will make New Year's resolutions, resolutions which invariably will not be kept. But there is a way that a brand-new beginning can be made, and irrespective as to what the past has been.

Too good to be true?

But yet, in the Lord Jesus Christ, it is true.

If you, Believer or unbeliever, will resolve at this moment to make Jesus the Lord of your life, realizing that every debt has been settled through the Cross, you truly can have a new beginning (Gal. 6:14).

For that beginning, a new beginning, first of all, one must realize that Jesus Christ, and Jesus Christ Alone, is

1

the Source; and we speak of the Source of all that you need, whatever it might be. However, the *"means"* by which Christ can do these great things in your heart and life is the Cross, as it is ever the Cross. Put your Faith in Him and what He has done for you at the Cross, and maintain your Faith in that Finished Work, and you, in effect, will have a new beginning, a miraculous, new beginning, and irrespective as to what the past has been (Jn. 3:16).

JANUARY

2

*a*nd the Earth was without form, and void; and darkness was upon the face of the deep. And the Spirit of God moved upon the face of the waters (Gen. 1:2).

The darkness that was here prevalent was taken away only by the *"Spirit of God,"* as He *"moved upon the face of the waters."* As someone has well said, *"The Moving of the Holy Spirit is the first sign of life."*

There is a darkness in the heart and life of every unbeliever. Regrettably, there is also a *"darkness"* in the hearts and lives of many Believers, because of wrong direction, erroneous doctrine, or failing to take advantage of God's Prescribed Order of Victory.

That *"darkness"* cannot be removed by humanistic psychology, by therapy, by a change of environment or scenery, or, in fact, by anything that man has to offer. But it can be removed!

Actually, the *"darkness"* that invades the soul of a man, bringing about guilt and condemnation, can only be

3

moved by the same manner in which God addressed the problem at the beginning of time. The Spirit of God moved, *"And God said, Let there be light: and there was light"* (Gen. 1:3).

That *"Light"* resides in Christ, for He said, *"I am the Light of the world"* (Jn. 8:12).

When you, as a Believer, put your Faith exclusively in Christ and what He has done for you at the Cross, the Holy Spirit will then move upon you, even as He did upon the *"face of the waters"* so long, long ago, and the darkness will go. It will be replaced by Light.

While it is the Holy Spirit Who will carry out the work, it is all through what Christ did for you at the Cross, which requires your Faith in that Finished Work.

At the very beginning, God gave the order. It is:

1. Darkness covers the unredeemed soul of man.

2. The Spirit of God moves upon the darkness of the unredeemed soul.

3. And God, said, *"Let there be Light,"* which redeems the soul.

JANUARY

3

*a*nd I will put enmity between you and the woman, and between your seed and her seed; it shall bruise your head, and you shall bruise His heel (Gen. 3:15).

This is the first mention of the Cross, although in shadow, after the Fall. The Lord told Satan through the serpent that victory would come by the *"Seed of the woman."* Ironically, woman has no seed, with the exception of One, Who was the Lord Jesus Christ. Christ bruised the head of Satan, and did so at Calvary's Cross. That's where Satan was totally and completely defeated (Col. 2:14-15).

The *"heel of Christ being bruised"* concerned the suffering, humiliation, and shame of the Cross (Heb. 12:2).

So, as to exactly how the Lord would do this, we now know after the fact; however, at the time that the Lord related this word to Satan, the Evil One knew that a Redeemer would be brought into the world through a woman, but no more information was given regarding how the Redemption would be effected.

God, however, keeps His Promises. For every person who will believe, and irrespective as to who that person is or what they have done, this which the Lord told Satan so long, long ago is now an accomplished fact. Satan's head was bruised at the Cross, and at great price, we might quickly add.

But here is the clincher:

All of it was done for you and me. Considering that, it is incumbent upon us to have the Blessing which the Cross affords. It is done simply by Faith, which pertains to placing our Faith exclusively in Christ and what He did for us at the Cross, and not allowing our Faith to be moved elsewhere. That is the secret of all blessings (Eph. 2:13-18).

JANUARY

4

*U*nto Adam also and to his wife did the LORD God make coats of skins, and clothed them (Gen. 3:21).

Immediately after the Fall, Adam and Eve lost the light which had enswathed them before the Fall; they are now naked, and more than all naked to the Judgment of God (Gen. 3:7). As a result, they *"sewed fig leaves together and made themselves aprons."*

Regrettably, man has been trying to cover his spiritual nakedness with fig leaves from then until now.

When they finally had to answer to the Lord, the Bible tells us that the LORD God *"made coats of skins, and clothed them."* For this to be done, the Lord had to kill one or more animals, which necessitated blood being shed. The skins were then taken from these animals and used to supply clothing or a covering for Adam and Eve.

The death of the animal or animals was the first symbol of Christ, Who would give His Life in order to cover the sins of man.

7

And let the Reader understand:

Anything man attempts to use to cover his sins, other than the Precious Shed Blood of the Lord Jesus Christ, is looked at by God as *"fig leaves,"* rating it totally unacceptable. The Blood of Jesus Christ alone can cleanse from all sin, which then makes possible the Righteousness of God as a covering — all made possible by the Cross (I Jn. 1:7).

JANUARY
5

*a*nd in process of time it came to pass, that Cain brought of the fruit of the ground an offering unto the LORD. And Abel, he also brought of the firstlings of his flock and of the fat thereof. And the LORD had respect unto Abel and to his offering: But unto Cain and to his offering He had not respect. And Cain was very wroth, and his countenance fell (Gen. 4:3-5).

There is no difference between the two brothers, Cain and Abel, but an eternal difference between their sacrifices. They are both corrupt branches of a decayed tree, both born outside Eden, both guilty, both sinners, no moral difference, and both sentenced to death.

The words, *"by faith"* (Heb. 11:4), teach that God had revealed a way of approach to Himself (Rom. 10:17). Abel accepts this way; Cain rejects it.

Abel's Altar speaks of Repentance, of Faith, and of the Precious Blood of Christ, the Lamb of God without blemish. Cain's altar tells of pride, unbelief, and self-righteousness. Abel's Altar is beautiful to God's eye and repulsive to man's; Cain's altar, beautiful to man's eye and repulsive to God's.

These *"altars"* exist today. Around the one, that is, Christ and His Atoning Work, few are gathered; around the other, many. God accepts the slain lamb and rejects the offered fruit; the offering being rejected, so, of necessity, is the offeror.

We must ever understand that God looks at the sinner not at all, because there is no point. He knows instantly what the sinner is. He looks at the Offering, and the only Offering that He will accept is the Sacrifice of Christ. Any other offering is immediately rejected!

The only way to God is through Jesus Christ (Jn. 14:6).

The only way to Jesus Christ is through the Cross (Lk. 9:23).

The only way to the Cross is by an abnegation of self (Lk. 9:23).

JANUARY

6

*a*nd Noah built an Altar unto the LORD; and took of every clean beast, and of every clean fowl, and offered Burnt Offerings on the Altar. And the LORD smelled the sweet savor . . . (Gen. 8:20-21).

Noah built an Altar and worshipped; not the Altar, but God. The Altar was the instrument of his Salvation, as the Cross was Paul's, and of every other Believer who has ever lived. But the Apostle did not worship the Cross, as multitudes do today, but worshipped Him Who died upon it.

The *"Altar"* built by Noah and the sacrifices offered upon it were symbols of Christ and what He would do to redeem the lost sons of Adam's fallen race. When Noah offered up his sacrifices, even as commanded by the Lord, the Scripture says that *"the LORD smelled a sweet savor."*

What could have been *"sweet"* about the carcass of an animal being burned to a crisp on an Altar?

The *"sweet savor"* had to do with what it represented,

which was the Coming Redeemer, Whose Coming and Sacrifice of Himself would redeem fallen humanity.

Let the Reader understand:

The Lord *"smells a sweet savor"* only as it regards our Faith in Christ and what He did for us at the Cross. This means that everything else is repugnant to Him, coming up rather as a *"stink"* in His nostrils.

That rules out every fad, every scheme, anything and everything for that matter, which is not anchored solely in *"Jesus Christ and Him Crucified"* (I Cor. 1:23).

Every single Believer should, therefore, check very carefully as to what his Pastor is preaching, or his favorite TV Evangelist, etc. If he or she is not preaching the Cross, there is no *"sweet savor"* going up to the Lord, but something else entirely!

JANUARY

7

*a*nd the LORD appeared unto Abram, and said, Unto your seed will I give this land: and there built he an Altar unto the LORD, Who appeared unto him (Gen. 12:7).

Abraham is referred to as the *"Altar builder."* Why did he build so many Altars?

Whenever the Lord spoke to Abraham, and Abraham heard and yielded, which was the moment of his conversion, the Lord also made it very clear to Abraham as to the manner in which man was to approach God. It only could be through the sacrifice of a clean animal, which necessitated the shedding of blood, all which symbolized Christ. That was the only way that God could converse with man — any man. God accepts nothing from humanity except it comes by the way of the Cross.

That's the reason that Abraham had to build a new Altar everywhere he went. There was no other way to converse with the Lord.

It has not changed even unto this moment. Man can

13

come to God only by the way of the Cross (I Cor. 2:2).

This means if the Church is not preaching the Cross, then whatever that particular Church is doing is totally unacceptable to God. This means every person who attends such a Church, for whatever reason they are attending, is not attending for the Lord, but for something else entirely. Such a course spells disaster!

Find a Church which *"builds the Altar,"* i.e., *"trusts in Christ and what He did at the Cross"*; there life and victory will be found (I Cor. 1:17-18, 21, 23; 2:2).

JANUARY

8

*a*nd he removed from thence unto a mountain on the east of Beth-el, and pitched his tent, having Beth-el on the west, and Hai on the east: and there he built an Altar unto the LORD, and called upon the Name of the LORD (Gen. 12:8).

"Beth-el" means "House of God." "Hai" means "garbage dump."

The Altar alone, typifying the Cross, can keep the Believer away from the garbage dump.

It is virtually impossible for the Believer to know the difference between the "House of God" and the "garbage dump" other than by the Cross. That's the reason we have so much false doctrine presently and so many Christians following false doctrine. For the last several decades, the Church has drifted so far from the Cross that it hardly knows any more where it has been, where it is, or where it is going. Because it no longer plants its doctrines on the foundation of the Cross, it has lost completely its moorings.

15

Without an understanding of the Cross, there is absolutely no discernment regarding false doctrine.

That's the reason that Paul said:

"Now the Spirit speaks expressly, that in the latter times (the times in which we now live) *some shall depart from the Faith, giving heed to seducing spirits, and doctrines of devils"* (I Tim. 4:1).

A *"departure from the Faith,"* i.e., *"Christ and Him Crucified,"* is the reason!

Never forget:

Satan dresses up his *"garbage dumps"* to look like something else altogether. In other words, they look like anything but garbage dumps; and, without an understanding of the Cross, invariably that's the way the Believer will go (Gal. 6:14).

JANUARY
9

*a*nd *he believed in the LORD; and He counted it to him for Righteousness* (Gen. 15:6).

If one properly understands this one Verse of Scripture, then one basically understands the entirety of the Bible.

What is it that Abraham believed?

First of all, *"he believed in the LORD."* And what does that mean?

Regarding the dealings of the Lord with Abraham, this means that Abraham believed that God ultimately would send a Redeemer into this world and would do so through his offspring. The Apostle Paul, in addressing this very thing, said, *"Now to Abraham and his seed were the Promises made. He said not, And to seeds, as of many; but as of One, and to your Seed, which is Christ"* (Gal. 3:16).

So, the entire nation of Israel, which would come from the loins of Abraham and the womb of Sarah, was but for one reason, and that was to bring forth *"One Seed, which is Christ."* That *"Seed"* was brought forth for one reason, and one reason only, and that was to go to the Cross, which was necessary, that is, if the terrible sin debt was to be paid, and man thereby redeemed.

In essence, *"Christ and Him Crucified"* presents the entirety of the story of the Bible. Consequently, that's where my Faith and your Faith had better be anchored (Rom. 4:3).

JANUARY
10

*a*nd Sarah saw the son of Hagar the Egyptian, which she had born unto Abraham, mocking. Wherefore she said unto Abraham, Cast out this bondwoman and her son: for the son of this bondwoman shall not be heir with my son, even with Isaac (Gen. 21:9-10).

The effect of the birth of Isaac was to make manifest the character of Ishmael. Ishmael hated Isaac and so did his mother, Hagar. Prompted by her, Ishmael sought to murder Isaac (Gal. 4:29), and, with his mother, was justly expelled. Both merited the severer sentence of death. Thus, the birth of Isaac, which filled Sarah's heart with joy, filled Hagar's with murder.

Isaac and Ishmael symbolize the new and the old natures in the Believer. Hagar and Sarah typify the two covenants of works and Grace, of bondage and liberty (Gal., Chpt. 4). The birth of the new nature demands the expulsion of the old. It is impossible, in fact, to improve the old nature. In the Eighth Chapter of Romans, the Holy

19

Spirit says it is *"enmity against God: for it not subject to the Law of God, neither indeed can be."*

If, therefore, the old nature cannot be subject to the Law of God, how can it be improved?

How foolish, therefore, appears the doctrine of moral evolution!

The Divine way of holiness is to *"put off the old man"* just as Abraham *"put off"* Ishmael. Man's way of holiness is to improve the *"old man,"* that is, to improve Ishmael. The effort is both foolish and hopeless.

The only way the *"old man,"* which refers to the old way, the way of the flesh, can be put off is by the Believer evidencing and maintaining Faith in Christ and the Cross. As the Cross is the only answer for *"sin,"* it also is the only answer for *"self"* (Lk. 9:23-24).

JANUARY

11

*a*nd Abraham lifted up his eyes, and looked, and behold behind him a ram caught in a thicket by his horns: and Abraham went and took the ram, and offered him up for a Burnt Offering in the stead of his son. And Abraham called the name of that place Jehovah-Jireh: as it is said to this day, In the mount of the LORD it shall be seen (Gen. 22:13-14).

The name, "Jehovah-Jireh," means "the LORD will see" or "provide."

Provide what?

He will provide a Redeemer, which all of this, as it regards the proposed offering of Isaac, represented.

The great test of Faith which the Lord required of Abraham, as it regards the proposed offering up of his son Isaac, was for the purpose of telling the great Patriarch how mankind would be delivered. It would be by and through the Death of God's Only Son, of which Isaac was a Type.

However, as the Lord told Abraham of the <u>manner</u> of

21

Redemption, which would be by death, He did not tell him <u>how</u> this death would be brought about, which would be by the Cross. That information would be given to Moses some 400 years later (Num. 21:8-9).

22

JANUARY

12

*a*nd Esau said to Jacob, Feed me, I pray you, with that same red pottage; for I am faint: therefore was his name called Edom. And Jacob said, Sell me this day your birthright. And Esau said, Behold, I am at the point to die: and what profit shall this birthright do to me? And Jacob said, Swear to me this day; and he swore unto him: and he sold his birthright unto Jacob (Gen. 25:30-33).

The birthright was to go to the firstborn. In this case, it was Esau. It pertained to the Father's Blessing involving Supremacy. It also included a Double Portion of the family estate. Last of all, it concerned the Domestic Priesthood.

The Domestic Priesthood meant that the oldest son acted as Priest for the family and offered the Sacrifices which God had commanded Adam and his sons to offer. Officiating the Sacrifices meant that the firstborn knew and understood that this was a symbol of the Coming Redeemer. But the Scripture says that Esau had no regard for any Coming Redeemer. He was interested only in the now and present. So it would not be as was intended, *"The God of Abraham, of Isaac, and of Esau."* Esau had no faith in that of which we speak.

Jacob, deplorable as was his character, valued Divine and Eternal Blessings. So he tried to purchase the Birthright; he found, to his dismay, that such cannot be done. God has nothing for sale. Everything He has is a *"Gift"* (Jn. 3:16). Had Jacob placed himself in God's hands at the beginning, the Prophecy made to his mother before he was born (Gen. 25:23) would have been fulfilled to him without the degradation and suffering which his own scheming brought upon him.

Regrettably, the entirety of the world and most of the Church, as Esau, have no regard for the birthright, i.e., *"the Cross of Christ."* And then the few in the Church who do regard the birthright, i.e., *"the Cross,"* all too often try to obtain it by means other than Faith.

It can be gained only by Faith (Rom. 5:1).

JANUARY
13

*a*nd he dreamed, and behold a ladder set up on the Earth, and the top of it reached to Heaven: and behold the Angels of God ascending and descending on it (Gen. 28:12).

Jesus spoke of this ladder when He began His public Ministry. He said to Nathanael, *"Verily, verily, I say unto you, Hereafter you shall see Heaven open, and the Angels of God ascending and descending upon the Son of Man"* (Jn. 1:51).

That ladder, as Jacob saw it, was closed to all but the Angels. In other words, due to the terrible sin debt upon man, even believing man, Heaven was closed to all. Believers who died before the Cross did not go to Heaven, but rather down into Paradise, where they actually were held captive by Satan (Eph. 4:8). They were comforted in Paradise; however, there was only a gulf which separated Paradise from Hell (Lk. 16:19-31).

But when Jesus died on the Cross, the sin debt was forever paid. Now that ladder is open not only to Angels, but also to all Believers.

25

The moment the Cross was a fact, Jesus went down into the nether parts of the Earth, and made those who had been all of this time captives of Satan, His captives, and took them with Him home to Glory. Now when a Believer dies, he instantly goes to be with Jesus (Phil. 1:23), all made possible by the Cross.

JANUARY

14

*a*nd Jacob was left alone; and there wrestled a Man with him until the breaking of the day (Gen. 32:24).

God had a controversy with Jacob because of his faulty life. When, as a consequence, he found himself in deadly peril and realized that God Himself was behind that peril, and that it really was not with Esau his brother that he had to contend, but rather with the Angel of Jehovah Himself, he then learned a valuable lesson. When sore broken by that Mighty Hand, when he ceased to wrestle and clung instead with weeping and supplication to the very God Who wounded him, it was then he got the victory and the glorious name of *"Israel."*

The great principle that God cannot give victory *"to the flesh"* appears in this night scene. It is the broken heart that begins to experience what Divine Power means. Better for the sun to rise upon a limping Israel than to set upon a lying Jacob.

Jacob, for his misconduct, was exiled from the

27

Promised Land, having nothing but his staff. He returns a wealthy prince, but lamed. So Israel, cast out of Jehovah's land because of her sin, also will return with abundance, but broken and contrite in spirit, all typified by Jacob.

God had to cripple the *"flesh"* in Jacob, as He has to cripple the flesh in us. It can only be done one way:

As you, the Reader, will learn in this Devotional, it is the Holy Spirit Alone Who can subdue the flesh. He demands only one thing of us, and that is that our Faith be anchored squarely in Christ and the Cross, never wavering.

Paul said:

"For the Law of the Spirit of Life in Christ Jesus has made me free from the Law of sin and death" (Rom. 8:2).

JANUARY

15

*a*nd Jacob called unto his sons, and said, Gather yourselves together, that I may tell you that which shall befall you
in the last days (Gen. 49:1).

The Holy Spirit, in Hebrews 11:21, points to Jacob's
action in this Chapter as the great faith action of his life.
Feeble and dying, and having nothing except the staff on
which he leaned and worshipped, he yet bestowed vast
and unseen possessions on his grandsons.

First he recited the Gift of the Land of Canaan to him
by God (Gen. 49:3-4). Then, making Joseph his firstborn
(Gen. 49:22), he adopts Joseph's two sons as his own
(*"Even as Reuben and Simeon, they shall be mine"*), and setting the younger above the elder, endowed them with the
firstborn's double portion. It was a beautiful picture of a
faith that was Divine, intelligent, and triumphant.

The double portion given to Joseph as the firstborn was
a conquered portion (Gen. 49:22). The possession given
by God to the Divine Firstborn among many brethren, the

29

Lord Jesus Christ, is also a conquered possession, i.e., it was done at the Cross, and it redeemed His People out of the land of the enemy — the Amorite, one might say.

Everything Jacob said came to pass, and everything our Heavenly Jacob has promised us will also come to pass. The Cross has made it all possible! (Rom. 6:1-14)

JANUARY
16

*S*peak ye unto all the congregation of Israel, saying, In the tenth day of this month they shall take to them every man a lamb, according to the house of their fathers, a lamb for an house (Ex. 12:3).

The lamb, and all that pertained to it, symbolized Jesus in His Atoning Work.

1. *"Your lamb shall be without blemish"*: Jesus was without blemish.

2. *"A male of the first year"*: Jesus was the Second Man, the Last Adam (I Cor. 15:45, 47).

3. *"And you shall keep it up until the fourteenth day of the same month"*: This was for further inspection in order that no blemish be found. For 33 1/2 years no fault was found with Christ. Satan had no part in Him.

4. *"The congregation of Israel shall kill it in the evening"*: Jesus would die at the time of the evening Sacrifice, 3 p.m.

5. *"And they shall take of the blood, and strike it on the two side posts and on the upper door posts of the houses"*: As

31

the blood of the lamb was shed, Christ shed His Life's Blood. As the blood of the lamb was to be applied to the houses, likewise, and by faith, it is to be applied to our hearts and lives (Eph., Chpt. 2).

6. *"And they shall eat the flesh, and let nothing of it remain"*: One must partake of all of Christ, which refers to believing all He did for us at the Cross.

7. *"The lamb was to be eaten with unleavened bread"*: This typified the perfection of Christ. There was no evil, i.e., *"leaven,"* in Him.

8. *"And you shall eat it; with your loins girded, your shoes on your feet, and your staff in your hand"*: As Israel was leaving Egypt (and they were to be prepared to leave at a moment's time), likewise, the believing sinner, upon accepting Christ, is to leave the world and its system behind, and do so forever.

JANUARY
17

*a*nd the blood shall be to you for a token upon the houses where you are: and when I see the blood, I will pass over you, and the plague shall not be upon you to destroy you, when I smite the land of Egypt (Ex. 12:13).

He said, *"When I see the blood,"* not *"When I see your particular Church,"* or *"your good works,"* or *"your particular Denomination,"* or whatever! It's *"When I see the blood, I will pass over you."*

The worthiness of the person is not taken into question, simply because, in the eyes of God, there is no worthiness. The goodness of the person is also not taken into question, simply because, in the eyes of God, no one can really be called *"good."* That which characterizes acceptance by God is that the Blood of His Son, the Lord Jesus Christ, which refers to what He did for us at the Cross of Calvary, be applied to our hearts and lives, which is done by Faith (Rom. 5:1; Eph. 2:8-9).

This simply means that both the believing sinner

and the believing Christian are to place their Faith exclusively in Christ and what Christ did for us at the Cross (Rom. 6:1-14).

The Holy Spirit states in I Corinthians 5:7 that the Passover pictured Christ's Sacrifice of Himself in order to save sinners sentenced to die. Two great facts appear in the first Passover: the certain doom of the firstborn and his certain Salvation. He was doomed to death by God, not because of his conduct, but because of his birth. This latter fact, he could not alter; and he was, therefore, hopelessly lost. He was, however, absolutely saved, because of the value of the life sacrificed for him. He knew he was saved because God had pledged Himself to most certainly save all who sprinkled the shed blood upon the door posts, all a Type of the price Jesus would pay on Calvary's Cross in order that we might be saved (Jn. 3:16).

JANUARY
18

*a*nd this day shall be unto you for a memorial; and you shall keep it a feast to the LORD throughout your generations; you shall keep it a feast by an ordinance forever *(Ex. 12:14).*

All sinners are justly doomed by God to death. But He loves them as He loved the firstborn; therefore, the Lamb of God has suffered that death. His Precious Blood, that is, His Priceless Life poured out, attests the fact.

The Word of God promises eternal safety to anyone who will seek Salvation in that Atoning Saviour. The Believer in Christ knows, therefore, that he shall never perish; and this knowledge is based on two facts outside of himself, which are:

1. The preciousness of Christ's Blood to God.
2. The Faithfulness of God to His Own Promise.

Israel was to keep the Passover *"for a memorial,"* and was to do so *"forever."* This referred to the fact that their Salvation, prosperity, freedom, and strength all were derived from *"the Blood of the Lamb."* It has not changed for the modern Believer. Everything we are, and I speak of Righteousness, can only be credited to the Shed Blood of the Lamb.

All of this represented the Cross, which means that it must ever be the anchor and the Object of our Faith (Eph. 2:13-18).

JANUARY
19

*t*hen sang Moses and the Children of Israel this song unto the LORD, and spoke, saying, I will sing unto the LORD, for He has triumphed gloriously: the horse and his rider has He thrown into the sea (Ex. 15:1).

The Red Sea and the Jordan River typify the Death and Resurrection of Christ. The Red Sea pictures death to sin; the Jordan, death to self. The one separates from Egypt; the other, from the wilderness.

Moses began and ended his wilderness life with a song. That of Deuteronomy 32:1-43 is the one referred to in Revelation 15:3. There was no singing in Egypt; there only was groaning. Singing only follows Redemption.

This, the song of Exodus 15, is the oldest song of praise in existence. The greatest poets unite in admiration of its surpassing beauty and sublimity. It is a song of praise; its theme is Jehovah-Jesus; and it praises Him for His destruction of the enemy. It begins with Redemption and ends with Glory. In fact, this is the first of ten songs of praise recorded in the Bible; the last is Revelation 14:3.

"Self" is absent from this song; it is all about Jehovah and His Power to save, all brought about by the death of the Pascal Lamb, which typified Jesus and the price that He would pay at Calvary's Cross. The Cross alone sponsors Redemption's song!

JANUARY

20

*a*nd he cried unto the LORD; and the LORD showed him a Tree, which when he had cast into the waters, the waters were made sweet: there He made for them a Statute and an Ordinance, and there he proved them (Ex. 15:25).

We find here that God tests faith in order to strengthen and enrich it. This test can come at any time, either before a great victory or after a great victory. Israel journeyed three days in the wilderness and found no water. When water was found, there was an added trial — the water was bitter.

The *"bitterness"* typifies life's journey. At times, it's not a pleasant journey. There is only one answer to the episodes of bitterness that come to every Believer; it is the Cross of Christ. As *"bitterness"* represented the pitfalls of life, which cannot be escaped, likewise, the *"Tree"* represents the Cross.

Facing the *"bitter waters,"* Moses *"cried unto the LORD."* That is what every Believer should do. An answer is guaranteed. It is found here in God's Word. The Lord told Moses to cut down a *"Tree"* which was growing nearby. It was to be *"cast into the waters."* That being done, *"the waters were made sweet."*

In this episode, the Lord is telling us that the Cross is the answer to every problem. If the *"Tree"* would be placed into the vicissitudes of life, we will find that the Lord will turn the bitterness into sweetness. As here enjoined, the answer is the Cross, always the Cross! (I Pet. 2:24-25).

JANUARY
21

*a*nd said, *If you will diligently hearken to the voice of the LORD your God, and will do that which is right in His sight, and will give ear to His Commandments, and keep all His Statutes, I will put none of these diseases upon you, which I have brought upon the Egyptians: for I am the LORD Who heals you* (Ex. 15:26).

In this episode of the bitter waters of Marah, we find that the Lord gives a great Promise to Moses, and, in fact, to every Believer. It is a Promise of Divine Healing, which addresses itself not only to physical needs, but also to emotional needs, typified by the *"bitter waters"* of Ex. 15:25.

But yet the Promise has a qualification, a qualification which is impossible for us as human beings to meet.

We are to *"give ear to His Commandments, and keep <u>all</u> His Statutes."* That being the case, He has promised to keep us free from *"diseases,"* etc.

But, as stated, what human being can say that he has always kept all of God's Commandments and Statutes?

41

The answer: None!

However, the door is not closed. There is One, only One, Who has always kept all of God's Commandments and Statutes. And that is all that is needed! The *"One"* is the Lord Jesus Christ. He did it all as the Second Man and the Last Adam (I Cor., Chpt. 15); He did it all on our behalf.

Our Faith and trust exclusively in Him and what He has done for us at the Cross guarantees us His Perfection and all the benefits which go with that Perfection.

Need I say more?! (Rom. 8:1-2, 11).

42

JANUARY

22

*a*nd when the Children of Israel saw it, they said one to another, It is Manna: for they wist not what it was. And Moses said unto them, This is the Bread which the LORD has given you to eat (Ex. 16:15).

The Manna prefigured the descent of the True Bread, of which if a man eat he shall live forever (Jn. 6:51). It was a test of appetite and of obedience. In Egypt, Israel had slave food; in the desert, Angel's food. The test quickly revealed that the natural man has no appetite for Heavenly things. The people soon called it *"light food."*

The Manna was so precious that it could not bear contact with the earth. It fell upon the dew and had to be gathered ere the sun was up, and freshly every morning. Yesterday's Manna did not do for today, nor today's for tomorrow (Num., Chpt. 9). Thus, must the Christian feed upon Christ every day, as He reveals Himself in the Scriptures (Lk. 9:23-24).

Israel in the desert presents a striking picture! Egypt

behind them, Canaan before them, the wilderness around them, and the Manna above them. They were a Heaven-born people and a Heaven-bound people; they ate Heaven-baked Bread.

In looking back toward Egypt, they murmured; when looking forward toward the Wilderness, they saw the Glory of the Lord (Williams).

Jesus as the Bread of Life, and He Alone is, can only be had by virtue of the Cross. As we have repeatedly stated, Christ is the Source, while the Cross is the means (Eph., Chpt. 1).

JANUARY
23

*a*nd he said unto them, This is that which the LORD has said, Tomorrow is the rest of the Holy Sabbath unto the LORD . . . (Ex. 16:23).

The Sabbath, the day of rest, here suddenly reappears after a silence of more than 2,000 years. Redemption being accomplished, the Sabbath is gifted to Israel. But man has no heart for God's rest. His nature is bad; he can neither rest with, nor work for, God. If God makes a rest for him, he will not keep it; and if God tells him to work, he will not do it.

In this Chapter, Israel refused the Sabbath as a gift; in Numbers 15, they disobeyed it as a Law.

The Sabbath was to be a day of *"rest,"* symbolizing the *"rest"* which one finds in Christ, and only in Christ. Hence He says, *"Come unto Me, all you who labor and are heavy laden, and I will give you Rest"* (Mat. 11:28).

Since the *"Sabbath"* is only a symbol of the *"rest"* that one finds in Christ, once the reality had come, the symbolism is no longer needed. Hence, the strict observance of this ritual was not carried over into the New Covenant. And yet, when one accepts Christ, following Him by placing one's Faith entirely in Christ and the Cross, this is the same as *"keeping the Sabbath,"* because the Sabbath prefigured Christ and His Rest (Heb., Chpt. 4).

JANUARY
24

*b*ehold, I will stand before you there upon the Rock in Horeb; and you shall smite the Rock, and there shall come water out of it, that the people may drink. And Moses did so in the sight of the Elders of Israel (Ex. 17:6).

It seems strange that God, Who professed to love them, should lead Israel into a desert, both foodless and waterless. But love led them there that they might learn the desperate unbelief of their own hearts and the unfailing faithfulness of God's Heart. Only in a desert could God reveal what He can be to those who trust Him; for only there was Israel dependent upon Him for everything. Without God — nothing; with God — everything.

The water from the Smitten Rock foretold the Living Water, the Holy Spirit, to be sent forth by the Smitten Saviour. The Holy Spirit was shed forth as the fruit of Christ's Sacrifice (I Cor. 10:4). The Rock was smitten by the very same rod of judgment that smote the land of Egypt.

The *"Rock"* was a Type of Christ being smitten by God

47

(Isa. 53:4), which was done at the Cross, and which brought forth Eternal Life, at least for all who will believe (Jn. 3:16).

The fact of the Cross guaranteed the payment of all sin, past, present, and future, the giving of Eternal Life, and the advent of the Holy Spirit in a new dimension, at least for all who will believe (Jn. 7:37-39).

JANUARY
25

*t*hen came Amalek, and fought with Israel in Rephidim (Ex. 17:8).

The reception of the Holy Spirit, symbolized by the Smitten Rock pouring out life-giving water, immediately causes war. *"Then came Amalek, and fought with Israel."* Up to this point, God had fought for them. Israel was to stand still and see His Salvation; but the Command now is to go out and fight.

There is an immense difference between Justification and Sanctification. The one is Christ fighting <u>for</u> us; the other, the Holy Spirit fighting <u>in</u> us. The entrance of the new nature is the beginning of warfare with the old.

Amalek pictures the old carnal nature. He was the grandson of Esau, who, before and after birth, tried to murder Jacob, and who preferred the mess of pottage to the birthright. This carnal nature wars against the Spirit. *"It is not subject to the Law of God, neither indeed can be"*; and God has decreed war against it forever.

49

The only way that *"Amalek,"* i.e., the flesh, can be defeated is by the Believer ever placing his Faith in the *"Smitten Rock,"* i.e., *"the Crucified Christ"* (Gal. 6:14). Otherwise there is no victory! (Gal. 2:20-21).

JANUARY
26

And Moses said unto Joshua, Choose us out men, and go out, fight with Amalek: tomorrow I will stand on the top of the hill with the Rod of God in my hand (Ex. 17:9).

God did not destroy Amalek, but determined to have war with him from generation to generation. He was to dwell in the land, but not to reign in it. The Sixth Chapter of Romans, which presents the blueprint for spiritual victory, says, *"Let not sin (the sin nature) therefore reign in your mortal body."* This Command would have no meaning if the sin nature did not continue to exist in the Christian. Amalek is a type of the sin nature.

The sin nature dwells in the Believer, but dwells and reigns in an unbeliever.

There is only one way for the Believer to have perpetual victory over the sin nature, and that is to understand, even as Paul told us in Romans 6:3-5, that we are baptized into the death of Christ, buried with Him by baptism into death, and raised with Him by the Glory of the Father, that we *"should walk in newness of life."*

The Cross of Christ is the foundation principle of our life, living, and victory. Our Faith must ever rest in that Finished Work. Only then will this *"fight"* be successful! (II Tim. 2:4)

JANUARY
27

*b*ut Moses' hands were heavy; and they took a stone, and put it under him, and he sat thereon; and Aaron and Hur stayed up his hands, the one on the one side, and the other on the other side; and his hands were steady until the going down of the sun (Ex. 17:12).

In brief form, we are here given the blueprint for victory:

1. *"But Moses' hands were heavy"*: When Moses *"held up his hands,"* Israel prevailed. When he *"let down his hands,"* Amalek prevailed. Functioning by his own strength, his hands grew heavy, symbolizing the flesh, which quickly wearies.

2. *"And they took a stone, and put it under him, and he sat thereon"*: The *"Stone"* is a Type of Christ. In Him, we rest, and only in Him can we rest. Resting in the midst of battle may seem strange, but the Lord's battles are fought with Faith, and not by the flesh.

3. *"And Aaron and Hur stayed up his hands, the one on*

the one side, and the other on the other side": Aaron is a Type of Christ as our Great High Priest, the Lord Jesus Christ, ever making Intercession for us. *"Hur"* is a Type of the Holy Spirit.

With the Intercessor and the Holy Spirit holding up our hands, they will then be *"steady."* Then our Heavenly Joshua will win the victory, all on our behalf, but only when our obedience is as it should be. Our hands must be held up, a posture which signifies our trusting solely in the Lord. Christ acts here as the High Priest and the Warrior. To follow His direction guarantees victory (I Jn. 5:4).

JANUARY
28

*a*nd you shall make an Altar of Shittim Wood, five cubits long, and five cubits broad; the Altar shall be foursquare: and the height thereof shall be three cubits (Ex. 27:1).

The great Brazen Altar, which sat in front of the Tabernacle, represented Jesus and Calvary. The brass (copper) pictured judgment and the enduring strength of His Atoning Sacrifice; its polished surface, His sinlessness; its measurements, three by five, His Deity and His Grace. Its shape, foursquare, expressed its provision and sufficiency for the four quarters of the Earth; and its position, in front of the entrance to the House, that the Crucified Lamb of Calvary is the One and Only Way to God.

It was borne by staves, thereby accompanying the people in their pilgrim way to Canaan, so teaching the lesson that there never comes a period in the Christian life where the Atoning Blood of Christ can be dispensed with.

The Brazen Altar, without a doubt, was the single most important piece of furniture in the entirety of the

Tabernacle. Some may argue that the Ark of the Covenant was the greatest; however, nothing could be reached in the Tabernacle, the Golden Lampstand, the Table of Shewbread, the Altar of Worship, and, above all, the Ark of the Covenant, without the Priests first going by means of the Brazen Altar. In other words, the Brazen Altar, typifying Christ and His Crucifixion, made possible the entirety of the Levitical Worship.

Presently, and forever it will be the case, the Believer will ever have access to the Throne of God, all because of Jesus and what He did at the Cross (Rev., Chpt. 5).

JANUARY
29

*a*nd you shall make a plate of pure gold, and grave upon
it like the engravings of a signet, HOLINESS TO THE LORD
(Ex. 28:36).

Aaron, the brother of Moses, was the first Great High
Priest of Israel, a symbol of the Lord Jesus Christ, Who is
forever our High Priest (Heb. 7:26-27).

Aaron, as the Great High Priest, wore a crown of sorts,
which was to bear on its front a golden plate bearing the
words, *"HOLINESS TO THE LORD."* In the coming Millennium, this engraving will appear on the bells of the horses
(Zech., Chpt. 14). The golden plate and its engraving pictured Israel as an election before God. Imperfect as Israel
was in herself, as thus represented by Aaron and his crown,
she was Holiness itself.

Believer, look away from your ten thousand failures,
and look upon the Lord Jesus Christ, Who is Holiness
Personified, symbolized by Aaron. Realize that your Holiness is, and ever shall be, altogether in Christ. Your Faith

in Him and His Perfect Sacrifice guarantees such Holiness, and a Perfect Holiness, at that, which is the only type of Holiness that God will accept.

Man cannot perfect Holiness within himself and by his own machinations, no matter how hard he tries. It is attained only by looking exclusively to Christ and His Atoning Sacrifice (Gal. 2:20-21).

JANUARY
30

*a*nd you shall make an Altar to burn incense upon: of shittim wood shall you make it (Ex. 30:1).

When Aaron and his sons were anointed, with the description given in the Twenty-ninth Chapter of Exodus, the sons were anointed with him, and not he with them. Everything is connected with Jesus, of which Aaron was a Type.

The Precious Blood of Christ had first to be poured out before the Spirit could be poured forth; and sinners must first be washed from their sins in that Precious Blood before they can be baptized with the Holy Spirit. Thus cleansed and sanctified, worship at the Golden Altar of Incense is possible; but not otherwise!

This Golden Altar of Incense sat immediately in front of the Veil which separated the Holy Place from the Holy of Holies in the Tabernacle. Coals of fire were to be taken from the Brazen Altar outside and placed on the Golden Altar, with Incense poured over the coals, which typified the Intercession of Christ on behalf of His People.

Having brought His People out of Egypt, God established the Brazen Altar outside the Tabernacle and the Golden Altar inside; He appointed a Mediator to maintain relationship with Him in order that He might dwell among them. That Mediator was Aaron, the High Priest. The Brazen Altar symbolized the perfection of Christ's Sacrifice for sin; the Golden Altar, the preciousness of His Person. The Golden Altar itself spoke of Jesus. The wood and the gold pre-figured His Humanity and Deity; it was crowned and it had staves to bear it so as to be the day and night companion of a pilgrim people.

The Incense burned upon it spoke of Him. Aaron himself, in his robes of glory, pictured Him; and the light of the Golden Lampstand foretold Him, Who, being the Light of that world that needs no sun, came into this world to be its Light. That Light is Jesus!

JANUARY
31

*a*nd Aaron shall make an Atonement upon the horns of it once a year with the Blood of the Sin Offering of Atonements: once in the year shall he make Atonement upon it throughout your generations: it is most holy unto the LORD (Ex. 30:10).

The fire of 30:7 and the blood of 30:10 teach that there can be no acceptable worship apart from Atonement. In the matter of Atonement, all worshippers stand on one common ground, and that is the Sacrifice of Christ.

The word *"Atonement"* means, in the Hebrew Text, *"a cover"*; it is not the English word *"at-one-ment." "Now our sins may all be covered with the Precious Blood He shed"* (Ps. 32:1).

The Brazen Altar was for the sinner; the Brazen Laver for the Saint. The former testified of the Blood of Christ; the latter, of the Word of God. The former cleansed the conscience; the latter, the conduct.

The sons of Aaron, already cleansed, clothed, and crowned, had nevertheless to wash their hands and feet

61

in the Laver before entering the Tabernacle or approaching the Altar. To maintain conscious fellowship with God and to be effective Ministers in Priestly service for man, the daily washing of the Word must never be neglected, lest death enter the soul.

Every Believer stands on the common ground of Calvary and the Word; in Old Testament times, the former was represented by the Brazen Altar, and the latter was represented by the Brazen Laver. Regrettably, most of the worship that is presently claimed to be unto the Lord is not based on the Atoning Work of Calvary, but rather on something else. And it doesn't really matter what else it is, if it's not the Cross, it's not acceptable to God (Eph. 2:13-18).

FEBRUARY

1

*W*hen you number them . . . This they shall give, every one who passes among them who are numbered, half a shekel after the shekel of the Sanctuary: (a shekel is 20 gerahs:) an half shekel shall be the offering of the LORD (Ex. 30:12-13).

Whenever the people of Israel were numbered, in other words, a census taken, every person from 20 years old and above had to give a half shekel, which was, in a sense, a tax. The *"shekel"* was of silver; in the Old Testament, silver was a symbol of Redemption. All, whether rich or poor, had to give the same amount, signifying that Redemption, of which all of this was a type, was the same for all.

This, no doubt, is one of the reasons the Lord grew incensed with David when he numbered the people. Every evidence is that David ignored the census tax, which meant that he, in effect, was ignoring the very basis of Israel's existence — the Shed Blood of the Lamb.

This is basically the reason that David responded as he did when he went to purchase the threshingfloor of

Araunah the Jebusite for the purpose of offering up sacrifice. The Jebusite offered it to David for nothing, but David said, *"No; but I will surely buy it of you at a price: neither will I offer up Burnt Offerings unto the LORD my God of that which does cost me nothing"* (II Sam. 24:24).

We are bought with a price, and that price is the Shed Blood of Jesus Christ.

FEBRUARY

2

You shall keep the Sabbath therefore; for it is holy unto you: everyone who defiles it shall surely be put to death: for whosoever does any work therein, that soul shall be cut off from among his people (Ex. 31:14).

"My Sabbath you shall keep." What distinguishes God's people is participation in God's rest. Christ is God's rest (Heb., Chpt. 4). The honor, or dishonor, done to the Sabbath was the test under Law; the honor, or dishonor, done to Christ, the test under Grace. Death was the penalty of dishonoring the Sabbath of the Old Testament; a similar penalty attaches to dishonoring Christ, i.e., spiritual death.

The Sabbath was associated with the Manna (Ex., Chpt. 16), with the giving of the Law (Ex., Chpt. 20), and with the building of the Tabernacle (Ex., Chpt. 31). Zeal in building the Tabernacle, enthusiasm in observing the Law, and energy in gathering the Manna were not permitted to disturb God's rest.

When Christ came, He in totality fulfilled the symbolism of the Sabbath, as well as everything else which pertained to the Mosaic Law. He, as stated, is our rest. Following Him constitutes keeping the Sabbath, which no longer pertains to a special day as it did in Old Testament times, but pertains presently to every day.

FEBRUARY
3

*a*nd he received them at their hand, and fashioned it with a graving tool, after he had made it a molten calf: and they said, These be your gods, O Israel, which brought you up out of the land of Egypt (Ex. 32:4).

Moses was on top of the mountain, dealing with Heavenly things, while, at the foot of the mountain, Aaron and the people sat at the feet of Satan, admiring a golden calf, and dancing and singing around it. The Devil can make men dance and sing, or writhe and scream, if either action can oppose or dishonor Christ.

The calf was the great god of the Egyptians. It was carried in the vanguard of their processions. Sacrifices were offered to it, and lascivious dances executed in its honor. It was worshipped as the generator of life.

People who are ignorant of the brute condition of fallen man's heart think it incredible that men and women who passed through the Red Sea, who daily looked upon the pillar of fire, who heard the Voice of God, and who witnessed the sublime terrors of Mount Sinai, could possibly have fallen, and in so short a time, into such gross idolatry. The Apostle Paul did not share this incredulity, for he declares that these facts admonish the Church (I Cor., Chpt. 10).

Moses had gone up on high, but because he delayed to return, Israel made a god they could see. So it is today. Christendom prefers a human priest and a little piece of bread that may be seen and handled to the Divine Priest Who has passed into the Heavens.

One of the depths of Satan is not to abolish God, but to represent Him by something visible. Hence the feast of Exodus 32:5 was proposed as a feast to Jehovah. Also Satan can, through a religious teacher like Aaron, associate idolatry with Christ, recognize the good in all religions, and provide a worship that appeals to man's natural heart. In fact, everything, as it regards the golden calf, was done by Aaron under the cover of *"religion."*

As someone has well said, *"The doing of religion is the most powerful narcotic in the world."* Anything and everything that departs from Christ and the Cross must be constituted as mere religion (Williams).

FEBRUARY

4

*i*f his offering be a Burnt Sacrifice of the herd, let him offer a male without blemish: he shall offer it of his own voluntary will at the door of the Tabernacle of the congregation before the LORD (Lev. 1:3).

There were five great Offerings in the Levitical Law: the Burnt Offering, the Meal Offering, the Trespass Offering, the Peace Offering, and the Sin Offering (Lev. Chpts. 1-7). God only accepted such Offerings as He Himself ordained. The worshipper, imperfect and sinful in himself, was accepted in the perfection of the Offering. The conscience under the old Levitical Law being a reflection of the Sacrifice remained imperfect because Levitical Sacrifices were imperfect. Christ's Sacrifice being perfect gives a perfected conscience; therefore, a peace that nothing can destroy.

The Burnt Offering typified Christ offering Himself without spot to God. It was a voluntary Offering. So Christ delighted to do God's Will. He laid down His Life

69

of Himself. Therefore, it is that the victim was a male without blemish. This signified the spotless Perfection of Christ's Manhood. The entire Sacrifice was burned on the Altar; that is, it was wholly for God. Such was the devotion of Christ's Heart.

The skin of the Sacrifice was given to the Priests. Only the mere surface of Christ's offering up of Himself to God can be apprehended by the Believer. The infinite depths of that great surrender are beyond human understanding.

The inwards of the Sacrifice were washed with water, so Christ's Emotions, as well as His Ways and Words, when judged by the Word of God, were found to be sinless. With respect to Him, all within and without had no blemish. Therefore, Faith in Him Alone and what He did for us at the Cross brings about acceptance by God.

FEBRUARY
5

*a*nd if his oblation be a sacrifice of Peace Offering, if he offer it of the herd; whether it be a male or female, he shall offer it without blemish before the LORD (Lev. 3:1).

The infinite fullness of the Atoning Sacrifice of Christ needed many Offerings to show forth, even faintly, its plenitude and veracity. The Burnt Offering pictured Christ dying; the Meal Offering, Christ living; and Leviticus, Chapter 3, presents Him as making peace by the Blood of His Cross, and so establishing for man communion with God (Eph., Chpt. 2).

The Burnt Offering was a male; the Peace Offering, male or female, in either case, without blemish.

When the Offering was presented, the worshipper laid his hand upon the head of the Offering, and its blood was sprinkled on the Altar round about; for fellowship is encircled by Atonement and only exists within it. Thus, God and the worshipper were brought into fellowship. Peace was established. Its eternal and unshakable foundation

71

was not the worthfulness of the worshipper, but the preciousness of the sprinkled blood.

All the fat was wholly burned upon the Altar as a sweet savor. The fat and the blood symbolized the priceless life and precious inward affections of the Lamb of God. All of this gave He for us on the Cross of Calvary, of which all of this in the Levitical Law was a type.

FEBRUARY

6

*S*peak unto the Children of Israel, saying, If a soul shall sin through ignorance against any of the Commandments of the LORD concerning things which ought not to be done, and shall do against any of them (Lev. 4:2).

The words, *"through ignorance,"* prove that man, whether he be a Chief Priest or a *"common person,"* cannot know, at least in totality, what sin is. This is humbling and comforting. It reveals that the efficacy of Christ's Atonement for sin is not to be measured by man's consciousness of sin, but by God's measurement of it. To believe this fact fills the heart with a Divine peace.

The Sin Offering was wholly burned outside the camp, but the blood and the fat were offered to God. This double action illuminates the Cross. Jesus suffered *"outside the camp,"* thereby showing how abhorrent to God is sin; yet, at the same time, was His Blood precious, and the fat, i.e., His inward Personal excellence *"most holy."* In fact, the Incense, the Shewbread, the Sin Offering, and the Meal

Offering are all named *"most holy."* Thus, the Spirit of God, when speaking of Jesus as a Man or as an Offering for sin, repeats with emphasis that He was, in His entire being, *"most holy."*

All of this was absolutely necessary if Christ was to serve as the most perfect Sacrifice for sin, at least a Sacrifice which God would accept. God could only accept perfection; therefore, Christ Alone could satisfy these requirements.

FEBRUARY

7

*a*nd the Priest shall put some of the blood upon the horns of the Altar of sweet incense before the LORD, which is in the Tabernacle of the congregation; and shall pour all the blood of the bullock at the bottom of the Altar of the Burnt Offering, which is at the door of the Tabernacle of the congregation (Lev. 4:7).

The *"Altar of Sweet Incense"* was the Golden Altar, which sat immediately in front of the Veil that separated the Holy Place from the Holy of Holies in the Tabernacle. Blood was to be applied to the four horns of this Altar, which pointed to all directions of the compass. This signified that Intercession by the Saviour is the same the world over, irrespective of race, color, or creed.

The Blood poured out *"at the bottom of the Altar of the Burnt Offering"* pertained to the Brazen Altar which sat in front of the Tabernacle.

All of this signified that a man is not sentenced to death because of some very great sin, but, in reality, because of any type of sin, irrespective as to how little it might be. In the Eyes of God, even the smallest sin is so great that to expiate its guilt, all the blood of the spotless Sacrifice must be poured out at the bottom of the Altar. So, to atone for, i.e., cover, the smallest conceivable departure from absolute sinlessness, even that done through ignorance, the whole of Christ's Blood must be shed. This shows us how terrible, how awful, how desperate that sin actually is, even that which we think to be small.

In order to obtain forgiveness of his sin, the man said nothing and did nothing except to lay his hand upon the head of the spotless substitute, thus transferring his guilt and its doom to the substitute. The Law claimed the man's life as the just penalty for his sin. The sin being transferred, the Law then claimed the life of the substitute; and directly that life was surrendered, the full claim of the Law was satisfied and the man thereby saved.

The knowledge that he was saved was founded upon two facts outside of himself, i.e., the value of the blood shed for him, and the trustworthiness of the Word spoken to him. On this Divine Foundation rests the Christian's peace. The knowledge that Christ's Blood is of infinite value to cleanse all sins, and the conviction that the Word of God, which declares that whoever trusts that Saviour shall never be confounded, is always trustworthy — this double knowledge establishes assurance of Salvation (I Jn. 1:9).

FEBRUARY

8

*C*ommand Aaron and his sons, saying, This is the Law of the Burnt Offering: It is the Burnt Offering, because of the burning upon the Altar all night unto the morning, and the fire of the Altar shall be burning in it (Lev. 6:9).

The Burnt Offering was to burn all night. In the morning, dressed in his clean linen garments, the Priest was to gather its ashes and place them beside the Altar. Then, in his garments of beauty, he was to bring them with befitting glory into a clean place, which symbolizes the coming cleansed Millennial Earth. Through this night of mystery, the fragrance of Christ's offering up of Himself to God ascends continually.

"In the morning," Christ will appear to His people Israel in His double glory as the white-robed Priest and the Glory-crowned Mediator; and it will then be demonstrated to the world, as here foreshadowed by the honorable treatment of the ashes, that His Person and His Work have been accepted of God.

The fire that consumed the Burnt Offering originally came from Heaven (Lev. 9:24), and was maintained perpetually burning by the unwearied ministry of the Priest. It testified, on the one hand, to the unceasing delight of God in the Sacrifice of Christ, and, on the other hand, to His unceasing hatred of sin. False teachers today put this fire out by denying the doctrines of the Atonement and of the Wrath to come.

Let it never be forgotten:

It is Atonement alone which assuages the Wrath of God (Williams).

FEBRUARY
9

*b*esides the cakes, he shall offer for his Offering leavened bread with the Sacrifice of thanksgiving of his Peace Offerings (Lev. 7:13).

The Peace Offering for thanksgiving was eaten the same day it was offered; the Peace Offering for a vow, the same day or the next day — because a vow or a voluntary offering necessarily affected the heart more than an ordinary thanksgiving.

This Law taught the offeror to closely associate the death and sufferings of the slain lamb with the blessing for which he gave thanks. It teaches men today the same lesson. To disassociate worship and thanksgiving from the anguish and the shedding of the Blood of the Lord Jesus is to offer to God an abomination (Lev. 7:18), and to bring death into the soul and into the Church.

Ceremonial cleanliness was obligatory before eating the Peace Offering (Lev. 7:20-21). Disobedience in this matter entailed death. To profess faith in the Person and

Atonement of Christ, and to claim fellowship with Him, but to be secretly unclean, insures the Wrath of God.

The Sacrifice of Christ and Faith in that Sacrifice purge sin from the Believer. To claim to believe such and then fail to exercise faith in what Christ has done for us at the Cross proclaim hypocrisy or unbelief, or both. Ultimately, judgment is inevitable.

FEBRUARY
10

*a*nd Nadab and Abihu, the sons of Aaron, took either of them his censer, and put fire therein, and put incense thereon, and offered strange fire before the LORD, which He commanded them not. And there went out fire from the LORD, and devoured them, and they died before the LORD (Lev. 10:1-2).

The fact that these two men were Priests made no difference. They suffered the Judgment of God because they ignored Calvary.

Coals of fire were to be taken from the Brazen Altar, which typified Calvary, and placed on the Golden Altar in the Tabernacle. Incense was then to be poured over those coals of fire, which would fill the Holy Place of the Tabernacle, signifying the Intercession of our Lord on behalf of all the Saints.

The *"strange fire"* they offered was that taken from some other ignition than the Brazen Altar. It had, therefore, no connection with the Atonement. It was the sin of Cain. It is a sin largely committed today. Jesus said, *"I am the*

81

Way, no man comes unto the Father but by Me."

Acceptable worship can only be in the energy of the Holy Spirit, in the truth of the Shed Blood, and in obedience to the inspired Word. The fire of the Holy Spirit associates itself alone with the Blood of the Crucified Saviour; all other fire is *"strange fire."* As a result of their disobedience, fire came out from the Holy of Holies and struck dead Nadab and Abihu.

From this we understand that the only thing standing between man and the Wrath of God is the Cross of Christ. That accepted, Wrath subsides. That ignored, Wrath remains!

FEBRUARY

11

*t*his shall be the law of the leper in the day of his cleansing: He shall be brought unto the Priest (Lev. 14:2).

The Priest alone could judge whether a man was a leper or not. Directly a person was declared to be a leper, he was placed without the camp, and compelled, by voice and clothing, to confess himself a leper. Leprosy was a type of sin.

The leper was cleansed by blood, by water, and by oil (Lev. 14:6, 14-15). These symbolized the Blood of Christ, the Word of God, and the Holy Spirit. This triple cleansing restored him to the camp, to the family, and to the Tabernacle. All were based upon the preciousness and efficacy of the shed blood. Apart from the Blood of Jesus moral reformation and spiritual power are impossible.

Excepting the washing of himself in water, the leper did nothing for his cleansing; the Priest did everything. The leper is the sinner, the Priest is Jesus.

The Priest *"went forth"* out of the camp to where the

leper was; the leper was *"brought"* to him. So Christ came down from Heaven to where the sinner is; the Holy Spirit brings the sinner to Him.

The carnal mind finds this Chapter tiresome, uninteresting, and unpleasant; however, to the spiritual mind it is humbling and comforting. Love untiring and infinite wisdom are the foundation of all of these Statutes given in these Chapters. The Reader finds himself as a moral leper in the tender, patient, wise, and loving hands of our Heavenly Priest; accordingly, we should study every word with humility and adoration.

FEBRUARY

12

*a*nd the leper in whom the plague is, his clothes shall be rent, and his head bare, and he shall put a covering upon his upper lip, and shall cry, Unclean, unclean. All the days wherein the plague shall be in him he shall be defiled; he is unclean: he shall dwell alone; without the camp shall his habitation be (Lev. 13:45-46).

Leprosy being a type of sin, we are here told the disposition of such sin.

1. *"His clothes shall be rent"*: The coat was to be ripped up the back, signifying, spiritually, that sinners are undone.

2. *"His head bare"*: Under Old Testament Law, the head bare signified that there was no protection against the Judgment of God.

3. *"He shall put a covering upon his upper lip, and shall cry, Unclean, unclean"*: When an individual is asked if they are saved, and they exclaim, *"I'm a member of thus-and-so Church,"* they are, in essence, saying, *"Unclean, unclean."*

No Church, nor anything else, can cleanse the sinner, that being effected only by the shed Blood of Christ and our Faith in that cleansing stream.

4. *"All the days wherein the plague shall be in him, he shall be defiled"*: As long as sin remains, and it will forever remain until the person confesses Christ as Saviour and Lord, such a person will be unclean. There is no cleansing for sin outside of the precious, shed Blood of Jesus Christ.

5. *"He shall dwell alone"*: Irrespective of the noise and the clamor of society, or association with people, there is a terrible loneliness to sin.

FEBRUARY

13

*S*peak unto the Children of Israel, and say unto them, When any man has a running issue out of his flesh, because of his issue he is unclean. Every bed, whereon he lies that has the issue, it is unclean: and every thing, whereon he sits, shall be unclean (Lev. 15:2, 4).

The lessons of this Fifteenth Chapter of Leviticus are:

First, the Holiness of God and of His Dwelling-place.

Second, the loving and minute interest that He takes in the habits of His Children. Nothing was too small or too private for Him. Their clothing and their health concerned Him deeply.

Third, the corruption of fallen nature; it defiled. Walking or sleeping, sitting, standing or lying, its every touch conveyed pollution — a painful lesson for proud humanity.

Fourth, the cleansing power of the Shed Blood and the sanctifying virtue of the Word of God are the only way of cleansing and Holiness.

Thus, the nature of sin is exhibited in this Chapter.

Even that which was unavoidable defiled.

One of the sins, perhaps the greatest sin, of the modern Church is that it seems to little understand the terrible horror of sin. To properly understand that horror, one must understand the price that was paid to assuage its stain — the Death of the Son of God.

Justification assures of Salvation from the guilt of sin; Sanctification effects separation from the filth of sin.

FEBRUARY
14

*a*nd this shall be a Statute forever unto you: that in the seventh month, on the tenth day of the month, you shall afflict your souls, and do no work at all, whether it be one of your own country, or a stranger who sojourns among you: For on that day shall the Priest make an Atonement for you, to cleanse you, that you may be clean from all your sins before the LORD (Lev. 16:29-30).

Leviticus, Chapter 16 describes the Great Day of Atonement. It occurred once a year. There was no other day like it. It dealt with the sins of the whole nation for twelve months. It foreshadowed the Lamb of God taking away the sin of the world (Jn. 1:29).

Abel's lamb redeemed one man; the Pascal Lamb, one family; the Day of Atonement Lamb, one nation; the Lamb of Calvary, the whole world (Jn. 1:29).

This was the only day in the year that the High Priest entered the Most Holy Place. Enveloped in a cloud of Incense, he presented the blood of the Burnt Offering and of the Sin Offering, which he sprinkled once upon the Golden Mercy Seat, for God, knowing its value, needed but the one presentation. Then the blood was sprinkled seven times before the Mercy Seat. *"Seven"* being God's number of perfection and totality, as well as universality, proclaimed the total effectiveness of the one presentation.

The Tabernacle and all connected therewith were cleansed, as well as the nation. The atoning Sacrifice of Calvary not only redeemed man so that he can dwell with God, and God can dwell with him, but also made the sin-drenched creation suitable for God. Calvary paid it all!

FEBRUARY

15

*S*peak unto the Children of Israel, and say unto them, Concerning the Feasts of the LORD, which you shall proclaim to be holy convocations, even these are My Feasts (Lev. 23:2).

Israel's sacred year contained one weekly and seven annual Feasts, but the annual Feasts were related to the weekly Feast. The weekly Feast was the Sabbath; the seven annual Feasts were: Passover, Unleavened Bread, Firstfruits, Pentecost, Trumpets, Atonement, and Tabernacles.

Leviticus 23:2 declares these to be *"Feasts of Jehovah,"* and the words, *"even these are My Feasts,"* are added for emphasis. Alas! When our Lord came in the flesh, they had ceased to be *"Feasts of Jehovah,"* and had become *"feasts of the Jews"* (Jn. 2:13; 5:1; 6:4; 11:55).

A similar change may be witnessed presently in what professes to be the Kingdom of God. The Feast of the Sabbath stood apart as being God's rest. It was a Prophecy and a Promise of the rest in Christ that remains to the people of God.

91

The foundation of the seven Feasts was Grace; the topstone, Glory; for the first Feast — Passover — proclaimed Redemption through the Blood, and the last Feast — Tabernacles — pictured the Millennium. Between these two Feasts came the sheaf of Firstfruits, i.e., the Resurrection of Christ; Pentecost, i.e., the descent of the Holy Spirit, made possible by the Crucifixion of Christ; and the Great Day of Atonement, when Israel shall look upon Him Whom they have pierced, and, repentant, receive the new heart predicted by Ezekiel.

The Command to do no servile work is repeated ten times in connection with these Feasts. Man's activities were forbidden to intrude themselves into a Salvation which was Divine and Perfect (Williams).

FEBRUARY
16

*t*his is the Ordinance of the Law which the LORD has commanded, saying, Speak unto the Children of Israel, that they bring you a red heifer without spot, wherein is no blemish, and upon which never came yoke (Num. 19:2).

Numbers, Chapter 19 contains the Law of the Red Heifer. Some claim that this was an invention by the Priests of Israel; however, if this sacrifice had been invented by the Jews, they would have put it in the Book of Leviticus. As it is, being in Numbers, this proclaims the fact of inspiration.

The heifer symbolized Christ. It was spotless externally, and without blemish internally. It was free from any bondage whatever. It was a female, and it was red. Christ, in His Humanity, was spotless within and without; He was also as gentle as a woman; He was never in bondage to any sin; the Law had no claim upon Him as a debtor; and He robed Himself with the red earth of Manhood.

Eleazar led the heifer forth without the camp; and

there was she slain. So was Christ led of the Spirit to Calvary, where He offered up Himself.

The blood of the heifer is only once mentioned in this Chapter. So Christ was once offered. It needed not that other heifers should be slain — the ashes of the first heifer sufficed, and lasted, no doubt, for many years.

Purification from the defilements unavoidable during the sojourn was effected by an application of the ashes of the burnt heifer with running water, i.e., Living Water.

Christ's Death need not be repeated in order that forgiveness be enjoyed concerning daily sins of the celestial pilgrim. It only needs that the meaning and perfection of His Death, typified by the burnt ashes, should be effectively applied to the conscience by the Living Spirit, symbolized by the running water, and the sense of forgiveness and cleansing is then enjoyed.

There were many things which required the ashes of the red heifer, the touching of a corpse or even a bone being examples. Death is the result of sin — original sin; therefore, it defiles! The only answer for sin and death is the Crucified Christ and Faith in His Finished Work, symbolized by the ashes of the Red Heifer.

FEBRUARY

17

god is not a man, that He should lie; neither the son of man, that He should repent: has He said, and shall He not do it? or has He spoken, and shall He not make it good? (Num. 23:19).

This Prophecy, as given by Balaam, proclaims God, and rightly so, as the God of Blessing. In fact, for those who truly follow Him, the Scripture plainly says, *"And He has blessed; and I cannot reverse it."* That's quite a Promise!

Nothing can stop the Blessings of God for those who truly follow the Lord.

The Prophecy then said, *"He has not beheld iniquity in Jacob, neither has He seen perverseness in Israel."* This is a proclamation of Justification by Faith. This great foundation truth of the Gospel appears in this Prophecy. Neither iniquity in Jacob nor perverseness in Israel were visible to the Divine eye, because that eye rested on the perfections of Him in Whom Israel was chosen.

Who could lay anything to the charge of those whom

God justified, i.e., declared righteous? (Rom. 8:33)

This simply says that proper Faith in Christ and what He did for us at the Cross means that God does not necessarily look at us, but rather at the One in Whom we have believed. There He sees nothing but perfection; He can, therefore, refer to all who follow Christ as being placed in the same position — perfection.

Then he said, *"And the shout of a king is among them."* Of course, as the Lord referred to Israel of that time, the *"King"* of Whom he spoke was the One Who would be born in Bethlehem, the Lord Jesus Christ. This means that all *"Blessing"* and all *"Justification"* come solely by and through Christ, all made possible by the what He did at the Cross.

FEBRUARY
18

*a*nd the LORD said unto Moses, Write this for a memorial in a Book, and rehearse it in the ears of Joshua: for I will
utterly put out the remembrance of Amalek from under Heaven.
And Moses built an Altar, and called the name of it Jehovah-
Nissi (Ex. 17:14-15).

It is remarkable that the first mention of the Bible
should be in connection with the hostility of the natural
man (Amalek) to the spiritual man (Israel). War has ever
since accompanied the Book. In fact, no Book (the Bible)
has been so hated and so loved.

Paul told Timothy: *"War a good warfare"* (I Tim. 1:18).
He also said, *"The weapons of our warfare are not carnal,
but mighty through God to the pulling down of strongholds"*
(II Cor. 10:4).

Moses building the *"Altar"* tells us the manner in which
victory is won. It is always through the Sacrifice of Christ
and our Faith in that Finished Work. In fact, Paul told us
exactly how this warfare is engaged, and how it is won.

97

We speak of the never-ceasing war against the flesh.

He said, *"But God forbid that I should glory, save in the Cross of the our Lord Jesus Christ, by Whom the world is crucified unto me, and I unto the world"* (Gal. 6:14).

The *"Cross"* was the occasion for the victory which Moses saw, even as it regarded the entirety of Israel; the Cross is the scene of our victory. There is no other manner of victory, simply because no other manner is needed.

FEBRUARY
19

*A*nd Joshua the son of Nun sent out of Shittim two men to spy secretly, saying, Go view the land, even Jericho. And they went, and came into an harlot's house, named Rahab, and lodged there (Josh. 2:1).

Rahab would seem to be an unlikely prospect for Salvation, but yet the greatest prospect of all, because Salvation is not gauged upon what a person has been, but the faith they now evidence. Rahab was a debauched member of a doomed race. Yet Grace saved her.

She based her plea for Salvation upon the fact that she was justly ordained by God to destruction. Many people refuse to claim Salvation because of the belief that, if they are ordained to be saved, they will be saved, and, if ordained to be lost, they will be lost. However, all sinners are justly ordained to be lost (Rom. 5:12); therefore, all sinners may be saved.

Rahab prefaced her plea for Salvation by declaring that she knew all were doomed to destruction, and, because of this Divine Judgment, she asked for a true token that would assure her of her safety in the Day of Wrath that was coming. She was immediately provided with a way of Salvation. It was very simple way. She had but to bind some scarlet thread in a window. A child could do that.

This means that Salvation from the Wrath to come is equally simple. Trusting in the Lord Jesus Christ and in His Precious Blood secures eternal Salvation.

Rahab lost not a moment in making her calling and election sure. She bound the scarlet thread in the window. Directly she did so, she was saved — that is, she was in safety and assured of safety. Prior to binding the scarlet line in the window, she was ordained to destruction. But from the moment she trusted that *"true token,"* she was ordained to Salvation.

FEBRUARY
20

*b*ehold, when we come into the land, you shall bind this line of scarlet thread in the window which you did let us down by: and you shall bring your father, and your mother, and your brethren, and all your father's household, home unto you (Josh. 2:18).

Rahab's Salvation was not necessarily based upon something she trusted within herself, but rather on outward evidence, that is, the scarlet line. In it was perfection because it symbolized the Shed Blood of Christ; in herself, imperfection. Looking upon that *"true token"* and believing the testimony respecting it, she was assured of deliverance in the Day of Doom that was coming.

Thus, the outward token gave an inward peace.

The Believer in Jesus enjoys a similar peace. The preciousness of Christ's Blood and the testimony of the Holy Scriptures concerning it are the outward tokens which bring assurance of Salvation to the heart that trusts Christ.

It was vain for Rahab to seek for Salvation upon the

basis of personal worthiness; for she was vile indeed. She was a harlot. It is equally vain for the most moral, whoever that might be, to claim Salvation presently; for all have sinned, none are righteous, and all are under sentence of death (Rom. 5:12).

A Faith that is born of God always evidences itself by seeking the Salvation of others. Rahab pleads for her father, her mother, her brothers, her sisters, and all belonging to them; and they were all saved.

The moral effect of this Divine Faith evidenced in Rahab, who previously had been a harlot, now proclaims her joining the People of God, marrying one of its Princes, and her name shines in the genealogy of Jesus Christ (Mat. 1:5). Thus, we see what the Gospel of Jesus Christ can do in the heart and life of one, anyone, even one such as Rahab.

FEBRUARY
21

*a*nd Joshua said unto the people, Sanctify yourselves: for tomorrow the LORD will do wonders among you (Josh. 3:5).

Entrance into the Promised Land pictured the Baptism with the Holy Spirit. The wilderness experience proclaims life without this Baptism.

The Priests were to carry the Ark upon their shoulders. Both the Ark and the Priests were types of Christ.

The people were to follow the Ark as it was carried by the Priests, yet there was to be a space of about a half mile between them and it. Due to the fact that the sin debt had not yet been paid, because the Cross was still in the future, mere mortals, except the designated Priests, could not come close to the Ark. Thank God, Calvary has changed all of that!

Before this journey, which would witness the miracle of the opening of the Jordan, the people of Israel were to *"sanctify themselves."* Under the Old Covenant, due to the fact that the Holy Spirit did not at that time reside within

103

Believers, because, as stated, the sin debt was not yet paid, Sanctification consisted mostly of externals. Now it is a Work of the Spirit, simply because the sin debt has been paid at Calvary.

Let it ever be known:

The Jordan did not open for the sake of the people, even as much as God loved them, but for the sake of the Ark, which, as stated, was a Type of Christ.

Because of the Cross, now Christ lives in our hearts and lives, and does so through the Person of the Holy Spirit (Gal. 2:20). Consequently, we now have a much Better Covenant, based on Better Promises (Heb. 8:6). Because of the Cross, we are now able to come near (Eph. 2:12-18).

FEBRUARY

22

*a*nd the Children of Israel did so as Joshua commanded, and took up twelve stones out of the midst of Jordan, as the LORD spoke unto Joshua, according to the number of the Tribes of the Children of Israel, and carried them over with them unto to the place where they lodged, and laid them down there. And Joshua set up twelve stones in the midst of Jordan, in the place where the feet of the Priests which bore the Ark of the Covenant stood: and they are there unto this day (Josh. 4:8-9).

If the Reader isn't careful, he will read over what is actually said here without really understanding what Joshua actually was ordered to do by the Lord. He was instructed to take twelve stones out of the riverbed of Jordan while the waters were pushed back, where the Children of Israel passed over, and take those twelve stones to the Canaan side of the crossing, where they were to set them up for a memorial of what the Lord had done here this particular day.

They also were to take twelve stones from the wilderness

side of the Jordan, which signified their wilderness wanderings, and, I might quickly add, great failures, and put those stones in the very place from where they had taken the first twelve stones. When the Jordan came back to its original position, the wilderness stones would be forever covered, which was the idea.

To the unspiritual eye, this would seem to be nonsensical; however, to those who understand what the Spirit was saying, He was telling Israel that their wilderness wanderings were over, their failures were buried deep in the Jordan, and they were not to be discussed any more.

The twelve stones buried in the Jordan River, taken from the wilderness side, signified the death and burial of Israel's forty years of unbelief and sinning in the wilderness; the stones set up at Gilgal signified Israel's new life of Resurrection power and Victory. The origin of these stones was the deep bed of Jordan; their purpose was to testify that Israel owed her entrance into the goodly land only, and wholly, to Divine Grace and Power.

The two monuments, so to speak, express the great truths of Romans and Ephesians. The first signifies the Baptism into Christ, as outlined in Romans 6:3-5, where the Believer dies to his old life and rises into a new life. There he was baptized into the Death of Christ, buried with Him by baptism into death, and raised with Him into newness of life.

As to our present position, the first monument of twelve stones set up in Gilgal reminds us that we are now on Resurrection ground and that we are daily to testify to the glory of Christ, the One and Only Saviour, Who brought us out of the miry clay. It is also a dire sin for Believers, concerning the second monument, to go digging around in the muddy bed of Jordan, attempting to find stones that were forever buried there, meant to surface no more.

What the Lord has buried and forgotten, we had better let stay buried and forgotten.

FEBRUARY

23

*a*t that time the LORD said unto Joshua, Make thee sharp knives, and circumcise again the Children of Israel the second time (Josh. 5:2).

Israel was now in the Promised Land, but they find that entrance into its blessings and glory is barred by the strong fortress of Jericho, which loomed in their path. In the natural, its conquest was impossible to Israel, for its walls were great and high.

The city, which was a type of hindrances to blessings, must be subdued. But God cannot give victory to *"the flesh,"* i.e., to *"self."* Hence, *"the flesh"* must be *"put to death,"* which can only be done by the Believer looking exclusively to Christ and what Christ has done for us at the Cross; this then gives the Holy Spirit, Who Alone can subdue the flesh, latitude to work within our lives.

To symbolize what Christ would do, of which all of this was a Type, the Lord gave instructions to Joshua that all the males of Israel had to be circumcised. This had been done nearly 40 years before (Lev. 12:3); however, evidently the generation of males born in the wilderness had not yet been circumcised. So Joshua was instructed now to carry out this rite.

The Lord was instructing Joshua to completely immobilize his entire fighting force. Moreover, they would remain that way for several days. Should they be attacked, the soreness would make it impossible for them to defend Israel. This was, however, what the Lord wanted, in order to show that Israel's strength was not in its physical power.

Circumcision symbolized the Cross and death to self. First of all, there was shedding of blood, which signified Christ shedding His Blood on the Cross of Calvary. Second, there was a cutting, or separation, of the flesh, which signified death to self. As someone has said, *"When Jesus died on the Cross, He died to save us not only from 'sin,' but also from 'self.'"* Circumcision signified both!

This tells us that the only way the Believer can have victory over the *"Jerichos"* in his life is by looking to Christ and what He did at the Cross, which means that self is no longer being trusted or leaned upon, but rather the Spirit, Who functions entirely by the means of what Christ did on the Cross (Rom. 8:2).

FEBRUARY
24

*a*nd the Children of Israel encamped in Gilgal, and kept the Passover on the fourteenth day of the month at evening in the plains of Jericho (Josh. 5:10).

After Circumcision, the Lord now commands the Children of Israel to partake of the Passover, which evidently they had not done for some time. By the public eating of the Passover, Israel proclaimed that both her Redemption out of Egypt and her position in the Land of Promise were alike due to the preciousness of the Blood of the Pascal Lamb. True spiritual victories can only be won where there is this testimony to the Person and Work of the Lord Jesus Christ, of which the Passover was a Type.

Each family was to kill a lamb, a male lamb without blemish, which, of course, signified Christ and His Death on the Cross. The lamb was to be wholly eaten with bitter herbs, signifying that Christ is to be partaken of in totality, hence, all being eaten. The *"bitter herbs"* typified the bitterness of the bondage of Egypt from which the Israelites were delivered.

This plainly tells us that we as Believers can walk in victory only by one way and method:

That one way is Faith and Trust in Christ and what He has done for us at the Cross. Ever making the Cross of Christ the Object of our Faith enables the Holy Spirit to work within our lives, Who Alone can give us the victory. If it is to be noticed, the way of the Cross doesn't change; it cannot change, and it doesn't need to change.

One of the great efforts of the human race is the *"improvement of self."* While self definitely needs to be improved, it can be improved in only one way. The Holy Spirit Alone can improve our lives.

Let the Reader understand that carefully:

It cannot be done any other way (Rom. 8:1-2, 11).

In order for the Holy Spirit to do this, He demands of us that the Cross of Christ ever be the Object of our Faith (Rom. 8:2). Unfortunately, virtually all of the ways and means proposed by modern Preachers is that *"self"* improve *"self."* Such is impossible!

Paul said, *"Because the carnal mind is enmity against God: for it is not subject to the Law of God, neither indeed can be.*

"So then they who are in the flesh cannot please God" (Rom. 8:7-8).

111

FEBRUARY
25

*a*nd seven Priests shall bear before the Ark seven trumpets of rams' horns: and the seventh day you shall compass the city seven times, and the Priests shall blow with the trumpets (Josh. 6:4).

The manner in which Jericho was to be taken had no semblance of military strategy, neither was it meant to have. Yet all of this serves as a type or symbol of the manner in which *"Jerichos"* can be subdued within our hearts and lives. One may refer to them as six principles of Faith which must be brought into exercise in the actual winning of victories in the Christian life. These six principles are:

1. The intelligence of Faith.
2. The obedience of Faith.
3. The exercise of Faith.
4. The folly of Faith.
5. The patience of Faith.
6. The victory of Faith.

The *"intelligence"* of Faith puts Jesus in the midst, just

as Israel, at God's Command, put the Ark in the midst, which was a Type of Christ.

The *"obedience"* of Faith observes exactly the Word of the Lord, as Israel, in this Chapter, minutely obeyed the many Divine directions.

The *"exercise"* of Faith is illustrated here in that Israel had to march silently around the city day after day for six days. Such exercise develops Faith.

The *"folly"* of Faith, as it looks to the world, is evidenced here by Israel's silent march, day-by-day, around the city; and by their using, instead of battering rams, trumpets made of the horns of rams! The soldiers on the walls could very well have mocked them.

The *"victory"* of Faith is seen in the fact that the wall fell down without the use of means that could account for its fall.

The Lord gives us victory presently on the same principles. It is always by *"Faith,"* but it must ever be remembered that Christ and the Cross must ever be the Object of Faith (I Cor. 1:17-18, 23; 2:2).

FEBRUARY
26

*a*nd you, in any wise, keep yourselves from the accursed thing, lest you make yourselves accursed, when you take of the accursed thing, and make the camp of Israel a curse, and trouble it. But all the silver, and gold, and vessels of brass and iron, are consecrated to the LORD: they shall come into the treasury of the LORD (Josh. 6:18-19).

The wall of Jericho was its strength; the wealth of Jericho, its security. Israel was to have no fellowship with either. As to the wall, faith was to destroy it; as to the wealth, faith was to devote it to God.

At Jericho, God and Satan were face-to-face. It was the first great battle in the Land. It was a crisis; therefore, God must be everything. The victory must be entirely wrought by Him; the spoil must be wholly His. To be sure, the Lord cannot misuse wealth, but His Children can, and, most of the time, do!

Later on, when further trained and taught, Israel could share in the spoil. So it is in the Divine life. Gifts which, at the beginning, would be a snare may, later on, be sources of legitimate joy; but only so if shared in fellowship with God. Fellowship in that which was the security of Jericho would have brought Israel into bondage to the world, just as accepting the wealth of Sodom would have robbed Abraham of his independence.

The Believer's security is to be spiritual if he would win spiritual victory; and his confidence is not to be in the might and wisdom of man, i.e., the wall of Jericho, but in the Word, which says, *"I have given Jericho into your hand."* The Lord is saying the same thing presently as it regards the *"Jerichos"* which seek to serve as hindrances to our Christian experience.

Let it ever be understood:

Victory can only be won in God's Way, which is the *"Way of the Cross."*

Paul said, *"But God forbid that I should glory, save in the Cross of our Lord Jesus Christ, by Whom the world is Crucified unto me, and I unto the world"* (Gal. 6:14).

FEBRUARY
27

*b*ut the Children of Israel committed a trespass in the accursed thing: for Achan, the son of Carmi, the son of Zabdi, the son of Zerah, of the Tribe of Judah, took of the accursed thing: and the anger of the LORD was kindled against the Children of Israel (Josh. 7:1).

Israel had won a great victory regarding Jericho. The victory, of course, belonged to the Lord. The Believer, however, as Joshua, is sometimes caught off guard after a great victory. It is easy at such a time to be overconfident, and, thereby, to forget prayer. Had Joshua prayed about Ai, sin would immediately have been discovered and defeat avoided.

A hidden sin was the cause of Israel's defeat at Ai. God had given the Command that none of the *"treasure"* of Jericho was to be taken by the people; all of it was to be dedicated to the treasury of the Lord. Achan had disobeyed that Command and had taken for himself some silver, gold, and a Babylonian garment (Josh. 7:21).

In the life of victory, God is the One and Only strength of the Believer. We have no other strength. But God cannot give that strength if we indulge in sin. If He did, He would deny His Own Nature, which is Holiness. When He acts in power in the midst of His People, He must act in harmony with His Own Nature; hence, He must judge sin in the camp of Israel with the same *"fierce anger"* with which He judged it in the city of Jericho. In both cases, that Judgment was death.

But if the judgment and discovery of sin be painful, and if there be faithfulness in dealing with it, then Grace gives both blessing and victory, and the valley of Achor becomes a *"Door of Hope"* (Hos. 2:15).

The valley of Achor was where Achan was executed for his sin and his refusal to repent, until forced by Joshua. Sin should be feared, and extremely so, but neither its bitterness nor its punishment should be dreaded; for if it is dealt with correctly, by confessing it to the Lord, then, as stated, the *"valley of Achor,"* which had been a valley of death, now becomes a *"Door of Hope"* (I Jn. 1:9).

The Christian fails when the Christian gets his eyes off Christ and the Cross and onto self, which denies such a one the help of the Holy Spirit. That being the case, the person is to be restored by telling them *"why"* they failed, and how, once again, to resume the road of victory, i.e., Christ and the Cross (Gal. 6:1).

117

FEBRUARY

28

*t*hen Joshua built an Altar unto the LORD God of Israel in Mount Ebal (Josh. 8:30).

There were two mountains in Israel, actually in the midst of the country, which were to be dedicated to the Lord. One was Mount Ebal, which was the Mount of Cursing; the other was Mount Gerizim, which was the Mount of Blessing. Both stood side by side (Deut., Chpts. 27-28).

The Lord commanded Joshua to build an Altar on Mount Ebal, which was, as stated, the Mount of Sin and the Judgment of Cursing. The Altar pictured Jesus and the price He would pay at Calvary's Cross. The Altar was to be built of *"whole stones,"* which meant that no tool was to embellish the Altar, which means that Calvary and what it stands for is never to be changed.

Unfortunately, the modern Church is attempting to build an Altar, that is, if it recognizes the Altar at all, on Mount Gerizim, the Mount of Blessing.

But let it ever be understood:

There can be no Blessing until we recognize that our problem is sin, typified by Mount Ebal, and that the only answer to sin is the Cross of Christ.

Unfortunately, we presently have *"Blessing Churches"* and *"Cursing Churches."* To major in either one to the exclusion of the other is wrong. The Church that is Biblical will understand that sin is the problem and the *"Altar"* is the answer. That being done, the *"Blessing"* will abundantly follow! Otherwise, there is no Blessing!

FEBRUARY
29

*a*nd they went to Joshua unto the camp at Gilgal, and said unto him, and to the men of Israel, We be come from a far country: now therefore make you a league with us. And Joshua made peace with them, and made a league with them, to let them live: and the princes of the congregation swore unto them (Josh. 9:6, 15).

The Gibeonites, which were inhabitants of the land of Canaan, deceived Joshua and the Elders of Israel into believing that they were from a far country and that a covenant of peace should be made with them. And so it was. But after three days, Israel found out that the Gibeonites were instead only a short distance away. However, Israel had sworn to protect them; irrespective of the deception, Israel must keep her oath (Josh. 9:18).

Several things here were wrongly done. In the first place, the Scripture says that Joshua made peace with them because he believed them without *"asking counsel at the mouth of the LORD"* (Josh. 9:14). This tells us that we must pray about everything. In other words, we cannot trust the flesh, which speaks of mere human wisdom, to do anything right. It is incumbent upon the Child of God to seek the Lord about anything and everything, irrespective as to how small it, at first, may seem to be. We must have His Leading and Guidance in all things (Jn. 16:18).

Second, the Gibeonites practiced deception, which was wrong. Had they come to Joshua and the Elders of Israel in humble supplication, the evidence is they would have been spared. This is proven by the place and position given to them by the Lord.

When most people come to the Lord, however, they little come for the correct and the right reasons. But yet, if faith is evidenced, God always honors it, no matter how misplaced, at least for the person coming to Christ. As an example, almost no believing sinner comes to Christ as a result of love for the Lord, but rather because they fear Hell, etc.

But Grace triumphed over the folly of the Gibeonites, which it always does. The Gibeonites became the Nethinim. This word means *"given,"* i.e., devoted to the Sanctuary of Jehovah. Their lives were spared because the Princes of Israel had taken an oath to them in the Name of Jehovah. But, because of their deceit, they were condemned to be drawers of water to the House of the Lord. They were not condemned to domestic slavery to the Israelites, but to bondage to *"the congregation."* This meant they were to make certain the Brazen Laver was always filled with water and there always was wood for the Brazen Altar.

Grace, therefore, brought them into the Glory and Joy of Psalms 84:10. It also instructed David to appoint them to high positions in the Temple (Ezra 8:20). Later on, they were carried away captive with Israel; however, they were among the first to return with Ezra and Nehemiah, pledging themselves to keep the Statutes given by God to Moses (Ezra 2:43-58; Neh. 8:60). We last read of them (Neh. 3:26; 10:28; 11:21) making their home outside the watergate of Jerusalem.

Why the watergate?

Because, by being near the water supply, they could more readily discharge the honorable bondage to which Joshua had condemned them, i.e., of being drawers of water to the Temple of Jehovah. Thus, a curse, justly pronounced by Law, becomes, by Grace, a blessing.

And so it does with us all, and all made possible by Jesus and His Sacrificial, Atoning Death.

MARCH

1

*a*nd the LORD said unto Joshua, Fear them not: for I
have delivered them into your hand; there shall not a man of
them stand before you *(Josh. 10:8).*

Gibeon had made peace with Joshua, although under
somewhat devious circumstances. But yet Joshua was
bound to defend them. When anyone makes peace with
the Divine Joshua, he brings upon himself the anger of
those who had once been his friends and companions.
Thus it was with Gibeon.

Five kings formed a confederation against Gibeon, not
understanding, I suppose, that Joshua would come to their
rescue. But to their help he would go; he would, in fact,
win a tremendous victory, because the Lord had given him
instructions. Not only did the Lord use Joshua and his
army, giving them superhuman strength, but *"the Lord cast
down great stones from Heaven upon them"* (Josh. 10:11).
These were hailstones, which wreaked havoc among the
enemy. But the greatest miracle was yet to come!

The day was far spent, and the victory had not yet been won. Joshua asked the Lord for one of the greatest miracles that had ever been performed, and that was for the Earth to stop in its rotation. He said, *"Sun, stand thou still upon Gibeon; and thou, Moon, in valley of Ajalon."*

Hebrew Scholars point out that the words, *"stand still,"* and *"midst"* are defective translations. The word *"Sun"* is to be understood as *"sunlight,"* as in many other Passages in the Bible. *"Stand still"* should be translated *"remain"*; *"midst"* means the *"half of,"* i.e., the horizon, for so they spoke in those days.

The hill of Gibeon at the moment when Joshua spoke was behind him to the east, and the sun was setting in front of him to the west. It was evening and a continuance of the daylight was needed in order to complete the victory. What Joshua said may, therefore, be thus expressed in modern English: *"Sun, keep shining upon Gibeon, and thou, Moon, in the valley of Ajalon!"* And the sunlight remained and the moonlight continued, until the people of God had avenged themselves on their enemies.

God is a miracle-working God; He will do the same presently for all who believe Him!

MARCH

2

*a*nd it came to pass, when they brought out those kings unto Joshua, that Joshua called for all the men of Israel, and said unto the captains of the men of war which went with him, Come near, put your feet upon the necks of these kings. And they came near, and put their feet upon the necks of them (Josh. 10:24).

The placing of the foot on the head or neck of someone speaks of total dominion. There is but one way to deal with sin and that is to place the triumphant foot of faith upon its neck, putting it to death. It is impossible to come to terms with sin, just as, in the Judgment of God, it was impossible for Israel to improve these five kings. Man, in his folly, tries to improve what is opposed to God; but the failure of his effort ever reveals its foolishness.

Sin, in some way, is ever the problem of humanity. The solution to the sin problem, and there is only one solution, is the Cross of Christ (Rom. 8:1-2, 11). Man keeps trying to improve self, and the Church leads the way.

Let it ever be understood:

Self cannot improve self. It is impossible!

While self definitely needs to be improved, it can only be accomplished by the Power and Person of the Holy Spirit.

And how do we get Him to carry out this necessary work within our hearts and lives, which, in effect, is the development of the *"Fruit of the Spirit"* (Gal. 5:22-23)?

Let us say it again:

One cannot come to terms with sin, not in any capacity. It must be totally and completely defeated and put out of our lives, typified here by the feet of God's warriors being placed on the necks of these enemies.

The method? There is only one.

"For the Law (that which we are about to give is a Law of God, devised by the Godhead in eternity past [I Pet. 1:18-20]; this Law, in fact, is *'God's Prescribed Order of Victory') of the Spirit* (Holy Spirit, i.e., *'the way the Spirit works') of Life* (all life comes from Christ, but through the Holy Spirit [Jn. 16:13-14]) *in Christ Jesus* (anytime Paul uses this term, or one of its derivatives, he is, without fail, referring to what Christ did at the Cross, which makes this *'life'* possible) *has made me free* (given me total Victory) *from the Law of sin and death* (these are the two most powerful Laws in the Universe; the *'Law of the Spirit of Life in Christ Jesus'* alone is stronger than the *'Law of sin and death'*; if the Believer attempts to live for God by any manner other than Faith in Christ and the Cross, he is doomed to failure" (Rom. 8:2).

MARCH
3

*a*nd Joshua at that time turned back, and took Hazor, and smote the king thereof with the sword: for Hazor beforetime was the head of all those kingdoms (Josh. 11:10).

Hazor was the center of power for this area. Conventional wisdom would propose to make it the seat of the new government, so that it should be that for God which it previously had been for the world — *"for Hazor beforetime was the head of all those kingdoms."* But God will in no wise allow this seat of power to become that of His People. They were to depend exclusively on Him, thereby allowing Him to lead them accordingly.

So Hazor is to be totally destroyed. Not a vestige of its former power must remain to compete with Gilgal, where the Lord then resided. The center and source of power must be all Divine. At that time, Joshua also destroyed the Anakims, who were giants, actually the product of the union of fallen angels and women (Gen. 6:4).

The Believer must ever understand that God demands

nothing less than total victory. Every work of the flesh must be subdued and destroyed. This can be done only by the Believer placing his Faith exclusively in the Cross of Christ, which then gives the Holy Spirit great latitude to work within our lives. What is impossible for us is totally possible for Him. He is God!

MARCH

4

*a*nd these are the kings of the country which Joshua
and the Children of Israel smote on this side Jordan on the
west . . . which Joshua gave unto the Tribes of Israel for a
possession according to their divisions . . . all the kings thirty
and one (Josh. 12:7, 24).

On the wilderness side of Jordan, Israel conquered
only two kings; on the Canaan side, thirty-one. So it is
in the Christian life. Those who are satisfied to stop
short of claiming and enjoying all the exceeding great
and precious promises of the New Covenant win but few
victories over sin, self, and the world, but those who go
on into a perfect Faith, which is Faith in Christ and the
Cross, win many victories.

It is encouraging and touching to read of these thirty-
one victories so definitely and individually recorded. There
were not just thirty victories, but thirty-one. Each victory
was important in the eye of God and precious to the heart
of God, however uninteresting and small it might appear

to man. No victory over the enemy is small to God's mind. The broken numbers in Scriptures, for example, the number of the firstborn of Israel, the number of David's mighty men, the number in the net of John, Chapter 21, etc., form a profitable Bible subject for study.

All victory is found in the Cross, and the Cross alone (Rom. 6:3-14).

MARCH
5

*n*ow Joshua was old and stricken in years; and the LORD said unto him, You are old and stricken in years, and there remains yet very much land to be possessed (Josh. 13:1).

Joshua was now about 100 years old.

The first seven, and perhaps the first twelve, Verses of this Chapter are the very words of Him Who said, *"In My Father's House are many mansions."* He here pointed out to His People the *"very much land"* that He had prepared for them. He desired to make them understand and know all that He had given them. He had a Perfect Plan for them, as He has for His Own today. There was nothing uncertain in His arrangements, but, on the contrary, everything was orderly and well defined.

The fact that these Verses are the very words of the Lord Jesus Christ makes them especially precious to the Christian, while, to the ordinary reader, they are uninteresting. The sad word, *"nevertheless"* (13:13), expresses man's response to the exceeding Great and Precious

Promises of the preceding Verses. Such is also the sad condition of most Believers presently. All spiritual blessings are ours in the Heavenlies in Christ, but how few of these are really possessed and enjoyed!

There is a difference between the Gifts of God and receiving and enjoying those Gifts; and, accordingly, how many enemies remain unsubdued in the hearts of Believers.

Please allow me to state that which we have stated again and again:

All that the Lord has for us can never be realized unless we make the Cross of Christ the Object of our Faith. If we try to possess these *"Promises"* by carnal means, it cannot be done!

As we have repeatedly said, the Holy Spirit Alone can make real to us the victories already won by Jesus Christ, and He ever does so by the Cross and our Faith in that Finished Work (I Cor. 1:18).

MARCH
6

*n*ow therefore give me this mountain, whereof the LORD spoke in that day; for you heard in that day how the Anakims were there, and the cities were great and fenced: if so be the LORD will be with me, then I shall be able to drive them out as the LORD said. And Joshua blessed him, and gave unto Caleb the son of Jephunneh Hebron for an inheritance . . . And the land had rest from war (Josh. 14:12-13, 15).

This Chapter is one of sunshine, simply because it is one of faith. In the midst of unbelief registered by all of the Tribes at one time or the other, Caleb's faith shines like the sun. His was a Divine Faith. Such a faith overcomes the world; and, accordingly, he claims the great mountains for a possession; he not only expels giants from thence, but even Arba, the greatest of the giants (14:15). Such was the energy of faith in the heart of this man! The result was that Kirjath-arba — that is, the city of Arba — became Hebron — that is, *"fellowship"*; and the land had rest from war, for whenever there is faithfulness,

133

there is rest.

Thus, Caleb, who was a slave on the plains of Egypt, became a prince upon the mountains of Hebron.

Giant sins entrenched on strong mountains cannot be dislodged by the religious ingenuity of man, but only by a Faith that is born of God. Such Faith, at least Faith that is honored by God, must ever have the correct object, which always is the Cross of Christ. There is only one answer for the evil passions with which Satan would afflict us, and that is the Cross.

That's the reason that Paul said, *"But though we, or an Angel from Heaven, preach any other gospel unto you than that which we have preached unto you, let him be accursed"* (Gal. 1:8).

Paul's Gospel was *"Jesus Christ and Him Crucified"* (I Cor. 1:23).

134

MARCH
7

*a*s for the Jebusites the inhabitants of Jerusalem, the Children of Judah could not drive them out: but the Jebusites dwell with the Children of Judah at Jerusalem unto this day (Josh. 15:63).

Judah, being the Royal Tribe, and Joseph, having the Birthright which was forfeited by Reuben, were the first to receive their portions in the Promised Land. It is delightful to read of this apportionment. When God enriches His People, everything is real, substantial, and definite. He gives largely; and His Blessings may, without fear of disappointment, be counted just as this Chapter records the 116 cities given to Judah.

But a life of Blessing with God has definite borders, just as the lot of Judah had its Divinely marked boundaries. It is important that God should choose a lot in life for each one of His People, and that they should be satisfied with that lot and its limitations.

Achsah's faith and intelligence were admirable. So

sure was she that the South Land given to her by her father was really hers, and would not be taken from her by the Canaanite, that she asked for springs of water to make that land fertile. Her father, gladdened by such faith and intelligence, gave her more than she asked. Even a South Land needs springs of water. Therefore, without the Holy Spirit the most happily circumcised life, or gifted Ministry, must be alike barren. If men give good gifts unto their children, as Caleb did to Achsah, how much more will the Heavenly Father give the Holy Spirit to them who ask Him! (15:16-19; Lk. 11:13).

Man, however valued, is never perfect, and, therefore, Jerusalem remained in the power of the Jebusite until David, a type of Israel's Mighty King, captured it. In how many lives is found a fortress opposed to Christ's government, which ought to have been conquered at the beginning? (Williams)

MARCH

8

*W*hen they had made an end of dividing the land for inheritance by their coasts, the Children of Israel gave an inheritance to Joshua the son of Nun among them (Josh. 19:49).

Several things are said here which open to us the possibilities of great things given by the Lord. They are:

1. *"They gave him the city which he asked"*: We have not, because we ask not, and, all too often, we ask out of covetousness rather than asking in the Will of God (James 4:2-3). And yet Jesus told us, *"Ask, and it shall be given you; seek, and you shall find; knock, and it shall be opened unto you"* (Lk. 11:9).

2. *"According to the Word of the Lord"*: The Elders of Israel found that it was God's Will for Joshua to be given that for which he asked. *"The Word of the Lord"* should ever be the criteria. If it's promised in the Word, then we can have it.

3. *"Even Timnath-Serah in Mount Ephraim"*: *"Timnath"* means *"portion that remains,"* and *"Serah"* means *"city of*

137

the sun." So, in effect, Joshua was asking for the *"portion that remains."*

Too many Believers are satisfied with the status quo. They never push on for the *"portion that remains,"* and thereby miss out on so much. It is ironical! The Lord made the sun stand still for Joshua (the rotation of the Earth ceased for a period of time), and *"Serah"* means *"city of the sun."*

4. *"And he built the city, and dwelt therein"*: The Lord seldom gives us a city, so to speak, that is already built and ready. He gives us instead the Promise, and then we are to build whatever it is that is designated, which oftentimes requires the expulsion of the enemy. This is done in order that our Faith may be strengthened.

MARCH
9

*a*nd the second lot came forth to Simeon, even for the Tribe of the Children of Simeon according to their families: and their inheritance was within the inheritance of the Children of Judah (Josh. 19:1).

There was a reason that Simeon's inheritance in Canaan was within the inheritance of Judah.

Simeon, because of his misconduct (Gen. 34:25-29), was under a curse (Gen. 49:5-7). So, whenever the Tribe of Simeon came into the Land of Canaan, which was about 250 years later, because of this curse, Simeon has no inheritance. Judah, which was given the largest inheritance of all, shared with Simeon.

Such is a perfect example of the lost sons of Adam's fallen race. The whole of humanity was, and is, to a certain extent, under a curse, all brought on by the Fall in the Garden of Eden. However, our Heavenly Judah (Jesus came from the Tribe of Judah) has such a bountiful inheritance that He has consented to share with us. And so, our inheritance is now within the inheritance of the Lord Jesus Christ.

Paul said, *"And if children, then heirs; heirs of God, and joint-heirs with Christ . . . ."* (Rom. 8:17).

Thus it was that Simeon, justly doomed to wrath, was taken up in Grace — the curse being turned into a blessing, which the Lord Alone can do — and given a seat among the sons at the King's table; for the Lord, as stated, sprang out of Judah (Heb. 7:14).

Simeon was saved by Grace, not by works. The name means *"hearing."* The Holy Spirit in Galatians 3:2 contrasts salvation by *"doing"* and Salvation by *"hearing,"* and teaches that only upon the latter principle can sinners be given a portion in the Heavenly Canaan.

MARCH
10

Speak to the Children of Israel, saying, Appoint out for you cities of refuge, whereof I spoke unto you by the hand of Moses (Josh. 20:2).

The cities of refuge were six in number; three westward of Jordan, and three eastward.

Hebrews 6:18 sets forth Christ as the City of Refuge for sinners guilty of His Blood; and the six cities appointed by Joshua display, by the meaning of their names, something of the sufficiency of that Saviour. For in Him is found: *"Holiness"* (Kadesh), *"Strength"* (Shechem), *"Fellowship"* (Hebron), *"Safety"* (Bezer), *"Uplifting"* (Ramoth), and *"Happiness"* (Golan).

God puts Holiness first and Happiness last. Man reverses this.

The individual who accidentally kills someone could flee to one of these Cities of Refuge. He was to remain there until the death of the High Priest, when he could then go free. The Avenger of Blood, one of the relatives of

141

the individual killed, symbolized the Law. It demanded the death of the man-slayer.

The death of the High Priest satisfied this claim and liberated the man-slayer. Christ's Death, not His Life, rent the Veil, and frees the sinner from the curse of the Law (Gal. 3:13-14). The man-slayer was then at liberty to return to his possession as a free man.

When Israel shall look upon Him Whom they have pierced, it will then be revealed to them that His Death restores them to the Land and the Family of God.

Thus, a City of Refuge stood almost at every man's door, because these cities were scattered over Israel; but to enjoy its safety, the man-slayer had to flee thither.

There were individuals who found neither refuge in the city nor liberty in the death of the High Priest. It was the murderer by intention. Sinners who flee to Jesus prove, by doing so, that they are not willingly guilty of His Blood; and they, therefore, find in Him both safety and liberty. But sinners who refuse thus to seek mercy in Him demonstrate, by their refusal, that they are verily guilty of His Death; and for these individuals there is no Salvation (Williams).

MARCH

11

*a*nd the LORD was with Judah; and he drove out the inhabitants of the mountain; but could not drive out the inhabitants of the valley, because they had chariots of iron (Judg. 1:19)

Clearly and plainly, the Scripture says, *"The Lord was with Judah."* But yet Judah failed to take advantage of the might and power of the Lord, which could have helped them do anything. While *"chariots of iron"* may have been a formidable obstacle to Judah, they were nothing to the Lord. But yet Judah did not depend entirely on the Lord as they should have, and the enemy remained.

They looked at the *"chariots of iron"* instead of looking at the *"Arm of the Lord,"* and so became the miserable bondmen of those whom they should have utterly destroyed. They first permitted to remain in their midst the inhabitants of the land, and then, very soon, became insensible of the existence of these sources of evil and misery.

Such is the sad history presently of many a Christian,

143

and many a Church.

The faith of a weak woman, Achsah, and the courage of her cousin, Othniel (Judg. 1:12-15), are here again recorded by the Holy Spirit; they stand out in contrast to the cowardice and unbelief of the Tribes.

By the victories given to Judah, Simeon, and Manasseh, God showed what he could do for the heart that trusted Him. But the ground won by faith can only be held by faith; and very soon, therefore, the Canaanite and the Philistine recovered possession of what they had lost, which proved to be a terrible thorn in the side of Israel, and was so all the days of the Judges, a time frame of over 400 years.

We learn from Judges that the *"Promise"* is different than the *"Possession."* The *"Promise"* does not contain a *"Possession"* free of the enemy, but, most of the time, filled with the enemy. However, as Faith claims the Promise, likewise, it must claim the Possession of the Promise.

The principle now is the same as then.

While Israel of old fought physical enemies, we today fight spiritual enemies, but, as stated, the principle is the same. The Lord has given us the Promise, but, if we do not trust Him, the *"chariots of spiritual iron"* will never be dispossessed.

MARCH

12

*A*nd an Angel of the LORD came up from Gilgal to Bochim, and said, I made you to go up out of Egypt, and have brought you unto the land which I swore unto your fathers; and I said, I will never break My Covenant with you. And you shall make no league with the inhabitants of this land; you shall throw down their altars: but you have not obeyed My voice: why have you done this? (Judg. 2:1-2).

Actually, Verse 1 should read, "The Angel of Jehovah," i.e., the Lord Jesus Christ. Christ is not an Angel, at least as we think of such, but, at times, the Holy Spirit uses the term "Angel" to refer to God, Angels (as we know of such), and men. In this case, it is the Lord.

The doctrine of this Chapter is that God cannot give victories to the "flesh."

"Gilgal" means "rolled away"; it refers to the reproach of the wilderness that is rolled away from the Children of Israel. It is a place of victory.

"Bochim" means "place of weeping"; it pertains to the

145

Israelites who failed to drive out the inhabitants of the land, abjectly disobeying the Word of the Lord, hence the reason for the admonition.

The Lord would not have told Israel to drive out the inhabitants of the land but that He would help them to do. With God all things are possible! The evidence, however, is that they ceased to rely on the Lord, and relied on their own ability and strength, i.e., *"the flesh,"* thereby, suffering defeat. So, *"Bochim"* is rightly called the place of weeping.

The Believer is admonished to gain the victory over all *"works of the flesh."* He can do so only by one means, which is by ever evidencing Faith in Christ and what Christ has done at the Cross, all on our behalf. Then the Holy Spirit, Who is God, will give us victory after victory; however, He will not help us otherwise (Rom. 8:1-2, 11). Defeat results from unbelief, and we speak of unbelief as it regards Christ and the Cross. In fact, that's where all unbelief centers up.

How many Believers are in a place of weeping because of defeat, which means they have tried to live this life by the means of the flesh instead of by Faith in Christ and the Cross?

146

MARCH
13

*n*ow these are the nations which the LORD left, to prove Israel by them, even as many of Israel as had not known all the wars of Canaan (Judg. 3:1).

We find in this Chapter that idolatry always leads to slavery. There was first bondage to Baal; then, as a result, bondage to Shushan. However, every time they cried unto Jehovah, He raised up a Saviour for them. When they cried, He delivered — no matter how guilty they were. There was no delay. *"If we confess our sins, He is faithful and just to forgive us our sins."* Forgiveness immediately follows true confession.

The word *"quarries"* (Judg. 3:19, 26) should read *"graven images."* How sad to learn (Judg. 3:19) that these idols had been set up at Gilgal, especially considering that this had been the dwelling-place of Jehovah. Gilgal pictures the broken and contrite heart in which God dwells. If He be grieved away from such an heart, it quickly becomes the home of graven images, i.e., idols.

147

Regrettably, the problem of *"idols"* did not cease with the Israelites of that time and place. They abound presently. That's why John the Beloved said, *"Little children, keep yourselves from idols"* (I Jn. 5:21).

An *"idol"* is anything in which we place our faith, other than Christ and the Cross. In fact, religion is the greatest idol of all, and the doing of religion is the greatest narcotic there is. That means that everything other than Christ and the Cross leads to defeat, abject defeat! (Gal. 2:20-21; 6:14).

MARCH
14

*a*nd the Children of Israel again did evil in the sight of the LORD, when Ehud was dead. And LORD sold them into the hand of Jabin king of Canaan, who reigned in Hazor; the captain of whose host was Sisera, which dwelt in Harosheth of the Gentiles. And the Children of Israel cried unto the LORD: for he had nine hundred chariots of iron; and twenty years he mightily oppressed the Children of Israel. And Deborah, a Prophetess, the wife of Lapidoth, she judged Israel at that time (Judg. 4:1-4).

This may be said to be the women's Chapter. The faith of Deborah reached out and won a great victory; the faith of Jael destroyed a great tyrant and saved thousands from certain death.

There was one heart that did not tremble before Sisera and his nine hundred chariots of iron. She *"sat as judge"* under a palm tree near Bethel. Her namesake, Rebekah's nurse, was buried there some 400 years back. This was Deborah.

Some would claim that God cannot use women in the preaching and teaching of the Gospel. However, both of these women were raised up and energized by God for their respective Ministries, as were also the great women of the Pauline Epistles. If the Scriptures be read accurately, it will be seen that God used women under the First Covenant and He continues to do so under the Second Covenant.

Under the First Covenant, the Lord used Deborah to defeat one of the mightiest heathen warriors of them all, Sisera. It says that he had *"nine hundred chariots of iron."* But through the faith of this woman, his army was defeated, plus all of his chariots.

The Scripture says, *"And the LORD discomfited Sisera, and all his chariots, and all his host, with the edge of the sword before Barak"* (Judg. 4:15). The word *"discomfited"* implies supernatural discomfiture. Jael, another woman, finished the task by driving a nail through Sisera's temple. *"So he died"* (Judg. 4:21).

The Holy Spirit points, in the Scriptures, to only two women as preeminently *"blessed among women."* The one was *"Jael"*; the other, *"The Virgin Mary."* The latter is associated with the Advent of Israel's Redeemer; the former, with the judgment of Israel's oppressor (Judg. 5:24; Lk. 1:42).

MARCH

15

*f*or the divisions of Reuben there were great searchings of heart. Gilead abode beyond Jordan: and why did Dan remain in ships? Asher continued on the sea shore and abode in his breaches. Zebulun and Naphtali were a people who jeoparded their lives unto the death in the high places of the field (Judg. 5:16-18).

The Holy Spirit here pinpoints the response of some of the Tribes of Israel, as it regards the great battle fought with Sisera and the ensuing victory. We should be careful to note that the Lord catalogs every single thing that we as Believers do.

The Holy Spirit said that the Tribe of Reuben had divisions in their ranks, and, as such, they did not respond to the battle. They stayed *"beyond Jordan."*

With the Tribe of *"Dan,"* it was business as usual. They did not respond either!

The Tribe of Asher, so to speak, was up a creek; consequently, they did not respond!

To contrary, the Tribes of *"Zebulun"* and *"Naphtali"* gave their all, even jeoparding their lives in this fight against the enemies of the Lord.

As well, *"Ephraim,"* *"Benjamin,"* and *"Issachar"* responded favorably, and were noted as such.

And then the Spirit of the Lord through Deborah said, *"Curse ye Meroz* (a town), *said the Angel of the LORD, curse ye bitterly the inhabitants thereof; because they came not to the help of the LORD, to the help of the LORD against the mighty"* (Judg. 5:23).

All of this tells us that the conduct of the Tribes is contrasted. First, reference is made to the fact that only a minority of the Chiefs and of the people volunteered for the enterprise; but that did not discourage Deborah, for Jehovah *"came down"* for her against the mighty.

Faith will always gain the victory!

MARCH
16

*a*nd there came an Angel of the LORD, and sat under an oak which was in Ophrah, that pertained unto Joash the Abiezrite: and his son Gideon threshed wheat by the winepress, to hide it from the Midianites. And the Angel of the LORD appeared unto him, and said unto him, the LORD is with you, thou mighty man of valour (Judg. 6:11-12).

Israel now finds herself again under the jack-booted heel of the oppressor, all because of sin. These were God's People, and, therefore, were to be the mightiest on Earth; however, irrespective as to who the person or persons might be, sin will make slaves of those who engage its wares.

When the Lord appeared to Gideon, He referred to him as a *"mighty man of valor."* What is He saying about me? About you?

Gideon was strong because he knew himself to be weak, and because he believed Jehovah to be mighty; the misery that he was in because of the Midianites caused him to lift his heart to God instead of accepting, as others did, the tyranny of the oppressor.

In response to the great visitation of Jehovah to Gideon, the Scripture says, *"Then Gideon built an Altar there unto the LORD, and called it Jehovah-Shalom,"* which means *"the God of Peace."* The *"peace"* to which he now refers has a twofold meaning:

First of all, it refers to peace with God. Gideon's victory with the Lord manifested itself in him destroying the idols in his own home. Public victories cannot be won in the absence of private victories. With sin removed, and done so by virtue of the slain lamb, all which typified Christ, peace is now restored.

Peace restored in the spiritual guarantees peace in every other capacity. In other words, the Lord would have Gideon destroy the oppressor, which he did. All victory is found in the Cross of Christ, and no victory is found outside of the Cross of Christ.

MARCH
17

*a*nd the LORD said unto Gideon, By the three hundred men who lapped will I save you, and deliver the Midianites into your hand: and let all the other people go every man unto his place (Judg. 7:7).

An Israelite had a dream in which he saw a barley cake, which is the poorest of all bread, tumble into the host of Midian; it *"came unto a tent, and smote it that it fell, and overturned it, that the tent lay along"* (Judg. 7:13).

In gathering the army that was to fight the Midianites, in accordance with Deuteronomy 20:8, the cowardly were given the option of returning home, and 22,000 did so. A further test dismissed 9,700 men. By laying their swords aside, and going down with deliberation on their knees to drink, they showed that they were concerned about their own needs and comforts. On the other hand, the 300 showed by their action that God and the fortunes of His Kingdom had the first place in their hearts; they would not let even the necessary needs hinder them in getting to the work.

So the Lord would save Israel by defeating, with only three hundred men, the vast army of the Midianites. But these were three hundred faith men.

God, Who knows the heart, planned so that Israel could not say, *"My own hand has saved me."* Man always wants to have a hand in his own Salvation; but listen to the song:

> *"Nothing, either great or small,*
> *"Nothing, sinner, no,*
> *"Jesus did it all,*
> *"Long, long ago!"*

MARCH
18

*a*nd the Children of Israel said unto the LORD, *We have
sinned: do Thou unto us whatsoever seems good unto You;
deliver us only, we pray You, this day. And they put away the
strange gods from among them, and served the LORD: and
His soul was grieved for the misery of Israel* (Judg. 10:15-16).

Israel now finds herself, because of sin, again oppressed by the enemy, and severely so! The Philistines on
the west and the Ammonites on the east *"vexed and oppressed them."* These words may be translated *"broke and
crushed them."* In earlier days when serving one false god,
they were oppressed but on one side. But now, serving a
multitude of idols, they are oppressed on both sides.

Sin has no stopping point, ever taking the person
deeper into its clutches. Its aim is total destruction!

But there was sufficient energy of life in Israel to bring
out the cry of confession. To be conscious of misery is a
sign of life. Because of the deceitfulness of the heart, and
because of the deceitfulness of sin, bondage is accepted

after a slight struggle; then, after a time, the slave becomes unconscious of the slavery.

The confession, *"We have sinned against You,"* showed true Repentance, for it showed a sense of injury done to God, not merely sorrow because of the miseries that lay upon themselves. Remorse is not repentance — mental distress because of the painful results of sin is not repentance; but a sense of the grief and dishonor occasioned to God and sorrow because He has been sinned against — that is Repentance.

David and Simon Magus illustrate true and false repentance. The one cried out, *"I have sinned against the LORD."* His first thought was God and His Glory. The other said, *"Pray for me that none of these things come upon me."* His first thought was himself and how to secure exemption from punishment (Ps. 51; Acts 8:24).

True Repentance demands that the Believer repent not only of the bad that has been done, but the good as well. To be sure, it is a struggle of the flesh to repent of the good. The *"good"* is our crutch, our bargaining power with God; however, we must come to the place that we utterly realize that we have no bargaining power with God. Our only hope is to throw ourselves on His Mercy and Grace, confessing the evil and repenting of the good, i.e., *"dependence on good things."* We must know that our only hope is Christ and what He has done for us at the Cross. Faith in that Finished Work always brings spiritual relief (Gal. 6:14).

MARCH
19

*t*hen three thousand men of Judah went to the top of the rock Etam, and said to Samson, Knowest thou not that the Philistines are rulers over us? What is this that you have done to us? And he said unto them, As they did unto me, so have I done unto them. And they said unto him, We are come down to bind you, that we may deliver you into the hand of the Philistines. And Samson said unto them, Swear unto me, that you will not fall upon me yourselves (Judg. 15:11-12).

The opposition of the world is bitter to the Believer, but the opposition of the Church is more bitter. The men of Judah said to Samson: *"Do you not know that the Philistines rule over us?"* They wished to live in peace under that government of tyranny; and they did not wish to have in their midst a Nazarite who would disturb that peace and excite the world against them. Samson's own people were quite ready to hand him over to a cruel death in order to maintain that peace, so-called! This condition of spiritual degradation marks, and has marked, the history of the Christian Church.

But just as the lion had no strength against Samson, so the Philistine had no strength against him. In this, Samson is a Type of Christ, Who destroyed him who had the power of death, that is, the Devil; and thus food and sweetness are brought out of death, as the honey out of the conquered lion.

God's victories are usually won with despised instruments. In fact, the most feeble instrument is destruction to the enemy if God be behind it! Many presently ridicule Samson; and this is, in no way, meant to place a seal of approval upon his wrong direction; however, had he the help of his own people instead of their opposition, things may have been different.

At any rate, we must never forget that, despite Samson's failures, one great victory shines greater than all, and I speak of his faith. The Holy Spirit listed him in the great hall of faith, placing him in the same category as David and Samuel (Heb. 11:32). Ultimately, Samson was an overcomer, for the Scripture says, *"This is the Victory that overcomes the world, even our Faith"* (I Jn. 5:4).

MARCH
20

*a*nd Ruth said, *Intreat me not to leave you, or to return from following after you: for where you go, I will go: and where you lodge, I will lodge: your people shall be my people, and your God my God: Where you die, will I die, and there will I be buried: the LORD do so to me, and more also, if ought but death part you and me* (Ruth 1:16-17).

The example of Ruth is the example of true Salvation. Millions who have never been Born-Again presently clog the Churches. Sinners are saved, not so much by their acceptance of Christ, but by God's acceptance of Christ on their behalf; but sinners must accept the Saviour in order to profit by the Divine acceptance of His Person and Work (Jn. 1:12).

Naomi is on her way back to Bethlehem. To accept Jehovah, Ruth must leave Moab, just as the sinner, spiritually speaking, must leave the world. Ruth was willing to do that! Not only did she tell Naomi that she would leave Moab, but even more so, *"Where you go, I will go."* Now we have full consecration. Not only will she leave Moab, never to go back again, but wherever Naomi leads, i.e., *"wherever Christ leads,"* I will go.

And then, *"Where you lodge, I will lodge."* In other words, your place of Ministry will be my place of Ministry, and whatever that might be. Furthermore, Ruth will no longer identify with the Moabite people, but rather with the people of God, accepting them as her people, and Israel's God as her God.

This commitment was for time and eternity. *"Where you die, will I die, and there will I be buried."* In other words, this was not a momentary decision of emotionalism. It was a decision for time and eternity, i.e., acceptance of the Lord of Glory, which means that she had to turn her back on her family, her land, her country, and all that she had once known. And so it is with those who follow Christ!

The consecration of Ruth is a perfect example. Her reward would be of far greater magnitude than she could ever even begin to ask or think. This Gentile girl, this cursed Moabitess, due to her faith, would find herself in the lineage of the Coming Messiah. Nothing could be greater than that (Mat. 1:5).

MARCH
21

*t*hen Naomi her mother-in-law said unto her, My daughter, shall I not seek rest for you, that it may be well with you? Wash yourself, therefore, and anoint you, and put your raiment upon you, and get thee down to the floor: but make not yourself known unto the man, until he shall have done eating and drinking (Ruth 3:1, 3).

Ruth forsook her people and her native land for her trust under the wing of Jehovah the God of Israel, and when, as a gleaner, she sought her daily bread from the Hand of that Gracious God Who had made this provision for the widow and stranger (Lev. 19:9), she little thought that she was to find a bridegroom among the great Princes of Judah.

Such is the experience of everyone who turns the back upon the best the world can offer, seeking spiritual daily bread in Christ and in the fellowship of His *"field"* and *"servants."* These little conceive the measure of the Grace of Him Who *"takes knowledge of them,"* Who *"lets fall handfuls on purpose for them,"* and Who reaches out the choicest dainties for them that they may eat.

Boaz, in his instructions to the reapers, directed them to give Ruth greater liberty than that commanded by the Law, that is, Boaz gave her far more than she could eat. Naomi's advice to Ruth was wise and astute. She pointed out that Boaz was a redeemer; that, as such, he had the right to redeem their property, which, through poverty, they had lost; that such a redemption involved a marriage with Ruth. So, Naomi, who now serves as a Type of the Holy Spirit, gives Ruth instructions as to how this is to be brought about.

This is what she said:

"Shall I not seek rest for you, that it may be well with you?" We must ever understand that the Lord seeks our best; through Him, and Him Alone, can we have that best!

"Wash yourself therefore": This speaks of the sinner coming to Christ, who is then singularly washed (I Cor. 6:11).

"Put new raiment upon you": Upon coming to Christ and being washed (which speaks of Sanctification), the sinner is made clean; he can now put on the robe of righteousness; however, it is imputed righteousness, meaning that we, within ourselves, have none; so Christ must give us His Righteousness, which He does.

"Get you down to the floor": This speaks of humility, without which the person can find neither Christ nor the Will of God for one's life.

"But make not yourself known unto the man": In other words, let God make plans for you, which He definitely will bless. All too often, Believers try to make the plans themselves and then ask God to bless them, which He never will do. He only blesses that which He plans!

164

So here we have Sanctification, Justification, and humility, which is what the Holy Spirit intends.

The culmination of this was the marriage of Ruth to Boaz. In order for this to happen, Boaz had to purchase Ruth from a kinsman who had a prior claim, but who declared that he could not redeem her. The Law has a prior claim to sinners, but it cannot redeem them. Christ, the Divine Kinsman, became Man in order to redeem. It cost Boaz nothing to redeem Ruth, beyond the setting aside of himself and his own interest, but it cost Christ everything to redeem sinners.

Thus, Ruth, a *"wild olive tree,"* was grafted into, and became a partaker of, *"the root and fatness of the olive tree,"* i.e., Israel; thus, she typifies the Gentile Church.

MARCH
22

*a*nd ere the Lamp of God went out in the Temple of the LORD, where the Ark of God was, and Samuel was laid down to sleep *(I Sam. 3:3).*

I Samuel 3:1 says *"The Word of the LORD was precious in those days; there was no open vision."* This means there was a scarcity of the Word of the Lord in Israel of that day. The nation and its people were in serious straits, which always is the case when the Word of the Lord is scarce.

There have never been more Churches in America than at the present time; however, there has never been less true Word of the Lord preached at any time since the Reformation than now!

Eli, the High Priest, was not only physically blind, but spiritually blind, as well. Consequently, Israel had no spiritual leadership. How so much that mirrors the present!

Then the Scripture says, *"And ere the Lamp of God went out in the Temple of the LORD,"* which proclaims the Golden Lampstand, which sat in the Holy Place, giving light so that the Priests could see to minister. Regrettably, it is unattended, which means the oil has not been replenished. Is the *"Lamp"* going out in the modern Church?

The phrase, *"Where the Ark of God was,"* proclaimed the Holy of Holies, and typified the Throne of God. In other words, access to the Throne was being seriously curtailed. But then God spoke. It was at this dark moment that He chose to reveal Himself; yet not to some influential personage, but to a little boy!

Many people say that it is wrong to speak to a child about the Wrath of God; however, this belief shows how even religious teachers are fallen from God's moral likeness. For His first Message to little Samuel was an appalling one!

Regrettably, if the modern Church doesn't like the messenger, they reject the Message.

However, let it ever be understood:

It is God Who chooses the messenger, and not man. Those whom man chooses are not accepted by God; sadly, those whom God chooses, it seems, are little accepted by man. Nevertheless, the Word of God holds true, irrespective as to the messenger.

Jesus did not meet with the approval of Israel, so they rejected Him. In rejecting Him, they rejected His Message, which was the only Message of Life.

Listen to the Message! If it's not the Message of the Cross, then it's not the Message of the Lord, for the entirety of the Tabernacle and all of its furnishings typified Christ and the Cross.

MARCH
23

So the people sent to Shiloh, that they might bring from thence the Ark of the Covenant of the LORD of Hosts, which dwells between the Cherubims: and the two sons of Eli, Hophni and Phinehas, were there with the Ark of the Covenant of God (I Sam. 4:4).

I Samuel, Chapter 4, is a dark and foreboding Chapter. It speaks of a nation, the only nation in the world, in fact, where Jehovah ruled, or rather was supposed to rule, but now finds itself in serious spiritual straits. Eli was physically blind, the Elders were spiritually blind, and the people were grossly superstitious.

A short time before, God had revealed Himself to the little boy Samuel. Whenever God reveals Himself, the hostility of the enemy is aroused. Directly God revealed Himself in Shiloh, the Philistine revealed himself in Aphek.

Verse 1 of this Chapter proclaims, by the Holy Spirit, the fact that the Israelites *"pitched beside Ebenezer."* This area, however, was not even named *"Ebenezer"* until some 20 years later (I Sam. 7:12). This is by design. On that day of defeat, faith looked forward to the future day of victory, and set up, on the stricken field, the *"Stone of Help,"* which the word *"Ebenezer"* means.

This fact should be full of comfort at this present time, since the moral condition of the modern Church so closely resembles that of the Hebrew Church of that day.

Instead of Israel disobeying the Bible, violating the Most Holy Place, and fetching the Ark of God to themselves, they should rather have taken themselves to the Ark of God, i.e., the Throne of God, and, at the Door of the Tabernacle of the congregation, confessed their sins, broken their idols, and thus returned to God. Then victory would have been the sure result.

As it was, Hophni and Phinehas boldly intruded into the Most Holy Place, into which none were permitted to enter except the High Priest, and that but once a year, and not without blood (Heb. 9:7). They treated the Ark of God like some type of magic talisman, thinking its presence, irrespective of their lack of faith and their sinful lives, would bring victory.

Is the modern Church at present any better?

The further the heart departs from God and His Word, the greater is the importance attached to symbols and ceremonies. Likewise, I might quickly add, it is attached to schemes and efforts devised by men, which claim to be Revelations from the Lord, but are, in fact, anything but!

Attending Church and being religious afford nothing with the Lord. There must be a personal experience, and such an experience can only be gained by Faith in Christ and what Christ has done for us at the Cross. Then, and then alone, will the Holy Spirit work mightily within our lives, because our Faith now has, as its correct Object, the Cross of Christ (I Cor. 1:17-18, 23; 2:2; Gal. 6:14).

MARCH
24

*a*nd the Ark of God was taken; and the two sons of Eli, Hophni and Phinehas, were slain (I Sam. 4:11).

Israel is now in serious straits, because its spiritual leadership is woefully lacking. The Philistines attack, for Satan sees his opportunity. Israel is defeated, with some 4,000 men dying on that fateful day.

As the people of God retreat in order to stem the tide of defeat, they think, *"Let us fetch the Ark of the Covenant of the LORD out of Shiloh unto us, that, when it comes among us, it may save us out of the hand of our enemies."*

They were to find that the Ark of God, without the Presence of God, was no more than a piece of furniture; consequently, it contained no power within itself; therefore, the end result would not be what they had hoped, but rather the very opposite.

I'm afraid the modern Church is all too often reduced to the same spectacle as Israel of old, i.e., rituals and ceremonies have taken the place of the Spirit of God. As with

Israel of old, Satan, of which the Philistines were a type, will play havoc with Believers.

As Israel of old, the modern Church has its ornaments; it has become, again as Israel, very adept at shouting (I Sam. 4:5-6); however, their *"shouting"* was no more than racket in the ears of God, and likewise, Satan. The results were awful:

1. Thirty thousand of the soldiers of Israel were killed in the battle. Coupling that with the 4,000 previously killed constituted 34,000 men dying in that one conflict.

2. The Ark of God was taken by the Philistines.

3. The two sons of Eli, Hophni and Phinehas, were killed.

When Eli, who was the Great High Priest, heard that the Ark of God has been taken by the Philistines, the Scripture says, *"he fell from off the seat backward by the side of the gate, and his neck broke, and he died"* (I Sam. 4:18).

Along with being High Priest, Eli also served as the Judge of Israel, a role he filled for some 40 years. Had he judged in fellowship with God and in obedience to the Scriptures, the disasters that befell on the day of his death would never have happened; and yet, in his death, he showed that the interests of God's Kingdom had a true place in his heart.

Israel, when confronted by the enemy, tried to use a symbol in place of the Substance. The modern Church does the same when it places its faith in things other than the Cross.

MARCH
25

*a*nd Samuel spoke unto all the House of Israel, saying, If you do return unto the LORD with all your hearts, then put away the strange gods and Ashtaroth from among you, and prepare your hearts unto the LORD, and serve Him only: and He will deliver you out of the hand of the Philistines (I Sam. 7:3).

Now commences the spiritual leadership of the Prophet Samuel, actually the first man to fill that office, even though there were Prophets before him. Consequently, this Chapter is like a beam of sunshine upon a dark and cloudy day. It records a great revival. This revival was doubtless the result of Samuel's faithful preaching.

His preaching, doctrinally, was reconciliation to God by the Death of His Son (I Sam. 7:9; Rom. 5:10), and, ethically, a turning to God from all idols to serve the Living and the True God. In fact, Israel had not ceased to worship Jehovah, but she had associated other gods with Him. This has ever been Satan's object as an angel of light; and, accordingly, multitudes presently worship Jesus Christ and the Virgin Mary, actually giving her a higher form of worship even than Him.

But God will not accept such worship, nor the association of other gods with Himself, for He said (Ex. 20:3): *"You shall have no other gods together with Me."*

God's true Servants always preach as Samuel preached. They arouse people to a consciousness of their sinful condition before God; they set forth the Lamb of God evidently crucified among them (Gal. 3:1), as the Divine Way of pardon and Righteousness; and they denounce all compromise with evil.

The Holy Spirit through the Prophet demanded four things of Israel. In fact, the Lord demands no less presently. These four things are:

1. Altercation: *"Return unto the LORD with all your hearts."*

2. Separation: *"Then put away the strange gods and Ashtaroth from among you."*

3. Preparation: *"Prepare your hearts unto the LORD."*

4. Designation: *"Serve the LORD only."*

On that basis, which looks to the Cross, we will emphasize in tomorrow's devotion, the Lord has promised to deliver. If there is no deliverance, this means we are failing in that which the Lord has said to do.

MARCH
26

*a*nd Samuel took a sucking lamb, and offered it for a Burnt Offering wholly unto the LORD: and Samuel cried unto the LORD for Israel; and the LORD heard him (I Sam. 7:9).

The Holy Spirit has Samuel now to do two things, which must be a lesson to us, as well.

At the sign of the Revival registered in yesterday's devotion, Satan once again comes against Israel. The Evil One will always test our faith, and, in fact, the Lord allows him to do such, but only up to a point. In response to the Evil One, symbolized by the Philistines coming against Israel, the Lord told His People to do two things:

They were to *"draw water and pour it out before the LORD"* (I Sam. 7:6). They also were to *"fast"* that day and admit that they had *"sinned against the LORD."*

The *"pouring out of water on the ground"* symbolizes two things:

First of all, *"water"* symbolizes the Holy Spirit.

Second, the pouring out of the water on the ground

symbolizes our utter helplessness (II Sam. 14:14). In fact, the Holy Spirit cannot help us until we realize and come to the place of utter helplessness. Otherwise, we will depend on the flesh, i.e., *"self."*

That's why Jesus said that if we were to follow Him, we must first of all *"deny ourselves"* (Lk. 9:23).

Coming to the position of helplessness, Samuel was then told to take a *"sucking lamb, and offer it for a Burnt Offering wholly unto the LORD"* (I Sam. 7:9). This is the reason that we said, a couple of devotions ago, that the preaching of Samuel was based on reconciliation to God by the death of His Son, of which the offering up of this lamb was a Type.

The Cross, and the Cross alone, is the place of victory for the Child of God. It was there that Jesus defeated Satan and all his minions of darkness; He did so by atoning for all sin (Col. 2:14-15).

If the Christian attempts to bring about victory in any way other than Faith in Christ and the Cross, such a Christian is doomed to failure (Rom. 6:3-14).

MARCH

27

*b*e glad then, you Children of Zion, and rejoice in the LORD your God: for He has given you the former rain moderately, and He will cause to come down for you the rain, the former rain, and the latter rain in the first month (Joel 2:23).

The terms *"former rain"* and *"latter rain"* have a spiritual meaning regarding the outpouring of the Holy Spirit.

The *"former rain"* speaks of the outpouring of the Spirit from the Day of Pentecost through the time of the Early Church, and then some beyond that. Regrettably, the Early Church went into apostasy, with the Catholic Church coming out of that apostasy.

The Reformation took place early in the Sixteenth Century, and completely revolutionized the Church, as the great Message of *"Justification by Faith"* once again began to be preached. During a period of several centuries, very few people were baptized with the Holy Spirit; in fact, very few people were saved. The Gospel was successfully cut off from the people, which plunged the world into what is referred to as the *"Dark Ages."* During that time, the Catholic Church was supreme; during that time untold thousands were tortured to death because they refused to give allegiance to the Pope.

But at the Reformation, things began to change. At approximately the turn of the Twentieth Century, the *"latter rain"* outpouring took place, and continues to this hour. From that time unto the present, millions have been baptized with the Holy Spirit, with the evidence of speaking with other tongues. I have been blessed by the Lord to be a part of this great *"latter rain"* outpouring.

In 1968, the Lord moved upon my heart to begin a Radio Ministry, which actually began, if I remember correctly, on January 1, 1969. It was a fifteen minute program aired Monday through Friday, which we called *"The Campmeeting Hour."* In a short time, we were on approximately 600 stations daily.

Almost at the beginning of the Radio Ministry, the Lord began to lay it on my heart to teach on the Holy Spirit, which we tried our best to obey. At any rate, the Lord used our Radio Ministry to stir the hearts of untold thousands toward the Holy Spirit. These were Baptists, Methodists, Catholics, Presbyterians, etc.

The Lord also instructed me to set aside at least one Service in our Meetings, which were being conducted all over the United States and other parts of the world, for people to be baptized with the Holy Spirit. He even told me that, if we would be faithful, He would baptize 1,000 people with the Holy Spirit in one Service.

The Lord did exactly what He had promised. We saw tens of thousands baptized with the Holy Spirit, with the evidence of speaking with other tongues. It was in the Meeting in New York City, at Madison Square Garden, where the Lord did that which He told He would do, regarding 1,000 being baptized in one Service.

That Sunday afternoon we saw many people brought to Christ. And then when I gave the call for people to be baptized with the Spirit, hundreds and hundreds began to come forward. In fact, the line reached down each aisle all the way to the back.

I knew there had been a mighty moving of the Spirit and that many, many hundreds had been filled with the Spirit, but I had not bothered to think about the exact number. The exact number, in fact, really didn't matter.

It was the next day that the Lord spoke to my heart, informing me that over 1,000 people had been baptized with the Spirit in that Service. He fulfilled exactly what He told me He would do.

At this present time, nearly 20 years after that occasion, even as I dictate these notes, the Church desperately needs an outpouring of power from on high (Acts 2:1-4).

MARCH
28

*t*hen Nahash the Ammonite came up, and encamped against Jabesh-Gilead: and all the men of Jabesh said unto Nahash, Make a covenant with us, and we will serve you. And Nahash the Ammonite answered them, On this condition will I make a covenant with you, that I may thrust out all your right eyes, and lay it for a reproach upon all Israel (I Sam. 11:1-2).

We find here that Saul began well, but he did not conclude that way. I Samuel 12:12 states that it was anxiety because of the threatened Ammonite invasion that influenced the people to demand a king. Their conduct illustrates the unbelief and rebellion of man's heart. They would rather lean upon a king whom they could see, and who was mortal, than upon a King unseen and Almighty. When God did give them such a king as they desired, they despised him (I Sam. 10:27).

When Satan, symbolized by Nahash the Ammonite, invaded Israel, the first reaction of God's People was to yield to the enemy, and, in fact, to serve him. Such characterizes far too many in the modern Church. They have made a covenant with Satan, which means they have compromised the Word of God, which means they have become slaves to the Evil One. Satan's demands are always more than one can afford to pay. There can be no covenant made with Satan, not in any form or fashion.

As stated, the demands of the Evil One were harsh. He demanded that every fighting man in Israel put out his right eye.

Why the right eye?

The shield, as held by the soldier of those days, covered the body, the shoulders, and the face, except for the right eye. With his right eye, the soldier would look over the top of the shield, thereby seeing how to fight the enemy. If that eye is blinded, he could not see to fight; he was, therefore, rendered useless. This is why Nahash demanded the blindness of the right eye.

If it is to be noticed, the modern Church accepts false doctrine readily, plus most anything else that Satan has to offer.

The reason?

It has made a covenant with the Evil One, and the price is the blindness of the right eye, spiritually speaking; now they cannot see what is right or what is wrong.

As stated, no covenant can be made with Satan — not of any nature.

And let it be understood:

If we make anything the object of our faith other than Christ and His Cross, we are, in effect, whether we realize it or not, making a covenant with Satan.

MARCH

29

*a*nd Jonathan said to the young man who bore his armor, Come, and let us go over unto the garrison of these uncircumcised: it may be that the LORD will work for us: for there is no restraint to the LORD to save by many or by few (I Sam. 14:6).

It is instructive to contrast Jonathan with his father, Saul. Jonathan acted in the energy of faith; Saul, in the energy of the flesh.

And we must ever understand:

That which seeks its strength in the wisdom and energy of man can never go beyond from which it springs.

Hence the moral and inward movements of faith are wholly unknown to it.

But that which energized the heart of Jonathan was the Divine Gift of Faith; because Divine, it was victorious over the world, despite the universal ruin which met Jonathan's eye on every side. For that which is born of God overcomes the world (I Jn. 5:4).

Thus Jonathan here stands as an animating figure for the servants of God today. Saul represents Christendom as officially the visible Kingdom of God upon Earth, but corrupted and enslaved. Yet, within this broken Kingdom it is still possible for faith to win her victories, as Jonathan won his.

But whenever faith acts, the world opposes; hence the Philistines are found quickly encamped at Michmash. Satan, who knows and dreads the power of faith, brought up his agents as the sand which is on the seashore in multitude. All that Israel could do was to hide themselves in holes, pits, thickets, and rocks.

However, in the midst of this terrible position in which the people of God now find themselves, faith on the part of Jonathan begins to shine. And wherever faith is found, God displays His Strength.

Faith never lessens nor creates difficulties. Her path is open, very narrow, and made difficult by sharp rocks on either hand. But these are not difficulties for God! Jonathan did not think of himself; and his words to his armor-bearer do not express doubt as to God's ability to overcome them, but assurance. Faith's fair flower looks never so fair as when blooming in such a rocky and savage defile beset with enemies, such as is pictured here.

Jonathan's faith was based upon God and His covenanted relationship to His People Israel. He did not say, "*Jehovah has delivered them into my hand,*" but, "*into the hand of Israel.*" He was to be nothing — the God of Israel was to be everything.

It is quite true that Israel at this time was a moral ruin; but faith forgets, or nullifies, circumstances and

183

builds upon Divine Promises. This characterizes faith. Though broken and sinful, yet was God with, and for, His People; not with, and for, the circumcised Philistines.

Faith's great passion ever is that God should manifest Himself; as well, Faith always realizes that numbers, whether little or large, have no relationship to God. As Jonathan said, *"For there is no restraint to the LORD to save by many or by few."* So the Lord that very day, through the Faith of Jonathan, brought about a great victory for Israel. Despite the present condition of the modern Church, a condition which is not good, still the Lord is looking for modern Jonathans who will exercise faith, daring to believe Him for great things, and who will not touch the glory, but will give it all to God!

MARCH

30

*b**ut Saul and the people spared Agag, and the best of the
sheep, and of the oxen, and of the fatlings, and the lambs, and
all that was good, and would not utterly destroy them: but
everything that was vile and refuse, that they destroyed utterly*
(I Sam. 15:9).

The Amalekites, as proclaimed in this Fifteenth Chapter of I Samuel, represent the flesh. Some 500 years before, when Israel was in the wilderness, having just come out of Egypt, the Amalekites attacked the People of God. At that time, the Lord said that He would *"have war with Amalek from generation to generation"* (Ex. 17:8, 16). As stated, Amalek represents the flesh.

Saul was given instructions to totally destroy Amalek. He said, *"Utterly destroy all that they have, and spare them not; but kill both man and woman, infant and suckling, ox and sheep, camel and ass"* (I Sam. 15:3).

Such instructions may seem to be harsh to most. Yet we must remember that God had given Amalek some 500 years respite for repentance — but in vain. That nation, like the southern nations of Canaan, resisted every Divine impulse; they finally became so corrupt that, in the interest of humanity, love decreed its absolute extinction. In other words, God was forced to perform major surgery on the human race, and for the good of the human race as a whole.

Saul, however, did not obey the Lord, but rather spared Agag, the king of the Amalekites, plus the best of the sheep and oxen, etc. This is symbolic of modern Believers who desire to eradicate the bad things of the flesh, i.e., those things which destroy, such as immorality, liquor, drugs, etc., in other words *"that which is vile and refuse"*; however, that which seems to be good, they seek to spare, just as Saul spared Agag, etc.

The *"good"* consists of our dependence on our good works, our religious associations, in fact, anything in which we place our faith, other than Christ and the Cross. We are loathe to separate ourselves from these *"good things."* But the Holy Spirit through the Prophet includes such direction to be *"rebellion."* Concerning that, he said, *"For rebellion is as the sin of witchcraft, and stubbornness is as iniquity and idolatry"* (I Sam. 15:23).

When Samuel approached Saul, the king was very religious and said, *"Blessed be thou of the LORD: I have performed the Commandment of the LORD."*

Then Samuel answered, *"What means then this bleating of the sheep in my ears, and the lowing of the oxen which I hear?"*

The modern Church also claims to have *"performed the Commandment of the LORD"*; however, the Lord says otherwise.

Let us say it again:

Anything which we make as the object of our faith, other than the Cross, is constituted as *"flesh,"* which the Lord cannot abide. He is still saying, *"Utterly destroy all!"* Not only must the *"bad"* flesh be destroyed, but the *"good,"* as well!

MARCH
31

*a*nd the LORD said unto Samuel, How long will you
mourn for Saul, seeing I have rejected him from reigning over
Israel? Fill your horn with oil, and go, I will send you to Jesse
the Beth-lehemite: for I have provided Me a king among his
sons (I Sam. 16:1).

At the very time that Samuel the Prophet was *"mourning"* for Saul, i.e., he saw no positive future for Israel, the
Lord was planning great things for His People.

Let me say that again:

Whatever the circumstances might be, however the situation may present itself, the Lord is planning great things
for us, that is, if we will only believe Him.

Look at it again!

At this very moment, and no matter how it may seem
to be otherwise, the Lord is planning great things for
you. To receive those great things, obedience is demanded,
but obedience which we can easily carry out, that is, if
we will truly follow the Lord. This means that there is no

reason that any Believer should *"mourn."*

Concerning Saul, the Lord told the Prophet, *"I have rejected him from reigning over Israel."*

There are untold numbers of Godly people who are spending their time and attention on something that God has already rejected. Some of you holding this small book in your hands are still trying to hold on to a Church, or even an entire Denomination, which the Lord has already rejected. Such a Church, even as Saul, may continue right on; however, if the Believer is to truly follow the Lord, he will have to look elsewhere, even as Samuel is here told to look elsewhere.

The Lord told the Prophet to quit his pity-party, and *"Fill your horn with oil, and go."*

"Oil" is a Type of the Holy Spirit. We readily see here that the Holy Spirit had departed from Saul. If the Holy Spirit is no longer present, we should find out where the Holy Spirit is moving, and there situate ourselves. Nothing else matters!

The Lord had already chosen another king. He would be in the family of *"Jesse the Beth-lehemite."* It was the Lord Who chose a certain member of this family, David; man had no choice in the matter.

The trouble with the modern Church is men appointing men; consequently, they wind up with Saul, whom God has rejected, rather than David, whom God has chosen.

Last of all, the Lord told Samuel, *"For I have provided Me a king among his sons."* Whatever we think, God has provided! We, unfortunately, all too often look in the wrong place.

The Lord didn't tell Samuel which one of the sons He

had chosen from the family of Jesse the Bethlehemite.

The reason?

The Lord was looking for faith on the part of Samuel; to be sure, such faith was ultimately found!

APRIL

1

*t*hen said David to the Philistine, You come to me with the sword, and with the spear, and with the shield: but I come to you in the name of the LORD of Hosts, the God of the armies of Israel, Whom you have defied (I Sam. 17:45).

When David, who was just a young stripling, probably sixteen or seventeen years old, went to the battlefront where his brothers were, he went there to bless them and do them good; however, like Joseph's brothers, when he was sent to bless them, he was met with envy and hatred. Thus it was with God's Beloved Son. His brothers, Mary's sons, did not believe on Him (Jn. 7:5), and, with her, sought to lay hold upon Him as being beside Himself (Mk. 3:32); His spiritual brethren, Israel, nailed Him to the tree.

When David offered to fight the giant, not for money, nor for the hand of the king's daughter — every man he spoke to had no higher thought than that — but David knew that the matter was more noble and more serious than this. He was to bring the Philistine giant and the

Living God face-to-face. What had a woman and her money to do with that?

Saul tried to get David to use his armor, but David knew that God could not give victories to *"the flesh,"* nor can faith use it. In the Name of the Lord, David had privately vanquished the *"lion"* and the *"bear."* This is one of the fundamental principles governing the Christian life. Public victories can come only after private victories are won.

Going toward the giant, David chose five smooth stones out of the brook. If the brook, with its living running water, pictures the Holy Spirit, then the five smooth stones picture Grace; to be sure, Grace won the day! The Stone, picturing Christ, smote the giant in the forehead; and he fell upon his face to the earth.

The Scripture then says, *"David ran, and stood upon the Philistine, and took his sword, and drew it out of the sheath thereof, and slew him, and cut off his head therewith"* (I Sam. 17:51). This is the posture for the Child of God. We are to stand as *"more than a conqueror"* on the head of any giant that may come against us, which we can do in Christ.

The Believer must understand that the terrible forces of darkness facing him are beyond his power and capabilities. As Goliath, Satan can only be defeated by and through Christ and what Christ has done for us at the Cross. To face the giants that come against us in any other fashion is to guarantee defeat. To place one's Faith in Christ and the Cross guarantees victory, and a total and complete victory, at that (Rom. 6:3-14).

APRIL
2

*a*nd David said in his heart, I shall now perish one day by the hand of Saul: there is nothing better for me than that I should speedily escape into the land of the Philistines; and Saul shall despair of me, to seek me any more in any coast of Israel: so shall I escape out of his hand (I Sam. 27:1).

Once the path of faith is abandoned, all the previous experience with the Lord is put on hold. Not only is there no advancement, but rather a regression! David, at least for a time, forgot the sure Promises of God, and succumbed to the fears of the flesh. Faith had told him, despite the actions of Saul, to dwell in the land of Judah (I Sam. 22:5); however, fear tells him, *"I shall one day perish by the hand of Saul."*

Saul, however, could no more have killed David than the idea that the sun is going to rise in the west. So David would go over to the land of Philistines, thinking to escape Saul. Forsaking the path of faith not only causes the loss of past experience, but it also leads into sin and sorrow. We must never forget that there is no halfway house between fellowship with God and fellowship with the Philistine. If the Philistine is made a refuge, then David must dwell in the midst of them, and declare himself ready to fight with them against the people of God (I Sam. 29:8).

In His Love and pity for His Servant, God overruled all for David's safety, but, at the same time, He also sorely chastened him (I Sam., Chpt. 30). David's action in joining Achish not only possibly delayed his possession of the Kingdom, but it became the occasion for teaching his 600 men to sin against light and knowledge. Faith does not deny the hindrances and obstacles, as some have been taught to do, but neither does it fear them.

We know what David should have done, but do we know what we ought to do?

We can know, and beyond the shadow of a doubt, if we will firmly anchor our Faith — it's always by Faith — in Christ and His Substitutionary Work on the Cross. Then the Holy Spirit will be certain and sure to *"guide us into all truth"* (Jn. 16:13).

APRIL

3

*i*s not this David, of whom they sang one to another in dances, saying, Saul slew his thousands, and David his ten thousands? (I Sam. 29:5).

Before coming to the Throne, the Twenty-ninth Chapter of I Samuel records the lowest point of David's experience with the Lord. He professes himself ready and eager to fight against God's beloved People, and to help Satan destroy them! All this shows how deeply a Child of God can fall when he leans upon the hand of man and not upon the Hand of God.

Concerning this, Williams says:

"*The path of faith is wearying to nature; and there is an ever present temptation to seek ease from the thorns through which that path sometimes leads.*

"*The persecution of Believers oftentimes has the effect of throwing them into the arms of the enemies of God; just as Saul's hatred drove David to the Philistines. But this only happens when the Christian follows his own will, and thinks,*

195

by doing so, to avoid the very difficulties which, had he walked with God, would have become channels of teaching and refreshment to his soul. The more glorious a work there is for faith, the more sure is nature to weary if faith grows feeble."

David dwelt in the country of the Philistines *"a full year and four months."* For that time, we might quickly say, he was totally out of the Will of God (I Sam. 27:7). To be out of the Will of God is the worst place in which a Believer can find himself. Such a position presents a load too heavy to bear, and a price we cannot afford to pay. Good never comes from such a position; to be sure, God always, and without exception, has a Perfect Will for each one of His Children. We must find that Will, get in that Will, and stay in that Will, no matter the seeming difficulties (Rom. 12:1-2).

APRIL

4

*a*nd David was greatly distressed; for the people spoke of stoning him, because the soul of all the people was grieved, every man for his sons and for his daughters: but David encouraged himself in the LORD his God (I Sam. 30:6).

David seeking the aid of the Philistines greatly hinders the Operation of the Holy Spirit in his life, as proven by the Amalekites taking advantage of the situation by invading the land and burning with fire Ziklag, David's home at that time. How so much we bring upon ourselves bitter troubles because we are out of the Will of God! If such a man as David, a man after God's own heart, who wrote over half of the Psalms, and, above all, through whose family the Messiah ultimately would come, could miss the Lord, as David obviously did, then we certainly should understand that any of us are also capable of such!

It was a bitter trial for David and his men to come back to Ziklag, where all of the wives and children were, and to see the city burnt with fire, and to find that all of their loved ones had been taken as slaves by the Amalekites. Suffering and loss accompany departure from the Lord; there must be chastisement in order that Restoration be effected. To be sure, chastisement is grievous, but it yields the peaceable fruit of Righteousness (Heb. 12:11).

Even though David had so grievously sinned against the Lord, still, the Lord was to David a present Deliverer and a gracious, forgiving Saviour.

At this time, looking at the ruins of what had been their homes, David's men grew fiercely angry with him, even threatening to stone him. It was truly the low water-mark of David's life; however, despite the past failures, and despite the present situation, which was bleak indeed, the Scripture says, *"David encouraged himself in the LORD his God."* He cast his burden upon the Lord, which is the only place for the Believer to go. Regrettably, the modern Church has opted, at times like this, to seek the help of other mere mortals, and I speak of humanistic psychology.

Let it ever be understood:

There is no help from that source. Its wisdom, if it has any at all, is sensual and devilish (James 3:15), while *"the wisdom that comes from above is first pure, then peaceable, gentle, and easy to be intreated, full of mercy and good fruits, without partiality, and without hypocrisy"* (James 3:17).

Let it ever be known:

As God was David's refuge then, He is our refuge now! Times may change, but the problems are the same; the solution is the same, as well.

Because *"David encouraged himself in the LORD,"* he

was able to recover every single thing he lost, plus much more besides (I Sam. 30:18-20). Let David's experience be a lesson to all. Whatever the problem, irrespective of the failure, if you will turn to the Lord, despite what others might say, you also can *"recover all."*

APRIL
5

*S*o *Saul died, and his three sons, and his armourbearer, and all his men, that same day together* (I Sam. 31:6).

It is believed that Saul was twenty years old when he was crowned king. He reigned forty years; therefore, he would be sixty at the time of his death. The sunny morning of his beginning ended in a black night of horror and death. It must be said that self-will wrecked his life and his reign (I Chron. 10:13-14). In that self-will, he found himself opposing God at every turn of his life. He disobeyed what he was commanded to do, and he opposed the one whom the Lord had called, namely, David.

Only one who is born of the Spirit can serve and please God. Saul was raised up, as a king after the people's heart, to deliver them from the Philistines and other enemies.

Please read the following words very carefully:

If it were possible for *"the natural man"* to do God's Will, and to win victories for the Lord, then Saul most definitely would have succeeded; but he didn't succeed. He rather failed, and failed miserably! He perished at the hands of the very enemies he set out to conquer! Such must ever be the result when *"the flesh"* attempts to do battle for God. And yet, most Christians, sadly and regrettably, attempt to live this life in the manner of Saul instead of the manner of David.

Most modern Christians simply do not know how to live for God; consequently, they make the attempt in all the wrong ways, which results in the words of the Apostle Paul being fulfilled in their lives, *"O wretched man that I am . . ."* (Rom. 7:24). Living for the Lord can be carried out successfully in only one way, and that is by the Believer understanding that everything we receive from the Lord comes to us exclusively through Christ as the Source and the Cross as the Means.

Ever maintaining the Cross as our Object of Faith guarantees perpetual victory (Rom. 6:14), and is the <u>only</u> manner of victory.

APRIL

6

*N*ow there was long war between the house of Saul and the house of David: but David waxed stronger and stronger, and the house of Saul waxed weaker and weaker (II Sam. 3:1).

As is obvious, there was contention and outright hostility for many years between *"the house of Saul"* and *"the house of David."* To be frank, fellowship between the two was impossible.

Concerning this, Williams says:

"As then, he who was born after the flesh persecuted him who was born after the Spirit, so is it now (Gal. 4:29). A carnal nature is the enemy of the spiritual; but victory is assured to the latter."

Why did the Lord allow *"Saul"* to continue? For many years, Saul caused David untold problems. As well, many of us presently struggle with difficulties, all the time knowing that God has the Power to eliminate those difficulties, and to do so immediately. But yet He oftentimes allows them to continue. Why?

First of all, the Lord minutely looks after His Children, even to the extent of numbering the very hairs of our heads (Mat. 10:30). This means that nothing can happen to us but that the Lord either causes it or allows it. Of course, He definitely doesn't cause us to sin, but He does allow us to do wrong, that is, if we are so foolish to do so. And if we do so, there will be negative results!

The Lord allowed Saul to continue as long as he did for many reasons. One of those reasons, no doubt, was the attempt to get Saul to repent. The Lord loved Saul; regrettably, that love was not reciprocated. However, the greatest reason of all, probably, for allowing Saul to continue was that David might learn trust and faith, which, despite what some say, can be learned no other way (II Cor. 12:9-10).

APRIL

7

*a*nd the king and his men went to Jerusalem unto the Jebusites, the inhabitants of the land: which spoke unto David, saying, Except you take away the blind and the lame, you shall not come in hither: thinking, David cannot come in hither. Nevertheless, David took the stronghold of Zion: the same is the City of David (II Sam. 5:6-7).

The Jebusites inhabited Jerusalem when David became king. Saul was never able to dislodge them. The Believer must remember this: If inward battles are not won (the Jebusites), then certainly we cannot hope to win the outward battles (the Philistines). In fact, the Philistines ultimately killed Saul.

The following also must be remembered:

That which God will use, Satan will make every attempt to sully, just as he did Jerusalem. The Evil One knew that Jerusalem would be chosen by God to be His City; consequently, he would place his strongest opponent to Righteousness, the Jebusites, there. This means that even though Zion was God's City, it was so completely in the power of the enemy that even the blind and the lame were deemed sufficiently strong to garrison it.

But David took the city, even though others before him had been unable to do so. As well, our Heavenly David has defeated the enemy, all on our behalf, but yet the same is required of us, spiritually speaking, as it was David of old.

How did he take the city?

First of all, immediately on becoming king, he recognized that his enemy in their very midst had to be defeated. We must look at the weaknesses in our personal lives in the same manner.

Second, the way that entrance was gained into the city was by the water gutter, which is a Type of the Holy Spirit. In other words, that which we personally need to be before Christ cannot be brought about by our own machinations, only by the Holy Spirit.

Third, the Jebusites taunted David by saying that he was so weak that the *"lame and blind"* could defend the city against him and his army. David's response was that he *"hated the lame and the blind,"* meaning, in the spiritual sense, that we should hate everything in our lives that makes us spiritually lame or spiritually blind.

David took the city and *"dwelt in the fort."* The Holy Spirit demands that we dwell in victory where previously had been defeat. Only then, as David, can we *"grow great, and the LORD God of Hosts be with us."*

APRIL

8

*a*nd David consulted with the captains of thousands and hundreds, and with every leader. And David arose, and went with all the people who were with him from Baale of Judah, to bring up from thence the Ark of God, Whose Name is called by the Name of the LORD of Hosts that dwells between the Cherubims (I Chron. 13:1; II Sam. 6:2).

As it regards the bringing up of the Ark of God into Jerusalem, this was a noble desire, no doubt placed in the heart of David by the Lord; however, as to the carrying out of this all-important task, David consulted not with the Lord, but rather with other men. Had he consulted with the Lord, success, and not disaster, would have resulted. But he consulted man, imitated the Philistine (placed the Ark on a new cart), and organized a great public function in which he and his plans largely obscured God and His Glory; consequently, the day ended in death, anger, and fear. All this was the planning of *"the flesh."*

The Ark of the Covenant was to be carried on the

shoulders of Priests, because Priests, under the Law of Moses, were types of Christ (Deut. 10:8; 31:9, 25). The results were that Uzzah put forth his hand to steady the Ark and died instantly — all because of David's disobedience.

What man has set up, he feels himself bound to sustain. But the God of Israel needed not, as the gods of the nations, a human hand to uphold Him. It was necessary that He should teach His People this lesson. He must be held in reverence of all them who are round about Him; and all must learn that God judged the *"flesh"* in an Israelite in the same manner as in a Philistine; for there is no difference.

Uzzah, no doubt, thought with exultation how the Ark of God was death to the men of Ashdod, but he never anticipated it being death to himself! But the Living God is a consuming fire to the actions of the carnal nature, whether inside or outside the family of Abraham. Thus, did He judge the presumption of the flesh in Uzzah. This should be a lesson to us, in that God judges the *"flesh"* wherever it is found.

Paul plainly said: *"So then they who are in the flesh cannot please God"* (Rom. 8:8). The *"flesh"* is our own self efforts. Placing our faith in anything other than Christ and His Cross constitutes *"walking after the flesh"* (Rom. 8:1).

APRIL
9

And David said, Is there yet any that is left of the house of Saul, that I may show him kindness for Jonathan's sake? (II Sam. 9:1).

Why did David, even after Saul was dead, desire to show kindness to the house of Saul, considering that Saul, when alive, had repeatedly tried to kill him? The reason was the covenant that David had made with Jonathan, Saul's son and David's close friend (I Sam. 23:16-18). Such a covenant was inviolable, meaning it was unbreakable. Whatever belonged to Jonathan, also belonged to David, and vice versa.

It was found that one son of Jonathan was still alive. His name was Mephibosheth. His very name meant *"the reproach of shame."* He lived in a place called *"Lo-debar,"* which means *"the desert place, no pasture."* He also was a cripple. Thus, he aptly pictured man as a rebel by nature, a sinner by practice, morally deformed, self-convicted, and far from God. Yet David, *"for Jonathan's sake,"* sought him, found him, pardoned him, enriched him, gave him a place among his sons, and brought him into his banqueting house, unfolding over him his banner of love!

The one condition which Mephibosheth fulfilled, and which made real to him his translation from hungry Lo-debar to the banqueting of Mount Zion, was that he surrender unreservedly to David. A similar surrender on the part of the sinner to the Saviour, the Lord Jesus Christ, of which all of this is a type, carries with it a consciousness of forgiveness, life, and glory.

When sitting at the king's table, Mephibosheth's eyes must have shone with admiration when fixed on David; but what self-abasement must have clothed his mind when his gaze fell upon his deformed feet! Yet the knowledge that he was there, *"for Jonathan's sake,"* and not because of any personal worthfulness, must have continually assured him of his position. So *"he did eat continually at the king's table."*

Grace saved him; the riches of that Grace endowed him; and its exceeding riches set him as a son at the king's table continually. And so will it be for all who look to the Grace afforded by Christ (Eph. 2:8-9).

APRIL
10

*a*nd Nathan said to David, You are the man (II Sam. 12:7).

As one reads this Chapter, one must come to the conclusion that it testifies to the inspiration of the Bible, for only the Holy Spirit could have (would have) recorded so faithfully its infamy and horror. It gives a true insight into man's nature as sinful and fallen. It teaches the reader the humbling lesson that such is the nature he possesses, and that, if Divine restraints are withheld and temptations sufficiently attractive and skillfully offered, there is no depth of evil, shame, and falsehood to which he will not fall.

Uriah, the husband of Bath-sheba, was one of David's thirty-seven mighty men (II Sam. 23:39). To make him the bearer of the letter arranging for his murder was a depth of infamy which is appalling; worse yet, it was committed by one of the Godliest men who ever lived — David.

David's efforts to shield Bath-sheba is the one redeeming feature in this sad history. But his plans were his own, and, unfortunately, they succeeded. Bitter fruit

210

usually follows from successful human plans. Had David, directly he had sinned against God, Uriah, and Bath-sheba, cast himself with anguish of heart upon God, the Lord would have made a way of escape and forgiveness consistent with Himself and morally instructive to David (Williams).

The Lord raised up David as a king to witness to the nature of Divine Government. In this matter of Uriah, David falsified that testimony; God, therefore, vindicated Himself by judging and chastening David in the sight of all men. He was accordingly disgraced by one son (13:14), banished by another (15:19), rebelled against by a third (I Ki., Chpt. 2), cursed by a subject (16:5), betrayed by his friends, and deserted by his people. His child was stricken with death; the sword never departed from his house. His whole subsequent history was a succession of sorrows and calamities.

Concerning this, Williams says, *"Thus God protects women, honors marriage, and strikes with burning judgments the sin which men lightly regard, clothe with poisonous poetry, or treat as a subject of humor and jesting."*

David's anger in Verse 5 concerning the lamb is a remarkable instance of how sensitive the moral judgment may be at the very time when the heart is blinded by sin! This fact illustrates the deceitfulness of sin (Heb. 3:13). And yet, David had a true knowledge of God. When his sin was pointed out by Nathan the Prophet with the awful words, *"You are the man,"* David's first thoughts were, not the punishment that would follow, but the injury done to God.

Psalm 51 witnesses to the depth and sincerity of the

king's Repentance; and his submission to the judgment that smote his child showed that, although more guilty than they, yet he had a spiritual knowledge of God which others did not possess. He laid open the tenderest emotions of his heart to God — the heart that God was wounding — but directly the Will of God was manifested, he at once submitted. This was the evident Work of the Holy Spirit in him.

David really loved Bath-sheba; and she was, in many respects, a woman of character. In fact, the last Chapter of Proverbs, written by her son Solomon, portrays Bath-sheba. The Holy Spirit sanctioned all that was written.

APRIL

11

*a*nd *Absalom sent for Ahithophel the Gilonite, David's counselor, from his city, even from Giloh, while he offered sacrifices. And the conspiracy was strong; for the people increased continually with Absalom* (II Sam. 15:12).

The rebellion and violent death of Absalom were, without a doubt, the greatest trials of David's life; more so because he felt that he was to blame. David was now 56 years old; Absalom, 24; and Solomon, 6 years of age. Absalom easily deceived the people by a profession of devotion to them (II Sam. 15:2-6), and as easily deceived his father by a profession of devotion to God (II Sam. 15:7-8).

Because man has fallen from God's moral image, he can readily deceive and be deceived (II Tim. 3:13).

Deception and rebellion are grievous in any case; however, for such to lodge in the heart of one's own son, and against David, presents injury of the highest sort.

Absalom reasoned that inasmuch as David had sinned with Bath-sheba and had planned the murder of her husband (actions which were heinous indeed), he could take the throne. Most of the people of Israel agreed with him! However, God had not selected Absalom to take the throne; God had selected David. Even though David had sinned terribly, the Lord had not deposed him as king. If Absalom had succeeded in his plan, it would have destroyed Israel.

At this time, Israel was one of the greatest nations in the world. It was prosperous far beyond most of the surrounding nations. This was all owed to David; however, most of the people did not recognize that, or else they didn't care. So they would put a deceiver on the throne.

Thus, the conqueror of Goliath was hunted from his throne and dishonored in his home by his own son — and that in fulfillment of the Word of the Lord! Such is God's holy wrath against sin. And such is the bitter fruit of sin — the sharp two-edged sword of the Word of God was unsheathed against David.

How just is God! But whom He loves, He chastens; and accordingly, while thus revealing His righteous Anger, He, at the same time, overruled these judgments to draw David into a closer fellowship with Himself. The Lord did this in order to discipline and teach his heart so that his sorrows, the fruit of his sins, became occasions of spiritual enrichment to him.

This account, consequently, is a valuable testimony that God does not cast off His People when they sin against Him; that He forgives them directly as they confess their faults; that He overrules all to enrich their knowledge of Himself; and that He furnishes them with expressions and sentiments proper to the Restoration of the soul.

APRIL
12

*a*nd David built there an Altar unto the LORD, and offered Burnt Offerings and Peace Offerings. So the LORD was intreated for the land, and the plague was stayed from Israel (II Sam. 24:25).

The Twenty-fourth Chapter of II Samuel, in point of time as it regards events, precedes those of the Twenty-third Chapter. This is designed by the Holy Spirit, inasmuch as Chapter 23 prefigures the glories of Christ and records the names of the companions of that glory. The Twenty-fourth Chapter speaks of the sufferings of Christ, as the Sin Offering, which He should accomplish at Jerusalem. David foreshadowed this, for no Priest is mentioned.

David had given orders that a census should be taken in both Judah and Israel. That, within itself, was not wrong, that is, if David's motives were right. The great wrong came in that David disobeyed the Word of God, in that a half-shekel was to be paid to the Sanctuary for every man who was numbered. This proclaimed the fact that

215

Israel's foundation was Redemption, in fact, the foundation upon which the Tabernacle stood. All were based on the Precious Blood of Christ. To ignore this was to invite a plague, which is exactly what happened (Ex. 30:11-16).

When the census was brought back, the number was 800,000 valiant men who drew the sword for Israel and 500,000 for Judah. And then the Scripture tells us that several things happened, which are:

1. *"David's heart smote him after that he had numbered the people"*: David's heart did not smite him until the sin was accomplished, though its pursuit occupied more than nine months. Sin, when accomplished, occasions disgust; it is the pursuit of it which has such a hateful attraction to the heart. Directly the sin is committed, Satan no longer cares to hide its ugliness.

2. David said, *"For I have done very foolishly"*: To be sure, sin makes fools of people! At this point, the Lord sent Gad the Prophet to David. The Lord gave David one of three choices:

   A.   Seven years of famine;

   B.   Defeated three months by his enemies; or

   C.   Three days' pestilence in the land, sent by the Lord.

Quickly was David's choice made: *"Let us fall now into the Hand of the LORD, for His mercies are great: and let me not fall into the hand of man."*

So the Lord sent a plague on both Israel and Judah. Seventy thousand men died in that three-day plague. The only remedy was the Cross of Christ, as the only remedy is the Cross of Christ. David purchased the threshingfloor of Araunah the Jubusite, which was in the heart of Jerusalem, in order to *"build an Altar unto the LORD, that the plague may be stayed from the people."* On that Altar, David *"offered Burnt Offerings and Peace Offerings,"* all serving as types of Christ and what He would do at the Cross.

The Cross alone stops the plague of sin in the human heart and life. Nothing else will, because nothing else can. The answer for sin in any form is the Cross, even as the answer always has been the Cross! (Rom. 8:2).

APRIL
13

even as I swore unto you by the LORD God of Israel, saying, Assuredly Solomon your son shall reign after me, and he shall sit upon my throne in my stead; even so will I certainly do this day (I Ki. 1:30).

David, one of the greatest men of God who ever lived now comes to the place that he must die. The giant-killer cannot evade death; because of Adam's Fall, death is passed on all men. Thank God, that enemy was defeated at Calvary; even though its effect will be the last to be destroyed, that day for certain will come (I Cor. 15:26, 54-57).

The Lord had promised David that he would give him a Son Whom God would raise up to Him, God being His Father, and He being His Son, Who should build the Temple of Jehovah and reign forever and ever. This was the Promise, and David himself knew it referred to Christ (II Sam., Chpt. 7).

But the words, *"If he commit iniquity . . ."* (II Sam. 7:14), expressed responsibility; and David understood

218

that this concerned Solomon and not the Christ of Glory. Solomon was God's choice to occupy the throne after the death of his father David; however, Adonijah, Joab, and Abiathar (the High Priest) set up their kingdom in opposition to God's elect king. God had no place in their hearts, and so Solomon did not suit them. God's choice never does suit man.

Adonijah, the fourth son of David, was now the eldest surviving son. Amnon, Chileab, and Absalom were all dead. Adonijah was Absalom's half-brother and, like him, very handsome and overindulged by his father. We find from all of this that men never make a common choice with God. Solomon, as stated, was God's chosen king; and the conspirators knew that very well.

If the plans of these evil men had succeeded, it would have meant the ruin of Israel. The glory under Solomon never would have transpired. Tragically, all too often, even presently, and especially presently, men are attempting to set up their kingdom in opposition to that which is desired by the Lord. Ruin is always the result!

Israel, in a sense, was the Kingdom of God on Earth. Consequently, the way of the Lord was much more obvious. Presently, the Kingdom of God is in the hearts of men, and it is not so obvious. Thus, the two kingdoms, man's religious kingdom and God's Kingdom, struggle side by side.

Accordingly, every Believer must make a choice. Will it be that of man, or will it be that of God? If the choice for the kingdom of religious man is made, spiritual wreckage will be the result, with even the possibility of the loss of the soul.

That's why Paul said: *"I marvel that you are so soon removed from Him* (the Holy Spirit) *Who called you into the Grace of Christ* (made possible by the Cross) *unto another gospel* (anything which doesn't have the Cross as its Object of Faith):

"Which is not another (presents the fact that Satan's aim is not so much to deny the Gospel, which he little can do, but to corrupt it); *but there be some who trouble you, and would pervert the Gospel of Christ* (once again, to make the Object of Faith something other than the Cross [Gal. 1:6-7])".

APRIL
14

*J*udah and Israel were many, as the sand which is by the sea in multitude, eating and drinking, and making merry. And Solomon reigned over all kingdoms, from the river unto the land of the Philistines, and unto the border of Egypt: they brought presents, and served Solomon all the days of his life (I Ki. 4:20-21).

Now we see the result of God's Way, which is always *"more abundant life"* (Jn. 10:10). The prosperity, the eating, drinking, and making merry (I Ki. 4:20), the abundance (4:22-23), the peace and safety (4:24-25), the extended dominion (4:21), the external honor (4:34), and the internal dignity (4:2) all resulted from the one fact that Solomon, God's choice, was king. The destruction of the rebels and the enthronement of God's elect prince originated this universal contentment and prosperity.

It is a forepicture, although feeble, of the happy day that awaits the Earth, when the rebels who now govern it and fill it with misery will be overthrown, and the Prince of Peace, the Greater than Solomon (Mat. 12:42), will take unto Himself His great Power and reign gloriously before His ancient People Israel. The present miseries that oppress the nations, which they, by repeated efforts, vainly try to remove, would at once all be put to an end and universal peace, happiness, and prosperity secured, if men would invite the Messiah to return and take the government of the world into His Mighty Hands. We all know, however, that the world is not going to do that; nevertheless, at the appropriate time, the Lord Jesus Christ is definitely going to come. That of which Solomon's reign was a forepicture will then be a reality (Rev., Chpt. 19).

APRIL
15

*a*nd Solomon made affinity with Pharaoh king of Egypt, and took Pharaoh's daughter, and brought her into the city of David, until he had made an end of building his own house, and the House of the LORD, and the wall of Jerusalem round about. And Solomon loved the LORD, walking in the Statutes of David his father . . . (I Ki. 3:1, 3).

Israel was forbidden to make affinity in marriage with the Canaanites; with respect to the Egyptians, such Passages as Isaiah 19:21, 23, 25; Zechariah 14:18; Deuteronomy 23:7; and, Ezekiel 29:13 suggest that they are vessels of mercy, prepared unto Millennial Glory, in union with Israel; and, as such, are representative of the future redeemed Gentile nations.

Solomon's marriage, therefore, with the daughter of Egypt and her introduction into the city of David, where the Ark was — symbol of the Covenant and of God's relationship with His People, brought her into that Covenant (Ps. 105:8-23). The Covenant was not made with

Pharaoh's daughter. But Grace placed her where the Ark, the symbol of the Covenant, was hidden; and thus was she safeguarded and sheltered by Him Who had made that Covenant with His People, and Who will, in the latter day, include in it all the nations of the Earth (Jer. 12:16).

At this time, the Brazen Altar was at Gibeon, where the Tabernacle was; however, the Ark was in Jerusalem, the city of David. The Brazen Altar was visible; the Ark was hidden. The Brazen Altar pictures Christ lifted up from the Earth in suffering, rejection, and death; the Ark of the Covenant pictures Christ hidden in the heavenlies awaiting the time of His manifestation in Glory.

In the sad days of the Judges and of Saul, the Tabernacle was forsaken and the Ark of the Covenant disrupted from the Brazen Altar, retired into the city of David, there hidden till the glory under Solomon was established. It was there that Solomon brought Pharaoh's daughter (where the Ark of the Covenant was), and not to Gibeon, where the Brazen Altar was. Such is the Grace which awaits the Gentile.

Having put away sin at the Brazen Altar (Calvary) by the Sacrifice of Himself, Christ has retired into the Heavens, and we Gentiles, like Pharaoh's daughter, shelter ourselves in that hidden Saviour. He, like Solomon, will build us a House with many mansions, and we, in union with Israel, will enter into the glory of His Millennial Kingdom.

All of this, therefore, which took place in the first part of Solomon's reign, pictures the Gentile Church; it also looks forward to the coming Kingdom Age.

APRIL
16

*a*nd it came to pass in the four hundred and eightieth year after the Children of Israel were come out of the land of Egypt, in the fourth year of Solomon's reign over Israel, in the month Zif, which is the second month (May), that he began to build the House of the LORD (I Ki. 6:1).

As the Tabernacle in every aspect of its structure presented Christ in His Atoning, Mediatorial, and Intercessory Work, likewise, the Temple did the same, but with one difference. Just as every whit of the Tabernacle symbolized the glories attaching to Christ in His First Advent, so all the dazzling splendor of the Temple prefigured the glories of His Second Advent. Both buildings were designed by God; nothing was left to the religious feeling, taste, or imagination of Moses, David, or Solomon (Heb. 8:5; I Chron. 28:19).

The Temple was built of stone, cedar, cypress, olivewood, and gold. The instruments of its service were largely copper. These materials set forth the Deity, the precious

225

and sinless humanity, and the strength, the grace, and the governmental Power of Christ.

As this Temple was built without outward noise, meaning *"there was neither hammer nor axe nor any tool of iron heard in the house, while it was in building"* (6:7), so was Christ, the True Temple, prepared of God without observation (Lk. 17:20; Heb. 10:5). In the Tabernacle, there was a Veil between the Holy Place and the Holy of Holies; however, no Veil is mentioned in the Temple. The figure here is not that of access to God, as was the Tabernacle, but of dwelling with God. There were folding doors which opened; for Millennial fellowship will be real and partial. Full fellowship will only be enjoyed in the new Heavens and the new Earth.

The Cherubim symbolized Judgment. Their wings met over the blood-sprinkled Mercy Seat and reached to either extremity of the Most Holy Place. In fact, the Most Holy Place was 30 feet wide, 30 feet long, and 30 feet high (6:20). The Great Brazen Altar (II Chron., Chpt. 4) also was 30 feet square; for Atonement and Glory are one. In other words, as great as the Throne of God, of which the Holy of Holies was a type, is the Redemption of God, symbolized by the Brazen Altar.

This is the reason the conversation on the Mount of Transfiguration was about the decease of Christ which He should accomplish at Jerusalem (Lk. 9:31). Atonement, it must ever be understood, is the theology of Heaven, and the entrance into Heaven is gained only by acceptance of the Atonement. Otherwise, the Holy Spirit will bar all entrance (Eph. 2:18).

The Cherubim of Gold, attached to the Mercy Seat

226

and made of the same mass of gold, looked downward upon the sprinkled blood; the Cherubim made of olive wood, which filled the Holy of Holies in the Temple, looked outward. This refers to the fact that God's Perfect Judgments will, in the Millennium, be enabled to look out from Calvary upon a kingdom wherein shall dwell Righteousness. This now is not possible, for Righteousness retreated to Heaven when Christ went back to the Father (Jn. 16:10).

But Jesus is coming back. He will establish a Kingdom which will incorporate the entirety of the world, of which Solomon's Temple was a forepicture.

APRIL
17

f or he cast two pillars of brass, of eighteen cubits (27 feet) *high apiece: and a line of twelve cubits* (18 feet) *did compass either of them about* (I Ki. 7:15).

The pillars of copper are mentioned seven times in the Bible (I Ki. 7:15; II Ki. 25:13; I Chron. 18:8; II Chron. 3:15; Jer. 27:19; 52:17; Rev. 3:12).

These Scriptures state that the copper was captured by David from the Syrians (I Chron. 18:8). David's incursion into these Gentile areas and the taking of the copper symbolize believing sinners being brought into the Kingdom of God. Before David took it, almost all of this copper (which consisted of lampstands, doorstops, altars to heathen gods, etc.) was dedicated to heathen gods, symbolizing believing sinners brought from the world into the Grace of God.

At the appointed time, Solomon took all of these ornaments and melted them together, thereby destroying their past identity, even as our wicked past is destroyed in Christ (II Chron. 4:17). We like to think that the talent and ability of the ungodly, should they come to the Lord, could be used greatly for Christ; however, none of it truly can be used for God. Everything of the world and of the flesh must be stripped away, with the Holy Spirit Alone having His Perfect Way.

These notable pillars were peculiar to the Temple, as distinguished from the Tabernacle; for, in the Tabernacle, God was the traveling Companion of His People, but, in the Millennium, He will be a Resident among them. The pillars were works of art, displaying strength, beauty, and grace of surpassing splendor. These pillars, therefore, pictured Christ as Israel's Millennial King; they voiced the strength, the grace, the beauty, the life, and the varied fruit of the Spirit, which will be seen in Him when He sets up His visible Kingdom over the Earth. Their dazzling splendor of polished copper, illumined by the rising sun (for the pillars faced the rising sun), prefigured the moral glory of Christ as the Door of the House of God.

And yet, our Lord tells us, *"Him who overcomes will I make a pillar in the Temple of My God"* (Rev. 3:12). This plainly tells us that every Believer, of which the pillars in the Temple were a type, will rule and reign with Christ.

APRIL
18

*t*hen Solomon assembled the Elders of Israel, and all the heads of the Tribes, the chief of the fathers of the Children of Israel, unto King Solomon in Jerusalem, that they might bring up the Ark of the Covenant of the LORD out of the city of David, which is Zion (I Ki. 8:1).

The Temple is now finished! It seems that approximately a year, or maybe even a little more time, had elapsed between its completion and its dedication. This great event occurred in the Year of Jubilee, during the Feast of Tabernacles, in connection with the Great Day of Atonement. The Feast of the Dedication lasted for seven days, then came the Great Day of Atonement, and finally the seven days of the Feast of Tabernacles. Thus are the circumstances of the dedication harmonized with the Grace and the Glory of the future Kingdom which was then foreshadowed, and we speak of the coming Kingdom Age.

The Ark of the Covenant was brought up from Zion, the city of David, where it had been lodged in a tent, to the neighboring hill of Moriah, upon which the Temple was built; and the Tabernacle of Moses was brought up from Gibeon, where it had been in the days of Saul. It may be assumed that the Tabernacle and its vessels were reverently laid up among the *"treasures of the House"* (I Ki. 7:51).

The Ark, having the Tables of the Law within it, was placed within the Holy of Holies. All was performed exactly as the Bible commanded; consequently, the Glory of Jehovah filled the House of Jehovah.

By God's Command (I Chron. 28:19), there were variations made in the vessels in the Temple as contrasted with those of the Tabernacle. These changes harmonize with the purpose of the Temple as an exposition of the coming Glory, but there was no alteration with respect to the Ark, for it was God's one and only Throne. Its staves, however, were withdrawn, and the Golden Pot of Manna and Aaron's Rod that budded, which were associated with the Tabernacle in the wilderness (Ex. 16:33; Num. 17:10; Heb. 9:4), are not mentioned. All this is harmonious.

The Ark entered its rest. The staves with which the Priests had borne it in the wilderness were withdrawn and became the memorials of that time of pilgrimage, testifying to the Grace and Faithfulness which had brought them into God's Rest. But Aaron's Rod and the Pot of Manna are not mentioned, for these, being types of that which would be substantial in the Millennium, necessarily disappeared — they would be out of place in the glorious reign and rest of Canaan.

Therefore, it was that Solomon, as Priest and King, in the presence of a manifested glory, displaced Aaron and his Priesthood; for he, and not the High Priest, dedicated the Temple and blessed the people, because Solomon represented Christ Who will reign supreme in the coming Kingdom Age.

The Ten Commandments remained in the Ark; for the Word of the Lord endures forever. It is mentioned with emphasis (I Ki. 8:9) that they, and nothing else, were in the Ark. This had to be; for the Law of God was hidden in the Messiah's heart (Ps. 119:11), as it was hidden in the Ark. That Law will be the basis and rule of the Righteousness which will govern in the coming Kingdom Age.

The Law, in fact, is kept now, and will be forever, through Christ and what Christ has done for us at the Cross.

232

APRIL
19

*a*nd Solomon offered a Sacrifice of Peace Offerings, which he offered unto the LORD, two and twenty thousand oxen, and an hundred and twenty thousand sheep. So the king and all the Children of Israel dedicated the House of the LORD. Now when Solomon had made an end of praying, the fire came down from Heaven and consumed the Burnt Offering and the Sacrifices; and the Glory of the LORD filled the House. And the Priests could not enter into the House of the LORD because the Glory of the LORD had filled the LORD'S House (I Ki. 8:63; II Chron. 7:1-2).

The Temple was the only building in the entirety of the world in which the One True God was worshipped.

There is every evidence that the Lord gave Solomon these instructions regarding the tremendous number of Sacrifices which were offered at the Dedication of the Temple. This proclaimed the fact that Israel's foundation, its only foundation, was the Precious Blood of Christ, of which the Sacrifices were a symbol. The tremendous number of animals

233

offered portrays the significance of what Jesus would do at Calvary; consequently, it is not possible to overemphasize the Cross of Christ, as here should be abundantly evident.

Before the abundant number of sacrifices were offered, appropriate sacrifices were placed on the Great Altar. The Scripture says, *"Fire came down from Heaven, and consumed them."* The fire that consumed the *"Burnt Offering"* at the Dedication *"came down from Heaven,"* but the fire that consumed the Burnt Offering at the Dedication of the Tabernacle *"came out from before the LORD,"* that is, came out from between the Cherubim within the Most Holy Place, where the Ark of the Covenant was kept. But in coming out from, and passing through, the Tabernacle, that fire did not burn even the Veil through which it passed, for that Tent, in essence, was Christ. This is characteristic. The fire from the Tabernacle is Christ in His First Advent; the fire from Heaven, Christ in His Second Advent, even as the Tabernacle portrayed the First Advent of Christ, while the Temple portrayed His Second Advent.

The latter has not yet come to pass, but it most assuredly shall!

The Sacrifice was offered, representing Calvary; the fire fell on the Sacrifice, consuming it, typifying the Judgment of God poured out on Christ instead of upon us who rightly deserved it. Then at that time the Glory filled the Temple to such an extent that the Priests could not even enter the Temple for the force of that power.

Let it therefore ever be understood:

The True Glory of the Lord will accompany nothing but Christ and His Cross. Any other professed glory is fake, as, of necessity, it must be. Everything must be based squarely on the Cross of Christ (I Pet. 1:18-20).

234

APRIL
20

*a*nd Elijah said unto all the people, Come near unto me. And all the people came near unto him. And he repaired the Altar of the LORD that was broken down (I Ki. 18:30).

For God to move, the Altar, which was broken down, and which was a Type of the coming Atonement of Christ, had first of all to be repaired. Presently, the Church, that is, if it is to see a Move of God, has to come back to the Cross. God will tolerate no other direction.

To repair the Altar, Elijah used *"twelve stones."* The number *"twelve"* is God's number of Government; however, it must ever be remembered that it is God's Government and not man's. His Government is His Word. That Government is centered up in the Cross.

Elijah next *"made a trench about the Altar,"* which speaks of separation. To be sure, the Cross of Christ separates Believers from the world; it alone will separate Believers from the world.

Then the great Prophet put the Bullock, cut in pieces,

235

on the Altar, which represented Christ on the Cross. The *"Bullock, cut in pieces"* represents the horror of sin. It is much more than a mere surface problem, but rather goes to the very vitals of the human being, hence the necessity of the Cross, which alone addresses sin, both its cause and its effect (Heb. 10:12).

He then *"filled four barrels with water,"* did it three times, and poured it on the Sacrifice that was to be offered; the water ran down and filled the trench. The *"water"* is a Type of the Word of God, which is to saturate everything. More than all, this typifies that the Cross of Christ alone fulfills the Word of God in every respect. In other words, if the Believer is not basing everything strictly on the Cross, what he is doing is not according to the Word and cannot be blessed by the Lord.

This being done, *"the fire of the LORD fell, and consumed the Burnt Sacrifice, and the wood, and the stones, and the dust, and licked up the water that was in the trench"* (I Ki. 18:38).

The fire falling represented the Judgment of God. It fell on Christ instead of on mankind; however, if the Cross is not ever the Object of one's Faith, to be sure, ultimately the fire of judgment will fall, and it will be on the individual instead of on Christ. Christ became our Substitute, thereby, taking our place; however, as God the Father cannot be approached except through Christ (Jn. 14:6), likewise, Christ cannot be approached except through the Cross (Lk. 9:23).

APRIL
21

*a*nd Elijah said unto Ahab, Get thee up, eat and drink; for there is a sound of abundance of rain (I Ki. 18:41).

Israel had suffered some three and a half years of drought, which had brought the nation to utter ruin. In fact, there was not a green thing to be seen, with all of the brooks in the land completely dried up. This drought, instigated by the Lord, was indicative of Israel's spiritual condition. Governed by Ahab and wicked Jezebel, the nation had completely lost her way with God.

I'm afraid that this drought is also indicative of the modern Church. Religion abounds, even as it did in Israel of old, but precious little true Moving and Operation of the Holy Spirit. The modern Church says, *"We are rich and increased with goods, and have need of nothing."* However, the Lord says, *"And knowest not that you are wretched, and miserable, and poor, and blind, and naked"* (Rev. 3:17).

Due, however, to the Altar being repaired, which means that Israel was brought back to the Cross, with the fire

237

falling, which means that God recognized the Cross, as God will always recognize the Cross, and, in fact, will recognize nothing else, then the land is ready for a deluge of rain. In fact, the Prophet Elijah tells Ahab, *"Get thee up, eat and drink; for there is a sound of abundance of rain,"* and that's exactly what happened! The Scripture says, *"There was a great rain"* (I Ki. 18:45).

All of this tells us that before the rain of revival can come, the Church must first of all come back to the Cross. In these last days, I do not hold out any illusion that religious Denominations are going to come back to the Cross. In fact, they aren't! However, the *"abundance of rain"* awaits any and every individual Believer who will come back to the Cross.

Jesus says, *"Behold, I stand at the door, and knock: if any man hear My Voice, and open the door, I will come in to him, and will sup with him, and he with Me"* (Rev. 3:20).

APRIL
22

*a*nd it came to pass, when they were gone over, that Elijah said unto Elisha, Ask what I shall do for you, before I be taken away from you. And Elisha said, I pray you, let a double portion of your spirit be upon me. And he said, You have asked a hard thing: nevertheless, if you see me when I am taken from you, it shall be so unto you; but if not, it shall not be so (II Ki. 2:9-10).

There have never been two Prophets quite like Elijah and Elisha. The name *"Elijah"* means *"Jehovah is God,"* and figures Law. *"Elisha"* means *"God is Salvation,"* and represents Grace. Elisha has now been some ten years with Elijah — a testing time — and the last test now comes.

The Scripture indicates that Elisha knew that Elijah was going to be taken. Exactly how, that he did not know! Consequently, Elisha will not let the great Prophet out of his sight. Irrespective that Elijah told him first to remain in Gilgal, then to remain in Bethel, and finally to remain in Jericho, Elisha, prompted by the Spirit of God, knew that he must not let Elijah out of his sight. He hungered and thirsted after Righteousness; consequently, he would be filled (Mat. 5:6).

And then, at the miracle of the parting of the waters of Jordan, Elijah said to his protégé, *"Ask what I shall do for you, before I be taken away from you."* The answer from Elisha was instant, *"Let a double portion of your spirit be upon me."* Elisha wanted the Power of God. He was little interested in anything else.

For what is the modern Church seeking?

Then Elijah said to him, *"You have asked a hard thing."* A better translation from the Hebrew would be, *"You have staked a great claim."* And that's exactly what the Holy Spirit wanted him to do. Far too many Christians presently are staking insignificant claims, or rather none at all. The Church desperately needs those who will *"stake a great claim,"* i.e., *"ask for the impossible."*

To be frank, it was impossible for Elijah to give any part of his spirit to Elisha, much less a double portion; however, the Lord could do such; to be sure, the Lord did so such! There only was one requirement:

Elisha was not to take his eyes off the great Prophet. If Elisha observed Elijah as he was translated, he would receive his request; if not, *"it shall not be so."* To be sure, the moment this tremendous spectacle occurred, i.e., the translation of Elijah, and done so by a *"chariot of fire, and horses of fire,"* Elisha was intently observing, and he received exactly that for which he asked — a double portion.

The *"double portion"* is exactly what I want from the Lord, and it should be exactly what you want. Grace promised it to Elisha, and Grace gave it to Elisha. Grace will do the same for us! We must not be satisfied with the status quo, or even what has been. There awaits a double portion for all who will believe.

Elisha got exactly that for which he asked. He performed exactly twice as many miracles as Elijah.

APRIL
23

*a*nd the men of the city said unto Elisha, Behold, I pray you, the situation of this city is pleasant, as my lord sees: but the water is naught, and the ground barren (II Ki. 2:19).

This would be the second miracle performed by the Prophet Elisha, the opening of Jordan being the first (II Ki. 2:14). Elisha now comes into Jericho and is met by the elders of the city. They tell him that the situation of the city is pleasant, but they have one great problem. The water is poisoned, and the ground is, therefore, barren. The Holy Spirit will give the Prophet a beautiful answer to this scenario, all typifying Christ.

The Holy Spirit told Elisha to tell the Elders to *"bring me a new cruse."* The *"cruse"* of which he spoke was made of clay. It symbolized the humanity of Christ, i.e., *"His Incarnation."* Furthermore, it was required that this cruse be *"new,"* which symbolized the fact that there never had been since Adam a human being like Jesus. Born of the Virgin Mary, which means that His conception was decreed by the Holy Spirit, He was truly *"new"* in character, aspect, and every form of being.

That's why Paul referred to Christ as *"The Last Adam"* and *"The Second Man"* (I Cor. 15:45, 47).

Elisha then told the men to *"put salt therein,"* which is a type of the incorruptible Word of God. This means that Jesus lived by the Word, functioned in the Word, abided by the Word in every respect, never failed the Word, and was, in fact, the Living Word (Jn. 1:1-2). The Scripture says that Elisha *"took the new cruse"* to the *"spring of the waters"* and *"cast the salt in there."* This refers to the fact that Jesus obeyed the Word in every aspect, *"even the death of the Cross"* (Phil. 2:8).

For the poisoned waters to be healed, which represent original sin in the heart and life of every human being, Jesus would have to go to the Cross, thereby, in effect, casting the *"salt,"* i.e., *"Himself,"* into that iniquity (II Cor. 5:21). Only then can the poisoned waters of man's soul be healed, even as the waters were healed in Jericho, which was a type.

Let it ever be understood:

Man can plant a garden around the poisoned well, even install a new pump, and even make the pump out of gold, but none of that will have any effect on what the well produces. For the poisoned waters to be healed, the problem has to be addressed at its source. Only Christ has done that, which, in fact, was done at the Cross.

That's why Paul said he would glory in the Cross, and in the Cross alone (Gal. 6:14).

APRIL
24

*t*hen he said, Go, borrow thee vessels abroad of all your neighbors, even empty vessels; borrow not a few (II Ki. 4:3).

A particular Prophet died, and his wife was left penniless. She went to Elisha, asking for help regarding her problem. Her situation was so acute that the creditors were about to come and take her sons away, forcing them into servitude.

Let it ever be understood:

When it comes to the world, "*the creditor is come.*" Satan is that creditor, and he will take all, steal all, and destroy all (Jn. 10:10).

The woman, however, took her problem to Elisha, i.e., "*the Lord.*" Unfortunately, the modern Church has come to the place that it advocates taking our problems to the psychologist. What a sorry trade! No help whatsoever can be expected from that source, much less miracles!

Elisha asked her, "*What shall I do for you?*" The Lord, in effect, and at innumerable times, asks us the same thing,

"What shall I do for you?" (Mat. 21:22; Mk. 11:24-25; Jn. 14:14; 15:7).

The Prophet then asked her, *"What have you in the house?"* Her answer was quick in coming. She said, *"A pot of oil."*

In the Bible, *"oil"* is typical of the Holy Spirit. The woman may not have had much of anything else, but she, in typical form, had the Holy Spirit. That being the case, there is no limit to what can be done.

The Prophet then told her that she was to go to all of her neighbors and to borrow as many empty vessels as possible, *"borrow not a few."* She was to expect great things!

What are you expecting? Are you expecting great things? If you are, you will want great containers.

One of our biggest problems as Christians is that we make God too small, thereby asking for too little. I will never forget the exhortation of my Grandmother, who, in effect, was my Bible School, my Seminary, etc. Over and over again, she told me, *"Jimmy, God is a big God, so ask big!"* I have never forgotten that, and it has helped me to touch the world for Christ.

After the woman gathered all the vessels, she was to take the lone pot of oil which she had and start pouring it into the vessels. She would find that her source would not run dry until there were no more vessels. In other words, God stops when we stop! I don't ever want to stop, because if I don't stop, He won't stop! The oil will keep coming.

She took the oil, sold it, paid her debts, and had plenty enough left over to live on. He has enough, and to spare!

APRIL

25

*A*nd Elisha sent a messenger unto him, saying, Go and wash in Jordan seven times, and your flesh shall come again to you, and you shall be clean (II Ki. 5:10).

This concerns Naaman, captain of the host of the King of Syria. The Holy Spirit says that he was a *"great man,"* *"honorable,"* and a *"mighty man in valor."* But the Holy Spirit added, *"but he was a leper."*

In those days, leprosy was tantamount to a sentence of death. In the Old Testament, leprosy was used by the Holy Spirit as a type of sin. There was no earthly cure for leprosy, just as there is no earthly cure for sin.

A little maid, whom the Holy Spirit desired to remain nameless, had been taken captive from Israel and was now serving in the household of Naaman. Upon overhearing the consternation that followed the news that Naaman had contracted leprosy, the Scripture says this little maid told her mistress about the Prophet Elisha in Samaria!

She said, *"He will recover him of his leprosy."* This

young lady, who had been taken captive and made to serve as a slave in a strange land, could easily have succumbed to depression, even blaming God for her predicament. After all, she was an Israelite; however, she allowed none of that to control her. She maintained her faith, attempting to serve God to the best of her ability where He had placed her.

What an example!

On the word of this little *"maid,"* Naaman departed for Israel, taking with him several millions of dollars in order to *"pay for his healing."* How so like the world, thinking that Salvation can be bought! Furthermore, before going to Elisha, Naaman went to the King of Israel, who, of course, could do nothing for him.

Let that be a lesson for all. Man has no answer for these problems.

Elisha heard about the situation and said, *"Let him come now to me, and he shall know that there is a Prophet in Israel."*

So Naaman came; however, the situation was not exactly to his liking. Elisha didn't even come out to greet him; he rather sent a lowly messenger with a ridiculous message, at least ridiculous to Naaman. Naaman was to *"Go and wash in Jordan seven times."* He grew furiously angry, exclaiming how much better the rivers of Syria were than the River Jordan.

It is true that the rivers he named in Syria were crystal clear, while Jordan was anything but that. Likewise, Calvary, typified here by the River Jordan, holds no attraction. The Cross, in fact, has no attraction at all; it rather is *"an offence"* (Gal. 5:11). The only thing that one can say about the Cross is, *"It works."* It alone will *"cleanse from the leprosy of sin."* No matter how sparkling clear and beautifully arrayed the other efforts are, whatever they are and wherever they are, they carry no healing process. The Cross alone does that.

Upon being told to wash in Jordan, Naaman, as stated, became enraged. Many today, when told about the Cross, do the same thing. But thankfully, Naaman ultimately obeyed and *"dipped himself seven times in Jordan, according to the saying of the man of God: and his flesh came again like unto the flesh of a little child, and he was clean"* (II Ki. 5:14).

Likewise is everyone who comes to that fountain. It may not be attractive to the world, but it cleanses from sin (Zech. 13:1).

APRIL
26

*a*nd he (Naaman) *returned to the man of God, he and all his company, and came, and stood before him: and he said, Behold, now I know that there is no God in all the Earth, but in Israel: now therefore, I pray you, take a blessing of your servant. But he (Elisha) said, As the LORD lives, before Whom I stand, I will receive none. And he urged him to take it; but he refused* (II Ki. 5:15-16).

After Naaman was healed, he obviously was very grateful. He goes back to the Prophet and offers to give him as much money as he wanted. But Elisha refused to take anything.

Why?

At times, Elisha did take gifts, or at least the indication is that he did. But this was different. All of this was a Type of what Christ did at the Cross, which affords Salvation free of charge to all who simply will believe (Jn. 3:16). No price is put on such, because no price can be put on such. So, Elisha was forbidden by the Lord to take anything. Had he done so, it would have spoiled the Type.

But after Naaman left, Elisha's servant, Gehazi, no doubt having overheard the conversation, ran and overtook the Syrian. Gehazi lied to Naaman, claiming that Elisha had changed his mind and would like some payment — *"a talent of silver, and two changes of garments"* (II Ki. 5:22).

The end result would not be pleasant. Because Gehazi spoiled the Type and lied to Naaman, Elisha was instructed by the Holy Spirit to tell him, *"The leprosy therefore of Naaman shall cleave unto you, and unto your seed forever."* Then, *"he went out from his presence a leper as white as snow"* (II Ki. 5:27).

This should be a powerful lesson for every person. Salvation cannot be bought. In fact, God has nothing for sale. Everything is a gift; and if we try to earn Salvation, we will find that the sin remains; it will remain forever, that is, if one continues on that path.

Such a direction completely destroyed Israel.

Paul said, *"For they being ignorant of God's Righteousness, and going about to establish their own righteousness, have not submitted themselves unto the Righteousness of God"* (Rom. 10:3).

Paul then tells the Church, *"For if God spared not the natural branches, take heed lest He also spare not you,"* meaning if God's Redemption Plan of the Cross is ignored, the results will be destruction (Rom. 11:21).

APRIL
27

*a*nd there were four leprous men at the entering of the gate: and they said one to another, Why sit we here until we die? (II Ki. 7:3).

Because of sin, the Northern Kingdom of Israel has been reduced to slavery and starvation. At the moment of the Text, the Syrians had surrounded the city of Samaria, placing it under siege. Soon the food ran out, with the situation becoming dire indeed!

There were four leprous men sitting at the gate of the city, because they were not allowed inside. They too were starving to death. In this abject condition, they reasoned among themselves, *"Why sit we here until we die?"* They would go into the camp of the Syrians, who might give them some food. If they die in the attempt, i.e., if they were killed by the Syrians, they were no worse off than at present. They were most assuredly going to die, so they had nothing to lose.

These four men showed Faith; to be sure, Faith is always attached to action. *"Faith without works is dead."*

How many modern Believers have simply given up? It may even be that you have sinned, and sinned greatly, typified by the leprosy. In this terrible condition, most in the modern Church would write you off. But you must realize that God has not written you off. God loves you; He paid a great price for your soul. But if you continue to sit in the place of despondency, refusing to act, there is nothing God can do. He awaits only your favorable response.

Why not say, as those four leprous men of so long ago, *"Why sit I here until I die?"*

When you get up, God gets up! Don't forget that.

When the four lepers went into the camp of the Syrians, the Lord made their footfall sound like a mighty army. The Syrians thought that Israel had hired Hittites and Egyptians to come against them. Consequently, the Syrians fled, leaving everything in their camp — money, food, garments, everything!

After the lepers had eaten and drank, they, in essence, said to themselves, *"This is a day of good tidings. We must not keep it to ourselves. We must tell it to all in the city."* And so they did! That which the Lord gives is of such magnificence and of such abundance, that it not only meets our every need, but we, at the same time, are to give this message of *"glad tidings"* concerning Salvation, which meets every need of every individual, to the entirety of the world.

The people in Samaria were starving to death. They are a type of the world without God. Admittedly, the world will not accept Christ and His largesse as readily as the starving people of Samaria accepted that which was left by the Syrians. Nevertheless, some few will. All who accept will find blessing untold.

As the lepers of old, it's up to us to tell them (Jn. 10:10).

APRIL
28

*a*nd King Ahaz went to Damascus to meet Tiglath-pileser king of Assyria, and saw an altar that was at Damascus: and King Ahaz sent to Urijah the Priest the fashion of the altar, and the pattern of it, according to all the workmanship thereof. And Urijah the Priest built an altar according to all that King Ahaz had sent from Damascus: so Urijah the Priest made it against King Ahaz came from Damascus* (II Ki. 16:10-11).

The correct name of King Ahaz, King of Judah, was *"Jehoahaz,"* which means *"the possession of Jehovah."* The man was so ungodly that the Spirit of God strikes the Jehovah-syllable out of his name, invariably calling him *"Ahaz,"* which simply means *"possession."* Such was his life. He was led, influenced, and possessed by anyone or anything except God.

His history illustrates how disastrous it is for the spiritual profit of a man when his own plans succeed. God, through Isaiah, earnestly counseled him not to invite the

King of Assyria to help him against the confederate kings of Israel and Damascus. He, however, followed his own counsel, and with success; but the ultimate result was ruin.

Not only did he worship the golden calf of the kings of Israel, but he introduced the horrible religion of Moloch, the god of fire, the red-hot iron arms of whose image received and burned alive helpless little children, possibly even hundreds. He completed his apostasy by displacing the great Brazen Altar of God's appointment, which sat in front of the Temple, setting up in its stead an altar inspired of Damascus.

So determined was Ahaz in his opposition to the Bible, that not only did he send to Urijah the High Priest a sketch of the idolatrous altar that he saw at Damascus, but he also sent with it a model; for that is the import of the words, *"the fashion of the altar, and the pattern of it"* (16:10).

Urijah the High Priest was just as guilty as Ahaz the king.

I'm afraid the modern Church is basically doing the same thing as Ahaz of old, replacing the Cross with a cross of their own design.

What do we mean by that?

Unless the Cross of Christ is totally the Object of our Faith, this means that we are also building another altar in conjunction with the Cross, whether we realize it or not. In fact, this is one of the most devious and crowning sins of the Evil One. He would like for Believers, so-called, to rid themselves of the Cross altogether, which most have done; however, barring that, i.e., if they want to cling to some semblance of the Cross, he will subtly suggest the substitution of another type of cross. Such is the Purpose Driven Life doctrine, or the Government of Twelve, or the Word of Faith, etc.

All false doctrine starts, in some way, with a wrong interpretation of the Cross, or else denies the Cross altogether.

APRIL
29

*t*herefore thus saith the LORD concerning the king of Assyria, He shall not come into the city, nor shoot an arrow there, nor come before it with shield, nor cast a bank against it. By the way that he came, by the same shall he return, and shall not come into this city, saith the LORD. For I will defend this city, to save it, for My Own sake, and for My servant David's sake (II Ki. 19:32-34).

From the accession of Hezekiah to the captivity, the Assyrian and the Babylonian overshadow the house of David, and call forth those exercises of heart which are painful to the flesh but profitable to the spirit. These enemies appeared because of Israel's unfaithfulness.

So is it in the Christian life. Fidelity to the Lord and to His precious Book saves the Christian from those trials which a want of fidelity surely brings; and yet, the pitying love and wisdom of God may use these very griefs as instruments of spiritual enrichment to those who, like Hezekiah and Josiah, really love Him, though that love be imperfect.

256

Hezekiah began his reign as a vassal of the King of Assyria, by whom he was placed upon the throne during the lifetime of his father, Ahaz. In 18:7, it is recorded that he rebelled against that monarch and defeated the Philistines. This victory over the Philistine, who was an internal enemy, and the later victory over the Assyrian, who was an external enemy, illustrate the fact that victory over both inward and outward temptation is promised to the overcomer.

Sennacherib, leader of the mighty Assyrian empire, had laid siege to Judah and was now threatening Jerusalem. In fact, he was demanding the surrender of the Sacred City. The Prophet Isaiah now appears for the first time on the pages of the Bible (II Ki. 19:2).

Isaiah the Prophet predicted victory, and great victory, at that. Not only would Sennacherib not take Jerusalem, but, furthermore, he would not even shoot an arrow against it. This great victory, however, was not because of any moral beauty in Hezekiah, but rather for His Own sake, and for David's sake, i.e., *"the True David, Christ."*

The Scripture says, *"And it came to pass that night, that the Angel of the LORD went out, and smote in the camp of the Assyrians an hundred eighty and five thousand: and when they* (the inhabitants of Jerusalem) *arose early in the morning, behold, they* (the army of Sennacherib) *were all dead corpses"* (II Ki. 19:35).

This shows us the power of prayer, and, above all, the Power of God. Never before had Sennacherib met such power. History records that he left immediately, going back to Assyria, where ultimately he was murdered by his own sons. Before his death, he made excursions into other parts of the world of that day, but never again toward Judah.

What a mighty God we serve!

APRIL
30

*b*ut when he was strong, his heart was lifted up to his destruction: for he transgressed against the LORD his God, and went into the Temple of the LORD to burn incense upon the Altar of Incense. And Azariah the Priest went in after him . . . and they withstood Uzziah the King, and said unto him, It appertains not unto you, Uzziah, to burn incense unto the LORD. . . . Then Uzziah was wroth . . . and while he was wroth with the Priests, the leprosy even rose up in his forehead before the Priests in the House of the LORD, from beside the Incense Altar (II Chron. 26:16-19).

Uzziah was *"marvelously helped,"* that is, God prospered him so greatly that people marveled. But when he was strong, he entered the zone of real danger. *"When we are weak, then are we strong,"* Paul said (II Cor. 12:10). Strong Christians, it seems, are in very great danger.

Uzziah went into the Holy Place of the Temple in order to burn incense on the Golden Altar, which was the duty of the Priests alone. In other words, no other person could enter this place, not even the king.

The Priests were types of Christ, and, thereby, offered up incense on the Golden Altar twice a day, which was a type of the Intercession afforded us by Christ. Uzziah was saying, in effect, that he really didn't need an Intercessor; he could be his own intercessor.

In the midst of his efforts to burn incense, while the Priests were pleading with him to stop, the Lord struck him with leprosy, and it began in his forehead.

Why his forehead?

On the forehead of the High Priest was the golden plate with the words inscribed upon it, *"Holiness to the LORD."* As it regarded Uzziah, the Lord was, in essence, saying that instead of Holiness, there was sinfulness.

Not only is our Redemption based strictly on the Cross of Calvary, but all Intercession by Christ is also based strictly on what He has done for us at the Cross. God accepts His Intercession only on that basis, i.e., *"the complete Sacrifice."* This simply means that when any Believer places his faith in something other than the Cross of Christ, he is, in effect, doing the same thing that Uzziah did, which, if continued, ultimately will incur the same result.

The greatest sin of all is rebellion against God's Prescribed Order, which is what Uzziah did, and what millions presently are doing! (Phil. 3:18-19)

MAY

1

*t*hen stood up Jeshua the son of Jozadak and his brethren the Priests, and Zerubbabel the son of Shealtiel, and his brethren, and built the Altar of the God of Israel, to offer Burnt Offerings thereon, as it is written in the Law of Moses the man of God (Ezra 3:2).

The Bible and the Atonement are the two great facts of this Third Chapter in Ezra — the one recognized as authoritative, the other confessed as necessary, and absolutely so.

Even though Israel had many enemies surrounding them, nations which were not at all in sympathy with Israel's restoration, dread of these surrounding nations did not impel Israel to seek safety in walls and battlements, but rather in Burnt Offerings and Sin Sacrifices. They, in effect, and in spirit, sought refuge in a Crucified Saviour. This means that they placed themselves under the wings of the God of Israel. This was a beautiful testimony.

Therefore, before they built the Temple, even before

they built the walls, they first of all built at Altar. Instructed by the Scriptures, they offered up the Burnt Offerings, and the Sin Offerings, thus publicly confessed themselves to be guilty sinners, and that only by the shedding of atoning blood could they be forgiven and brought back to God. It hasn't changed from then until now.

The safety, protection, strength, and power of the individual Christian is found entirely in the Cross, and only in the Cross, of which all of this was a type. When Paul, guided by the Holy Spirit, proceeded to give instructions how the Believer is to live a perpetually holy life, he took us straight to the Cross. We find it in the Sixth Chapter of Romans.

First of all, it must be remembered that Paul is dealing with Believers, and not the unredeemed. So he tells Believers in the first two Verses of the Sixth Chapter of Romans that sin is the problem. Whatever the difficulty, sin is the problem. And then he tells us the cure for sin, and the only cure for sin, which is the Cross. That is found in Romans 6:3-5.

Actually, if one doesn't properly understand the Sixth Chapter of Romans, then one simply doesn't know how to live for God. To be sure, a person can be saved and not understand this Chapter, but they cannot walk in victory.

As Israel after the dispersion proclaimed this fact, and actually as it is proclaimed throughout the entirety of the Bible, the Believer must ever understand that the entirety of the Message of the Word of God is *"Jesus Christ and Him Crucified"* (Gen. 3:15; Isa., Chpt. 53; Rom. 6:1-14; I Cor. 1:17-18, 21, 23; 2:2).

MAY

2

*t*here was a man in the land of Uz, whose name was Job; and that man was perfect and upright, and one who feared God, and eschewed evil (Job 1:1).

Job is the oldest Book in the Bible, and thereby the oldest Book in the world. It was written by Moses (Lk. 24:27, 44). It explains the problem of why good men are afflicted. It is in order to bring about their Sanctification. It is interesting that this difficult question should be the first taken up and answered in the Bible.

In the Book of Job, the discovery of the worthlessness of self is the first step in Christian experience. Then we discover the worthfulness of Christ, which is the second step. However, the worthfulness of Christ can never be reached until we fully understand the worthlessness of self.

The Book of Job does not symbolize an unconverted man, but rather a Believer. It was necessary that one of God's Children should be chosen for this trial; for the

262

subject of this Book is not the conversion of the sinner, but the consecration of the Saint. It is evident that an unconverted man needs to be brought to the end of himself; but that a man who feared God, who was perfect in his efforts to serve the Lord, and who hated evil, should also need this, such presents itself as a mystery to most Christians. God chose the most consecrated man on the face of the Earth at that time to portray the fact that *"self"* is a problem, and that it must be dealt with, and that dealing with it is never easy, but always extremely difficult.

The effect of all that happened to Job was that he ultimately came to *"abhor himself"* (Job 42:5-6). This language shows that previously, i.e. before his great trial, he had thought well of himself. His creed was orthodox, for he approached God through Sacrifice, and his conduct was faultless, for he was a just man and hated evil. But these sharp trials, and especially the anger which the unjust accusations of his friends stirred up in his heart, revealed to himself unknown depths of moral ugliness; and, finally, his being challenged to measure himself with God made him conscious that in him, that is, in his *"flesh,"* there dwelt no good thing. This is a deep and painful experience which all Christian people have not reached, but yet must be reached, if we are to be what we ought to be in Christ (Williams).

*n*ow *there was a day when the sons of God came to present themselves before the LORD, and Satan came also among them. And the LORD said unto Satan, Have you considered My servant Job, that there is none like him in the Earth, a perfect and an upright man, one who fears God, and hates evil?* (Job 1:6, 8)

From the experience of Job we find many truths given to us. Some of them are as follows:

1. Satan is a created being, originally created by God as a righteous Angel, who, sometime in eternity past, fell, and who, in fact, led a revolution against God — a conflict which continues even unto this hour (Isa. 14:12-15; Ezek. 28:13-19).

2. We learn that Satan must appear before the Lord periodically to give account of himself.

3. We learn from Chapters 2 and 3 of Job that Satan can do only what the Lord allows him to do, and no more! In other words, Satan has to ask permission for whatever

he desires to do, and then minutely must follow directions laid down by the Lord.

4. We learn from Job's three friends the impotence of man and his efforts. With Eliphaz it was *"human experience"*; with Bildad, *"human tradition"*; and with Zophar, *"human merit."*

5. We learn from all of this that everything that happens to a Believer, irrespective as to what it might be, is either *"caused"* by the Lord or *"allowed"* by the Lord. Of course, the Lord never causes any Believer to sin, but He does allow such, that is, if such a Believer is so inclined; however, the penalty is always posted.

6. We learn that the discovery of the deep corruption of the heart is the most painful and humbling that a Believer can make.

So the Patriarch had to crucify all his goodness as truly as all his badness, and sit in wood ashes as a public confession that he merited death because of his sin-defiled nature. This moral principle governs the Salvation of the sinner as well as the Sanctification of the Saint.

7. We learn from the narrative of Job that everyone had to change except God! Job had to humble himself, and to pray for God to bless these three *"friends"* who had so despitefully used him and persecuted him. The three *"friends"* had to confess themselves worthy of death, and to seek forgiveness from God through the Precious Blood of Christ, as foreshadowed in the Sacrifices of Chapter 42.

8. We also learn that Job's latter end was better than his beginning. God gave him twice as much as he had before; and such is ever the result in the spiritual life. Increased spiritual wealth results from the death of self, i.e.,

the death of bad self and also of good self.

So, the subject of this book is not how God justifies a sinner, but how He sanctifies a Saint. Consequently, none but a good man could have been chosen for the process, or have profited by it. It is plain to all that a wicked man should die to self, but that a perfect man should also need to die to self is not so clear. And yet, this is the offense of the Cross. All of the goodness and beauty which men recognize in themselves and in others must be nailed in death to the Cross; and the only Man Who is to live must be the Risen Man, Christ Jesus.

True self-abhorrence comes not from self-examination, but in looking away from self to Jesus, the Perfecter and Author of Faith (Williams).

MAY
4

*h*e restores my soul: He leads me in the paths of righteousness for His Name's sake (Ps. 23:3).

The beauty of the Twenty-third Psalm knows no comparison. It is called *"The Shepherd's Psalm,"* and it written from the position of the sheep, who look exclusively to the Shepherd for leading and guiding. The Third Verse is particularly insightful.

At times, a sheep would stray from the *"correct path."* A sheep, being a sheep, i.e., comparatively dumb, he would soon get lost and find himself in a rocky defile, unable to find his way home; consequently, the sheep would begin to bleat, and then the shepherd would come, taking his crook and lifting the sheep out from the rocky crevice where he had become pinned, and place him back safely with the flock. In fact, this might happen several times, with the shepherd always coming and retrieving the recalcitrant one.

But after a period of time, after the sheep has left the

"*path of righteousness*" again, finding himself lost once again, despite his "*bleating,*" the shepherd doesn't come. Finally, when his voice is gone, and becoming very fearful that he will be overtaken by a bear or a lion, panic sets in. Why hasn't the shepherd come, even as he always has?

Then, with darkness settling in, the shepherd, who was there all the time, finally reaches down, and, with his crook, retrieves the wayward one. But then the shepherd does something totally different from what has previously been done. He picks up the lamb, stretches out one of its forepaws, takes his staff, and then smartly cracks the fore-paw, breaking the bone. That is chastisement! Carefully, he then sets the broken leg and carries the little sheep with him, actually close to his heart, until the leg is healed.

The little one then is placed once again on the "*path of righteousness.*" But now, he is not so quick to desert that path. In a sense, that is the story of the Twenty-third Psalm.

"*Surely goodness and mercy shall follow me all the days of my life: and I will dwell in the House of the LORD forever*" (Ps. 23:6).

MAY

5

*M*y God, My God, Why have You forsaken Me? Why are You so far from helping Me, and from the words of My roaring? (Ps. 22:1).

This Psalm portrays Christ as the Sin Offering, and doing so for all of mankind. Here, at the Cross, He atoned for all sin, past, present and future. There, the altogether righteous justice of a thrice-Holy God was perfectly satisfied, in that the perfect Sacrifice offered up satisfied every requirement.

Four degrees of suffering appear in this Psalm:

1. Suffering from the Hand of God; for, in effect, God smote Christ on the Cross (Vss. 1-6; Isa. 53:4).

2. Suffering from the rejection of Israel, in effect, His Own People (Vss. 7-8).

3. Suffering from the demons who gathered round His Cross in exulting and hellish triumph, or at least that which they thought was triumph (Vss. 12-13).

4. The physical suffering of the Crucifixion, which

was one of the most painful forms of death (Vss. 14-18).

Had the Messiah been only Man, He would have put His physical sufferings first and His spiritual sufferings last. But to Him, as the Only Begotten Son of God, there was no anguish so infinite as the hiding of the Father's Face. His physical sufferings were exquisitely agonizing, but his mental sufferings from the onslaught of demon spirits were even more terrible. The pain of His wounded Heart, however, because of those He loved and came to save, was a depth of agony deeper still; but an agony unspeakable was His being forsaken of God, at least after a fashion, even for a short period of time, i.e., from 12 noon until 3 p.m.

During His Ministry on Earth, Christ spoke of God as His Father and resumed the title after He had triumphantly shouted *"Finished."* But while suffering Divine Wrath as the Sin Offering, He addressed Him as *"God"* (Vss. 1-2, 10). In fact, the price He paid will never fully be understood; consequently, the victory He won in the paying of that price is likewise beyond comprehension.

Those who believe on this atoning Saviour shall be regarded as a new race — a generation of which the Messiah would be the Head (I Cor. 15:22; Isa. 53:10-11). We shall continually serve Him; we shall keep coming and shall keep declaring unto nations yet to be born that God's Righteous One accomplished this annihilation of sin by the oblation of Himself as the Sin Offering.

The last word in this Chapter in the Hebrew Text is *"accomplished,"* which corresponds to the word *"Finished"* in the Greek Text of Jn. 19:30.

Let it ever be known:

It was at the Cross where it was all *"accomplished"*!

MAY

6

*h*ave mercy upon me, O God, according to Your lovingkindness: according to the multitude of Your tender mercies blot out my transgressions (Ps. 51:1).

The Fifty-first Psalm presents the greatest example of a prayer of Repentance found anywhere in the Bible. It was given by the Holy Spirit to David when, his heart broken and contrite because of his sin against God, he did plead for pardon through the atoning Blood of the Lamb of God, foreshadowed in Exodus, Chapter 12. Thus was David not only fittingly provided with a vehicle of expression regarding Repentance and Faith, but he also was used as a channel of prophetic communication, which we shall see.

Concerning this, Williams says, "David, in his sin, Repentance, and Restoration, is a forepicture of Israel; for as he forsook the Law and was guilty of adultery and murder, so Israel despised the Covenant, turned aside to idolatry, and murdered the Messiah. Thus the scope and structure of the

271

Psalm go far beyond David: they predict the future confession and forgiveness of Israel in the day of the Second Coming of the Lord Jesus Christ, Israel's Messiah. They will look upon Him Whom they pierced and they shall mourn and weep (Zech., Chpts. 12-13; Rev. 1:7). *The first seventeen Verses are personal to David; the last two are national for Israel."*

Here appears the great principle that only those who have truly experienced forgiveness and pardon themselves can be true messengers of the Gospel. This principle is, in the first part of the Psalm, personally illustrated by David (Vs. 13); and in the latter part nationally illustrated by Israel (Vss. 18-19). These last two Verses, consequently, are not, as some think, a meaningless addition to the Psalm by some later writer. Both Verses belong to the structure and prophetic scope of the Psalm. They refer to that which is spoken of in Amos 9:11-12 and Acts 15:15-17. David's sin, confession, and Restoration illustrate this future Chapter in Israel's history. Their idolatry (*"adultery"*) and murder forgiven, they will go forth as messengers of the Gospel to win other nations to wholehearted faith and service in and for Christ. This concerning Israel will take place in the coming Kingdom Age.

MAY

7

*S*urely He shall deliver you from the snare of the fowler, and from the noisome pestilence (Ps. 91:3).

Moses wrote the Ninetieth Psalm and it is believed that He very well may have written the Ninety-first Psalm also.

The Psalm comforts and encourages the most timid Believer, for it assures him that what God was to His dearly beloved Son in His journey through the wilderness of this world, He will be to the weakest of His Children. We can prove Him to be what Christ proved Him to be.

In the earthly sojourn of Christ, for this is what this Psalm is all about, we find that the Messiah's path through the desert of this world was one of dependence upon God. Satan's effort in the temptation was to move Him to the place of independence; but he failed. Jesus walked a path of perfect submission, obedience, and dependence, all as a perfect example for us.

As the Evil One, however, repeatedly came against Christ, he will do the same to the Believer. Satan means to "*steal, kill, and destroy*" (Jn. 10:10). As Peter said, he goes about "*seeking whom he may devour*" (I Pet. 5:8).

And yet, we have this great Promise, illustrated in this Chapter, that whatever type of "*snare*" that Satan, here called the "*fowler*," may lay for us, the Lord has stated, "*Surely He shall deliver us.*" It is not merely, "*He shall deliver*," but rather "*Surely He shall deliver.*" This also refers to the "*noisome pestilence*," which refers to "*extreme wickedness.*"

All deliverance, without exception, is effected through the Cross. There Jesus defeated Satan and all his minions of darkness, doing so by atoning for all sin (Col. 2:14-15). To effect victory and to maintain victory, therefore, the Saint must ever make the Cross of Christ, where the victory was accomplished, ever the Object of his Faith. That being done, the Holy Spirit, Who is God, will work mightily in one's life. To be sure, Satan can easily stand up to us, but in no way can he stand up to the Holy Spirit.

Remember: When faith is properly placed, the Lord has said, "*Surely*"! Not "*Maybe,*" but "*Surely*"! (I Cor. 1:17-18, 23, 2:2; Gal. 6:14).

MAY
8

*h*ow sweet are Your Words unto My taste! Yea, sweeter than honey to My mouth! (Ps. 119:103).

The theme of this Psalm is the authority and sufficiency of the Bible as the only revealed Truth in the world. It, and it alone, is the rule of life. Its theme is the Word of God hidden in the heart and obeyed in the life. The Lord Jesus Christ is the Blessed Man Who fully satisfies its language. For He Himself is the Word of God. They only, who, like Him, are subject to that Word, are blessed.

This Psalm is an acrostic. There are 22 letters in the Hebrew alphabet and there are 22 stanzas in the Psalm. Each stanza contains 8 Verses. There are, therefore, 176 Verses in all.

In this Psalm, the Bible is given ten different titles, which, in effect, correspond to the Ten Commandments. Those titles are: "Way," "Testimonies," "Precepts," "Commandments," "Law," "Judgments," "Righteousness," "Statutes," "Word," and "Words."

This Psalm portrays the pilgrim walking through this world on a dangerous road on a dark night, wholly dependent upon a lamp to light his way and guide his feet (II Pet. 1:19). The lesson of the Psalm is that the lamp may be wholly trusted, and that whoever follows its light will be preserved from the squalors of the way, saved from the dangers of the path, and surely led to its desired end. This lamp is the Bible (Williams).

MAY

9

*l et every thing that has breath praise the LORD. Praise ye
the LORD* (Ps. 150:6).

This song, and all the Psalms are songs, will be sung
on that coming day after Israel has finally accepted the
Lord Jesus Christ as both Saviour and Lord. As a result,
and in her rightful place, even as the Lord originally intended, the whole world is in harmony, because the Prince
of Peace reigns supreme. As a result, the entirety of the
world will function in the world of *"Praise"* to the Lord.
He will be praised in His Sanctuary, which refers to the
Millennial Temple in Jerusalem. He also will be praised
for the *"firmament of His power,"* which refers to every problem being solved.

Then everyone's lips will be praise to the Lord because
of *"His mighty acts,"* which will be evident throughout the
entirety of the Earth. Men have tried to magnify their personal greatness, when, in reality, they have no greatness;
however, the Lord of Glory will truly have *"greatness,"* and,

277

on top of that, *"excellent greatness."*

Every musical instrument in the world will be used in praise to the Lord, which will bring the very elements into harmony with peace and prosperity. In other words, there will be no more tornados, hurricanes, famines, tidal waves, earthquakes, etc. Those things will be things of the past.

All sickness will be done away with, death placed in abeyance except in particular circumstances. All poverty will be eliminated, all war will be a thing of the past, superstition and ignorance will forever be laid aside, and the whole world will be at rest; then, and only then, will *"everything that has breath praise the Lord. Praise ye the LORD."* This will be in the coming Kingdom Age.

MAY

10

*i*f the clouds be full of rain, they empty themselves upon the Earth: if the tree fall toward the south, or toward the north, in the place where the tree falls, there it shall be (Eccl. 11:3).

In this one Chapter, we are given God's Formula for success. It is as follows:

Verse 1: The *"bread"* is the Word of God. The *"waters"* constitute the Holy Spirit. The Holy Spirit will function only upon the True Word of God, and it is guaranteed to bring home the blessing, whether in few or many days.

Verse 2: The number *"seven"* is God's Perfect Number. It refers to His Perfect Salvation, which is *"Jesus Christ and Him Crucified"* (I Cor. 1:23). The number *"eight"* pertains to Resurrection, for it was on this day that Christ rose from the dead. If we proclaim the Perfect Gospel of the Cross, *"we shall also be in the likeness of His Resurrection,"* i.e., *"Resurrection Life"* (Rom. 6:5).

Verse 3: If the Believer functions according to the Word of God, which means to function according to the

279

Message of the Cross, it really doesn't matter where the person is, or what the circumstances are, blessings will follow. In other words, the tree can fall toward the south, the north, etc. Wherever it falls, the person can be blessed, but only if they go God's Way.

Verse 4: The Believer is not to observe circumstances, but rather the Promises of God.

Verse 5: It is not known or understood exactly how a baby grows in its mother's womb. Likewise, we cannot know exactly how God will bring to pass His Promises, but bring them to pass He definitely shall, that is, if we will believe Him!

Verse 6: We are to sow the seed of the Word of God, not looking at circumstances, but rather continuing to believe the Lord, and then watch God work, even in ways that seem least likely. The Promise is: *"Cast your bread upon the waters, for you shall find it after many days"* (Eccl. 11:1).

MAY
11

*t*hen flew one of the Seraphims unto me, having a live coal in his hand, which he had taken with the tongs from off the Altar: And he laid it upon my mouth, and said, Lo, this has touched your lips; and your iniquity is taken away, and your sin purged (Isa. 6:6-7).

When men, like Isaiah, see themselves in the Divine Light, they cry out like the Prophet that they are *"undone."* The word *"undone"* means justly doomed to death. In the light of the Throne of God, which Isaiah saw, the Prophet learned that he was a moral leper; that his people were moral lepers; and that they altogether were as vile as King Uzziah, who was a leper (II Ki. 15:5).

If, in the Presence of the thrice-Holy LORD of Hosts, the sinless Seraphim had to veil both their faces and their feet, how hopeless was it for a moral leper such as Isaiah to stand in such a light! He needed a cleansing and covering of his sin: the living coals from off the Altar of Burnt Offering, symbolizing the fire of the Wrath of God and the Blood of the Lamb of God, when brought in contact with his *"unclean lips,"* removed his iniquity and expiated his sin.

There is no other way of cleansing and expiation than through the Wrath of God and the Atoning Blood of Christ. These are revealed and glorified at Calvary. There God judged sin infinitely and eternally in the Person of Christ; His Precious Blood there shed is the one and only perfect expiation for, and covering of, sin.

The modern Church must come back to the place that it knows and understands that the problem is sin, as the problem has always been sin. Understanding that, and understanding it properly, it will then come to realize that the only answer for sin is the Cross of Calvary.

Paul said: *"But this Man, after He had offered one Sacrifice for sins forever, sat down on the Right Hand of God;*

"For by one Offering He has perfected forever them who are sanctified" (Heb. 10:12, 14).

MAY
12

*a*nd there shall come forth a Rod out of the stem of Jesse, and a Branch shall grow out of his roots: And the Spirit of the LORD shall rest upon Him, the Spirit of Wisdom and Understanding, the Spirit of Counsel and Might, the Spirit of Knowledge and of the Fear of the LORD (Isa. 11:1-2).

Isaiah here sees the explanation of what John saw on the Isle of Patmos. John said, *"And I beheld, and, lo, in the midst of the Throne and of the four Beasts* (Living Ones), *and in the midst of the Elders, stood a Lamb as it had been slain, having seven horns and seven eyes, which are the Seven Spirits of God sent forth into all the Earth"* (Rev. 5:6).

There aren't *"seven Holy Spirits."* This phrase rather stands for the seven attributes of the Spirit of God, or, one might say, *"His sevenfold fullness."* Those attributes are:

"Spirit, Wisdom, Understanding, Counsel, Might, Knowledge, and Fear."

In this *"sevenfold fullness,"* we find all the *"help"* that we need in order to live this life and to be what we ought to be in the Lord (Jn. 14:16-18).

Tragically, the modern Church seeks to live for God without the help of this *"sevenfold fullness."* Even though the Holy Spirit most definitely resides in the heart and life of every single Believer, irrespective of the spiritual condition of such a Believer, still, what He can do is only potential. In other words, His help is not automatic.

But every single Believer can have this *"sevenfold fullness"* if the Believer will place his faith absolutely and exclusively in the Cross. The Holy Spirit always works within the parameters of the Finished Work of Christ. The Cross ever being the Object of our Faith, then the Holy Spirit will work mightily on our behalf, giving us the benefit of *"His sevenfold fullness,"* but only if our faith is properly placed in Christ and the Cross. He tells us this in Romans 8:2.

<u>MAY</u>
13

*t*he wolf also shall dwell with the lamb, and the leopard shall lie down with the kid; and the calf and the young lion and the fatling together; and a little child shall lead them. And the cow and the bear shall feed; their young ones shall lie down together: and the lion shall eat straw like the ox. And the sucking child shall play on the hole of the asp, and the weaned child shall put his hand on the cockatrice' den. They shall not hurt nor destroy in all My holy mountain: for the Earth shall be full of the knowledge of the LORD, as the waters cover the sea (Isa. 11:6-9).

Most of the evidence of the Fall will be eradicated and eliminated in the coming Resurrection of Life. At the Second Coming, which will begin the Kingdom Age when Christ shall rule and reign Personally from Jerusalem, the entire complexion of everything will be changed.

For instance, the animal kingdom will revert back to the manner of its original creation. Now, many animals are carnivorous (meat eaters). Then, in the coming Kingdom

Age, every animal will be docile. The wolf, the leopard, and the lion will no longer be fierce, but will be as the little lamb and the young calf; even a little child will play safely among them.

The cow and the bear, the latter being one of the most ferocious beasts in the world, shall, in that coming day, *"feed together."* Even the venom of the serpent will be gone forever; a little child will play with reptiles, even those reptiles which once were extremely venomous and deadly, but which now are totally changed. In fact, anything and everything that once was an instrument of *"hurt"* or *"destruction"* will be no more.

Why? How?

"The Earth shall be full of the knowledge of the LORD, as the waters cover the sea." The one spoken of as the *"LORD"* is Jesus Christ. *"His Rest shall be glorious."* Jesus is the *"Why"* and *"How."*

What this world has wanted and desired, trying repeatedly, in one way or the other, to bring it about, all to no avail, will then take place. It is, however, impossible to recreate the Garden of Eden without the Tree of Life.

Jesus is the Tree of Life. With Him superintending the affairs of Earth, which He most definitely will do in the coming Kingdom Age, the world will finally know the peace, prosperity, and security that the Lord all along intended.

This will be a time, one thousand years, such as the world has never before seen, but which it could have had all along, but especially when Jesus first came; however, Israel rejected Him, which submitted the world to now some 2,000 years of continued war, starvation, pain, suffering, and want. However, as surely as He came the first time, He most definitely will come the second time. Then Peace will reign!

MAY
14

*a*ll *we like sheep have gone astray; we have turned every one to his own way; and the LORD has laid on Him the iniquity of us all* (Isa. 53:6).

If two men, moving at the same speed, were to advance toward each other, one starting with Moses and the other from Christ, they would meet exactly in the middle of the Fifty-third Chapter of Isaiah, and, more particularly, Verses 5 and 6. Here is the simple doctrine of the Gospel — the death of Christ. This is the unique glory of the Gospel. All other founders of religions base their claims upon their life and their teaching — their death was a calamity, and without significance. But Christ's Death was His Glory and forms the imperishable foundation of the one and only Salvation. In fact, His Purpose in coming to this Earth was to die (I Cor. 15:1-4).

A young man was asked once if he was saved. His answer was to the point: *"I simply don't understand how to be saved."*

The Preacher who asked the question had to leave to catch a train, so he gave the young man his own personal Bible, along with these brief instructions: *"Read Isaiah 53:6. Go in at the first 'all' and come out at the last 'all.'"*

A few days later he saw the young man again and asked him if he had followed the instructions. The face which the Preacher had left some days earlier had been dour, but now a bright smile covered the young man's countenance. He replied, *"Oh yes. I read that 6th Verse. I went in at the first 'all' and came out at the last 'all.' Then I knew what Salvation was."*

"All" of us are sinners; Jesus Christ paid the price at Calvary's Cross for us *"all."* In fact, ladies and gentlemen, it is just that simple!

MAY
15

f or My people have committed two evils; they have forsaken
Me the fountain of living waters, and hewed them out cisterns, broken cisterns, that can hold no water (Jer. 2:13).

The people of Jerusalem, God's Own Chosen People,
had sunk to a level that was morally lower than the heathen. They committed two evils. First, they forsook Jehovah; second, they embraced idolatry. They exchanged a
living fountain for a broken cistern. The heathen were
only guilty of one evil, that is, of idolatry. For God had
not revealed Himself and His Law to them.

Is it possible that the modern Church is in worse condition spiritually than even the heathen?

For all practical purposes, with some few exceptions,
the modern Church has forsaken the Cross. To forsake
the Cross is to forsake Christ.

The modern Church no longer believes the answer is
found in the Cross of Christ, and only in the Cross of
Christ. In place of the Cross, it has substituted humanistic

psychology. Never mind that such wisdom is *"earthly, sensual, and devilish"* (James 3:15). They have opted for that in place of the *"wisdom that is from above,"* which is *"first pure, then peaceable, gentle, and easy to be intreated, full of mercy and good fruits, without partiality, and without hypocrisy"* (James 3:17).

So, as Israel of old, the modern Church also has committed two evils. First of all, it has abandoned the light of the Gospel; second, it has adopted the ways of the world. As an excellent example, the false direction of the book, *"The Purpose Driven Life,"* has been adopted by the Church, by the Mormons, by the Catholics, by secular interests of the world, and even by some Muslims; however, the Church is so spiritually blind that it cannot see that the whole thing is a *"broken cistern,"* which will *"hold no water."* Something accepted by all <u>cannot</u> be spiritually valid, as should be obvious!

To forsake the Cross is to forsake Christ. They cannot be separated. And, to be sure, the modern Church has forsaken the Cross. When this is done, and it has been done in a wholesale way, then the Church becomes a ready recipient of false doctrine. Without the Cross, there are no spiritual bearings.

MAY
16

*i*s Israel a servant? Is he a homeborn slave? Why is he
spoiled? (Jer. 2:14).

What did Jeremiah mean by Israel being a *"homeborn
slave"*? He meant they were a slave to their evil passions,
to their sins, and to their bondages, which is the greatest
enslavement of all. Tragically, they were slaves and didn't
even know it.

The best way to explain it, I think, is according to the
following:

To use the leopard as an example, if such an animal is
born in a zoo and raised in a zoo, it is a slave without
really knowing it. It does not know, and will never know,
the freedom of being able to bound across the grasslands
or the forest floor. There are a thousand and one things
that a leopard cooped up in a zoo will never know, but
that such an animal should enjoy.

This is typical, in fact, of most modern Christians.
Most Christians do not know the freedom of a victorious,

overcoming life. They are *"homeborn"* slaves without even knowing it. To say the least, that is tragic! There is only one way out of such bondage, and that is by the way of the Cross (Rom. 6:1-14; 8:1-2, 11). If the individual doesn't know the Message of the Cross, he cannot know true freedom; he cannot know what he is missing.

Every single Christian in the world, at least those who are truly Born-Again, has *"more abundant life"* (Jn. 10:10). However, only the Christians who understand the Cross and what it means to our everyday living actually live and enjoy this *"more abundant life."* The rest are *"homeborn slaves."*

Considering the price that Christ has paid, it's a shame not to have all of that for which He did pay such a price. The choice is yours!

It's the Cross of Christ which brings victory and freedom, or it's works, which bring slavery, i.e., a *"homeborn slave."*

*a*nd Jabez was more honorable than his brethren: and his mother called his name Jabez, saying, Because I bore him with sorrow. And Jabez called on the God of Israel, saying, Oh that You would bless me indeed, and enlarge my coast, and that Your hand might be with me, and that You would keep me from evil, that it may not grieve me! And God granted him that which he requested (I Chron. 4:9-10).

Like a beautiful gem, the Lord drops this glorious testimony in the midst of these genealogies. In Jewish culture of old, it was the mother who usually named the child that was born. The name *"Jabez"* means *"sorrow,"* which evidently pertained to the fact that something very grievous had happened in this family; consequently, Jabez, like untold millions, was born into a situation over which he had no control and which spelled hurt for him.

Most children never climb out over a negative childhood. In other words, if they are abused at an early age, it scars them for life. In fact, only the Lord can address such a problem, thereby turning bitter waters into sweet. So Jabez had two strikes against him even before he began, as do most in the world.

But Jabez turned to the one Source Who could change the situation, and it was God. Beautifully enough, that privilege is available to every human being in the world, that is, if they will only take advantage of its potential. There is nothing that the Lord cannot change. In fact, the very First Miracle that Jesus performed in His earthly Ministry was the changing of the water to 'wine at the marriage feast of Cana (Jn. 2:1-11). The Holy Spirit designed this in order that all may know and understand that despite adverse circumstances, or how bad they might be, the Lord Jesus Christ, as He changed the water to wine at Cana, can change any situation, if men will only call on Him and believe Him (Mk. 9:23).

All too often, however, men look to other men for help and get what help man can provide, which is little or nothing. If we call on God, as stated, there is nothing that He cannot change, nothing that He cannot do.

The prayer of Jabez was as follows:

1. *"Bless me"*: We learn from all of this that the Lord desires that we ask Him to bless us, and in every capacity. In fact, He is a blessing God. He wants to bless financially, domestically, physically, and, above all, spiritually. We have but to ask Him!

2. *"Enlarge my coast"*: The word *"coast"* actually means *"border."* In other words, Jabez was asking the Lord to get him out of this problem into which he had been born. Most people never break out of that which imprisons them, because they look to all the wrong sources. Only

the Lord can enlarge your borders. He only waits for you to ask Him!

3. *"That Your hand might be with me"*: The way this is given speaks of the Right Hand of God, which is the Hand of blessing and power. It can be judgment or it can be blessing. For Jabez it was blessing, because Jabez put his trust in the Lord. If you will put your trust in the Lord, it will be blessing, as well, for God is no respecter of persons.

4. *"That You would keep me from evil, that it may not grieve me"*: This, in effect, is the same prayer that Jesus told all of us to pray when He said, *"And lead us not into temptation, but deliver us from evil"* (Mat. 6:13). Actually, all the *"blessing"* depended on Jabez being kept from evil, which the Lord Alone could do. Jabez realized that, within himself, he could not bring about this place and position of freedom from evil. But the Lord could bring it about, and the Lord did.

As Believers, if we are to have the *"Blessing of Jabez,"* we must, at the same time, depart from all evil, which can be done only in Christ and our Faith in what He did for us at the Cross (Rom. 6:3-5).

The Bible plainly tells us that *"God granted him that which he requested."* He will do the same for anyone who, as Jabez, will dare to believe Him.

That means that you can pray the prayer of Jabez. The Lord, in fact, had it placed here that we might follow suit; however, He buried it in these genealogies in order that only the hungry and the thirsty would find it.

Believe the Lord, and allow Him to prove Himself to you, exactly as He did to Jabez so long ago!

MAY
18

*a*nd it shall come to pass, if you shall hearken diligently unto the voice of the LORD your God, to observe and to do all His Commandments, which I command you this day, that the LORD your God will set you on high above all nations of the Earth (Deut. 28:1).

In this tremendous Chapter, we have a promise of Blessings which are absolutely unparalleled. Some may argue that the Lord did these things for Israel under the Old Covenant, but will not do them for modern Christians under the New Covenant. There is nothing in the Word of God that even remotely lends credence to such an idea. We presently have, in fact, a much better Covenant, based on better Promises than anything in the Old Covenant (Heb. 8:6).

In this panoply of Promises, five great things are said. They are:

1. *"And all these blessings shall come on you, and overtake you"*: This literally means that the blessings of the

297

Lord will literally chase down the individual. What a promise! (28:2).

2. *"The LORD shall command the blessing upon you"*: At this moment, if we will only believe it, the Lord is commanding blessing upon us. We must believe it, expect it, and receive it (28:8).

3. *"And the LORD shall make you plenteous in goods"*: *"Plenty"* is what the Lord here promises. The word *"goods"* means everything that we need, whatever it might be (Deut. 28:11).

4. *"The LORD shall open unto you His good treasure"*: The Lord here tells us that we Believers literally have access to the treasure house of Heaven. Again, what a Promise! (28:12).

5. *"And the LORD shall make you the head and not the tail"*: To use an earthly vernacular, someone, regarding an Alaskan dog-sled team, has well said, *"If you're not the lead dog, the view never changes."* To continue to use the earthly vernacular, the Lord intends for His People to be the *"lead dog"* (28:13).

All of this is made possible by the Cross!

MAY

19

*W*hen I say unto the wicked, You shall surely die; and you give him not warning, nor speak to warn the wicked from his wicked way, to save his life; the same wicked man shall die in his iniquity; but his blood will I require at your hand (Ezek. 3:18).

The Lord, in effect, has made every single Preacher of the Gospel a *"watchman."* We are to watch for people's souls. We are to watch for false doctrine — especially for false doctrine.

If the Preacher sees wrong direction being followed, it is incumbent upon him to point out that wrong direction, and, if necessary, to the ones who are leading the false way. The Scripture is abundantly clear on the subject.

If the person or people aren't warned, they will still die lost, because ignorance is not Salvation; however, their blood will be required at the hands of Preachers who were silent when they should have spoken up. That's the sin of the modern Ministry, i.e., *"Don't rock the boat!"*

Let me also say this:

If it is any message other than the Cross, then it's false doctrine. The Apostle Paul said so (Gal. 1:8-9).

MAY
20

t herefore, thou son of man, prophesy against Gog, and say, Thus saith the Lord GOD; Behold, I am against you, O Gog, the chief prince of Meshech and Tubal: And I will turn you back, and leave but the sixth part of you, and will cause you to come up from the north parts, and will bring you upon the mountains of Israel (Ezek. 39:1-2).

Chapters 38 and 39 of Ezekiel give an account of the coming Battle of Armageddon. This will be the doom of the Antichrist, also of Satan and all of his cohorts of darkness. It will be the time of the Second Coming, when Israel will finally be brought to Christ.

At this present moment, the Church is awaiting the Rapture (I Thess. 4:13-18). At some point after the Rapture (also can be referred to as the Resurrection), the Great Tribulation will commence. It will be a time of trouble such as the world, especially Israel, has never seen before. Jesus said so (Mat. 24:21).

During this time, the Antichrist will make his debut,

attempting to take over the entirety of the world; however, he will have it in his spirit to completely annihilate Israel. In fact, the present problems between the Palestinians and Israel are leading up to this conflict. At the beginning, the Antichrist will seem to solve this problem. However, he will soon show his true colors, revealing himself for what he actually is — a hater of God, and especially the Jews.

At the midpoint of his seven-year pact with Israel, he will break that covenant and attack this tiny nation. Israel will suffer her first defeat since becoming a nation again in 1948. Then will begin the last effort at the *"final solution."* The Antichrist will attempt to do what Haman, Herod, and Hitler failed to do. He will come close!

But during the Battle of Armageddon, Israel will cry to the Lord for help as never before. If He doesn't help them, they will be totally annihilated. The Second Coming will be the answer of the Lord to the plea of His ancient People. At that time, Israel will be snatched from the jaws of defeat.

All of this, the fulfillment of all the futuristic events recorded in the Word of God, is made possible by the Cross (Heb. 13:20).

MAY

21

*a*fterward He brought me to the gate, even the gate that looks toward the east: And, behold, the glory of the God of Israel came from the way of the east: and His Voice was like a noise of many waters, and the Earth shined with His glory (Ezek. 43:1-2).

Some 500 years before Christ, the Prophet Ezekiel saw the Holy Spirit leave the Temple at Jerusalem. He could no longer remain. The idol-worship of the people had become so acute that there was no place left for the Lord. So He was forced to leave (Ezek. 11:23).

The return of the Holy Spirit will be after the Second Coming when Israel will finally have accepted Christ as Saviour and Lord. The Temple, which Ezekiel describes in the last eight Chapters of his Book, the new Millennial Temple, will then be occupied by the Holy Spirit, because Israel is finally right with God.

Israel is God's prophetic time clock. In other words, one can look at this newly formed nation and pretty well tell the lateness of the prophetic hour.

Concerning this, Jesus said: *"Now learn a Parable of the fig tree; When his branch is yet tender, and puts forth leaves, you know that summer is near"* (Mat. 24:32).

Israel is here likened to a *"fig tree."* For the first time in nearly 2,000 years, that branch is starting to *"put forth leaves."* This refers to Israel becoming a nation in 1948 and following. So, looking at Israel as a prophetic time clock, we *"know that it is near, even at the doors"* (Mat. 24:33). The Dispensation of the Church is about to end, which will usher Israel once again back to her rightful place, but, as stated, through much trouble (Jer. 30:7).

The Spirit of God will return, but only after Israel has accepted Christ.

Please understand:

They are going to have to accept the Christ of the Cross. The Prophet Zechariah said so (Zech. 13:6).

S *on of man, wail for the multitude of Egypt, and cast them down, even her, and the daughters of the famous nations, unto the nether parts of the Earth, with them who go down into the pit* (Ezek. 32:18).

The last Prophecy concerning Egypt (Vss. 17-32) presents, in vision, Pharaoh, his armies, and the armies of his allies, helpless captives, covered with shame, and shut up in the dungeon of Sheol (Hell), in company with other kings and their armies. When on Earth, all these were mighty and caused terror; but in the world of the dead, they suffer a common misery, ignominy, and helplessness.

These Scriptures present a momentary glance into the dreadful mystery of the spirit-world.

Many of the other monarchs listed in this Chapter had honorable burial in their armor, their swords beneath their heads, which was the custom in those days. But not so Pharaoh. He was, according to history, strangled.

Thus close these seven Prophecies concerning Egypt.

She sought, in self-will and the pride of nature, to take the place which God had given to Babylon, i.e., the leader of the world at that time. The mighty empire of Assyria had had to bend to God's gift of supremacy to Nebuchadnezzar; and Pharaoh, though he owned no god but himself (Ezek. 29:3, 9), was no better than other monarchs in power and might. He was uncircumcised like the others, that is, not owned of God, nor upheld by Him.

Pride and self-will characterized Egypt. Regrettably, she had been the confidence of God's People (Ezek. 29:16), but should be so no longer; for how could such a principal ever furnish the victories given only to Faith? Egypt shall have her place in the future (Isa., Chpt. 19), but never as a ruler; her judgment secures Israel's blessing, for the will of man in Pharaoh cannot frustrate the purpose of God in Grace.

We learn from all of this that the nations of the Earth, even the mightiest, are nothing in God's Hands; one day, every nation in the world will worship the Lord Jesus Christ. It will be in the coming Kingdom Age. The Prophet Isaiah said so (Isa., Chpts. 11-12).

MAY
23

*a*nd He said unto me, Son of man, can these bones live? And I answered, O Lord GOD, You know (Ezek. 37:3).

During World War II, some six million Jews died at the hands of the Nazi butchers. It was Satan's effort to destroy these ancient people, because he knew that the time had come for the beginning of their restoration. He did not succeed, but it was not for lack of trying.

Out of that funeral pyre, the death camps of Nazi Germany and Poland, the question asked some 2,500 years ago by the Lord of the Prophet Ezekiel now takes on meaning, *"Can these bones live?"* In 1948, the nation of Israel was reborn, one might say, thereby beginning the fulfillment of the Thirty-seventh Chapter of Ezekiel.

Within themselves, it was not possible, and is not possible, for them to live again. Within themselves, there is no hope, as should be overly obvious!

However, listen to what the Lord told the Prophet some 2,500 years ago:

"*Therefore prophesy and say unto them, Thus saith the Lord GOD; Behold, O My people, I will open your graves, and cause you to come up out of your graves, and bring you into the land of Israel*" (Ezek. 37:12).

And that's exactly what the Lord did. Out of the holocaust, He brought vagabond Jews from all over the world in order to establish the nation of Israel once again.

Concerning Israel and her restoration, some 500 years after the Prophecy of Ezekiel, the Apostle Paul said, "*And so all Israel shall be saved: as it is written, there shall come out of Zion the Deliverer, and shall turn away ungodliness from Jacob:*

"*For this is My Covenant unto them, when I shall take away their sins*" (Rom. 11:26-27).

Actually, Paul was quoting both Isaiah and Jeremiah (Isa. 27:9; Jer. 31:31).

Israel is God's prophetic time clock. In other words, one can look at Israel and tell just how late the time actually is. To be sure, it is late. Israel is about to enter into the worst time of her existence, called the "*Great Tribulation*" (Mat. 24:21).

Zechariah prophesied that two-thirds of the people of Israel will die at that time (Zech. 13:8-9). Then, and only then, actually during the Battle of Armageddon, when it seems as if Israel will be completely destroyed, will they then begin to call upon the Lord. He will answer that cry. That is the Second Coming, the time that Israel will finally accept the Lord Jesus Christ.

It's a shame that Israel will have to undergo such sorrow; however, millions in their own way have had to undergo trouble before they finally would say, "*Yes,*" to Jesus Christ.

MAY
24

*a*nd it shall come to pass, that everything that lives, which moves, whithersoever the Rivers shall come, shall live: and there shall be a very great multitude of fish, because these waters shall come thither: for they shall be healed; and everything shall live whither the River comes (Ezek. 47:9).

This of which Ezekiel speaks will take place in the coming Kingdom Age. The Temple will be rebuilt in Jerusalem, called the *"Millennial Temple."* Jesus will rule and reign supreme (Isa., Chpt. 11).

The Scripture tells us that *"waters,"* i.e., *"a river,"* will issue out from under the threshold of the Temple and flow eastward. These waters will *"come down from under the right side of the house, at the south side of the Altar,"* which means that the channel is the Altar of Jehovah, i.e., Calvary.

This River is a type of the Holy Spirit. Even though it will be a literal river in the coming Kingdom Age, still, its properties will be very similar to the Spirit of God.

First of all, *"The Man with a line in his hand"* is the Lord

Jesus Christ. He Alone can measure, because the measurement is His.

At first, the waters were only to the *"ankles"*; this typifies the Holy Spirit changing our *"direction."* Next, the waters were to the *"knees"*; this addresses our prayer life. Then, the waters were to the *"loins,"* speaking of our procreation abilities, i.e., the bringing of children into the Kingdom of God. Then, finally, it was *"waters to swim in, a river that could not be passed over."* The Holy Spirit, of which all of this is a Type, is of such magnitude that no one has ever exhausted His potential, and no one ever will!

The waters will be living and life-giving; but there shall be no healing for the miry places (Vs. 11). Imperfection will continue to exist during the Millennium, for man will still be under trial. He will have freedom of choice. If he accepts Messiah's rule, he will enjoy the blessings pictured in Verses 1 through 10 and Verse 12; but if he rejects that Government, he will be turned over to judgment, for Grace despised involves bitterness and death.

Millennium blessing will be powerful and abiding; it will greatly surmount and almost efface evil, but not entirely. For only in the New Heaven and New Earth will there be perfection (Rev., Chpts. 21-22).

MAY
25

*a*nd by the River upon the bank thereof, on this side and on that side, shall grow all trees for meat, whose leaf shall not fade, neither shall the fruit thereof be consumed: it shall bring forth new fruit according to his months, because their waters they issued out of the Sanctuary: and the fruit thereof shall be for meat, and the leaf thereof for medicine (Ezek. 47:12).

The trees mentioned here will grow on both sides of the river and will perpetually bring forth new fruit. They will do so because they are nourished by waters issuing from the Sanctuary. The fruit and leaf will heal as well as nourish. Such is the character of a life and ministry based upon Calvary, and energized by the Holy Spirit.

In the coming Kingdom Age, there will be two types of people on Earth, i.e., human beings, as we think of such, and human beings with Glorified Bodies. Those with Glorified Bodies will not need this particular fruit; however, the *"fruit for meat"* and the *"leaf for medicine"* will be needed by the regular human beings. The *"fruit"* and *"leaf"* will

311

give the human body perfect nutrition and will also drive out all sickness and disease.

This *"fruit"* and these *"leaves"* will no doubt be shipped all over the world in copious quantities.

The Kingdom Age, for this is when such will transpire, will be a time of peace, prosperity, and the Power of God as the world has never known before. These *"trees"* will be similar to, if not identical with, the Tree of Life.

Some wonderful things await the world on that coming Glad Day.

MAY
26

*Y*ou saw till that a Stone was cut out without hands, which
smote the image upon his feet that were of iron and clay,
and broke them to pieces. Then was the iron, the clay, the
brass, the silver, and the gold, broken to pieces together, and
became like the chaff of the summer threshingfloors; and the
wind carried them away, that no place was found for them:
and the Stone that smote the image became a great mountain,
and filled the whole Earth (Dan. 2:34-35).

The Lord gave Nebuchadnezzar a dream of the statue
of a man, which predicted a succession of five monar-
chies. The first four are the Babylonian, the Persian, the
Grecian, and the Roman. The last will be that of the Antichrist, typified by the feet and the toes. The other empires
are history, while the last one is just ahead. The Antichrist
will be the last and greatest emperor. He and his government will be destroyed by the Messiah, Who will be the
Stone unshaped by human agency, and Whose apparition
will destroy all these kings, represented simultaneously by

the two feet and the ten toes of the statue.

These Verses completely destroy the popular belief that the Gospel gradually will conquer the world. Modern Gospel teaches that the world is getting better and better, and that Christianity will ultimately come to terms with Islam and other religions. Then, when all is sweetness and light, the Church will then beckon Jesus to come back. Nothing could be further from the Truth.

This Passage in Daniel teaches that the end will not be sweetness and light, but rather cataclysmic. Jesus Christ, as stated, represented by the Stone, will come from Heaven and will smite the feet, which represent the various nations then under the Antichrist. It will be a violent and powerful overthrow, which will take place at the Second Coming of Christ. Up unto that time, the world will get worse and worse (II Tim. 3:1-5).

The Kingdom which will be set up by our Lord will "*become a great mountain, and fill the whole Earth*" (Dan. 2:35). Furthermore, the Scripture says that "*the Kingdom shall not be left to other people, but it shall break in pieces and consume all these kingdoms, and it shall stand forever*" (Dan. 2:44).

When Jesus comes back the second time without sin unto Salvation, He will have with Him every Saint of God who has ever lived, even as is described in Revelation, Chapter 19.

As the song says, "*What a day that will be!*"

MAY
27

*i*f it be so, our God Whom we serve is able to deliver us from the burning fiery furnace, and He will deliver us out of your hand, O king. But if not, be it known unto you, O king, that we will not serve your gods, nor worship the golden image which you have set up (Dan. 3:17-18).

The erection of this image and the demand that it be worshipped, especially considering that this is done so soon after the events of the previous Chapter, illustrate the darkness and incurable rebellion of the natural heart. These events prove that, apart from a new spiritual birth, no circumstances, however powerful, can teach man to know and worship God.

All monarchs recognize that to consolidate their power they must have a state religion. This is man's wisdom. Otherwise religion, the most powerful motive of the heart, becomes a dissolvent to the authority of the Throne. Man naturally likes supreme power blended by religion into one solid body around the head of State, because this helps to obscure the appearance of authority. But the religion chosen must be one that will suit and gratify man's will — hence, idolatry.

This is the great feature that characterizes the dominion of man in the Earth from the first king of Babylon, Nebuchadnezzar, to its last king, the Antichrist. God is disowned by the Gentile, but acknowledged by a little group of suffering Believers.

These moral features will reappear most vividly during the final and future days of Gentile government. God will allow His faithful witnesses, typified by Shadrach, Meshach, and Abednego, to be cast into the fiery furnace so as to be tried in the place where evil exists. But He will walk with them in the fiery trial; He will deliver and glorify them, but with this distinction; He will permit their bodies, in most cases, to perish (Rev. 13:7, 15).

The great image erected suggests that it was a phallus, this being held to represent the life-giver. It was marked by three sixes, i.e., "666": sixty cubits high, six cubits broad, and proclaimed by six instruments of music (Vss. 1, 15).

When they were pointed out, the three Hebrew children emphatically stated that they would not fall down and worship the image. They further stated that God could deliver them. "But if not," they would die before they would bow.

Some in these modern times may conclude that the three Hebrew children did not evidence a good confession when they uttered the words, "But if not"! I maintain that "truth" is never a bad confession. In view of their consecration, the Scripture emphatically states that the Lord did in fact deliver them, and did so gloriously.

Every Believer should have this type of consecration. If the Lord delivers us, wonderful! *"But if not,"* we still will remain faithful!

317

MAY
28

*i*n the same hour came forth fingers of a man's hand and wrote over against the candlestick upon the plaister of the wall of the king's palace: and the king saw the part of the hand that wrote (Dan. 5:5).

The iniquity of the Gentile comes to a head in this Chapter; and its insolence and blasphemy reveal its ignorance and weakness. The king threw down a bold challenge to Jehovah. He and the companions of his orgy drank wine out of the sacred vessels of the Temple of God, and praised the idols, six in number, of gold, silver, brass, iron, wood, and stone.

The Divine response was the destruction that very night of the king in all his glory.

Daniel, though subject to the king, did not invite him to repentance, as he did Nebuchadnezzar, or treat him with the same respect. He announced his coming doom; this prefigures the judgments which will fall upon the last king of Babylon, who is to be cast into the Lake of Fire.

For Babylon has given its own character to all the governments which have succeeded it; and however forbearing with these governments God has been, and is, all was already lost for them, even in the days of Nebuchadnezzar.

Belshazzar was co-regent with his father, Nabonidus, and reigned in Babylon while his father was warring against Cyrus. Years ago, the hall in which he held his drunken orgy was found. It is some 60 feet wide and 172 feet long; its walls are beautifully decorated.

After the handwriting appeared on the wall and none of his wise men could read the writing, then was Daniel brought in. The king, true to fallen man's unchanging action, sought help from God as a last resource, not as the first. Even then this great big pompous fool condescendingly says, *"I have heard of you."* He does not add that *"the Spirit of the Holy God is with you,"* as the Queen-Mother had said, but rather *"the spirit of the gods is in you."*

He offered great gifts to Daniel, but the Prophet-Statesman rejected them all.

Stark terror filled Belshazzar's heart, as it did the hearts of all who were there — with the exception of Daniel. Every evidence is that the visible fingers which had written the message were still poised in the air beside the inscription.

The message, as Daniel read it, carried no tinge of mercy. It was final! It was judgment!

For how many presently is *"the handwriting on the wall"*?

MAY
29

*t*he beginning of the Word of the LORD by Hosea. And the
LORD said to Hosea, Go, take unto you a wife of whoredoms
and children of whoredoms: for the land has committed great
whoredom, departing from the LORD (Hos. 1:2).

The name *"Hosea"* means *"Salvation."* His prophecies
covered more than 60 years. His ministry and probably his
life terminated at the destruction of the Northern Kingdom.

The Prophecy is mainly addressed to the Ten Tribes
shortly before their dispersion. The nation, because of its
devotion to idols and its forsaking of Jehovah, is appealed
to under the figure of an unfaithful wife.

The word *"whoredom"* is to be read *"idolatry."* The
Prophet, who was a spiritual son of Abraham, and perhaps of the children of Judah, was commanded to marry
a wife belonging to the Northern Kingdom and to have
children by her.

That which the Lord demanded of Hosea, i.e., to marry
a harlot, was beyond, far beyond, what He had asked many

to do. There is no evidence that the Lord explained Himself to the Prophet, nor that He ever did so. All of this was to be an example of Israel's backsliding, and also of her coming Restoration.

Gomer, for that was the woman's name, lived with Hosea for a period of time, and then forsook him and her children to go back into the world of vice and shame. This portrays Israel forsaking Christ.

After some time, possibly several years, the Lord told the Prophet to go and purchase Gomer, for she was now to be sold as a slave. So he purchased her off the auction block for fifteen pieces of silver and a couple of bushels of grain (Hos. 3:2). By now her beauty was gone. Used up, she stands before the crowd. For all the obvious reasons, no one wants her. But Hosea did! So he bought her back.

This pictures Israel in a coming day, forsaken by the entirety of the world and the Antichrist close to annihilating her completely. No one cares and no one desires her. She is used up. However, the Lord Jesus Christ, the Heavenly Hosea, still loves her, and He will buy her back. Not only that, He will restore her to the beauty she once had (Hos. 3:5).

This glorious Message is not only to Israel. It is to every person who has once known God but has lost their way. Jesus Christ has already paid the price in order to purchase you back. All you have to do is say, *"Yes"*!

MAY
30

O *Israel, return unto the LORD your God; for you have fallen by your iniquity. Take with you words, and turn to the LORD: Say unto Him, Take away all iniquity, and receive us graciously: so will we render the calves of our lips. Asshur shall not save us; we will not ride upon horses: neither will we say any more to the work of our hands, You are our gods: for in You the fatherless find mercy* (Hos. 14:1-3).

Hosea now gives an Altar call! It is for Israel, but yet it is just as succinctly applicable for any and every person.

What the Holy Spirit gives through the Prophet is a perfect example of what the Lord wants and desires from anyone who comes to Him. It is as follows:

1. Israel is commanded to *"return unto the LORD your God"*: This is the first step that must be taken, and the only direction that holds an answer, irrespective of the problem.

2. *"For you have fallen by your iniquity"*: Sin was the problem of Israel, as sin is the problem of the entirety of the human race. Someone has well said, *"If the economy was the*

322

problem, the Lord would have sent an economist. If manufacturing was the problem, the Lord would have sent an engineer. If construction was the problem, the Lord would have sent a carpenter. But the problem was sin, so God sent a Saviour."

3. *"Take with you words, and turn to the LORD"*: Not sacraments, nor ceremonies, nor rituals, but *"words."* This is a confession of sin.

4. *"And receive us graciously"*: This is a cry for forgiveness upon the principle of Grace and not of merit.

5. *"So will we render the calves of our lips"*: This corresponds to the sacrifice of praise, and refers actually to the Cross.

6. *"Asshur shall not save us"*: Israel's sin was trusting man (Assyria and Egypt) and idols for salvation. Trusting man is still our sin.

7. *"We will not ride upon horses"*: We will not place any trust in the Egyptian cavalry.

8. *"Neither will we say any more to the work of our hands, You are our gods"*: *"Self"* cannot save self. Our efforts are constituted by the Lord as idolatry.

9. *"For in You the fatherless find mercy"*: Jehovah was to be the Father of Israel; however, Israel had forsaken Jehovah and was now fatherless. But her cry is, as it should be ours: *"The Lord shows mercy to the fatherless."*

THE ANSWER OF THE LORD TO THE REPENTANCE OF ISRAEL (AND ANY INDIVIDUAL, FOR THAT MATTER)

10. *"I will heal their backsliding"*: The *"backsliding"* referred to apostasy and idolatry. Forgiveness based

upon Grace, not upon merit, can pardon the most desperate sins.

11. *"I will love them freely"*: The statement means *"without a just cause."* In other words, even though Israel will give the Lord no reason to love her, He will, just the same, extend his love, just as He will for all who come to Him in humble supplication.

12. *"My anger is turned away from him"*: True Repentance cools the anger of God.

13. *"I will be as the dew unto Israel"*: *"Dew"* speaks of the Holy Spirit, Who will be freely given to Israel, and, again, to anyone who meets God's terms.

14. *"He shall grow as the lily"*: The *"lily"* speaks of Righteousness, freely given!

15. *"And cast forth his roots as Lebanon"*: Like a tree planted by the waters.

16. *"His branches shall spread, and his beauty shall be as the olive tree"*: Israel will now bring forth fruit, which, of course, will take place in the coming Kingdom Age.

17. *"And his smell as Lebanon"*: This speaks of the cedars of Lebanon. It is a fact that no insect or serpent can be found where there are Cedar trees, or any of the Cedar family. This tells us of the protection of the Children of God — protection from demon spirits.

18. *"They who dwell under His shadow shall return"*: This is the resting place for the Child of God, *"under His shadow"* (Hos. 14:4-7).

To close this great Book, the Prophet, under the inspiration of the Holy Spirit said, *"Who is wise, and he shall understand these things? Prudent, and he shall know them? for the ways of the LORD are right, and the just shall walk in them: but the transgressors shall fall therein"* (Hos. 14:9).

MAY

31

*a*nd it shall come to pass afterward, that I will pour out My Spirit upon all flesh; and your sons and your daughters shall prophesy, your old men shall dream dreams, your young men shall see visions: And also upon the servants and upon the handmaids in those days will I pour out My Spirit (Joel 2:28-29).

Joel is the Holy Spirit Prophet of the Old Testament, the one quoted by Simon Peter on the Day of Pentecost (Acts 2:16-21).

Before the Cross, the Holy Spirit, even though working mightily in the world, still, was very limited as to what He could do, because the blood of bulls and goats could not take away sins (Heb. 10:4). In other words, the Holy Spirit could not come into the hearts and lives of Believers before the Cross and abide there permanently. He came into the hearts of some to help them accomplish particular works, but He was still very limited, due to the fact that the sin debt could not be paid with animal blood.

That's the reason that Jesus said of John the Baptist, that even though he was the greatest Prophet born of woman, still, the least in the Kingdom of God was greater than John (Lk. 7:28).

What did Jesus mean by that?

He didn't mean that we are greater in character than John. Not at all! He meant that the Cross would afford greater privileges and opportunities than John ever thought of having.

That's why Paul said that the "New Covenant," which was made possible by the Cross, is a much better Covenant, based on better Promises (Heb. 8:6).

Now, due to the what the Cross has made possible, in that it atoned for all sin, the Holy Spirit comes into the hearts and lives of all Believers, and does so to remain forever, and to constantly help us (Jn. 14:16-17).

The Cross, by the shedding of the Precious Blood of Christ, atoned for all sin, past, present, and future, at least for those who will believe. The sin debt was thereby forever paid. Consequently, the Holy Spirit now, even at conversion, comes into the heart and life of the Believer in order to abide forever. As long as faith is maintained in Christ, He most definitely will there abide. He desires to help us, lead us, and guide us as we live this life for the Lord (Jn. 16:7-15).

Every single thing done in our lives, as it regards the Fruit of the Spirit, Christlikeness, Righteousness, Holiness, in fact, all Spiritual Growth, must be carried out by the Holy Spirit. That's what makes false doctrines so wrong. They are attempting to sanctify people by the means of the flesh. Such cannot be done.

Anything done in our hearts and lives for the Lord must, and without fail, be instituted, instigated, carried out, and accomplished by the Holy Spirit.

And how does He do such?

He only requires of us that we evidence Faith in Christ and the Cross, and not allow our faith to be moved from that correct Object, which then will give Him the latitude to do all the things that need to be done. He works entirely within the confines and parameters of the Finished Work of Christ. He will not work outside of those parameters (Rom. 8:2).

JUNE

1

*t*hen Jonah prayed unto the LORD his God out of the fish's belly, And said, I cried by reason of my affliction unto the LORD, and He heard me; out of the belly of Hell cried I, and You heard my voice (Jonah 2:1-2).

Jonah was the first of the Prophets after Elijah and Elisha. He was the only Prophet sent to the Gentiles, and he was the only Prophet who tried to conceal his Message. The reason for that attempt at concealment was that the prosperity of Nineveh, the city to which Jonah was being sent, meant the subjection of Israel. Conversely, the destruction of Nineveh would mean the prosperity of Zion. So Jonah had great problems going to preach to the Ninevites.

Nineveh was founded by Nimrod (Gen. 10:11). The name signifies *"City of Nimis,"* i.e. Nimrod.

The Book of Jonah is unique in that it is more concerned with the Prophet himself than with his Prophecy. The condition of his soul and God's loving discipline of him instruct and humble the Reader.

Despite Jonah's effort to get away from God and thereby not have to preach the Message of repentance to Nineveh, the Holy Spirit declares that Jehovah is still Jonah's God. When disciplined and restored in soul, Jonah could say, *"My God."* Fellowship may be broken, but relationship? Never! That is, if the person keeps believing.

In the belly of the whale, Jonah begins to cry to God. He said, *"But I will sacrifice unto You with the voice of thanksgiving; I will pay that that I have vowed. Salvation is of the LORD"* (2:9).

"Salvation is of Jehovah." This is the last lesson that proud man consents to learn; for it teaches him that he cannot contribute to his own salvation — for what could Jonah do inside the great fish? And so if man is to be saved, the Salvation must be wholly Divine.

Jonah was a *"sign"* to the Ninevites (Mat. 16:1-4; Lk. 11:30); that is, he was a personal illustration of the Wrath and the Grace of God. The word *"sign"* makes it evident that the facts of his entombment in the fish and his deliverance preceded him and were known to the people of Nineveh. Hence, their acceptance of his message.

The Message was straight and to the point. Unless Nineveh repented, in forty days judgment would come. It is not stated exactly how this judgment would come; but, evidently, knowing of Jonah's experience, the Holy Spirit used this to bring about one of the few times in history that true Repentance was forthcoming upon the announcement of impending judgment.

The last two Verses contain the great lesson of the Book. Jonah needed the gourd, which he himself had not made, and grieved at its destruction. God created the inhabitants of Nineveh; His love needed them. How much greater, therefore, would be His grief in their destruction, as it is with any soul!

JUNE

2

*a*nd the LORD answered me, and said, Write the Vision, and make it plain upon tables, that he may run who reads it. For the Vision is yet for an appointed time, but at the end it shall speak, and not lie: though it tarry, wait for it; because it will surely come, it will not tarry (Hab. 2:2-3).

For Habakkuk, it was a perplexing problem that God's People would suffer and the wicked go free. He realized that because of Israel's sin, punishment was imminent; but there was a dilemma in trying to understand how a Holy God could use the wicked Chaldeans to chasten His Children. The Prophet, however, came to recognize that whatever God did was best and He would take care of the situation.

The word *"Faith"* is mentioned only two times in the Old Testament (Deut. 32:20; Hab. 2:4). In fact, the statement made by Habakkuk, *"The just shall live by his faith,"* presents the very foundation of the New Covenant. So, the Lord was telling the Prophet the following:

Irrespective as to the condition that Israel was in presently, the Lord gives a ray of hope to the Prophet; it was probably during the time of the Prophet Jeremiah, just before Judah was destroyed by the Babylonians.

The Lord said:

1. *"Write the Vision"*: That's exactly what Habakkuk did. The Promise was short, but oh so powerful. It spoke of *"Justification by Faith."*

2. *"Make it plain upon tables"*: This Gospel Message, so important it was, must be clear and easy to read.

3. *"That he may run who reads it"*: In essence, the Lord is saying that while situations in the near future are going to be difficult, victory is coming.

4. *"For the Vision is yet for an appointed time"*: It was not in doubt, the time had already been set, and by the Lord of Glory. In fact, the Vision would be fulfilled in Christ, and, more particularly, when the meaning of the New Covenant was given to the Apostle Paul. That meaning was *"Justification by Faith."*

5. *"But at the end it shall speak, and not lie"*: Nothing will be able to stop its fulfillment.

6. *"Though it tarry, wait for it"*: In other words, it's not coming at the moment, but it will come.

7. *"Because it will surely come, it will not tarry"*: In other words, Israel will see many hard times between the present and the fulfillment; however, at the appointed time, it most definitely would come. And so it did! And so it will!

JUNE
3

*i*s the seed yet in the barn? Yes, as yet the vine, and the fig tree, and the pomegranate, and the olive tree, have not brought forth: from this day will I bless you (Hag. 2:19).

When the Children of Israel came back from Babylonian captivity, those who returned came back to what might be referred to as a moonscape. In other words, Judah and Jerusalem had been completely destroyed.

First of all, they laid the foundation of the Temple, but then work stopped, and did so for a number of years. During this time, the people built their houses, attending to their own needs and desires, but neglected the House of God. Also during this time, the Lord visited judgment of sorts upon Israel for their lack of diligence regarding the Temple, causing their crops to not be what they should have been and their business activities to fall into the same category.

Then Haggai began to prophesy, with the Lord speaking through him. Basically, the first admonition given was *"Consider your ways"* (Hag. 2:18). Regarding their harvest, when they expected to get twenty bushels out of a particular piece of ground, they got only ten. When they expected to get fifty vessels of oil, they got only twenty (2:16). In essence, the Lord is telling them that He caused this to be brought about in this fashion in order that they might know that the Lord was displeased with them.

They were told to go to work on the Temple and finish it. Then the Lord gave a Promise which was, by and large, unlike any other Promise. If they would obey Him, *"From this day will I bless you."* He even specified the day that the blessing would begin, the twenty-fourth day of the ninth month.

From this we learn that the blessings of the Lord have to do with our diligence to His Work. That's why Jesus told us, *"Seek ye first the Kingdom of God, and His Righteousness; and all these things shall be added unto you"* (Mat. 6:33). Israel suffered from not attending first of all to God's business. Millions of Christians presently are following in the same manner.

We should look at our situation and *"Consider our ways"*!

JUNE

4

*i*n that day there shall be a fountain opened to the House
of David and to the inhabitants of Jerusalem for sin and for
uncleanness (Zech. 13:1).

This fountain of which Zechariah speaks was histori-
cally opened at Calvary, but will be consciously opened to
repentant Judah in the future day of her repentance; but
the fact and function of that fountain only become conscious to the awakened sinner. A true sense of sin and
guilt in relationship to God awakens the sense of the need
of cleansing; so the shed and cleansing Blood of the Lamb
of God becomes precious to the convicted conscience. The
fear of punishment does not come in here to impair the
character and depth of Judah's sorrow and repentance.

The ever-living efficacy of Christ's atoning Work and
its power to cleanse the conscience and the life is justly
comparable to a fountain. The sense of the Hebrew Text is
that this fountain shall be opened and shall remain open.

Of all sinners, the Jerusalem sinner may be accounted

the greatest. It was Jerusalem that stoned the Prophets and that crucified the Messiah. Great sinners, therefore, may hope for pardon and cleansing in this fountain open for the House of David.

The entrance of Christ judges sin, unmasks its true character, and arouses a moral consciousness which approves that judgment. Israel must accept Christ and what He did at the Cross in order for sin to be judged, the same as any other believing sinner.

JUNE

5

*f*or I will gather all nations against Jerusalem to battle; and the city shall be taken, and the houses rifled, and the women ravished; and half of the city shall go forth into captivity, and the residue of the people shall not be cut off from the city. Then shall the LORD go forth, and fight against those nations, as when He fought in the day of battle (Zech. 14:2-3).

This signifies the Second Coming, which will be the most cataclysmic event in human history. It will take place during the Battle of Armageddon, when it looks like Jerusalem is lost and Israel is annihilated.

The Old Testament records many instances when the Lord fought for Israel. He will do the same at that coming time, in fact, in a greater way than ever.

The Thirty-eighth and Thirty-ninth Chapters of Ezekiel give an account of this battle. This particular day when the Lord does come back will be a day unlike any other. The Scripture says, *"That the light shall not be clear, nor dark"* (Zech. 14:6). After Israel accepts Him as Saviour and Lord, which they will do immediately, then the Lord Jesus Christ will be the One God of the whole Earth. There will be no religious Denominations at that time, consequently no divided Church.

The world, with Jesus Christ at its Head, will enter into the greatest time of peace and prosperity it has even known. The Prince of Peace will then be reigning. As a result, peace will envelop the world, which it has never seen before. The Prophet Isaiah predicted this day by saying:

"And He shall judge among the nations, and shall rebuke many people: and they shall beat their swords into plowshares, and their spears into pruninghooks: nation shall not lift up sword against nation, neither shall they learn war anymore" (Isa. 2:4).

At that time, every Saint who has ever lived, beginning with Abel and coming through unto the time of the First Resurrection, will have Glorified Bodies and will help the Lord administer the affairs of the universe. That includes every Believer now alive, and, of course, all who have died.

This is the Kingdom that Israel rejected upon the First Advent of Christ, but will accept at the Second Advent of Christ.

JUNE
6

*b*ring ye all the tithes into the storehouse, that there may be meat in My House, and prove Me now herewith, saith the LORD of Hosts, if I will not open you the windows of Heaven, and pour you out a blessing, that there shall not be room enough to receive it (Mal. 3:10).

While this great Promise was given under the Law, still, tithing predates the Law by several hundreds of years. The first mention of tithing in the Bible is when Abraham paid tithes to Melchizedek (Gen. 14:20). Some claim that while God blessed Israel economically, at least when they did somewhat right, He will not do such to the Church, our blessings only being spiritual! Nothing could be further from the truth.

In fact, whatever the Lord did for Israel of old, He will do for His People presently, and even greater. How could He do less now under a greater and better Covenant than He did for Israel with an inferior Covenant?

If any Believer will faithfully believe the Lord, will ask

Him to meet our every need, irrespective if that need is financial, physical, domestic, or spiritual, to be sure, the Lord will answer that prayer. As stated, we now have a better Covenant, based on better Promises (Heb. 8:6).

"We have not, because we ask not."

And then, all too often, our motives aren't right. If that is the case, God cannot honor any request. *"You ask, and receive not, because you ask amiss, that you may consume it upon your lusts"* (James 4: 2-3).

If, under the Old Covenant, the Lord said that He would *"open the windows of Heaven, and pour out a blessing, that there would not be room enough to receive it,"* He definitely will do the same identical thing now for those who will believe Him.

JUNE
7

*i*n those days came John the Baptist, preaching in the wilderness of Judaea, And saying, Repent ye: for the Kingdom of Heaven is at hand. For this is He Who was spoken of by the Prophet Isaiah, saying, The voice of one crying in the wilderness, Prepare ye the Way of the LORD, make His paths straight (Mat. 3:1-3).

The preaching of John the Baptist wasn't exactly according to diplomatic skills. It was personal, abrupt, powerful, forceful, and straight to the point. It minced no words. People sometimes speak of the spirit of the New Testament being different from that of the Old Testament, but Matthew 3:1-7 overthrows this belief, as do many other Passages, notably those of the Book of Revelation.

How could God's attitude towards sin change?

The Baptist called these individuals children of Satan; he declared the Wrath of God was coming, that the ax of judgment was even then lying at the root of the tree of religious profession, and that if these moralists did not repent, they would be burned up as chaff in the unquench-able fire.

To strike off a branch of a tree is partial destruction, but to lay the ax at the root means total destruction. To be sure, John the Baptist used the tree as a symbol to picture the professors of religion.

The voice of John the Baptist was the first voice of a Prophet heard in Israel in some 400 years. Without the voice of the Prophet, Israel became bogged down in legal-ism. Without the voice of the Prophet, this is the direction the Church always takes.

It should be noticed that John's preaching carried very little foretelling; almost all was in the class of *"forthtelling."* In other words, John was a powerful Preacher of Righ-teousness, which is the major calling of the true Prophet.

John was the last of the Prophets under the Old Cov-enant; he would be the greatest of all, simply because he went immediately before the face of Jehovah-Messiah. In fact, he introduced Christ!

How much preaching presently measures up to that carried out by the Baptist?

JUNE

8

*t*hen was Jesus led up of the Spirit into the wilderness to be tempted of the Devil (Mat. 4:1).

The First Adam was tempted in a Garden; the Second Man, the Last Adam, was tempted in a wilderness.

"Tempted" means *"to be put to the test."* Adam was tested in innocence; Jesus was tempted knowing both good and evil, though He, in Himself, was sinless. He entered the wilderness of this world's misery and evil to render in it a life of absolute obedience and dependence; it was, therefore, necessary for that Perfect Obedience and Dependence to be tested. It demanded that He should have no other Will than that of His Father; and that He would accept that Will and delight in it, no matter what might be the consequences to Himself. We should remember that!

It was this Obedience and Dependence that the tempter sought to impair. So he invited Him to use His Privileges as the Son of God, as the Messiah, and as the

Son of Man, to work a miracle in His Own favor, to manifest Himself to Israel, and to take up the sovereignty of the Earth promised to Him. But Satan failed!

The manner in which Jesus was tempted is the manner of all temptation. The act performed, whatever it might be, is the result of the real temptation, that being to step outside of the Will of God. Oftentimes we tend to look at the act and not the cause. In doing so, we miss the point altogether. Worse yet, we will not find victory in such a pursuit.

We Believers cannot meet Satan on the same terms that Jesus met him. We are foolish if we think we can. Our way of escape, the only way, in fact, of escape, is to look exclusively to what was done at the Cross by Christ, Who is our Substitute, and Who, with His Perfect Life and Perfect Sacrifice of Himself, defeated the powers of darkness on all counts.

Paul said, *"Blotting out the handwriting of ordinances that was against us, which was contrary to us, and took it out of the way, nailing it to His Cross;*

And having spoiled principalities and powers, He made a show of them openly, triumphing over them in it" (Col. 2:14-15).

Faith in Christ and the Cross, ever making the Cross the Object of our Faith, is the only pathway to victory, simply because no other pathway is needed.

JUNE
9

a *nd seeing the multitudes, He went up into a mountain:*
and when He was set, His disciples came unto Him: And He
opened His Mouth, and taught them, saying (Mat. 5:1-2).

Two sermons, both delivered on mountains, opened
and closed the Lord's public Ministry. The first, which
we are now discussing, was upon a mountain near
Capernaum; the last, upon Olivet, near Jerusalem (Mat.,
Chpt. 24). The theme of each was the Kingdom from
the Heavens.

Of the nine Beatitudes, the first four proclaim the Salvation experience. They are:

1. *"Blessed are the poor in spirit: for theirs is the King-*
dom of Heaven": First of all, the individual must know and
realize that he is morally and spiritually bankrupt. That is
what is meant by being *"poor in spirit."* It is hard for man
to understand that's what he is, and harder still for him to
admit it. But entrance into this Kingdom of Heaven demands that man admit what he is.

2. *"Blessed are they who mourn: for they shall be comforted"*: This does not speak of sadness or mourning at funerals. It refers to being sorry for one's undone condition before God. Once again, we go back to admitting what we are, and we are sorry, very sorry!

3. *"Blessed are the meek: for they shall inherit the Earth"*: The proud will not come to God; if they do, they will not admit what they are, so they leave without having received anything. In fact, the key to all the Beatitudes is the first, i.e., *"poor in spirit."* Realizing that, one *"mourns,"* which results in *"meekness."* The only personal thing that Jesus ever said about Himself was that He was *"meek and lowly in heart"* (Mat. 11:29).

4. *"Blessed are they which do hunger and thirst after Righteousness: for they shall be filled"*: Having fulfilled the first three, such will guarantee a hunger and thirst after Righteousness. This being the case, it is guaranteed of fulfillment. .

Those first four Beatitudes being carried out, the balance will fall into place.

I might quickly add:

The only way that any person can be what these Beatitudes state is that Faith is ever in Christ and what He did for us at the Cross. Only when one sees the Cross, and sees it properly, can one come to the place of being *"poor in spirit,"* which, as stated, is the key to all the other Beatitudes.

JUNE
10

*b*eware of false prophets, which come to you in sheep's clothing, but inwardly they are ravening wolves (Mat. 7:15).

The preachers of falsehood are now at once introduced; they deny the need of Christ and the Cross; they stand in contrast to the Preachers of Truth.

The moral fruit of these false teachers is corruption in the Church and corruption in the world. Any way that one desires to put the account, false teachers are workers of iniquity, however attractive their personal character may be. All false doctrine propagated by false preachers has its beginning in a faulty understanding of the Cross. The Cross is the foundation on which all doctrine must be built (I Pet. 1:18-20); if doctrine is not built on that foundation, it will, in some way, be specious. Unless there is a proper understanding of the Cross, false doctrine and false prophets are going to be, in some way, the result.

Our Lord plainly tells us in these Passages (Mat. 7:15-20) that no good fruit can come from a corrupt tree. It's

348

not possible! It may look promising to begin with, but the end result will not be favorable at all.

How does one recognize a false prophet?

Jesus told us! *"Therefore by their fruits you shall know them."*

A false way is always loaded down with religious machinery. Those ensnared are always hard at work at their religion; consequently, there is much outward activity, but no inner change, i.e., *"no spiritual growth."* True Spiritual Growth comes about only by and through one's Faith in Christ and His Finished Work on our behalf.

JUNE
11

*a*nd behold, there came a leper and worshipped Him, saying, Lord, if You will, You can make me clean. And Jesus put forth His Hand, and touched him, saying, I will; be thou clean. And immediately his leprosy was cleansed (Mat. 8:2-3).

Having exhibited on the mountain the Statutes of the Kingdom which He proposed to set up on the Earth, our Lord descended, and, in the midst of the people, demonstrated His Power as God over disease (Vss. 2-16), over nature (Vss. 24-26), and over demons (Vss. 28-32), and His Ability, by banishing evil, to fill the Earth with happiness and destroy the works and kingdom of the Devil. But men preferred Satanic domination, disease, demons, and swine (Vs. 34).

It was against the Mosaic Law for one to touch a leper. To do so made one ceremonially unclean.

Did Jesus break the Law?

Leprosy was a type of sin and was looked at by Israel of old as a judgment from God. Not only was the disease

350

loathsome, but many even thought that a leper could not be saved. Luke said that this man was *"full of leprosy,"* which means that he was near death (Lk. 5:12). Desperate, even though the Law forbade such, he came close to Jesus, close enough to touch Him.

He did not doubt the Power of Christ to cleanse the leprosy, only the Will of Christ. Knowing his terrible condition, he made the statement, *"If You will, You can make me clean!"*

Upon this declaration, coupled with the man's faith, Jesus *"put forth His hand, and touched him."* As His hand was going toward the leper, He said, *"I will; be thou clean!"*

No! Jesus did not break the Law by touching the leper. The Greek Text implies that His Word healed the leper, and not His touch. In fact, when His hand touched the leper, he had already been cleansed, so no Law was broken. The Scripture says that he was *"cleansed immediately"*!

Everything that Jesus did was meant not only to help the individual in question, but also to serve as a great Spiritual Truth. The *"cleansing of the leper"* portrayed His Power to cleanse from all sin, and to do so immediately upon a proper confession of faith.

JUNE
12

*W*hen Jesus heard it, He marveled, and said to them who followed, Verily I say unto you, I have not found so great faith, no, not in Israel (Mat. 8:10).

The Centurion comes to Christ, asking our Lord to heal his servant, who was *"sick of the palsy, grievously tormented."* The answer of Christ was immediate, *"I will come and heal him."* The Centurion surprised the Lord by saying, *"I am not worthy that You should come under my roof: but speak the Word only, and my servant shall be healed."*

The intelligence of this man was remarkable. He argued that the soldiers had to obey him because in his person resided the authority of the emperor; similarly, disease obeyed Jesus because in Him was the authority of God. And he was right!

When Jesus heard this statement, *"He marveled."* This records one of only two times He marveled: at the *"faith"* of this Gentile, and at the *"unbelief"* of the Jews (Mk. 6:6).

The Lord followed His reaction by saying, *"Verily I say*

unto you, I have not found so great faith, no, not in Israel." This is a portrayal of the fact that the Gentiles would accept Christ while Israel would not. Jesus then did exactly what the Centurion requested. He said to him, *"Go your way; and as you have believed, so be it done unto you."*

The Scripture is emphatic when it says, *"And his servant was healed in the selfsame hour."*

This great miracle by Christ portrays the fact that *"faith"* is the chief ingredient demanded by the Lord on our part.

But let the following ever be understood:

Then the faith had to be registered solely in Christ, and for the obvious reasons. Now that the Cross is a fact, we must ever realize that while Christ is the Source, the Cross is the means. Then our faith will ever be honored.

JUNE
13

*b*ut when the Pharisees heard it, they said, This fellow
does not cast out devils, but by Beelzebub the prince of the
devils (Mat. 12:24).

To attribute the Power of God to demon spirits is blasphemy. This is, in fact, the worst blasphemy of all, blaspheming the Holy Spirit, for which there is no forgiveness.

The Pharisees, who, incidentally, were the religious leaders in Israel during Jesus' day, could not deny the healings and miracles performed by Christ, nor did they have a rebuttal for His messages. So they claimed that the power He evidenced was furnished by the Devil, and not by the Holy Spirit. They were, therefore, attributing the Work of the Holy Spirit to the Devil. That is the sin of blaspheming the Holy Spirit (Mat. 12:24-32).

There are two groups of people who can blaspheme the Holy Spirit: those who have once know the Lord and then turned their back upon Him, or else professors of religion, as these Pharisees. An individual who has never

354

known the Lord and who makes no religious profession cannot blaspheme the Holy Spirit, simply because he doesn't have enough knowledge to do so.

A person who has truly blasphemed the Holy Spirit, even as these Pharisees, will have no desire to come to Christ, no desire to function Scripturally. The idea is patently unscriptural that a person may want to come to the Lord but cannot do so because they think they have blasphemed the Holy Spirit. The very fact that a person wants to come to the Lord means that such a desire has been generated by the Holy Spirit. To be sure, the Holy Spirit would not generate such a desire if there was no hope.

Considering this exceedingly important subject, I fear for those who malign, as being of the Devil, speaking in tongues, or any other thing truly done by the Holy Spirit.

"*Wherefore I say unto you* (addressing the most fearsome statement), *All manner of sin and blasphemy shall be forgiven unto men* (that is, if they properly confess the sin to the Lord [I Jn. 1:9]): *but the blasphemy against the Holy Spirit shall not be forgiven unto men*" (Mat. 12:31).

JUNE
14

*a*nd He commanded the multitude to sit down on the grass, and took the five loaves, and the two fishes, and looking up to Heaven, He blessed, and broke, and gave the loaves to His Disciples, and the Disciples to the multitude. And they did all eat, and were filled: and they took up of the fragments that remained twelve baskets full (Mat. 14:19-20).

An order is developed here which characterizes the life and living of Believers, at least if they want to truly follow the Lord. That order is:

1. *"He took"*: His taking the five loaves and two fish characterize Him taking us when we were Born-Again.

Let it be understood:

As these were multiplied to feed thousands of people, He desires to multiply us, as well. If we will truly follow Him, in other words, follow the order that is laid out here, thousands will be spiritually fed and spiritually healed.

2. *"He blessed"*: Almost immediately after the person is saved, the blessings of the Lord begin. They come from

all directions in order to encourage the new convert. It is a blessed time; however, we cannot remain in that particular position, simply because the Lord has something much greater for us.

Many Christians, in this state, attempt to give the *"blessing"* to others, but the conclusion is that self is glorified instead of the Lord. Consequently, the end result is of no positive benefit.

3. *"He broke"*: After the blessing comes the breaking, and this is the part that none of us enjoy. However, if we are to be what we must be in the Lord, it is inevitable, meaning absolutely necessary, that we experience the breaking process. It is painful and hurtful, but necessary!

This is what John the Baptist was speaking of when, concerning Jesus, he said, *"Whose fan is in His Hand, and He will thoroughly purge His Floor, and gather His Wheat into the garner; but He will burn up the chaff with unquenchable fire"* (Mat. 3:12).

4. *"He gave"*: Only after we have been properly broken can we then be successfully given. And now there is a great difference. Instead of *"self"* being glorified, the Master is glorified. We can now be multiplied, which will then spiritually feed the multiplied thousands who are in such desperate need.

Unfortunately, many do not survive the breaking process. They quit, lose faith, lose heart, and, thereby, miss the greatest blessing of all.

JUNE

15

*b*ut *He answered and said, It is not meet to take the children's bread, and cast it to dogs. And she said, Truth, Lord: yet the dogs eat of the crumbs which fall from their masters' table. Then Jesus answered and said unto her, O woman, great is your faith: be it unto you even as you will. And her daughter was made whole from that very hour* (Mat. 15:26-28).

The lesson taught here is remarkable indeed! A Gentile lady comes to Christ and requests deliverance for her daughter.

As a Minister of the Circumcision for the Truth of God to fulfill the Promises made to the Fathers, Christ refused to answer the Gentile petition addressed to him as Son of David. Obedience must dominate pity. As Man, He was *"sent"*; He was, therefore, a Servant. Hence, the silence of Verse 23, i.e., *"He answered her not a word."*

As stated, there was a reason for that, so He will take another tact. He said to her, *"It is not meet to take the children's bread, and to cast it to dogs."*

Her answer was classic. She said, *"Truth, Lord: yet the dogs eat of the crumbs which fall from their masters' table."*

She had previously addressed him as Son of David, to which He could not respond, because she was a Gentile. Now she addresses Him as *"Lord."* As God, He has liberty of action; in Grace, He could respond to the need which Faith presented to that Grace. Otherwise, He would have denied His Own Character and Nature as God.

Her plea, *"Lord, help me,"* was better than her first one. But she did not get blessing until she added, *"I am a dog."* This was the same ground the publican took when he said, *"Be propitiated to me the sinner."*

If deliverance from the power of sin and Satan be a crumb, what must the whole loaf be!

JUNE
16

*W*hile he yet spoke, behold, a bright cloud overshadowed them: and behold, a Voice out of the cloud, which said, This is My Beloved Son, in Whom I am well pleased; hear ye Him (Mat. 17:5).

The transfiguration presents a portrayal of the Glory of Christ. The Glory did not shine upon Jesus, but shone out from Him through His raiment. When Moses and Elijah appeared on the mountain with Him, Moses did so as a portrayal of the Law, while Elijah did so as a portrayal of Grace.

The gist of the conversation of Jesus with these two men, one who had been dead for about 1,500 years, and the other who had been translated that he did not see death, is interesting indeed! They spoke with Him of His atoning death (Lk. 9:31). This tells us that this Doctrine, the Atonement, is the great theme of Heaven (Rev. 1:5; 5:6, 9; 7:14).

Peter made a foolish statement about building three

tabernacles, *"one for Jesus, one for Moses, and one for Elijah."* However, the answer from above was quick in coming. God will not have even the greatest Saints associated with His Beloved Son in worship or teaching. Both Moses and Elijah were, in fact, immediately withdrawn and the Divine Voice said, *"Hear Him, and Him Alone!"*

This means that all prayers to Saints, even prayers to the Virgin Mary, will avail nothing. The Command from God the Father is stark, crisp, and to the point, *"Hear ye Him!"*

JUNE
17

*a*nd, behold, one came and said unto Him, Good Master, what good thing shall I do, that I may have eternal life? And He said unto him, Why do you call Me good? There is none good but One, that is, God: but if you will enter into life, keep the Commandments (Mat. 19:16-17).

Why did Jesus tell this rich young ruler to keep the Commandments, when He knew it couldn't be done?

Putting together the facts from the three Evangelists, this man was young, noble, wealthy, strong, courteous, educated, and religious. Most men would esteem him to be perfectly happy; however, despite all of his claims of keeping the Law, he was conscious that he had no *"life."* He desired to get it, and he asked what he should do.

Christ answered him in the way He did for two reasons:

First of all, Christ, as a Minister unto the Circumcision under the First Covenant, replied that a perfect obedience to the Law would be rewarded with everlasting life.

Second, the Lord would draw him out, thereby proving

the foolishness of his claims.

The young nobleman affirmed that he had rendered perfect obedience. But yet, something was lacking. Spiritually, the young man was blind.

As to the requirement to keep the Commandments, his ridiculous answer was, *"Which?"*

Jesus was patient with him and named several Commandments, when, in reality, they all had to be kept, and kept all the time, if life was to derived from that source, which, of course, was impossible!

Jesus then hit at the heart of the young man's problem, which was money. The Lord told him to sell all he had, *"And come and follow Me."*

The Scripture is clear. *"He went away sorrowful: for he had great possessions"* (Mat. 19:22).

Overhearing the exchange, the Disciples were astonished that it should be impossible for a highly moral man, such as this ruler, to go into the Kingdom. They did not understand that there is no good in man; and they quite forgot the declaration of Psalm 14.

Entrance into the Kingdom of God by man, as man, however cultivated and moral, is here declared by the Infallible Judge to be impossible. It is quite impossible for a man to change his color or a leopard, his spots, because that which he exhibits externally is in his nature. But God can do it, for with Him all things are possible. What then cannot be obtained by merit may be received by gift; for the Gift of God is eternal life (Rom. 6:23).

The condition of man, even moral man, is the reason for the Cross!

JUNE
18

*b*ut woe unto you, Scribes and Pharisees, hypocrites! For you shut up the Kingdom of Heaven against men: for you neither go in yourselves, neither suffer you them who are entering to go in. You serpents, you generation of vipers, how can you escape the damnation of Hell? (Mat. 23:13, 33).

The Jesus of this Chapter is not the Jesus of the modern pulpit or the fashionable way, for this Jesus denounced eight *"Woes"* upon the Preachers of that day; in terrific language, He condemned them to the damnation of Hell.

The first twelve Verses are addressed to the Disciples and the multitude; the remainder, to the Scribes and Pharisees, who, in effect, were the religious leaders of Israel of that day.

The phrase, *"Sit in Moses' seat"* (23:2), means that they were the official custodians and teachers of the Bible. But, actually, they shut up the Kingdom of Heaven, took away the key, i.e., the Bible, for they withheld it from the laity, and they nullified it with their own traditions.

364

Presently, the Bible is under attack as never before. It is not so much ridiculed as it is corrupted. Untold translations, so-called, are making their debut, which actually are no more than interpretations or paraphrases. As a result, many modern Believers, if you could call them that, little know what the Word of God actually says.

For those who pervert the Word of God, would appellatives, such as *"serpents," "hypocrites,"* and *"vipers,"* be suitable?

The outburst of Verse Thirty-seven is extremely moving. The God of Israel stands in His Temple. He suddenly turns from these blind and impure hypocrites. The sinless anger that burns on His Face and in His Eyes melts into anguish and pity, as, it may be assumed, spreading out His Arms, He looks down upon the city spread before and beneath Him, and cries out, *"O Jerusalem, Jerusalem. How often would I have gathered you!"*

Then, once more addressing the Pharisees, He says, *"Behold your House is left unto you desolate,"* after which He goes out and departs from the Temple.

Men only saw a simple man leaving the Temple, but the Angels saw the God of Glory and the Glory of God forsaking it. The Glory of God dwelt in Solomon's Temple; but, in the Second Temple, as predicted by Haggai, the God of Glory Himself!

JUNE
19

*a*nd as He sat upon the Mount of Olives, the Disciples came unto Him privately, saying, Tell us, when shall these things be? And what shall be the sign of Your coming, and of the end of the world? (Mat. 24:3).

Jesus, the God of Israel, having forsaken His House, it becomes morally leprous — as all become that He forsakes — and in harmony with Leviticus 14:45, He predicted that not one stone of it should be left upon another. He began His Ministry on a mountain, the Mount of Beatitudes, and closed it on another mountain, the Mount of Olives.

Christ offered the Kingdom to Israel, but He and it were refused. Consequently, even as He will say in this Twenty-fourth Chapter, this subjected the world to continued wars, famines, earthquakes, etc. — a continued time frame which has lasted now for nearly twenty centuries.

Most of this Chapter refers to Israel; however, the first fourteen Verses refer to the Church Age directly, and the

Church, per se, indirectly. Three particulars stand out. They are:

1. *"Deception"*: *"For many shall come in My Name, saying, I am (of) Christ; and shall deceive many."* Deception is one of Satan's most powerful weapons. The answer to deception is a firm understanding of the Word of God, which translates into a firm understanding of Christ and the Cross.

2. *"False prophets"*: *"And many false prophets shall rise, and shall deceive many."* If the Message is not *"Jesus Christ and Him Crucified,"* then the person must be labeled a *"false prophet."*

3. *"The Gospel"*: *"And this Gospel of the Kingdom shall be preached in all the world for a witness unto all nations; then shall the end come."* Despite the false apostles and the false ways, the prediction is that the Gospel of the Kingdom will be preached *"unto all nations."* It does not say, *"all people"*; but it does say, *"all nations."* We have personally aired Gospel programming by Television in approximately 35 nations, with the Message translated into their language, whatever that language might have been.

The phrase, *"And then shall the end come,"* plainly tells us that the Gospel of Jesus Christ being preached all over the world proclaims the fact that the Church Age is about over.

The Fifteenth Verse of the Twenty-fourth Chapter of Matthew signals the Great Tribulation. All of this means that the Church should be getting ready for the Rapture (I Thess. 4:13-18).

JUNE
20

*a*nd then shall appear the sign of the Son of Man in Heaven: and then shall all the Tribes of the Earth mourn, and they shall see the Son of Man coming in the clouds of Heaven with power and great glory (Mat. 24:30).

This speaks of the Second Coming, which will be the single most cataclysmic event in the annals of human history. The Coming of the Son of Man to deliver His ancient People will not be secret, but Worldwide. In fact, during the Great Tribulation, many false messiahs will arise, claiming to be the one which Israel desperately seeks.

At the beginning of the Great Tribulation, the Antichrist, the greatest of them all, will make his debut, with Israel announcing to the world that he is the Messiah. In fact, he will sign a seven-year treaty with Israel guaranteeing their protection. He also will enable them to rebuild their Temple.

But in the midst of the Great Tribulation, he will show his true colors and attack Israel, in which she will suffer her first defeat since again becoming a nation in 1948.

That's what Paul was speaking of when he said, *"For when they* (Israel) *shall say, Peace and safety; then sudden destruction comes upon them, as travail upon a woman with child; and they shall not escape"* (I Thess. 5:3). Israel would then be destroyed, but events will draw away the Antichrist and he will leave Israel for another day — the Battle of Armageddon.

When all of these false messiahs come forth at that time, Jesus said, *"Believe it not!"* Then He said, *"For as the lightning comes out of the east, and shines even unto the west; so shall the Coming of the Son of Man be"* (Mat. 24:27). In other words, it will be obvious and on a Worldwide basis, with the entirety of the heavens putting on a display of glory such as it has never done before, because the King is coming home. There will be no doubt as to Who He is!

As stated, this is the Second Coming!

JUNE
21

*a*nd they came to Jericho: and as He went out of Jericho with His Disciples and a great number of people, blind Bartimaeus, the son of Timaeus, sat by the highway side begging (Mk. 10:46).

The healing of blind Bartimaeus presents one of the greatest recorded miracles found in the Bible.

There is no evidence that Jesus had been to Jericho before this. In fact, it was only a few days before the Crucifixion. He had come from Galilee, and had come the long way around, and did so by crossing the Jordan and coming down on the east side. He would have crossed back to the west side at Jericho, hence Him going through the city.

I firmly believe that the Holy Spirit had Jesus to go through Jericho in order that Zacchaeus be saved and Bartimaeus be healed and saved. There is a good possibility that both of these men had earnestly sought the Lord that Jesus would come this way. If they had, their prayer was now answered.

Upon ascertaining that it was Jesus, Bartimaeus began to cry out, saying, *"Jesus, Thou Son of David, have mercy on me."* He was, in effect, publicly confessing that Jesus Christ was the Messiah, the Lord of Glory. He asked for mercy.

Let it ever be said:

No one has ever asked mercy of the Lord but that they received it!

Many tried to stop Bartimaeus from shouting out to Jesus, but he only shouted the louder. Sadly, there isn't much of a helping hand, as it regards people coming to the Lord. There should be, but there isn't!

The more they told Bartimaeus to shut up, the louder he cried.

The Scripture then says, *"Jesus stood still, and commanded him to be called."* This was Bartimaeus' day.

In a sense, the Lord, at this very moment, is commanding certain people to be called.

Are you ready for that call? Will you respond favorably?

The Scripture says, *"Casting away his garment, he rose, and came to Jesus."* This was a garment carried by beggars, which would be used as a receptacle to catch a few coins during the day, and as a garment to ward off the chill at night. Bartimaeus threw it away because he knew that he would no longer need it. In other words, in just a few moments, he would no longer be blind and he would no longer be a beggar.

The way his name is given in the Sacred Text insinuates that he may have once come from a well-to-do family. If that was the case, fortune had not shined on him too well, and now he is reduced to begging. But his day is about to change.

Jesus said to him, *"What will you that I should do unto you?"*

What a question!

The answer was immediate, *"Lord, that I might receive my sight."*

He was immediately healed and followed Jesus. Tradition says that he became a stalwart in the Church in Jerusalem and remained so until the day of his death.

The lesson is clear. Jesus can change things!

JUNE
22

*i*n *the beginning was the Word, and the Word was with God, and the Word was God* (Jn. 1:1).

In this First Chapter of the Gospel of St. John, we are given a compendium of the entirety of the Word of God.

The first Verse tells us that Jesus, as the Living Word, is the same as the Written Word. This means that the entirety of the Bible, in some way, is the story of Jesus Christ and Him Crucified, and unequivocally so. Then the Scripture says, *"And the Word was made flesh, and dwelt among us, (and we beheld His Glory, the Glory as of the Only Begotten of the Father,) full of Grace and Truth"* (Jn. 1:14).

We are told here that *"the Word was made flesh, and dwelt among us,"* which means that He came to this world for a specific purpose. To do what He had to do, God would have to become Man, hence the Incarnation. The Creator would become a creature. Unthinkable! But yet it happened.

The Scripture then said, *"The next day John* (John the

Baptist) *sees Jesus coming unto him, and said, Behold the Lamb of God, which takes away the sin of the world"* (Jn. 1:29).

Why did John refer to Christ as *"the Lamb of God"*? Why not *"the Lion of the Tribe of Judah"*?

The Holy Spirit had John to refer to Jesus as *"the Lamb of God"* for a specific purpose and reason. He would be what all the millions of lambs had represented since the dawn of time, the Perfect Sacrifice. That is the reason He came!

The destination of the Son of God was the Cross, ever the Cross!

Concerning this, the Prophet Isaiah said, *"I gave My back to the smiters, and My cheeks to them who plucked off the hair: I hid not My face from shame and spitting.*

"For the Lord GOD will help Me; therefore shall I not be confounded: therefore have I set My face like a flint, and I know that I shall not be ashamed" (Isa. 50:6-7).

Calvary was ever before Him because His mission was to liberate the fallen sons of Adam's lost race.

And that He did!

374

JUNE
23

*b*ut He turned, and said unto Peter, Get thee behind Me,
Satan: you are an offense unto Me: for you savor not the
things that be of God, but those that be of men (Mat. 16:23).

Any number of times, Jesus told His Disciples that He
would go to Jerusalem, be killed, and raised again the
third day (16:21). They seemed to understand not at all
what He was saying, despite the several times He related
this to them. There was a reason for that.

In their thinking, there was no place in the picture for
a *"Cross."* Jesus was going to take the Throne of Israel,
use His mighty power to throw off the Roman yoke, and
make Israel, once again, they thought, the leading light in
the world. They could see nothing else!

Jesus had come to this Earth in order to redeem the
entirety of the world, not just Israel. Further, Israel was a
long way from being ready for that of which the Disciples
spoke. As becomes overly obvious, the religious leaders
of Israel passionately hated the Lord Jesus Christ.

When Jesus mentioned the terrible Sacrifice which was soon to come, *"Then Peter took Him, and began to rebuke Him, saying, Be it far from You, Lord: this shall not be unto You."*

Concerning this, Williams says, *"The poor human heart likes position and glory, and is quite willing to exalt the Messiah even to Heaven, but it shrinks from self-mortification, shame, hatred, persecution, and death."*

Unfortunately, the term *"Cross"* encompasses all this. If anyone wishes to go after Jesus, he must consent to share His reproach, and, if need be, to die with Him.

"At the door of the Roman Court of Justice, crosses were piled high, and the condemned, on leaving, took up a cross and carried it to the place of execution. The Believer must follow Christ in that path.

"Those who take up that cross lose their life in relation to this world, but find it in Christ; those who refuse safeguard their life in this world, but suffer eternal loss."

The *"loss"* is far greater than that which they think to gain. Those who, in action, take up the Cross will be rewarded with *"life"*; others will lose *"life"* (Mat. 16:24-25).

Jesus turned and said unto Peter, *"Get thee behind Me, Satan: you are an offense unto Me: for you savor not the things that be of God, but those that be of men"* (Mat. 16:23).

Let it ever be understood:

Any Message that belittles the Cross, lessens the Cross, denigrates the Cross, or tries to bypass the Cross, is said to be, by the Lord Jesus Himself, of Satan. That which is of God follows the pattern of the Cross, and follows the pattern of the Cross exclusively! Those who, in action, take up the Cross will be rewarded with *"life"*; the others will lose *"life."*

JUNE

24

*a*nd it came to pass also on another Sabbath, that He
entered into the Synagogue and taught: and there was a man
whose right hand was withered (Lk. 6:6).

What a blessing it must have been to have heard Jesus
teach! And yet, those whose hearts were not right with
God found no substance in His Words of Life, just as those
presently! That's why Jesus was constantly saying, *"He
who has ears to hear, let him hear"* (Lk. 8:8).

There was a man in the Synagogue *"whose right hand
was withered."* This portrays the entirety of the human
race, spiritually withered as a result of the Fall, especially
the *"right hand."* Considering that the man, as are most,
was right-handed, his activities, of necessity, would have
been greatly curtailed. This pictures the entirety of the
human race, which is in the same condition.

Concerning this, Paul said, *"For the flesh (in this case,
evil desires) lusts against the Spirit (is the opposite of the
Holy Spirit), and the Spirit against the flesh (it is the Holy*

Spirit Alone, Who can subdue the flesh; He does so, as we have repeatedly stated, by our Faith being placed exclusively in the Cross): *and these are contrary one to the other* (these two can never harmonize; as Paul has stated, the old nature must be cast out, which the Holy Spirit Alone can do): *so that you cannot do the things that you would.* (Without the Holy Spirit, Who works by the Cross, the Believer cannot live a Holy life [Gal. 5:17].)

It must be remembered that Paul is speaking here to Believers. He is simply telling us that, due to the *"withered hand,"* we simply cannot function as we ought to, even though we are saved and are new creations in Christ Jesus (II Cor. 5:17). Consequently, we must function according to the pattern laid down by Christ.

Unfortunately, the Scribes and the Pharisees greatly opposed His healing the man. They were more concerned about their petty rules, which, incidentally, were man-made, than about the restoration of this man. That is a perfect picture of religion.

Despite their opposition, the Christ of Glory told the man to stand up in obvious view of the entirety of the crowd, and then told Him, *"Stretch forth your hand."* The man did so, *"and his hand was restored whole as the other."* That is the only cure for the fallen sons of Adam's lost race. The Church, at least for the most part, however, has unfortunately adopted the ways of the world, and I speak of humanistic psychology, in trying to meet this problem. There is no help from that source, even as there cannot be any help from that source.

Let all know and realize:

No matter how badly withered is the right hand, Jesus can restore it. That's His business!

JUNE
25

*a*nd they arrived at the country of the Gadarenes, which is over against Galilee. And when He went forth to land, there met Him out of the city a certain man, which had devils long time, and wore no clothes, neither abode in any house, but in the tombs (Lk. 8:26-27).

As stated in other accounts, every miracle of healing that Jesus performed was not only for the person or persons involved, but also was meant to teach a great spiritual truth. The deliverance of the maniac of Gadara presents an excellent example.

Matthew mentions two demoniacs; but, Mark and Luke, mention one. If there were two, there certainly was one. He is here individualized as being probably both the fiercer and better known of the two; he also alone asked to be permitted to remain with the Lord, becoming an effective Preacher. The other demoniac presented no such peculiar interests and is, therefore, not mentioned by Mark or Luke.

The man described by Luke was demon-possessed, so controlled by demons, in fact, that he could no longer function in society. He wore no clothes, cut himself with stones (Mk. 5:5), and dwelt in tombs among the dead bodies. Spiritually speaking, this is a perfect description of much of the world. They are controlled by demon spirits; death, in many and varied ways, is the result, i.e., all unredeemed, in a sense, are dead while they live (I Tim. 5:6).

According to the Scripture, when the demoniac saw Jesus, he ran and worshipped Him (Mk. 5:6). This tells us that demon spirits worship the Lord more than many who call themselves "Christians." When Jesus questioned him, asking him his name, he answered, "Legion." This means that a host of demon spirits occupied this man, at least 2,000 (Mk. 5:13).

The demons asked if they could go into the swine which were nearby, and Jesus permitted them to do so. Upon the entrance of the demons, the swine immediately ran into the lake and were drowned.

The only answer for possessed, dissipated, disconcerted, displaced humanity is the Lord Jesus Christ. To be sure, humanistic psychology holds no answer whatsoever. Jesus Alone holds the answer; but, regrettably, psychology is preached in most Churches, and Jesus little, if at all!

The Gadarenes took no interest in the Salvation from Satan's power of a fellow human being, but they viewed the loss of their property, i.e., the hogs, with deep concern. They have many successors today. The deliverance of people from the powers of darkness, be it alcohol, drugs, etc., excites no one in the world, but the destruction of a distillery by fire causes much excitement.

The delivered man wanted to come and be with Jesus, which is easy to understand; however, Jesus told him to go and *"Show what great things God has done for you."* The young ruler was commanded to follow Christ (Mk. 10:21); the leper was forbidden to speak of Christ (Mk. 1:43); but the former demoniac was ordered to publish what great things Jesus had done for him.

JUNE
26

*a*nd it came to pass afterward, that He went throughout every city and village, preaching and showing the glad tidings of the Kingdom of God: and the Twelve were with Him. And certain women, which had been healed of evil spirits and infirmities, Mary called Magdalene, out of whom went seven devils, And Joanna the wife of Chuza Herod's steward, and Susanna, and many others, which ministered unto Him of their substance (Lk. 8:1-3).

Man magnifies sacraments and ceremonies and belittles preaching. God magnifies preaching. It pleases Him, by the foolishness of preaching, i.e., preaching the Cross, to save men (I Cor. 1:21). Christ preached incessantly, and so did the Apostle Paul, the Twelve, and the Seventy. To be sure, that is our example. If we are to see spiritual results, we will have to follow that example.

Satan does not fear ceremonies, but he greatly fears the anointed preaching of the Gospel.

Women are prominent and honorably mentioned in

Luke. Some of these women were wealthy and they used their money to minister to the Lord's necessities. His were the cattle on a thousand hills; with a few loaves, He could feed thousands. But He did not feed Himself. For sustenance, He depended on these women and others. Thus, He proved that He was a Man like his fellowmen; at the same time, He tested their fidelity to, and their affection for, Himself. True Disciples, now as then, minister to Him; mere professors do not.

"*Susanna*" is mentioned only here. Nothing whatever is known of her, and yet is her name known throughout the whole world because it is recorded in this one Verse. Here, as elsewhere, it seems that women worked and men talked.

Mary Magdalene was delivered from Satanic dominion; she, therefore, loved Him greatly. She was, in fact, the very first one to preach the Gospel of the Resurrection (Mk. 16:9-10).

It must have been difficult for these women to face the scorn and contempt of the religious leaders of Israel; yet they were faithful to the end. It was not a woman who betrayed the Lord for thirty pieces of silver; it was not women who forsook Him and fled; nor was it a woman who thrice denied that she knew Him. But it was women who wailed and lamented when He was led forth to be crucified; it was women who stood to the last by His Cross; and it was women who were the first to visit His Tomb on the Resurrection Morning.

It was Jesus, therefore, Who liberated women from the stigma of Eve being the first to fall (Gen. 3:1-6).

383

JUNE
27

*a*nd *a woman having an issue of blood twelve years, which had spent all her living upon physicians, neither could be healed of any, Came behind Him, and touched the border of His garment: and immediately her issue of blood stanched* (Lk. 8:43-44).

There is a tremendous lesson on faith in the illustration of the woman who touched the hem of Jesus' garment. This lesson is applicable to all!

The woman had been sick for some twelve years. The implication is that she had been financially well off, but had spent all that she had on physicians, "*neither could be healed of any.*" This is not meant to be a diatribe against doctors, for Luke himself was a physician. It simply meant that they couldn't help her, just as doctors presently are helpless in many cases. The implication also is that some pretended to help her only to get her money.

As Jesus came, hundreds thronged Him. No doubt, the woman wanted to appeal to Him personally, but there was no way it could be done. Too many people were pushing and shoving; besides that, she was frail and weak.

Faith, however, does not quit. She said, *"If I may touch but His clothes, I shall be whole"* (Mk. 5:28). The great lesson presented here is that if Christ doesn't touch us, we can touch Him. So that opens the door to all, at least all who will believe. When she touched Him, she was healed immediately.

Jesus then asked her to give her testimony, which she did. *"And He said unto her, Daughter, be of good comfort: your faith has made you whole; go in peace"* (Lk. 8:48).

There is one more great lesson here! In Verse 43, she was addressed merely as *"a woman."* But now Jesus calls her *"Daughter,"* which means that He claimed her.

Of this woman, one might say the following:

1. She was chained: She was chained by sickness and sin.

2. She was changed: There is only One Who truly can change people, and that is the Lord.

3. She was claimed: She was merely *"a woman"* previously, but now she is *"Daughter."*

The Lord *"claims"* all those whom He *"changes."*

JUNE
28

*a*nd, *behold, there came a man named Jairus, and he was a ruler of the Synagogue: and he fell down at Jesus' feet, and besought Him that He would come into his house: For he had one only daughter, about twelve years of age, and she lay a dying. But as He went the people thronged Him* (Lk. 8:41-42).

Love descends rather than ascends. Hence parents love their children more than children love their parents. So God loves man, but man does not love God. With one exception (Mk. 1:30), the Gospels do not record children coming to Jesus on behalf of their parents, but cases of parents coming to Him on behalf of their children are frequent.

Jairus would have Jesus come to heal his daughter, who was at the point of death. In fact, the little girl died while her father was gone to get Jesus. When the child grew ill, Jesus was across the Sea of Galilee, delivering the maniac of Gadara. Jairus was undoubtedly desperate for Jesus to return, and when He returned, the man hastened to Him.

But Jesus was delayed again by the woman who touched the hem of His garment. Finally, he is told, *"Your daughter is dead. Trouble not the Master."* Jesus, however, says, *"Fear not: believe only, and she shall be made whole."* What thoughts ran through Jairus' mind when Jesus made this statement?

When the Master went to Jairus' home, He asked only Peter, James, and John to go with Him. Three times He did this. Why these Three?

1. He would raise the child from the dead, showing these Three His *"Power."*

2. At the Mount of Transfiguration, He would show these Three His *"Glory"* (Lk. 9:28).

3. In the Garden of Gethsemane, He would show these Three His *"Suffering"* (Mat. 26:37).

When Jesus told the mourners that the child was only sleeping, they laughed Him to scorn. What the Lord meant was that the child was not going to stay dead! He spoke of death as sleeping, because He would take all fear out of death; He would do so by defeating death at the Cross.

Mark said they *"entered in where the damsel was lying"* (Mk. 5:40). The Greek word for *"entered"* here means *"to go on a journey."* To be sure, it was a journey of unprecedented proportions for His Three Disciples and the parents. They would witness the child being raised from the dead. Any and every person who makes Christ the Saviour and Lord of his life enters on a journey of staggering proportions, so staggering, in fact, that it is impossible presently to comprehend it all.

Jesus took the child by the hand and said, *"Maid, arise."* Then *"her spirit came again, and she arose immediately."* This fact demonstrates the separate existence of the spirit, independent from the body. Evidently, the spirit of the child went to Paradise, but was, as is obvious, abruptly called back.

Jesus *"charged them that they should tell no man what was done."* He sought neither publicity nor admiration. His appeal was to the heart and to the conscience. His mission was to bring people to Repentance and to forgiveness of sins. There can be no understanding of the Person and Work of the Lord Jesus Christ apart from this consciousness of sin against God and the need of pardon.

To work great miracles and yet seek to hide them is foreign to human nature. Men love admiration and publicity; shallow streams make the most noise (Williams).

JUNE
29

*a*nd, behold, a certain lawyer stood up, and tempted Him, saying, Master, what shall I do to inherit eternal life? (Lk. 10:25).

In the Israel of Jesus' day, a lawyer was one who devoted himself to the study of the Law of Moses. This lawyer meant to test Christ's knowledge of the Law. Eternal life is man's greatest interest; no more tremendous question could be asked than that of this Verse.

In His reply, the Lord immediately points to the Bible as an infallible authority. In the lawyer's answer, which, incidentally, was correct, is revealed a clear knowledge of God and of Truth which men in Israel possessed at that time, or at least could possess, if they so desired. It was knowledge immeasurably in advance of that of other parts of the world.

Greece, with its pagan poets and philosophers, claimed great knowledge; they had, however, no knowledge of the things that really counted.

Sadly, the lawyer, though he answered correctly, did not evidence faith correctly, because he was self-righteous. He was determined to win Heaven by religious self-efforts.

At a point in his Ministry, Spurgeon was criticized for not speaking enough about science, etc. His answer to the accusation was revealing. When he took the pulpit on the Sunday morning in question, he laid his Bible on the podium, and then said:

"There is a woman in this audience who recently lost a child. To know where that child presently is, she cannot go to science. She must go to the Bible."

The great Preacher was, in essence, saying that the answers that really matter are found only in the Word of God. No person truly can be said to be educated, no matter how many university degrees they might hold, unless they are properly educated in the Word of God.

This is one of the reasons that many of the modern translations, so-called, of the Bible (which are really mere paraphrases) are so dangerous. Jesus didn't say, *"Man shall not live by bread alone, but by every thought . . . ,"* but rather, *"Man shall not live by bread alone, but by every Word that proceeds out of the Mouth of God"* (Mat. 4:4).

In the Christian life, the daily study of the Word of God (but make certain that it actually is the Word of God that you are studying) must have first place. All other duties must give way to it.

JUNE
30

*a*nd He said unto them, *Which of you shall have a friend, and shall go unto him at midnight, and say unto him, Friend, lend me three loaves; For a friend of mine in his journey is come to me, and I have nothing to set before him?* (Lk. 11:5-6).

Here we are taught a great lesson. It might be called *"The Parable of the Three Loaves."* A man went to a friend at midnight requesting that he lend him *"three loaves,"* because a friend of his on a long journey had stopped by his home, but he had no food to set before him. That's why he needed to borrow the bread.

Evidently, he awakened his friend, because it was midnight. The man answered immediately; his reply was that the door was shut and that he could not arise. But Jesus said the man at the door kept knocking and would not take *"No"* for an answer. Because of his persistence, the friend arose and gave the man as much as he needed.

The moral is this:

When we ask the Lord for something, whatever the

circumstances may be, whatever the situation may seem to be, if the answer doesn't come immediately (and most of the time, it doesn't), we should not quit; we should *"keep asking," "keep seeking,"* and *"keep knocking."* Jesus clearly said that if we did this, we would *"receive,"* we would *"find,"* and the door would be *"opened."* Jesus further said that we will receive that for which we are asking, i.e., if we ask for bread, we will not receive a stone, etc.

The problem with many Christians is that we *"quit asking,"* we quit *"seeking,"* and we quit *"knocking."* We must understand that *"delay"* is not *"denial."* We also must understand that everything the Lord does with us and for us, especially answers to prayer, all are meant to increase our faith, our trust, and our dependence upon Him. He is very mindful of all our needs, more mindful, in fact, than we would ever know.

However, we should carefully ask for that which we truly need, even as this man needed three loaves. Too often we ask for things for which we have little need.

The moral of this is:

If what we are asking is in the Will of God, we must not allow delay to discourage us. We must *"keep asking," "keep seeking,"* and *"keep knocking."*

392

JULY

1

*t*hen said one unto Him, Lord are there few who be saved? And He said unto them, Strive to enter in at the strait gate: for many, I say unto you, will seek to enter in, and shall not be able (Lk. 13:23-24).

The Lord has just given several Parables, all which stress the fact that few would be saved.

In essence, the Lord ignored the man who asked the question of Verse 23, but seized the opportunity suggested by the question to address an earnest appeal to all standing around Him, to let nothing prevent them pressing through the narrow door of conversion which alone gave entrance into the true Kingdom of God. For directly the Master of that house shut the door, they would vainly seek to enter (13:25-28). When that door is shut, multitudes will repent too late, and believe too late, and sorrow for sin too late, and begin to pray too late.

Earth is the only place in creation where there is infidelity. There is no unbelief in Hell. These Verses

393

(13:24-28) destroy the theory of repentance and salvation after death.

Men may ask religious questions and so flatter themselves that they are religious; further, they may have an ecclesiastical relation to Christ (13:26), and yet be shut out from Heaven. To be shut out from Heaven is to be shut into Hell, with its hopeless weeping of remorse and its hopeless gnashing of despair. Here, as everywhere, Christ's teaching conflicts with almost all modern thought.

There is only one way of Salvation, and that is by Faith and Trust in Jesus and what He did for us at the Cross (Jn. 8:32; 14:6).

JULY

2

*t*hen drew near to Him all the Publicans and sinners for to hear Him. And the Pharisees and Scribes murmured, saying, This Man receives sinners, and eats with them (Lk. 15:1-2).

The point of the three Parables in this Chapter, *"The Parable of the Lost Sheep," "The Parable of the Lost Coin,"* and *"The Parable of the Prodigal Son,"* is God's joy over repenting sinners. They unveil the sentiments of His Heart and not those of the repentant sinner, as is usually taught. He did not sit still in Heaven pitying sinners, just as the shepherd, the woman, and the father did not idly bewail the lost sheep, the lost silver, and the lost son. The word *"found"* (15:24) reveals the Divine activities in secret in the conscience and heart of the prodigal. Christ left the starry crown of Heaven for the thorny crown of Earth in the activity of the love that seeks the lost till it is found.

The shepherd rejoiced, the woman rejoiced, and the father rejoiced. Such is the joy of God when sinners come to Jesus. This Grace is a Grace that seeks and a Grace that receives. The first two Parables describe the former; the third Parable, the latter. Grace convicts the conscience, but attracts the heart.

The measure of that Grace is the measure of the love that begets it. The son's reception and position were decided by the energy of that love, and not by the measure of the son's repentance. The father's position decided that of the son. All was measured by the sentiments, not of the prodigal's heart, but of the father's heart.

The stupidity, the insensibility, and the depravity of the sinner are expressed in the three Parables. If the doubling of the dream to Pharaoh (Gen. 41:32) assured its certitude, how much more does the trebling of this Parable make certain the attitude of God's heart to lost man!

(The information on the three Parables was derived from George Williams.)

JULY

3

*a*nd He said, A certain man had two sons: And the younger of them said to his father, Father, give me the portion of goods that falls to me. And he divided unto them his living. And not many days after the younger son gathered all together, and took his journey into a far country, and there wasted his substance with riotous living (Lk. 15:11-13).

The Parable of the Prodigal Son portrays the only time in Scripture that God, personified in this Parable by the Father, is pictured running. In that for which, and to which, He ran, provides a fitting example of Who God is and What God is. He is love!

The spiritual declension of the son took place while he was in his father's house. He fell from the moment he desired the father's goods without the father's company; and it only needed a few days to find him in the far country. Backsliding begins in the heart and very soon places the feet with the swine.

His only occupation was the degrading one — to a

397

Jew — of a swine-herd, and his only food the husks that the swine did eat. No man gave to him; for in the Devil's country, nothing is given, everything must be bought, and bought at a terrible price.

First of all, the Prodigal *"came to himself"* (15;15); then he *"came to his father"* (15:20). Such is the action of the Holy Spirit first upon the conscience and then upon the heart. While the boy was a great way off, the father saw, had compassion, ran, fell on his neck, kissed him, and said to the servants, *"Bring . . . "* (15:20-22). All these activities express the grace and love that welcome true Repentance.

Grace ran to kiss the Prodigal in his rags; Righteousness hasted to dress him in its robes; for he could not sit in his rags at the father's board. The Prodigal had not to provide the best robe, the ring, the sandals, and the fatted calf. They were provided for him, and they declared that his Repentance had been accepted; for servants were not thus arrayed and feasted. We must understand that there were no reproaches, rebukes, or reproofs for the past, no irritating admonitions for the future, because the Father and His Joy are the subjects of this story rather than the moral condition of the son.

The elder brother pictured the Pharisee. He neither understood nor shared in the Father's joy. On the contrary, he was covetous and refused to sympathize, although his Father entreated him to do so. Self-righteous, he claimed to have given a perfect obedience. But his desire to make merry with his friends showed that morally he was as much lost to his Father as was his brother.

Christ, as *"The Way,"* is symbolized in the robe, the

ring, the sandals, and the fatted calf, for He is Righteousness (II Cor. 5:21), Eternal Life (Jn. 11:25), Sonship (Jn. 1:12), and Peace (I Cor. 5:7-8). The death of the sinless calf was a necessity ere the feast could be enjoyed. Had the Prodigal refused this raiment and claimed the right to enter the Father's house in his rags and nakedness, he, like Cain, would have been rejected. His was true Repentance, and so it accepted these gifts, assuring purity, perpetuity, position, and provision.

This Parable, in fact, destroys the argument that no Atoning and Mediating Saviour is needed between God and the sinner.

JULY

4

*t*here was a certain rich man, which was clothed in purple and fine linen, and fared sumptuously every day: And there was a certain beggar named Lazarus, which was laid at his gate, full of sores (Lk. 16:19-20).

No one ever spoke so plainly about Hell as the Lord Jesus. The illustration given, regarding the rich man and Lazarus, is not a Parable, as claimed by some, but actually the portrayal of a literal happening. From this illustration, we draw several conclusions about Hell. They are:

1. Hell is a locality. It is a place, actually in the heart of the Earth (Mat. 12:40).

2. At death, the rich man instantly went to Hell, which tells us what immediately happens to the unconverted when they die. On the other hand, Lazarus, upon death, was immediately taken to Paradise by Angels.

3. The rich man went to Hell, not because he was rich, but because he failed to accept the Lord. Lazarus went to Paradise, not because he was a poor beggar, but

because he had made the Lord his Saviour (Lk. 16:31).

4. This illustration given by Jesus completely blew to pieces the thinking of most Jews. They reasoned that financial blessings translated into Salvation, while poverty translated into that which was otherwise. Jesus tells them here that neither thing, riches or poverty, has anything to do with Salvation.

5. We learn from this illustration that all who die, whether they are in Hell or Heaven, maintain intelligence through their soul and spirit. The rich man is represented as having eyes, ears, a mouth, a tongue, and a tortured body, i.e., "in spirit form."

6. We learn here that the fires of Hell are real.

7. We learn that all those in Hell are in torment.

8. We learn that Hell is eternal, for the rich man asked that Lazarus might be sent to his five brothers. He did not ask this grace for himself, for he knew that he was eternally entombed. It is easy to step into Hell, but impossible to step out.

9. We learn that there are no unbelievers in Hell, nor is there any Salvation.

10. We learn that the rich man repented, but it is too late. There is no Salvation after death. The Lord Jesus here destroys that doctrine.

11. We learn from this illustration that the Scriptures contain all that is necessary to Salvation. A person who would return from the dead could add nothing to the Scriptures; and a man who will not listen to the Bible will not listen to a multitude if raised from the dead (16:31).

JULY
5

*t**ake heed to yourselves: If your brother trespass against you, rebuke him; and if he repent, forgive him. And if he trespass against you seven times in a day, and seven times in a day turn again to you, saying, I repent; you shall forgive him* (Lk. 17:3-4).

The Lord warns His Disciples here not to think only of the sins of the Pharisees, but also of their own, especially of the sin of an unforgiving spirit. The repentant Brother was to be forgiven seven times *"in a day"*; and when Peter, on another occasion, asked the Lord (Mat. 18:21) if he were to stop at seven times, Jesus said, *"No; not until seventy times seven,"* i.e., four hundred ninety times. This is an important number in the history of God's moral government of sinning Israel. It means endless forgiving.

Only twice prior to Pentecost do we read of the Apostles, as a body, asking the Lord for spiritual energy. Here they ask Him to increase their faith; on another occasion, they begged to be taught how to pray.

The searching doctrine of Verses 1 through 4 made the Apostles conscious that something higher than fallen human nature alone could obey such teaching. The Lord replied (17:6) that Faith was a power so real that its smallest provision could remove the greatest moral obstacles. He used a tree as an example. The removal, in fact, of trees and mountains were proverbial figures of speech among the Jews at that time, expressing the overcoming of great difficulties.

Then in order to forewarn the Apostles about flattering themselves that they would be entitled to admiration if they lived without injuring others, if they practiced perpetual forgiveness, and if they worked wonderful miracles, He now adds that, having fulfilled all these conditions, they would be no better than unprofitable servants (17:7-10), that is, they would, in no way, have benefited their Master. This is a fatal blow to the doctrine of Salvation by works.

From this we learn the following:

The Disciple is to say, *"I am an unprofitable servant."* The Master will then say, *"Well done, good and faithful servant"* (Mat. 25:21).

JULY
6

*a*nd as it was in the days of Noah, so shall it be also in the days of the Son of Man. Even thus shall it be in the day when the Son of Man is revealed (Lk. 17:26, 30).

The Doctrine of 17:23-37 strikes against the expectation of many that the world will grow morally better and ultimately become the Kingdom of God. But here the Lord gives a fearful picture of the state of the world and the professing Church at the time of His Second Coming.

More than once Jesus pointed to Noah and the state of society in his day (Mat. 24:37) as prefiguring the condition of the nations when He shall appear. The Second Coming will contrast with His First. The First Chapter of II Thessalonians describes the Second Coming. It will not be local, obscure, or with great humility, but universal, powerful, and glorious. The glories of that day will have a relation to, and will be the result of, His Atoning Sufferings at Calvary. It will find the world as indifferent and corrupt as in the days of Noah and of Lot (17:26-30).

404

All will perish, who, like Lot's wife, have their hearts in Sodom, though, like her, they make a profession of having left it, as also will all those who put any interest, even life itself, above the claims of Righteousness. The Second Coming will be, in fact, the most cataclysmic event in the history of mankind.

When the Lord comes the second time, He will not come to be mocked, criticized, jeered, and rejected. He will not come to be beaten and nailed to a Cross. Instead, He will come as *"KING OF KINGS, AND LORD OF LORDS"* (Rev. 19:16). Every Saint of God who has ever lived, all the way up through the First Resurrection, will accompany Him at that glorious time. Then the very creation will rejoice, because the Saviour of men is at last coming to take control. And take control He shall! (Isa., Chpt. 11).

JULY
7

*a*nd He spoke this Parable unto certain which trusted in themselves that they were righteous, and despised others: Two men went up into the Temple to pray; the one, a Pharisee, and the other a Publican (Lk. 18:9-10).

The Parable of the Pharisee and the Publican, as given by Christ, proclaims, in no uncertain terms, the rudiments of relative righteousness, works righteousness, and imputed Righteousness; only the last one is acceptable to the Lord.

The Pharisee projected, first of all, *"relative righteousness."* In other words, he measured his supposed righteousness by comparing himself with others. Those who rely on such always select those who they think are worse than they themselves; somehow, this seems to make them feel better. God, however, can never accept relative righteousness.

The Pharisee also was relying on *"work righteousness,"* which spoke of his twice-weekly fasts and his paying tithe on all that he possessed (or at least this was his claim). Millions in the world today, like this Pharisee of old, trust in *"works righteousness,"* which God also will never accept. The two, *"works righteousness"* and *"relative righteousness,"* are the two types of supposed righteousness which are claimed by most of the world.

The *"Publican, standing afar off,"* which meant he was probably in the Court of the Gentiles, began to pray, but would not so much as *"lift up his eyes unto Heaven."* He felt his acute unworthiness, and conducted himself accordingly. When the Scripture says, *"he smote upon his breast,"* it means that he kept doing this over and over. When he said, *"God be merciful to me a sinner,"* the original Text actually says, *"the sinner,"* meaning that, in his own eyes, he felt he was the greatest sinner in the world.

Every afternoon at 3 o'clock, the evening lamb was offered up as a propitiation for the sins of that day. The Publican pleaded forgiveness and acceptance because of the merit of that atoning blood. It foreshadowed the atoning death of the Lamb of God, Who was Himself the Propitiation, i.e., the *"Mercy Seat."* As a result, the Lord imputed unto him a perfect Righteousness, all made possible by the atoning death of the Lamb of God.

"Imputed Righteousness" is Righteousness that we do not earn, and cannot earn, and neither can we merit such. It is freely given to the believing sinner upon confession of Faith in Christ. It is the only type of Righteousness that God will accept, because it's based on the perfect Righteousness of Christ. It is obtained by evidencing Faith in Christ and His Perfect Sacrifice of Himself.

The Scripture says that this man *"went down to his house*

justified rather than the other." In other words, he was declared a righteous man. The Pharisee was not justified at all. There are no degrees in Justification. The Verse does not mean that the Pharisee was partly justified and the Publican fully; it means that the one was wholly justified and the other, not at all.

In reference to all of this, the Lord said, *"For every one who exalts himself shall be abased; and he who humbles himself shall be exalted"* (Lk. 18:14). The Lord evidently repeated this frequently (Mat. 23:12).

JULY
8

*a*nd the Lord said, Simon, Simon, behold Satan has desired to have you, that he may sift you as wheat: But I have prayed for you, that your faith fail not: and when you are converted, strengthen your brethren (Lk. 22:31-32).

Simon Peter now faces the greatest trial of his life. It is primarily because of his boasting, as evidenced in 22:33. It seems that Satan had asked permission to tempt Peter and had evidently been given permission. Such permission, however, was not to please Satan, not at all, but rather as a lesson for Simon Peter. Satan can only do what the Lord allows him to do.

The Lord said to Peter, *"I have prayed for you, that your faith fail not."* We must ever realize that every attack by Satan against us, whether it's in the realm of the physical, financial, domestic, or spiritual, is always but for one purpose, and that is to completely destroy our faith, or at least seriously weaken it. Satan's attack is always delivered against Faith, for if that fails, all fail.

So Satan said to Eve, *"Has God said?"* When that doubt had done its work, he boldly added, *"You shall not surely die."*

Jesus told Peter that He would pray for him. He never said anything like that concerning Judas. He knew there was no hope for Judas, and He also knew that Peter would pull through.

The appointed time contemplated in this prayer was not the moment of Peter's denial, but the dark moment of despair when he went out and wept bitterly. Then Satan, no doubt, must have whispered to him: *"You have committed spiritual suicide. Now are you mine!"* But the Lord's look (22:31) was the means that upheld his faith, and so Christ's prayer was answered, as all such like prayers are always answered!

Jesus said, *"And when you are converted, strengthen your brethren"* (22:32). The word *"converted,"* as used here, does not mean to get saved again, as it normally does, but rather *"to come back to the right way."* Peter most definitely would do that; then he was also able to *"strengthen his brethren."*

Did Peter fall?

No! He failed, but he did not fall. To *"fall"* is to lose faith, thereby to quit believing. This is what happened to many of the Hebrew Believers, which occasioned Paul to write the Book of Hebrews (Heb. 6:4-6; 10:26-29). They had quit believing in Christ and the Cross.

As long as one keeps believing in Christ, and what Christ did at the Cross, while there might be failure, there will not be a Fall.

410

JULY
9

*a*nd He came out, and went, as He was wont, to the Mount of Olives; and His Disciples also followed Him (Lk. 22:39).

Here in the Passion of Christ is the great lesson of surrender taught. It comes, in essence, in three stages. They are:

1. *"The place of surrender"*: The Scripture said, *"And when He was at the place, He said unto them, Pray that you enter not into temptation"* (22:40).

Before a Believer can surrender totally to the Lord Jesus Christ, he has to first come to the *"place of surrender."* There is a Gethsemane for every Believer. The problem of self-will is acute in the hearts and lives of all, even the best of Christians. There is only one way for self-will to be conquered, and that is for the person to come to the *"place"* where they understand that the Cross of Christ is the only answer.

Jesus died on the Cross, not only to save us from sin, but also to save us from *"self."*

411

2. *"The price of surrender"*: What is the price? Jesus tells us what it is.

He said, *"Father, if You be willing, remove this cup from Me: nevertheless not My Will, but Yours, be done"* (22:42).

The price of surrender is our personal wills being swallowed up in the sweet Will of God. The Cross is the only means by which the will of the individual can properly acquiesce to the Will of God. If the Believer attempts to pay the price himself, instead of looking to the One Who has already paid the price, this will only breed self-righteousness. Making the Cross the Object of one's Faith, and the Cross alone, will have the effect of us looking to Christ, and only Christ!

3. *"The peace of surrender"*: Once that surrender was made, *"There appeared an Angel unto Him from Heaven, strengthening Him"* (22:43).

This didn't mean that the struggle grew less intense, for, in fact, it increased; however, the extra strength provided by the Angel was sufficient. Angels also ministered to Him in the Temptation (Mk. 1:13).

All want the *"peace of surrender,"* which is a peace that passes all understanding, but many do not want to come to the *"place"* or pay the *"price."* There is, however, no other way! (Jn. 14:27).

JULY

10

a*nd He said to them all, If any man will come after Me, let him deny himself, and take up his cross daily, and follow Me"* (Lk. 9:23).

In this short Passage, we have before us that which the Lord expects in our proposed serving Him and service to Him. There are three things that must be done. They are:

1. **The individual must deny himself:** Self-denial, which is demanded here, is not asceticism, as many think. Incidentally, asceticism is the denial of all things which are pleasurable or comfortable, etc. So, many think if they make things abnormally hard for themselves, then this denotes some type of holiness, etc. It doesn't!

The denial of self of which Jesus here spoke refers to one denying one's own strength, ability, and prowess, i.e., *"the flesh."* This is, in fact, one of the greatest hindrances to the Child of God. The Believer attempts to do for himself that which he cannot do, and which, in fact, the Lord has already done.

2. Take up the Cross: As many people misunderstand self-denial, they also misunderstand the taking up of the Cross. Most think it refers to suffering. In fact, it does. It is not, however, the suffering of the individual that here is demanded, but rather the Suffering of Christ.

The idea, as here presented, pertains to the Believer understanding that Christ is the Source and the Cross is the means; consequently, we are speaking of the benefits of the Cross; such benefits include everything man lost in the Fall. That's what Jesus meant by taking up the Cross. That is altogether different from what most people think. Taking up the Cross is the understanding that everything we receive from the Lord comes by way of the Cross.

3. Daily: The idea lends toward a daily renewal of Faith. It is somewhat like the Manna of old. There would be a fresh supply each day; the Children of Israel were to enjoy what was given that day, and trust the Lord for the next day.

Satan is ever vigilant. That's the reason we have to watch and pray. We must not take the great Redemption process for granted. We must every day make the decision to look solely to Christ, which means to trust Him for what He did for us at the Cross, and Him Alone!

JULY

11

*a*nd *he said unto Jesus, Lord, remember me when You come into Your Kingdom. And Jesus said unto him, Verily I say unto you, Today shall you be with Me in Paradise* (Lk. 23:42-43).

The conversion of the thief is peculiar to Luke. It is one of the most remarkable conversions in the Bible. In one flash of light, the Holy Spirit revealed Christ to him and taught him of the Lord's future Kingdom of Glory, though, at the moment, He was hanging in shame and agony on the tree.

The thief did not ask for any physical relief to his pain, but only for a remembrance in the future Kingdom. They were in the same condemnation — he justly, but the Lord only as a Sin Offering — and He prayed that they might be together in the same Glory. So the Precious Blood, then flowing for his sins, cleansed him so effectually that it made him at that moment as fit to enter Paradise as Christ Himself.

The Divine Nature of the thief's Repentance was evidenced by six steps:

1. His concern about his companion (23:40).
2. His confession of his own sinfulness (23:41).
3. His confession of Christ's innocence (23:41).
4. His faith in Christ's Power and willingness to save him — he called him Lord, and declared his belief that He had a Kingdom (23:42).
5. He prayed to Him (23:42).
6. He asked for no great thing, but only to be remembered; this was humility.

The thief's short prayer embodied a great creed; he believed:

A. That his soul lived after death;
B. That the world to come would be one of felicity or misery;
C. That a Crucified Jew was the Lord of Glory;
D. That His future Kingdom was better than this present world;
E. That Christ intended to have pardoned sinners in that Kingdom;
F. That He would receive into it the truly penitent;
G. That the key of that Kingdom was hanging at Christ's girdle, though He Himself was hanging naked on the Tree; and,
H. That by resting his soul for eternal Salvation upon this dying Saviour, he had that Kingdom assured to him.

The thief's spiritual intelligence seemed to exceed that of most all of the Apostles prior to Pentecost.

Near the Cross of the dying thief stood the Apostle John, the Virgin Mary, her sister, Mary the wife of Cleophas, and Mary Magdalene. But to none of these exalted Saints did the malefactor turn for help. He turned from them and prayed directly to Jesus, with nothing and nobody between his sin-stained soul and the sin-atoning Saviour.

He did not cry, *"Oh Holy Mother of God! Refuge of sinners, pray for me! I put my whole trust and confidence in the power of your intercession."* Nor did he appeal to her sister, as being the Holy Aunt of God, nor to John, as being the Beloved Apostle of God. Had he trusted any one of these great Saints, he would have perished, for Salvation is in Christ and in none other. He is the One and only refuge of sinners (Acts 4:12).

JULY
12

*t*hen He said unto them, O fools, and slow of heart to believe all that the Prophets have spoken: Ought not Christ to have suffered these things, and to enter into His Glory? (Lk. 24:25-26).

Verses 13 through 53 are peculiar to Luke. He Who walked on the road to Emmaus was *"this same Jesus"* (Acts 1:11), but *"in another form"* (Mk. 16:12). It is impossible for us to realize what were the powers of the Lord's Glorified Body after the Resurrection.

Like Joseph's action with his brothers, so the Lord did not discover himself to these two Disciples until He had brought them into a fitting condition of soul. When Jesus used the words, *"Ought not,"* it meant *"Was it not necessary, because it was predicted?"* This emphasizes the word *"all"* in Verse 25. These two Disciples had confined their Bible study to that which the Scriptures promised respecting the Messiah's Glory and Kingdom, but they had been blind to the multitude of types and Prophecies foretelling His Sufferings as an Atoning Saviour.

Jesus then directed these two men to the Bible, which then was the Old Testament. In a sense, He divides it into two parts, *"the Law"* and *"the Prophets."* This makes the Bible, because it is inspired, the supreme authority as to Faith and Doctrine. Its subject is the Sufferings and Glories of Christ — His Sufferings as Sin Bearer, i.e., Sin Offering (Phil. 2:6-10); His Glories as Sin Purger (Heb. 1:3). The story of the Bible is the story of Jesus Christ and Him Crucified. If we understand it as we should, we will see that everything ultimately points to Him and His Sacrifice of Himself.

Concerning all of this, it might well be said that Christ went, Bible in hand, into death, and that He came out, Bible in hand, from among the dead. He insisted that it predicted His Death and Resurrection in relation to sin and its judgment. So, immediately prior to His Death and immediately subsequent to His Resurrection, He made more than thirty quotations from the Inspired Word.

If the Word was the Light to Christ, it most definitely must be our Light as well (Ps. 119:105).

JULY
13

O you sons of men, how long will you turn my glory into shame? how long will you love vanity, and seek after leasing? Selah" (Ps. 4:2).

In this Verse, David refers to the sin of Absalom, which characterizes the sin of all men.

THREE SINS LISTED

There are three sins listed in this Second Verse, which, in fact, are universal sins. They are:

1. Turning God's Glory to shame (Rom. 1:22-32). God's greatest Glory is His Creation of man; however, due to the Fall, man has turned after the ways of unrighteousness, thereby turning the Glory of God into shame.

Other than the few hours Adam lived righteously before the Fall, the only True Man Who has ever truly lived is the Lord Jesus Christ.

2. Unredeemed man loves vanity (Rom. 8:20; Eph.

4:17; II Pet. 2:18). Vanity stems from pride, which, within itself is the foundation sin of the human race (Prov. 6:16-17; I Jn. 2:16).

3. Leasing: This word means *"lying"* or *"falsehood"* (Prov. 17:4; 19:22). Satan is the father of lies; consequently, all of his children are liars. Actually, almost the entirety of the human race, in its pursuit of life outside of Christ, is based on a lie.

The sins listed in Verse 2 are the reason that Absalom rebelled against his father; the Scribes and the Pharisees rebelled against Christ; and all men rebel against God.

JULY

14

*a*nd when they wanted wine, the mother of Jesus said unto Him, They have no wine. This beginning of miracles did Jesus in Cana of Galilee, and manifested forth His Glory; and His Disciples believed on Him (Jn. 2:3, 11).

The First Miracle that Jesus performed in His earthly Ministry was the changing of water to wine in the little village of Cana of Galilee. Why did the Holy Spirit want this, the changing of the water to wine, to be His very First Miracle?

From the description, this family evidently was poor. If they had not been poor, they would not have run out of wine. Incidentally, this was not an intoxicating beverage, but rather grape juice. The Greek word used here for wine is "oinos," which means either fermented or unfermented wine. This was the unfermented variety.

The Holy Spirit desired this to be the First Miracle of Christ in order that all may know and understand that Jesus can change things. He can change sorrow to happiness, sickness to health, sin to Salvation, death to life. That is His Business, to change things, and, above all, to change men, which He Alone can do!

Four hundred and fifty years had now elapsed since the last public miracle of the Old Testament. It was that of Daniel, Chapter 6. As an aside, many point to this incident in support of the doctrine of the value of the intercession of the Virgin, for Mary went to Christ and told Him of the depletion of the wine. But the answer of Christ given to her, *"What have I to do with you,"* destroys that hypothesis. The answer to His question is *"Nothing."*

In every instance, the contrast is between the carnal nature, which is sinful, and the Holy Spirit. The Spiritual Kingdom has no contact with the carnal. There is an impassable abyss between them. There could, therefore, be no union between the sinless nature of Christ and the sinful nature of Mary. Nor could He admit her authority. This is declared in the words, *"My hour is not yet come."* That is, *"the moment for Me to act will be revealed by My Father, and His Voice is the only one to which I hearken."*

Mary, to her credit, recognized her error, stepped at once aside from between these needy people and the Almighty Giver of every good and perfect gift, telling the servants to turn from her to Him. When she was out of the way, He spoke directly to them, and, in a moment, the water was wine!

We learn from this First Miracle that Jesus can change things — anything! We also learn that we are to appeal directly to Him, and not to an intermediary.

JULY

15

*t*here was a man of the Pharisees, named Nicodemus, a ruler of the Jews: The same came to Jesus by night, and said unto Him, Rabbi, we know that You are a Teacher come from God: for no man can do these miracles that You do, except God be with Him (Jn. 3:1-2).

We learn from this Chapter that entrance into the human family is by natural birth and into the Divine Family by Spiritual Birth. As it is impossible to enter the human family except by birth, so is it impossible to enter the Divine Family. This is the great Doctrine of this Chapter.

Nicodemus was an important man in Israel. Not only was he rich, but he also was a member of the vaunted Sanhedrin, the ruling body of Israel. Jesus ignored the statement made to Him by Nicodemus, promptly telling him, *"Except a man be born again, he cannot see the Kingdom of God"* (3:3).

Jesus then told Nicodemus how the Born-Again experience is brought about. He said, *"And as Moses lifted up the serpent in the wilderness, even so must the Son of Man be lifted up: That whosoever believes in Him should not perish, but have Eternal Life"* (3:14-15).

Man demands a reasonable faith, based on evidence and scientific demonstration. The way of life preached to Nicodemus must, therefore, be unacceptable to them, for how could looking at a piece of copper heal disease, i.e., the serpent being lifted up on the pole in the wilderness? (Num. 21:9). Copper contains no healing properties discoverable by science. Therefore, how could a look to the Saviour on Calvary's Tree effect a New Birth? Both are impossible to the fallen intelligence of sinful man.

Christ at once raised the moral question with Nicodemus. He immediately stopped a religious discussion by telling this most religious man and professed Believer that he was so sinful, so hopelessly corrupt and fallen, as to be incapable of reformation, so darkened morally that he could neither recognize nor experience spiritual phenomena unless born from above. This fundamental truth is obnoxious to man, for it humbles him.

In this discussion, the Lord unveiled what man really is. He is a sinner, having responsibility, but no life. He is lost; he must seek life and pardon outside of himself, that is, in Christ, Who meets his failure in responsibility and gives him Eternal Life.

Unfortunately, the modern Church, borrowing the ways of the world, seeks to reform man. It cannot be done! While the message of morality, i.e., *"self-improvement,"* sounds good to the carnal ear, and thereby appeals to the flesh, such is impossible, even for a Believer.

In all of this, by noting the lifted up serpent in the

wilderness, Jesus leads Nicodemus, and all others, for that matter, to the Cross. The problem, whether for the unredeemed or the redeemed, is sin. The only answer for sin, as evidenced here, is the Cross. Fallen man must be miraculously changed, which can only come about through the Born-Again experience. The Cross made that possible. The Believer must be cleaned up! This can only be done by Faith in Christ and the Cross. As the Cross is the only answer for the unredeemed, it is also the only answer for the redeemed, as evidenced in this Chapter.

Incidentally, Nicodemus, despite being very religious, was unsaved. It would take the Cross to change that (Jn. 19:38-42).

JULY
16

*J*esus answered and said unto her, Whosoever drinks of this water shall thirst again: For whosoever drinks of the water that I shall give him shall never thirst; but the water that I shall give him shall be in him a well of water springing up into Everlasting Life (Jn. 4:13-14).

This scene at Jacob's well is one of the most amazing in human history. The dread Judge of the quick and the dead and one of the vilest of sinners are met together. But He is there not to condemn her, but to seek and to save her. The Mighty God, the Everlasting Father, the Prince of Peace, was sitting, weary and thirsty, by a well, but had no means even to quench His thirst. He, as Man, was dependent on an outcast woman for a little water.

His Grace and Love, rejected by Israel, now pour out their fullness upon an impure Samaritan — for Love is pained unless enabled to act. The floodgates of Grace lifted themselves up to bless the misery which Love pitied. Man's heart, withered with self-righteousness, cannot

427

understand this. Thus, sinners respond to the Grace which Pharisees proudly refuse; for Grace flows in the deep channels dug by sin and misery.

These two isolated hearts met — His, isolated by Holiness, for He was separate from sinners; hers, by sin, for she was separate from society — and this encounter of Holiness and sinfulness resulted in the Salvation of the sinner, for Jesus is *"the Saviour."*

Apparently ashamed to come with the other women in the cool of the morning to draw water, she was obliged to come alone in the burning heat of the noonday sun. As with Nicodemus, so with the Samaritan, the Lord hastened to raise the question of sin in the conscience. Nicodemus was highly moral and the Samaritan, grossly immoral; yet was there no difference between them. Both were sinners needing cleansing and Salvation. But how different was the Lord's method with each of them! The moralist was at once met with the abrupt word, *"You must be born again,"* but to the sinner, and One Who knew she was a sinner, He said, *"Give Me to drink"*!

A profession of faith in Christ which ignores the question of sin, the Holiness of God, the spirituality of worship as distinct from sacerdotal ceremonies, the need of pardon, and the condition of trust in an atoning and revealed Saviour — such a profession is worthless.

We learn from all of this that the Holy Spirit seeks people (16:13-15); the Father seeks worshippers (4:23); and the Son seeks sinners (Lk. 19:10).

Jesus did not pointedly reveal Himself to Nicodemus, but He did reveal Himself to this Samaritan woman.

Why not Nicodemus?

The sinner, exampled by the woman, accepts such, but self-righteousness, exampled by Nicodemus, could never accept such! Merit, in the one case, did not admit into Eternal Life, and demerit, in the other, did not exclude from it.

When Jesus, concerning the Messiah, said to the woman, *"I am He!"* — she was then saved by that Revelation (Mat. 11:27); for intelligence in Divine things comes by conscience and revelation and not by intellect.

Upon accepting Christ, *"The woman then left her waterpot, and went her way into the city, and said to the men (religious leaders of the city), Come, see a Man, which told me all things that ever I did: is not this the Christ?"* (4:28-29). This woman, who had been married five times, thus became the first Preacher of the Gospel to the Gentiles. So effective was her preaching that it caused a Revival. She became a vessel to receive and then to minister the gift of life.

And so can all who make Jesus the Saviour and the Lord of their lives.

429

JULY

17

t *he nobleman said unto Him, Sir, come down ere my child die. Jesus said unto him, Go your way; your son lives. And the man believed the Word that Jesus had spoken unto him, and he went his way* (Jn. 4:49-50).

Someone has well said, *"Desperation always precedes revelation."* More than likely, that is more true than not. This individual was a *"nobleman,"* which means that he was wealthy; however, his wealth didn't stop the difficulties of life, such as the near death of his son.

Living in Capernaum, actually the Headquarters of Jesus, he heard that Jesus would be in Cana, which was approximately 10 miles west. So he went to Jesus and *"besought Him that He would come down, and heal His son: for he was at the point of death."*

The Holy Spirit evidently informed Christ as to the thinking of this man, for Jesus said unto him, *"Except you see signs and wonders, you will not believe."* The Lord's seemingly rough answer to the nobleman's request, similar to that addressed to Nicodemus, was designed to test and deepen his faith; for Jesus knew his heart, its unbelief, and its demand for signs and wonders. Strengthened by this rebuke, the cry of anguish burst from him: *"Lord, come down ere my child die!"*

Jesus simply said to him, *"Go your way; your son lives."* That was it!

So the man had a choice. He could believe the Word of the Lord, or not believe it.

That's all that he had, the *"Word"* given him. One can well imagine the consternation that filled his heart. According to what Jesus had said to him, he may have thought that Jesus would come with him to Capernaum. After all, he was a very wealthy man. Or, there would be some type of demonstration that instantly would make obvious the great Power of Christ. He had, however, only the simple word, *"Go your way; your son lives."*

To be frank, that is enough! That is what every single person in this world has, the Word of the Saviour, i.e., *"The Word of God."* Do we believe it, or do we not believe it?

Evidently, the nobleman believed. He probably had to stay the night in Cana, departing the next morning to go back to Capernaum. What would he find when he arrived home? It seems his servants were some distance on the road toward Cana, awaiting his coming. For they met him and told him, saying, *"Your son lives,"* actually, the identical words that had been used by Christ.

What joy must have filled this man's heart! He asked his servants about the exact time the boy began to get better. They replied, *"Yesterday at the seventh hour the fever left him."* That was the same hour that Jesus had pronounced the boy's healing. His Word was enough!

The Scripture says that the nobleman believed, as well as the entirety of his house, which, of course, meant the entire family. This man had the "*Word*" of the Lord, and he found that it was enough. Today, we have the Word of the Lord. And I, as well as millions of others, can assure you, "*That is enough!*"

JULY
18

*a*fter this there was a Feast of the Jews; and Jesus went up to Jerusalem. Now there is at Jerusalem by the sheep market a pool, which is called in the Hebrew tongue Bethesda, having five porches. In these lay a great multitude of impotent folk, of blind, halt, withered, waiting for the moving of the water (Jn. 5:1-3).

The Sabbath, the Passover, and the Feast of Tabernacles, as forms and witnesses, were fulfilled when Christ, Who ordained them, appeared. Man had degraded them so that they became merely *"Feasts of the Jews"*; their impotency to give life is contrasted here with Him Who is Life. Sadly and regrettably, men cling to forms and festivals all the more strongly when lacking the life which these forms and festivals symbolized under the First Covenant of works; they used these forms to fight against Him of Whom the forms witnessed.

We will find that the healing of the impotent man contrasts the quickening Power of Christ with the powerlessness of the Law. It demanded strength on the part of the sinner in order to obtain the life it promised. But man is without strength (Rom. 5:6). So what the Law could not do because of the weakness of that upon which, and through which, it was to act, i.e., the carnal nature of man, Christ, as sent by God, effected, for He brought with Him the power to accomplish that which Grace willed. A single word from Him sufficed.

Jesus asked the man, *"Will you be made whole?"*

That is, in effect, the same question that the Lord is asking all. Man is undone, impotent, wandering as a lost sheep, all because of sin. So, down through the ages comes the cry, just as potent today as it was then: *"Will you be made whole?"*

And yet, it is so hard for men to believe.

The man answered Christ, saying, *"Sir, I have no man, when the water is troubled, to put me into the pool."*

In those words, we have the plight of the entirety of the human race. They are looking to other men, but the other men to whom they are looking are just as impotent as they are. While some men definitely may have this world's riches, still, that which man really needs cannot be supplied by man. If we look to man, we always will be disappointed.

Jesus said to the man, *"Rise, take up your bed, and walk."*

This man had been sick for 38 years, the same period of time that Israel spent in the wilderness. All of this time, the impotent man vainly sought life in the Pool of Bethesda, just as Israel had vainly sought life in the Law. In both cases, strength was required on the part of the person who sought what was promised, but they found that they could not receive.

Upon the Word of Christ, *"immediately the man was made whole, and took up his bed, and walked."* What a day that was for him! He was a picture of helpless humanity, unable to help himself, and finding no one who could help him.

But Jesus came. . .!

The man not only now could walk, he also carried his bed, that which once had carried him. More still, it was sin that had caused the sickness in the first place. To be sure, sin is the cause of all problems. So Jesus told him, *"Behold, you are made whole: sin no more, lest a worse thing come upon you"* (Jn. 5:14).

While we should relish that which the Lord did, and rejoice thereby, still, we must also not fail to take in the lesson that continued sinning brings continued judgment.

JULY
19

*t*hen Jesus said unto them, *Verily, verily, I say unto you, Except you eat the flesh of the Son of Man, and drink His Blood, you have no life in you. Whoso eats My flesh, and drinks My Blood, has Eternal Life; and I will raise him up at the last day. For My flesh is meat indeed, and My Blood is drink indeed. Jesus answered them, Have not I chosen you Twelve, and one of you is a Devil? He spoke of Judas Iscariot the son of Simon: for he it was who should betray Him, being one of the Twelve* (Jn. 6:53-55, 70-71).

The question is often asked, *"Why did Judas do what he did?"* How could he have been personally chosen by Christ, walk with Him for some three and a half years, witness the greatest array of miracles the world had ever known, and then betray the Master? The answer is found in the last half of this Sixth Chapter of the Gospel of John.

Judas did not appreciate the Message of the Cross, for that's what the Message here was. Judas, in fact, totally rejected God's Redemption Plan, which was the Cross of Calvary.

When Jesus spoke about *"eating His flesh"* and *"drinking*

His Blood," He was speaking of the Cross, i.e., the Sacrifice He would make there. He would offer up His Perfect Body as an Atonement for sin, thereby, in the giving of His Life, pour out His Precious Blood. This was the price that God demanded, and this was the price that Jesus would pay.

In this Message, more particularly Verses 53 through 56, Jesus proclaims the fact that the believing sinner must so embrace the Cross of Christ, that is, what Jesus did there, that he, in essence, and by Faith, becomes a part of Christ and what Christ did. It could be explained no better than Jesus, when He said, *"He who eats My flesh, and drinks My Blood, dwells in Me, and I in Him"* (6:56).

Whether Judas that day totally understood what Jesus meant, we cannot know; however, he most definitely came to understand what Jesus meant, and he fully rejected it. That's why Judas betrayed the Lord! He did not want the Cross, nor any part of the Cross, just as millions presently follow the same path.

Regrettably and sadly, the far greater majority in the modern Church have also rejected the Cross. As Cain of old, they see no need for a Sacrifice. They are willing to accept Jesus as a great Prophet, a great Statesman, even a great Miracle Worker, but the Cross? No!

However, the following should be noted:

1. The only way to God is through Jesus Christ (Jn. 14:6).

2. The only way to Jesus Christ is through the Cross (Lk. 9:23).

3. The only way to the Cross is by and through a denial of self (Lk. 9:23).

4. The only way to deny self is by looking to Christ and the Cross (Rom. 6:3-5).

JULY
20

*i**n the last day, the great day of the Feast, Jesus stood and cried, saying, If any man thirst, let him come unto Me, and drink. He who believes on Me, as the Scripture has said, out of his innermost being shall flow rivers of Living Water. But this spoke He of the Spirit, which they who believe on Him should receive . . .* (Jn. 7:37-39).

The scene that opens before us is magnificent, to say the least. The Temple Mount could have held as many as a half million people. It was the eighth day, the great day of the Feast, and it was a Sabbath. It was a day of ecstatic joy, of loud jubilation, and of sounding of trumpets. On this day, this great day, a Priest, bearing a golden vessel full of water, which had come from the Pool of Siloam, would approach the Altar in front of the Temple, while the rejoicing people sang: *"With joy shall you draw water out of the wells of Salvation"* (Isa. 12:3).

At the appropriate time, with the Priest holding up the golden vessel full of water above the great Altar, the people would have grown silent for a few moments, observing the very solemn but joyous scene, watching as the water poured from the golden vessel to the great Altar.

It was at this supreme moment that Jesus stood, no doubt on some elevated position, and shouted, *"If any man thirst, let him come unto Me and drink"* (Isa. 55:1). These Words of the Lord were given, and they rang out over the tremendous crowd there assembled, with a powerful anointing of the Holy Spirit, that must have shaken the entire vast assemblage. That day, all who heard that great invitation would have to choose between two alternatives — either to say, with Caiaphas, *"He is guilty of death,"* or to exclaim, with Thomas, *"My Lord and My God."*

To believe on Him and what He did at the Cross is to drink of Him. In Truth, this great cry of Christ harked back to the smitten Rock, when the river of water poured out, as Moses smote it in the wilderness (Ex., Chpt. 17).

The quotation in Verse 38 refers to the Messiah and not to the Believer. Christ is the Eternal and Inexhaustible Source of all Spiritual Blessings (Isa. 12:3; 55:1; 58:11; Ezek. 47:1; Joel 3:18; Zech. 13:1; 14:8). The Cross, of which all of this is a type, made possible the forgiveness and cleansing of sin, the giving of Eternal Life, and the Believer having now the privilege of being filled with the Holy Spirit. Of all of this, Christ is the Source and the Cross is the Means.

The contrast here is between the lifeless water, quickly exhausted, which a mortal Priest carried in a golden vessel, and the life-giving water flowing in eternal and inexhaustible fullness from out of the Divine and human affections of the great High Priest, the Lord Jesus Christ.

The lesson to be learned is that ceremonies, however magnificent, venerable, and Scriptural, can never satisfy the deep thirst of the soul. That thirst can only be satisfied by personal union with the Lord Jesus by faith. For He Alone is the Smitten Rock, Who, in Resurrection Power, sends forth a stream of life to dying men and to a thirsty world.

JULY
21

*t*hey say unto Him, Master, this woman was taken in adultery, in the very act. Now Moses in the Law commanded us, that such should be stoned: but what do You say? (Jn. 8:4-5)

As Jesus taught that morning in the Temple, probably in the Court of the Gentiles, He was interrupted by the Scribes and the Pharisees. That's about all that religion does, interrupt Him!

They had brought unto Him a woman taken in adultery, thinking to embarrass Him, or to force Him to take a position which would bring Rome, or even the people, down on His Head. Whatever decision He rendered would put Him in a vulnerable position, or so they thought. They seemed never to learn Who He really was; He was miles ahead of them in every respect!

Here stands the little, trembling creature, dying in shame, expecting to be stoned at any moment. There was no doubt about her guilt! And yet, why didn't they also bring the man? The Law of Moses demanded that

441

both be stoned!

Here stands the woman and her accusers in front of the great crowd who had come to hear Jesus teach. The Pharisees demanded of Him, *"What do You say?"*

The crowd grew silent, wondering what He would say and do. He stooped down and wrote in the dust on the pavement at His feet — for the Temple Court was paved. His action in stooping down to write in the dust recalled His action in stooping down from Heaven to Mount Sinai and writing with His Finger upon the stone tables of the Law, for He was the Author of the Law (Ex. 31:18). Almighty God, now manifested in the flesh, once more stooped Earthwards; once more He wrote upon stones — but now not that which condemned to death, but that which ordained to life. How the heart wishes that the Spirit had willed to record what was written!

The Pharisees brought forth this woman in the hope of confounding Jesus; for He was not a Saviour if He condemned her — the Law did that — and if He let her go, He despised and disallowed the Law. How foolish they were!

His action in writing on the pavement should have opened their eyes as to Who He was. He did not excuse or deny the woman's guilt, or the fact that the Law justly doomed her to death, but He announced that only those who were themselves innocent of the sin of which she was condemned could accuse her and execute the sentence of the Law.

The words in Verse 7, *"without sin,"* do not mean *"sinless,"* but they mean *"without her sin."* How could accusers guilty of the same sin as the accused carry out the sentence of a sinless Law?

Accordingly, these impure hypocrites, by slinking away, convicted themselves, and so were themselves found out *"in the very act"* of which they triumphantly accused their victim. Confused, they separated from one another, each caring for character rather than conscience, he who had the most reputation to save being the first to retire.

How could men who were themselves sentenced by the Law to be stoned to death for adultery, stone another for the same sin?

The Lord wrote twice on the stones at His Feet. He wrote twice at Sinai. One table related to the God; the other, to man, as to obedience and responsibility. But yet, Christ could not break the Law. So how did this dilemma solve itself?

He said to the woman the greatest words she had ever heard, *"Neither do I condemn you: go, and sin no more"* (8:11). How could He justify that in relationship to the Law, which demanded her death?

He justified His decision regarding her in the same manner that He justifies His decision concerning us, concerning all who ever have believed in Him, by going to the Cross and paying the price that she should have paid, that we should have paid, but couldn't pay.

On the Cross, He, in totality, fulfilled the requirements of the Law, and in every respect (Col. 2:14-15).

JULY
22

*h*e answered and said, Whether He be a sinner or no, I know not: one thing I know, that, whereas I was blind, now I see (Jn. 9:25).

Williams says, *"The Light that justified the adulteress and exposed and confounded her accusers (Jn., Chpt. 8) now enlightened the blind man and put to shame his haters; having brought these lost sheep into the fold, that same Light revealed their safety, and the Grace and Truth of their Shepherd. So Grace saved them, and Truth enlightened them.*

"This woman and this man symbolized Israel — as a Church, adulterous; as a nation, blind."

The man of our Text was blind from birth, which, of course, means that he had never seen anything and had no way to relate to anything except by touch and feel. Israel was morally blind; so are all men. But Jesus gave this man sight. He produced in him that which he previously did not have. He was darkness, but now became light in the Lord because enlightened by the Lord.

444

When the Disciples observed this man born blind, they asked the question, *"Why is he blind?"* thinking that his parents had done some terrible thing to occasion his malady. Jesus put that thought to rest by exclaiming that the man was blind, not because he had committed some terrible sin known by the Lord even before his birth, neither had his parents. So, with this one statement, Christ puts to rest the foolish, erroneous doctrine of the family curse.

In essence, He told His Disciples to forget about that. Whatever the problem, and whatever the cause, which, in effect, was original sin, would be set straight by *"the works of God which would be made manifest in him."* And Jesus Alone would manifest those works, for He Alone is *"the Light of the World."*

Our Lord then did something very unusual; He *"spat on the ground and made clay of the spittle."*

Why did He do this?

In this case, the clay symbolized His Humanity, and the moisture of His Lips, the Life that animated it.

The Lord then *"anointed the eyes of the blind man with the clay."* However, just as the man saw nothing after the clay had been put upon his eyes, so men are blind to the Person and Work of Christ, though He places Himself right before their very eyes.

The Work of Christ in the changing of men's lives, symbolized by this man born blind receiving his sight, can only be completed at the Cross, which is symbolized by *"the pool of Siloam."* This is a great truth which must not be forgotten; regrettably, it seems to be forgotten in most Church circles presently.

When the blind man went and washed, as commanded by Christ, the Scripture says, *"he came seeing."* When, for the first time in his life, his eyes were opened to all the beauty of nature, what thoughts and feelings must have entered this man's heart and mind? Those of you who are washed in the Blood of Christ know exactly how this man felt. Before you were saved, you had no knowledge of all that the Lord is. But upon conversion, as instantly as sight came to this former blind man, spiritual sight came to you.

Spiritual sight cannot be imparted without the action of the Cross, no matter what is done previously. Hence, the man had to go wash in the pool of Siloam.

The Pharisees were angry that Jesus had opened the eyes of this formerly blind man, because it was the Sabbath Day. To confirm the miracle, they went to the man's parents. The parents, it seems, waffled in their recognition of Christ, probably because anyone who confessed Christ would be *"put out of the Synagogue,"* which meant to be excommunicated, which carried all type of penalties (9:22).

The Pharisees then went to the former blind man, asking him to identify the One Who had healed him. The man, it must be remembered, had never, as of yet, seen Christ. So he did not know Him by sight. When the religious leaders began to malign Christ, actually calling Him *"a sinner,"* etc., the man answered, saying, *"Whether He be a sinner or no, I know not: one thing I know, that, whereas I was blind, now I see"* (9:25).

The courageous testimony of this man to these Priests and rulers of the Synagogue is inspiring; it also contrasts with the cowardice of his parents. Transported with rage, the rulers had him thrown out into the street, no doubt proceeding to excommunicate him from the Synagogue. But then he met Jesus!

The man now received, as well as his glorious miracle, Eternal Life.

Let it be understood:

It was either Christ or the Synagogue. It could not be both. One or the other had to go. Regrettably and sadly, it is very similar presently!

*V*erily, verily, I say unto you, He who enters not by the door into the sheepfold, but climbs up some other way, the same is a thief and a robber. But he who enters in by the Door is the Shepherd of the sheep. Verily, verily, I say unto you, I am the Door of the sheep (Jn. 10:1-2,7).

The Scribes and Pharisees claimed to be shepherds. Jesus contrasted Himself with them. He was the Good Shepherd. He came in by the door into the sheepfold, and He was Himself, at the same time, the Door of the sheep.

Let it be understood:

The Door of which He spoke was a blood-splattered Door; it was typified by the blood-splattered door of the first Passover in Egypt (Ex. 12:7).

The True Shepherd came in by the Door. That is, He submitted to all conditions ordained by Him Who built the sheepfold. These conditions were given through Moses. Accordingly, Christ was born of a woman under the Law, was circumcised, and fulfilled all that the Law demanded and predicted concerning the Messiah.

He was Jehovah's Perfect Servant, living by every Word that proceeded out of the Mouth of God, continually doing those things that pleased Him. Consequently, on presenting Himself at the Door, the doorkeeper, i.e., the Law, immediately admitted Him, and the sheep recognized His Voice. He, therefore, had access given to Him and to His sheep, despite the Pharisees and Priests.

Out from under the condemnation of the Law, He led His sheep — He Himself going before them to Calvary. The sheep followed Him, for their safety consisted in knowing the One Voice which was Life to them.

Further, He was the Door of the sheep. He was their authority for going out and their means for entering in. The sheepfold, which to them had been a prison, He turned into a refuge; so they went in for safety and went out for pasture. The sheep enjoyed safety and liberty.

He plainly said, *"I am the Door."* This means that the Church is not the Door to Christ, as the Roman Catholic Priests teach, but Christ is the Door to the Church, one might say! Salvation is, therefore, very simple! He promises Eternal Life to all who base their claim for entrance upon Him Alone.

The Good Shepherd died for the sheep; the Great Shepherd lives for the sheep (Heb. 13:20); and the Chief Shepherd comes for the sheep (I Pet. 5:4).

*a*nd when He thus had spoken, He cried with a loud voice, Lazarus, come forth. And he who was dead came forth, bound hand and foot with graveclothes: and his face was bound about with a napkin. Jesus said unto them, Loose him, and let him go (Jn. 11:43-44).

The impotent man (Jn., Chpt. 5), the blind man (Jn., Chpt. 9), and Lazarus picture Israel as morally impotent, blind, and dead. Of these three demonstrations of Christ's Deity, the last, as would be obvious, was the greatest. The sick may be healed, but there is no remedy for death.

Death convicts man as being a sinner and conducts him to judgment, for, because of sin, original sin, it is appointed unto man once to die, and after this the judgment. So Jesus waited for sin to do its utmost in Lazarus' body, and then went to manifest His Divine Glory in raising it to life.

When told of Lazarus' sickness, the Master said, *"This sickness is not unto death, but for the Glory of God, that the*

Son of God might be glorified thereby" (11:4). The Greek Text actually says, "*he shall not fall prey to death,*" which is the way it should have been translated. The Lord does not get glory out of sickness, but He most definitely does get Glory out of the sick being healed.

Now He will raise Lazarus from the dead, a miracle of astounding proportions, especially considering that Lazarus had been dead for four days. No one ever died in the Presence of Jesus, not even the two thieves.

As Jesus was on the way to the home of Lazarus, Martha went to meet Him, saying to Him, "*Lord, if You had been here, my brother had not died*" (11:21). But Jesus calmly told her, "*Your brother shall rise again.*" Martha answered by saying, "*I know that he shall rise again in the Resurrection at the last day*" (11:23-24).

Jesus probably had Martha stand before Him and He may have put His Hands on her shoulders so she would look straight at Him, even though the Bible does not clearly say this. Then He, in essence, said to her, "*Martha, you are looking at the Resurrection. I am the Resurrection, and the Life: he who believes in Me, though he were dead, yet shall he live*" (11:25).

Our Lord was telling Martha that the Resurrection is not a philosophy or even a doctrine or dogma, but rather a Person. It is the Lord Jesus Christ. He is the Resurrection, exactly as He is the Way, the Truth, and the Life (Jn. 14:6). This means that all the power of Resurrection, all the power of Life, is lodged in His Person.

Resurrection is the end of death; consequently, death has no more to do with the redeemed. It has done all it can do. It is finished. The redeemed live in the Life that put an end to it. For them, the old life and its death and judgment no longer exist.

When Jesus was on His way to the tomb, and when He stood before the tomb, five things happened:

1. *"He groaned in the Spirit and was troubled"*: He literally groaned indignation, most probably because of the malice of Satan in bringing such sorrow upon man.

2. *"Jesus wept"*: Once again, this was for the plight of the human race because of the Fall. Man was never meant to die, but sin brought death, with all of its attendant horror.

3. *"Jesus said, You take away the stone"*: It might be said that one can take away the stone, or one can throw stones. Which are you doing?

4. *"Jesus prayed"*: He didn't have to pray at this time, because He already knew the Will of the Father; however, for the people's sake, He prayed. Prayer must ever be our mainstay.

5. *"He cried with a loud voice, Lazarus, come forth"*: As someone has well said, *"There was such power in His Command, that if Jesus had not called Lazarus by name, all of the Righteous in the graves would have come forth."*

The Scripture then says:

"And he who was dead came forth, bound hand and foot with graveclothes: and his face was bound about with a napkin. Jesus said unto them, Loose him, and let him go" (11:44).

So this great Miracle portrays the fact that Jesus is the Resurrection and the Life; as such, He is also able to raise man from spiritual death, thereby giving him Eternal Life. For all who will believe, the Word is: *"Loose him and let him go."*

JULY
25

*t*hen took Mary a pound of ointment of spikenard, very costly, and anointed the feet of Jesus, and wiped His Feet with her hair: and the house was filled with the odor of the ointment (Jn. 12:3).

Before the Crucifixion, it seems that Mary, the sister of Martha and Lazarus, was the only one who actually believed that Jesus would rise from the dead. What she did that day, in taking this very costly ointment, which some believe would be worth approximately $10,000 in 2005 currency, i.e., using it to anoint the feet of Jesus, was totally misunderstood by even His closest Disciples. Man may have misjudged her, but Jesus vindicated her and understood her.

By doing what she did, she unconsciously erected to herself an eternal monument as lasting as the Gospel and linked with it. Jesus predicted the enduring remembrance of Mary's action, which Matthew recorded (Mat. 26:13). Somehow she learned the fact that on the third day He would rise again. So the spikenard she had prepared for His dead body, she now poured *"beforehand"* on His Living Body.

It was a testimony to His Resurrection, and she knew that she would have no other opportunity. She was not found at the empty sepulcher; she was too intelligent to be there. Judas objected to this anointing, claiming that it was a waste, proclaiming the fact that he had no understanding at all of Who Jesus actually was and What Jesus would actually do.

It's amazing! The news media says not one negative word about the millions of elderly people who take their meager income and purchase lottery tickets; however, they have much to say about elderly people who give to the cause of Christ! The only thing that is truly not a waste is that which is given to the Lord.

JULY
26

*h*e rose from supper, and laid aside His garments; and took a towel, and girded Himself. After that He poured water into a basin, and began to wash the Disciples' feet, and to wipe them with the towel, wherewith He was girded (Jn. 13:4-5).

The action presented here, Jesus washing His Disciples' feet, plays out to several particulars.

First of all, and concerning this, Williams says, "Nothing is more amazing than the fact of God assuming Manhood in order to serve man. Man could only be saved through the self-humiliation of Christ — 'if I wash you not,' etc. — such is sin; its cleansing demanded such a humiliation!"

Second, the feet only were washed.

Under the Mosaic Law, when the Priests went into the Holy Place, they had to wash both their hands and their feet at the Brazen Laver. To not do so could bring death.

So why didn't Jesus also wash the hands of His Disciples, along with their feet?

Under the Law, the entire episode presented a constant

"doing," hence, the necessity of the hands also being washed.

Under Christ, the *"doing"* has already been *"done,"* hence, the necessity of washing the feet only. The washing of the feet addressed our *"walk"* before the Lord. Despite the fact that we are Sanctified in Christ, which means to constantly be *"made clean,"* nevertheless, the very fact of living in this evil world pollutes, sullies, and stains, necessitating the need for constant washing.

What Christ did was only a symbolism, and not meant to be repeated, because ceremonies cannot cleanse. The Believer is constantly cleansed by placing his Faith exclusively in Christ and the Cross, thereby adhering strictly to the Word of God.

Last of all, what Jesus did presents the pattern for all Believers. The pattern is:

1. *"He laid aside His garments"*: This speaks of His Incarnation, when He laid aside the expression of His Deity, while not losing the possession of His Deity.

2. *"And took a towel"*: This represented the Service He would perform for mankind. The Believer is to never be a lord over others, but rather a servant to others, here exampled by Christ.

3. *"And girded Himself"*: When He laid aside His garments of Deity, He then *"girded Himself"* with the mantle of humanity, i.e., the Incarnation.

4. *"After that He poured water into a basin"*: This represents the Holy Spirit working through the Master, carrying out the work of obedience regarding the Father's Will.

The example for us is obvious! (Jn. 13:13-17).

JULY
27

*a*nd I will pray the Father, and He shall give you another Comforter, that He may abide with you forever; Even the
Spirit of Truth; Whom the world cannot receive, because it sees
Him not, neither knows Him: but you know Him; for He dwells
with you, and shall be in you (Jn. 14:16-17).

Jesus said more about the Holy Spirit the last week of
His Life than all the balance of His Ministry put together.
There was a reason for that. He is now about to leave His
Disciples. So now He will tell them how the Holy Spirit will
be sent back to them in a completely new dimension, a
dimension, in fact, that Believers had not heretofore known.

Before the Cross, the Holy Spirit only dwelt *"with Believers,"* only coming into hearts and lives occasionally,
and then only for a period of time to enable certain individuals to carry out the work designed for them by the
Lord. However, even among the great Prophets and Sages
of the Old Testament, still, the Spirit's Work with them
was severely restricted and limited, even though He helped

457

them to do great things on many occasions.

John the Baptist was the one who would introduce Christ, the One to Whom all the other great Prophets had pointed. So, John could be rightly said to be the greatest Prophet born of woman under the Old Covenant. But, because of the new dimension of the Holy Spirit's Work in the lives of Believers after the Cross was a Finished Work, Jesus said that the least Believer under the New Covenant was greater than John the Baptist (Lk. 7:28).

That didn't mean that modern Believers would be greater in character, etc., but rather greater in privileges, all because of what Christ has done at the Cross.

Before the Cross, animal sacrifices served as a substitute until the Substance would eventually come, Who, of course, would be Christ; however, the blood of animal sacrifices was woefully insufficient to retire the sin debt (Heb. 10:4). The sin debt, therefore, remained, which meant that the Holy Spirit was limited in what He could do.

But since the Cross, where the price was paid for sin — past, present, and future — and in every capacity, at least for all who will believe (Jn. 3:16), man, as a vessel, by evidencing Faith in Christ and what Christ did at the Cross, can be clean in every capacity, thereby a fit subject for the permanent indwelling of the Holy Spirit. Of all the great things the Cross afforded, one could probably say, without fear of contradiction, that the enabling of the Holy Spirit coming now in a new dimension is undoubtedly the greatest help of all.

Before the Law, the Holy Spirit, in a sense, accompanied the Sacrifices, at least those ordained by God. During the time of the Law, the Holy Spirit occupied the Holy

458

of Holies, actually residing, so to speak, between the Mercy Seat and the Cherubim. During the time of Christ, He resided exclusively within the Lamb of God, because He was no longer residing in the Holy of Holies in the Temple.

Some 500 years before Christ, in fact, Ezekiel saw the Holy Spirit leave the Temple in Jerusalem because of Israel's rebellion against the Lord regarding the worshipping of idols (Ezek. 11:23). But when Jesus died on the Cross, and then was resurrected and ascended to the Father, due to what He had done at the Cross, He could now send back the Holy Spirit in this glorious new dimension, which He most definitely did, Who now resides in the hearts and lives of Believers, and does so permanently, all made possible, as stated, by the Cross (I Cor. 3:16).

JULY
28

a *nd now I am no more in the world, but these are in the world, and I come to You. Holy Father, keep through Your Own Name those whom You have given Me, that they may be one, as We are* (Jn. 17:11).

Five times in this one prayer, incidentally, the longest recorded prayer of Christ, Jesus prayed for unity among Believers. Five is the number of Grace, signifying that this unity can be reached only by and through the Grace of God. But considering that He prayed five times in this one prayer for that petition to be fulfilled, we should then know and realize just how important this is for which He prayed.

The five times are found in Verses 11, 21 (two times in this one Verse), 22 and 23.

What did Jesus actually mean concerning Believers being *"one"*?

First of all, this certainly cannot be done unless Believers are properly in Christ. Jesus said, *"that they also may be one in Us"* (17:21). This is so important, being

460

properly in Christ, that Paul used this phrase (i.e., *"in Christ)* or one of its derivatives (i.e., *"in Him, in Whom,"* etc.) over one hundred times in His fourteen Epistles. So, unity is impossible without all being in Christ.

The next requirement is the critical issue. It pertains to the great Plan of God, consummated in Jesus Christ, which refers to the price that Christ paid on the Cross of Calvary. In other words, the *"unity"* here addressed must be in the Message of the Cross. Immediately after this prayer, Jesus went to the Cross. He gave to the Apostle Paul the meaning of the Cross, which, in effect, is the meaning of the New Covenant. Therefore, the *"oneness"* of which our Lord spoke must be centered up in His atoning, Substitutionary, Efficacious, and Vicarious Work on the Cross. This was Paul's Message as well!

In the First Chapter of I Corinthians, Paul warned greatly about division and then summed it up by saying, *"For Christ sent me not to baptize* (meaning that the unity is not to be found in Church ordinances), *but to preach the Gospel* (now he tells us what the Gospel actually is): *not with wisdom of words, lest the Cross of Christ should be made of none effect"* (I Cor. 1:17). There, and there alone, Christ and the Substitutionary Offering of Himself in Sacrifice, must be the sphere of unity, as it alone can be the sphere of unity.

For those who preach another Message, the Word is clear, *"Let him be accursed"* (Gal. 1:8).

JULY
29

*a*nd the Glory which You gave Me I have given them; that they may be one, even as We are One (Jn. 17:22).

It can be said, I think, that the Holy Spirit through Christ explained the Trinity in this Seventeenth Chapter of the Gospel of John as no place else in the Word of God. While there are three Personalities in the Godhead, there is but One God; Jesus here explains what He means by "One."

These three Personalities, are, above all, One in Essence, and are manifested in "God the Father," "God the Son," and "God the Holy Spirit." All three, as stated, are God, but there aren't three Gods, just One; One in Unity, One in Purpose, and One in Essence.

Jesus used the word "One" six times in this Seventeenth Chapter. The word, as He used it, was not as a number, but rather as Unity and Purpose.

Concerning Himself and the Father, He used the pronouns, "We" and "Us" (Vss. 11, 21, 22), denoting plurality.

Jesus was praying to the Father, and the Holy Spirit was helping Him pray, which denotes the Trinity.

If Jesus and the Father are One and the Same, as some teach, then Jesus was here praying to Himself, which is ridiculous! No! He was praying to His Father in Heaven, which means that He and the Father, although *"One"* in Unity, Purpose, and Essence, are two distinct Personalities. The confusion concerning the Trinity comes in because of Three manifestations being One; however, Jesus explains it perfectly in this Seventeenth Chapter. *"One"* is not referred to as a number, but rather as a description. If it is understood in that light, then problems regarding the Trinity are cleared up, becoming, in fact, easy to understand, at least as far as we poor human beings can understand such.

As well, if a person wants to know what God the Father is like, that person only has to look at the Lord Jesus Christ.

Philip said to the Lord, *"Show us the Father."* Jesus answered him by saying, *"Have I been so long with you, and yet have you not known Me, Philip?"* (Jn. 14:8-9). Jesus wasn't meaning that He was the Father, but rather that He was the same as the Father in Essence. So, if you've seen Jesus, you've seen the Father (Jn. 14:10-11).

JULY

30

*P*ilate therefore said unto Him, Are You a King then? Jesus answered, You say that I am a King. To this end was I born, and for this cause came I into the world, that I should bear witness unto the Truth. Everyone who is of the Truth hears My voice. Pilate said unto Him, What is Truth? (Jn. 18:37-38).

In the jaded world of Pilate's day, the governor had grown cynical. So he asks Christ, *"What is Truth?"* He really did not expect an answer, but the answer had already been given.

Some have claimed that *"All truth is God's truth."* They are trying to justify the foray of the Church into humanistic psychology, claiming that God gave this *"truth"* to Sigmund Freud. Nothing could be further from the truth!

In the first place, truth is not a philosophy or a culture. Truth is a Person, the Lord Jesus Christ. Of Himself, He said, *"I am the Way, the Truth, and the Life"* (Jn. 14:6). So, when one knows Christ, one know Truth; and until one knows Christ, one cannot know Truth.

464

There is what are commonly referred to as *"subjective"* and *"objective"* truth. The word *"subjective"* means that truth, at least as it is claimed, is subject to circumstances, surroundings, happenings, culture, etc. As such, it changes by the hour, because there are no absolutes in subjective truth, so-called! Therefore, such cannot honestly be called *"truth,"* even to the slightest degree.

"Objective" truth doesn't change, because truth cannot change. While the label of *"true"* might change, and does, in fact, change, *"truth,"* within itself, cannot change, because it is impossible for it to change. If it is truth, not only can it not change, it doesn't need to change.

Whatever truth was 3,000 years ago, truth is presently! That's the reason the Holy Spirit could say of our Lord, *"Jesus Christ, the same, yesterday, and today, and forever"* (Heb. 13:8). That's the reason it can be said of God the Father, *"For I am the LORD, I change not"* (Mal. 3:6).

The idea that God would give *"truth"* to unconverted men is palpably untrue. Concerning this, the Holy Spirit through Paul said, *"But the natural man receives not the things of the Spirit of God: for they are foolishness unto him: neither can he know them, because they are spiritually discerned"* (I Cor. 2:14).

JULY
31

*W*hen Jesus therefore had received the vinegar, He said,
It is finished: and He bowed His head, and gave up the ghost
(Jn. 19:30).

What was finished?

The great Plan of God, which had been formulated in
the Mind of the Godhead from before the foundation of
the world (I Pet. 1:18-20), by the death of Christ on the
Cross, was now finished. The story of Jesus Christ and
Him Crucified is, in fact, the emphasis of the entirety of
the Bible. All of eternity marched toward this one great
happening. Every act on this Earth, at least that which
was of the Lord, had, as its goal, only the Cross of Christ.
That which the First Adam had lost, the Last Adam now
purchases back with the death of Himself.

The phrase, *"He gave up the ghost,"* is, in the Greek
Text, quite another word from *"expired."* In John, the Holy
Spirit emphasizes the voluntary nature of His Death. The
special word found here is never used in this way in the

Bible, except in this Passage in reference to Christ.

Verses 33 through 35 and Verses 38 through 42 are fundamentally valuable as affirming beyond controversy the actual death of Jesus Christ. The added testimony of the Centurion (Mat., Chpt. 27) is also most valuable. For the doom to which the sinner is justly sentenced was death under the Wrath of God; if Christ did not really die and suffer that Wrath, then the Divine sentence has not been satisfied and the sinner is not released.

But thank God, the Divine sentence was satisfied; all are released from the terrible debt of sin, at least all who will believe (Jn. 3:16).

The moment that Jesus died on the Cross, the Scripture says, *"And, behold, the Veil of the Temple was rent in twain from the top to the bottom; and the Earth did quake, and the rocks rent"* (Mat. 27:51). This means that Redemption was now complete. The price had been paid, meaning the sin debt has been lifted; the way is now open to God, even to His very Throne, at least for all who put their Faith and trust in the Lord Jesus Christ and what He did for us at Calvary's Cross.

The *"finish"* of that great Plan did not await the Resurrection, even though the Resurrection was most definitely necessary, as would be overly obvious. The reason it did not await the Resurrection is simply because Jesus atoned for all sin on the Cross, past, present, and future, which guaranteed the Resurrection. If Christ had failed to atone for even one sin, then Jesus could not have been raised from the dead. The reason is simple! *"The wages of sin is death"* (Rom. 6:23). But due to the fact that all sin was atoned, the Resurrection was in no way in doubt.

It was at the Cross where the terrible sin debt was paid; at the Cross where the Righteousness of God was completely satisfied; at the Cross where a thrice-Holy God had His Holiness vindicated; at the Cross where the way to God was made completely open; at the Cross where the lost sons of Adam's fallen race could make peace with God!

It is finished!

AUGUST

1

*a*nd when she had thus said, she turned herself back, and saw Jesus standing, and knew not that it was Jesus. Jesus said unto her, Woman, why do you weep? Whom do you seek? She, supposing Him to be the gardener, said unto Him, Sir, if You have borne Him hence, tell me where You have laid Him, and I will take Him away (Jn. 20:14-15).

In the Twentieth and Twenty-first Chapters of John's Gospel, the Holy Spirit records four appearances of the Lord after He rose from the dead, and these appearances banished four great enemies of the human heart: "sorrow," "fear," "doubt," and "care."

The first appearance was to Mary Magdalene. She was overcome with sorrow, which, regrettably, characterizes the human family. The world is filled with sorrow of every stripe and description. When Jesus appeared to her, He, in answer to this problem, said, "I ascend unto My Father, and your Father; and to My God, and your God" (20:17). His Ascension to the Father portrays the fact that Calvary is

469

a Finished Work; in the Cross, all sorrow ultimately will be banished.

The second appearance recorded by John banished all *"fear."* On that Sunday evening, the *"Disciples were assembled for fear of the Jews,"* meaning they were in seclusion somewhere in Jerusalem, fearing that they, too, would be killed. But, all of a sudden *"came Jesus and stood in the midst, and said unto them, Peace be unto you"* (Jn. 20:19).

Peace cannot be had where there is fear; when true peace comes, and it can only come in Christ, fear is banished. There is now a sense of knowing that everything is going to be all right. Once again, the Cross is brought into view, with Jesus *"showing unto them His Hands and His Side,"* i.e., *"the nail prints and the wound in His Side."*

The only people in the world who truly have conquered fear are those who have placed their Faith and trust exclusively in Christ and what Christ has done at the Cross. The Holy Spirit then will guarantee the Peace of God.

The third great life problem that was conquered here is *"doubt,"* which took place with the third appearance recorded by John.

When Jesus appeared to the Disciples of the second account, Thomas was not present. When Thomas was told by the other Disciples that Jesus had appeared unto them, he expressed doubt, even great doubt. But after some eight days, the Disciples were again gathered and Thomas was with them. The Scripture says that Jesus suddenly appeared again, which was the third appearance, and stood in their midst. Again He said, *"Peace be unto you."*

Even as He had done so with the others, He takes Thomas to the Cross. The Lord tells Thomas to *"reach hither your finger, and behold My Hands; and reach hither your hand, and thrust it into My Side: and be not faithless, but believing"* (20:27). Thomas then gave the greatest exclamation and confession of our Lord to date. He said, *"My Lord and my God."*

The appearance of Christ and the sign of the Cross, which pertained to the wounds of the Master, which, incidentally, He will ever bear, addressed the great problem of *"doubt."* This means there is no excuse for anyone ever to doubt the veracity of Christ.

The last appearance recorded by John addressed the problem of *"care."* The other three appearances had been in Jerusalem. This appearance would be in Galilee. Some of the Disciples had gone fishing. This was not recreation, not at all! Inasmuch as Jesus had been crucified, and even though He had risen from the dead, they did not know how they could care financially for their families. So these particular seven Disciples resorted to the only way they knew to make a living, which was fishing. To be sure, this problem of *"care,"* i.e., how they would care for their families, loomed large in their minds.

Even though they fished all night, the Scripture says, *"They caught nothing."*

All of a sudden, they heard a Voice from the shore saying, *"Children, have you any meat?"*

This was more than a call for breakfast; it was a question that really addressed itself to their livelihood — in other words, *"Do you know how you will care for your families?"* They answered him, *"No!"* Then He told them to *"cast the net on the right side of the ship, and you shall find."* This they did. They instantly caught so many fish that they

471

could not draw the net back up into the ship. So, they had to drag it to shore, which was close.

Somewhere in that procedure, they recognized that He was the Lord.

Jesus then said unto them, *"Come and dine"* (21:12).

In essence, this stated that the problem of *"care"* was handled. He would not tell them to *"come and dine"* to an empty table. He was telling them that, as He had provided this miraculous catch, likewise, He would provide for them. And so He did! And so He does!

These four appearances recorded by John addressed the four life problems of *"sorrow," "fear," "doubt,"* and *"care."* Consequently, there is no reason for any Believer to succumb to any one of these maladies. Jesus has already addressed and handled the situation.

472

AUGUST

2

*S*o *when they had dined, Jesus said to Simon Peter, Simon, son of Jonas, do you love Me more than these? He said unto Him, Yes, Lord; You know that I love You. He said unto him, Feed My lambs* (Jn. 21:15).

The Lord will now wound Peter's heart in order to train and fit him for the high position of shepherding that which was most precious to Christ, the sheep. The questions posed by Christ concerning Peter's consecration will also address the past. There is no hint of condemnation.

The first question was, *"Peter, do you love Me more than these other men love Me, even as you did declare?"* (Mk. 14:29). In the Greek, the word used by Christ was *"agape,"* which means *"the God-kind of love."* In other words, He was asking Peter about the depth of his love.

When Peter answered, *"I have an affection for You,"* he used the Greek word for love, *"phileo,"* which is a lesser kind of love than the word used by Jesus, and which actually means *"affection."* However, the answer Peter gave was the answer he should have given. After the recent past, he no longer desired to boast of his love. Now he was even afraid to exclaim that he truly loved the Lord. How could he?

However, the position he now takes fits him, as nothing else would, for the God-kind of love!

The second question posed by Christ omitted the words, *"more than these,"* i.e., *"Do you love Me at all?"* Peter answered, *"I have an affection for You."*

The third question posed by Christ employed Peter's feebler term; it actually asks, *"Do you have even as much as an affection for Me?"* The Lord's use of this word plus His putting the question three times (in the evident remembrance of Peter's three denials) probed Peter's heart to the very depths.

Peter cried out with anguish, *"Lord, You know all things, You know that I have an affection for You."* He was still too heartbroken and miserable to use the stronger term, which again was what he should have felt and done.

The first time in this series of three questions posed by Christ, the Lord said, *"Feed My lambs."* The last two times, He said, *"Feed My sheep."* In essence, He was telling the Apostle that his true usefulness had not ended, but, in fact, had only begun. He would truly feed the sheep. And so he did, even unto the day of his death.

What is the moral of all this? To show us that we are never as strong as we think we are; and whatever it is the Lord wants us to be, He Alone can make of us!

AUGUST
3

*a*nd being assembled together with them, commanded them that they should not depart from Jerusalem, but wait for the Promise of the Father, which, said He, you have heard of Me. For John truly baptized with water; but you shall be baptized with the Holy Spirit not many days hence (Acts 1:4-5).

First of all, we must understand that the first eight Verses of the First Chapter of Acts proclaim the last recorded words of Christ before His Ascension. As all know, the last words of anyone, especially those of Christ, are of immense significance. Christ could have dealt with any subject He so desired, but we are led to believe that the subject He dealt with, the Baptism with the Holy Spirit, was, and is, the most important.

In essence, He was saying to His Disciples and all His followers, "Do not go try to establish Churches, do not attempt to go witness, do not attempt to do anything for Me, until you are first 'baptized with the Holy Spirit.'" As should be obvious, this tells us how utterly significant the Holy Spirit is

475

to our life, living, and work for the Lord, irrespective as to the person.

In fact, the *"Promise of the Father"* (Isa. 28:11; Joel 2:28-29), i.e., the Baptism with the Holy Spirit, is absolutely imperative, that is, if the person is to be spiritually effective. Whatever is done for the Lord must be conceived by the Spirit, birthed by the Spirit, and carried out by the Spirit. We Believers are merely channels through which the Holy Spirit works.

Even though Jesus' Disciples personally had been with Him for some three and a half years, which means they were privileged to have the greatest teaching that any human beings had ever heard, still, our Lord emphatically tells them, and, in fact, all His followers, that they must be Baptized with the Holy Spirit. This tells us how important this great *"Baptism"* actually is!

Someone has well said, *"The Moving of the Spirit is the beginning of life"* (Gen. 1:2). Without the Moving of the Spirit, there is no life!

AUGUST

4

*A*nd when the Day of Pentecost was fully come, they were all with one accord in one place. And suddenly there came a sound from Heaven as of a rushing mighty wind, and it filled all the house where they were sitting. And there appeared unto them cloven tongues like as a fire, and it sat upon each of them. And they were all filled with the Holy Spirit, and began to speak with other tongues, as the Spirit gave them utterance (Acts 2:1-4).

The word *"Pentecost"* in the Hebrew means *"fifty"* or *"fiftieth."* It refers to fifty days after the Passover. The *"Day of Pentecost"* was one of the great Feast Days of the Jews. It occurred probably in late May.

It was on this *"Day"* that the Holy Spirit came to this world in a completely new dimension, all made possible by the Cross. Incidentally, the scene of this outpouring, as described in this Chapter, took place in the Temple, probably in the Court of the Gentiles. It took place fairly early in the morning.

477

The great characteristic of this outpouring was that, for all who were there that day, possibly 120 or more, when they were *"filled with the Holy Spirit,"* they all *"began to speak with other tongues, as the Spirit gave them utterance."* In fact, the Bible teaches that speaking with other tongues is the initial, physical evidence that one has been baptized with the Holy Spirit. There is no infilling without this particular sign. The Prophet Isaiah, in fact, some 750 years prior, had predicted this phenomenon, and was quoted by Paul (Isa. 28:11; I Cor. 14:21).

There are five accounts of outpourings of the Holy Spirit in the Book of Acts. Three of those accounts emphatically state that the recipients spoke with tongues (Acts 2:4; 10:26; 19:1-7). The other two occasions give no details, just saying, *"They received the Holy Spirit"* (8:17; 9:17). This doesn't mean they didn't speak in tongues, only that it is not mentioned. In fact, there is evidence they did.

Regarding the revival in Samaria, when Peter and John laid hands on these individuals that they might *"receive the Holy Spirit,"* Simon the Sorcerer saw this taking place and offered the Apostles money that he also may have power to do such. Peter answered him forthwith, *"Your money perish with you . . . You have neither part nor lot in this matter"* (8:20-21). The word *"matter"* in the Greek is *"logos,"* which should have been translated *"utterance, talk, word."* This strongly implies that they spoke with other tongues.

When Ananias prayed for Paul to *"be filled with the Holy Spirit,"* the Scripture doesn't tell us what happened. But Paul, concerning himself, said, *"I thank my God, I speak with Tongues more than you all*" (I Cor. 14:18). So, the Biblical evidence is replete that all Believers will, without exception, speak with other tongues upon being baptized with the Holy Spirit.

Tongues are not incoherent babble or chatter, but rather a language known and spoken somewhere in the world, but not by the speaker who has been baptized with the Spirit. A perfect example of this is found on the Day of Pentecost. When the Jews were filled with the Spirit, there were other Jews in the Temple, many hundreds, no doubt, who were from all parts of the Roman Empire, and who also spoke the language of their respective area. They heard these "*Galilaeans*" speak their languages (Acts 2:7-13).

Some foolish souls have maliciously stated that speaking with other tongues is of the Devil. Of course, the statement is false, to say the least. But, for the sake of argument, we will say the following: If it is of the Devil, then it's the only thing the Devil has which makes people love the Lord supremely, love His Word supremely, and desire the things of God supremely!

Furthermore, when Peter began to minister on the Day of Pentecost, he didn't say, "*This fulfills that spoken by the Prophet Joel*," but rather, "*This is that which was spoken. . . .*" *This* means it began on the Day of Pentecost, and it continues unto this hour.

<u>AUGUST</u>
5

i thank my God, I speak with Tongues more than ye all (I Cor. 14:18).

Regarding speaking in tongues, many have asked the question, *"What good does it do?"* Perhaps the following will be of some help:

1. It is the Holy Spirit Who said that speaking with tongues would be a part of the Believer's experience. He said it some 750 years before the fact (Isa. 28:11).

2. Paul said, *"Wherefore Tongues are for a sign, not to them who believe, but to them who believe not"* (I Cor. 14:22). This means that speaking with other tongues is a sign to the entire world, and we speak of unbelievers, that we are coming down to the end. Jesus is about ready to come.

3. When one speaks in tongues, one is speaking unto God (I Cor. 14:2). To be sure, anything that one speaks to God, especially when controlled by the Holy Spirit, cannot be anything but beneficial.

480

4. Paul also said, *"Howbeit in the Spirit he speaks mysteries"* (I Cor. 14:2). The word *"mysteries"* actually means that the person speaks *"secrets"* unto God.

5. Luke wrote, *"We do hear them speak in our tongues the wonderful Works of God"* (Acts 2:11). So, when a person speaks in tongues, he is not only declaring secrets to the Lord, but also *"the wonderful Works of God"* (Acts 2:1-13).

6. Paul said, *"He who speaks in an unknown tongue edifies himself"* (I Cor. 14:4). Every Believer needs edification.

7. Tongues and interpretation are used to give Messages from the Lord to the people. Anything from the Lord is of great blessing (I Cor. 14:13).

8. Jude said, *"But you, Beloved, building up yourselves on your most Holy Faith, praying in the Holy Spirit"* (Jude, Vs. 20). This tells us that speaking with other tongues builds up the Believer regarding *"Faith."*

9. Isaiah, in predicting the coming time when Believers would be baptized with the Holy Spirit, with, we might quickly add, the evidence of speaking with other tongues (Isa. 28:11), also stated, *"This is the rest wherewith you may cause the weary to rest"* (Isa. 28:12). As one goes through life, one periodically needs *"rest."* Speaking with other tongues helps provide that *"rest."* The Bible says so!

10. In the same Verse, Isaiah also said, *"And this is the refreshing."* So, not only is *"rest"* provided, but speaking with other tongues rejuvenates the Believer also. It is sad that the modern Church has, by and large, opted for humanistic psychology, which holds no answers whatsoever (Isa. 28:11-12).

11. Concerning the episode involving Simon Peter and Cornelius, Luke wrote, *"For they heard them speak*

with tongues, and magnify God" (Acts 10:46). We are plainly told here that speaking with other tongues magnifies God. Anything that does this is beneficial, as should be readily understood.

12. Concerning the Day of Pentecost, Luke also wrote, *"And they were all filled with the Holy Spirit, and began to speak with other tongues, as the Spirit gave them utterance"* (Acts 2:4). Anything which the Holy Spirit originates is profitable.

13. Speaking with other tongues is the fulfillment of Bible Prophecy. Peter said so, quoting the Prophet Joel (Acts 2:16-18).

14. Concerning praying in tongues, Paul said, *"For if I pray in an unknown Tongue, my spirit prays"* (I Cor. 14:14). One's spirit praying is the highest form of prayer and of worship, that which every Believer ought to desire.

I think the Biblical account is replete, not only with the veracity of tongues, but also of its advantages and profitableness.

AUGUST

6

*i*nsomuch that they brought forth the sick into the streets, and laid them on beds and couches, that at the least the shadow of Peter passing by might overshadow some of them. There came also a multitude out of the cities round about unto Jerusalem, bringing sick folks, and them which were vexed with unclean spirits: and they were healed every one (Acts 5:15-16).

This must have been a sight to behold: scores of people so sick that they had to lie on beds and couches, lined up on the streets, along with other ill people who were able to stand, all hoping that Peter would pass their way. Even as he walked by them, his shadow touching them caused *"every one of them to be healed."* Without a doubt, this entire episode constituted a miracle of unprecedented proportions.

When we consider that Simon Peter was denying his Master just a few weeks earlier, but now he is being used by God in such a spectacular way, we have to ask ourselves the question, *"How could it be?"*

First of all, when the Lord forgives someone, they are

483

forgiven totally, completely, and absolutely. We must understand that there is no such thing as a 50 percent Justification, etc. One is either fully justified or not at all justified.

The modern Church has a problem with this. Before good graces can be gained again, if, in fact, they ever are gained, punishment has to be invoked. This is because the modern Church little understands the Cross, if at all. Much of the Protestant world, in fact, adopts the same direction as the Catholic Church, i.e., demanding *"Penance"* of some sort. Such a position, of course, completely abrogates the Finished Work of Christ.

The Lord has nothing for sale. Everything He has is a *"Gift"* (Rom. 6:23). But it is hard for the modern Church to accept that. Irrespective of the modern Church, Simon Peter was mightily used of the Lord as it regards the establishment of the Early Church.

The type of miracles mentioned here and the way they were carried out did not continue, even though sporadic Moves of God in this capacity did continue, continuing, in fact, unto this hour. The degree of miracle working power specified here was carried out by the Holy Spirit in order to establish the Early Church on a sound footing, which it very much helped to do.

From the pattern of the Early Church laid down in the Book of Acts, we learn what Church is to be like. The earmarks were laid down nearly twenty centuries ago by the Holy Spirit. If the modern Church doesn't carry those earmarks, then what is now referred to as *"Church"* is not referred to as such by the Lord at all! This means that every Church must be compared somewhat with the Early Church, that is, if it cares about following the pattern laid down by the Holy Spirit.

AUGUST

7

*t*hen Peter and the other Apostles answered and said, We ought to obey God rather than men. The God of our fathers raised up Jesus, Whom you killed and hanged on a tree. Him has God exalted with His Right Hand to be a Prince and a Saviour, for to give repentance to Israel, and forgiveness of sins (Acts 5:29-31).

From reading the Text, it becomes overly obvious that Simon Peter subscribed not at all to the modern method espoused by the Church of embracing all things and saying nothing negative about anything. So, we can follow the modern method, which is totally unscriptural, or we can follow the Bible. We cannot follow both!

Peter's use of the titles, *"a Prince"* and *"a Saviour to Israel,"* expresses Royalty and Atonement. Not only is the Lord Jesus the Medium of forgiveness and life, but He is the Dispenser of both. He gives, not sells, Repentance and Forgiveness. Forgiveness of sins means release from the eternal punishment of sins, and Repentance expresses

485

and involves a moral revulsion against sin and a determined breach with it. Repentance is a Divine Gift, as Forgiveness is a Divine Gift.

However, God cannot forgive sins of those who will not seek such or do not believe such. True Repentance is when we say of ourselves what God says of us. We must admit the full bore of our spiritual condition, which is negative, to say the least. This is the reason it so hard to get people to repent. They do not want to admit what they have done, which, in essence, says what they are. Sinners are not condemned so much for what they do as for what they are. True Bible Repentance goes to the heart of the problem, which alone can bring about forgiveness of sin (I Jn. 1:9).

For such to be, Holy Spirit conviction must be the order of the event. However, Holy Spirit conviction comes only by a proper Ministry of the Word. Regrettably, the Holy Spirit is sorely lacking in much of the modern Church. That being the case, there is little True Repentance and little resultant forgiveness of sins.

The True Gospel of Jesus Christ either makes men mad or glad; it seldom, if ever, leaves them neutral!

AUGUST
8

*a*nd he trembling and astonished said, Lord, what will You have me to do? And the Lord said unto him, Arise, and go into the city, and it shall be told you what you must do (Acts 9:6).

The conversion of Saul of Tarsus was, without a doubt, one of the greatest conversions in the annals of human history. There is a good possibility that Stephen's words and behavior had a great effect on him. He watched Stephen being stoned as he called upon God, saying, *"Lord Jesus, receive my spirit."* Saul was also watching as the martyr knelt down and cried with a loud voice, *"Lord, lay not this sin to their charge"* (Acts 7:59-60).

This is where conviction on Saul by the Holy Spirit began.

However, Saul reacted to that conviction, even as many do, by exhibiting more hatred against the followers of Christ. *"He made havoc of the Church, entering into every house, and haling men and women committed them to prison"* (Acts 8:3). His anger became so pronounced that the Holy

487

Spirit recorded him as *"breathing out threatenings and slaughter against the Disciples of the Lord"* (Acts 9:1).

It was with this frame of mind, fighting conviction by being ever more oppressive, that Saul went to Damascus in order to extend his violent reach. But something happened that would change his life forever, something so dramatic that he oftentimes was compelled to relate the experience.

As he came near Damascus, the Scripture says, *"Suddenly there shined round about him a light from Heaven"* (Acts 9:3). He then heard a voice and he also saw the Lord (Acts 9:17). One glimpse of Jesus undid all his arguments, discomfiting him in every capacity. Zealous as he was for the Law, yet found he that he was fighting against God and destroying his people.

The Scripture says, *"And he trembling and astonished said, Lord, what will You have me to do?"* (Acts 9:6). At that moment, Saul of Tarsus gave his heart and life to Jesus Christ. It is amazing that when he asked, *"Who are You, Lord?"* the Lord answered him by using the name that Paul hated the most, *"Jesus"* (Acts 9:5).

Ironically enough, it was to this man that the Lord would give the meaning of the New Covenant, which was, and is, the meaning of the Cross. He would be the Masterbuilder of the Church (I Cor. 3:10). The Lord would show Paul the victory of the Cross, not only as it refers to the Salvation of the soul, but also to the Sanctification of the Saint (Rom., Chpt. 6).

Some have asked the question, *"What is the origin of Western Civilization?"* If you know your Bible, the answer is simple. The little Jew from Tarsus is more responsible for Western Civilization than any man who has ever lived. It was his Gospel that pushed west, touching most of Europe, finally going to England, and then ultimately to the United States and elsewhere in the world. Paul is responsible for that which we refer to as *"Western Civilization."*

This Civilization, the envy of the world, enjoying the greatest prosperity and the greatest freedoms of all, can trace its origin to the Jew from Tarsus, i.e., *"the Gospel of the Lord Jesus Christ."*

AUGUST
9

Who shall tell you words, whereby you and all your house shall be saved (Acts 11:14).

The conversion of the Gentile, Cornelius, and his household opened up the Gospel to the Gentile world, all according to the Grace of the Cross. However, on a personal basis, the story of Cornelius affords us a great look into the Gospel and its reception. The Scriptures say many wonderful things about Cornelius; but yet, despite those wonderful things, he was still unsaved. The Scripture says this about him:

1. He was *"a devout man"*: This means he was a moral man.

2. *"He feared God with all his house"*: Despite the fact of being a Gentile, he recognized there was a God, and feared Him greatly.

3. *"He gave much alms to the people"*: He was generous with his money, helping the poor, etc.

4. *"He prayed to God always"*: While wondrously

commendable, still, Cornelius wasn't saved.

5. *"He had a Vision which definitely was from the Lord"*: What a wonderful experience, but yet, still, he wasn't saved.

6. In the Vision, he saw *"an Angel of God"*: This presented an experience of unprecedented proportions, but still he was unsaved.

7. The Angel told him that his *"prayers and alms had come up for a memorial before God"*: This means the Lord had noted everything that Cornelius had done and was doing, and was extremely favorable toward this Gentile. But yet, Cornelius was unsaved.

To be sure, most all the world, even a great segment of the modern Church, would automatically conclude this man to be saved. But despite all these wonderful things happening to him, and despite his efforts at morality, he still was unsaved.

Why didn't those things save him?

Salvation only comes one way, and that is by and through the Message of the Lord Jesus Christ, and what He has done for us at the Cross, and our Faith in that Finished Work.

Peter said, *"Neither is there Salvation in any other: for there is none other Name under Heaven given among men, whereby we must be saved"* (Acts 4:12).

To the inquiry of the Philippian jailer, Paul said, *"Believe on the Lord Jesus Christ, and you shall be saved, and your house"* (Acts 16:31).

Peter, and those who were with him, came to the house of Cornelius and began to minister to those who were gathered; when he came to the place in his message where he said, *"To Him* (Jesus) *give all the Prophets witness, that through His Name whosoever believes in Him shall receive remission of sins,"* evidently Cornelius and those in the house instantly believed, because *"the Holy Spirit fell on all them which heard the Word"* (Acts 10:43-44).

All of this simply means that there is no way that one can be saved except by accepting Jesus Christ as one's Saviour and Lord (Jn. 3:16). It must ever be understood that it is Jesus Christ Who died on the Cross, thereby paying the price for man's sins, thereby satisfying the demands of a thrice-Holy God. No other did that, only Jesus; consequently, it is in Him that one must believe, or else one cannot be saved, whether they are Jew or Gentile (Jn. 3:16).

What we have just stated, the world does not like! As Cain, they desire to effect their own Salvation; then they demand that God accept it. He won't! It is Christ, Christ Alone, Who is the Way, the Truth, and the Life (Jn. 14:6).

AUGUST

10

*t*hen Peter said, Silver and gold have I none; but such as I have give I thee: In the Name of Jesus Christ of Nazareth rise up and walk (Acts 3:6).

This lame man of our Text had no doubt heard of Jesus. There is no way that he could not have heard of Jesus of Nazareth. Knowing that Christ could heal any disease, he longed for Jesus to pass his way; however, it never happened! Then he heard that Jesus had been crucified. With that, his hopes were dashed to the ground. He would never be healed!

One can imagine the sorrow and the heartache of not being one of the thousands who had been healed by Christ, and now Christ was gone!

When the lame man arose that day, it would be a day like any other: humiliation, shame, a burden on his loved ones, reduced to begging, that was his lot in life. Being lame from his mother's womb, he had to be carried everywhere he went, as on all other days. As usual, they would lay him daily *"at the gate of the Temple which is called Beautiful, to ask alms of them who entered into the Temple"* (Acts 3:2).

This day had begun like all others. Why should it be any different?

No doubt, he had been deposited there early that morning. Now the day is moving along. A few shekels are handed to him. It is drawing close to 3 o'clock in the afternoon. Little would he know when 3 o'clock would come and go. Beside that, what did it matter?

He did not realize it, but this particular time was going to become the greatest moment in his life! At 3 p.m., *"Peter and John went up together into the Temple at the hour of prayer"* (Acts 3:1). As Peter and John started to go through the Gate Beautiful, the lame man *"asked an alms."* This was not unusual, because he asked alms of all who came through that Gate.

He never really looked up. His despondency caused him to cast his eyes downward. About all he ever saw was the feet of men and women.

As Peter and John drew abreast of him, mechanically he requested their help. But then he hears one of the men say something to him. Both men are looking at him, and they say, *"Look on us."*

He then looks up, *"expecting to receive something of them."* But Peter said to him, *"Silver and gold have I none; but such as I have give I thee: In the Name of Jesus Christ of Nazareth rise up and walk"* (Acts 3:4-6).

The man heard two things:

First of all, they had no money. His hopes must have fallen when he heard that. But then he heard something else. He heard the Name *"Jesus Christ of Nazareth."*

What did they mean by that? Why were they using His Name, when He had been crucified? But, upon hearing that Name, he was immediately quickened, because he linked that Name with healing.

Peter reaches out his hand, motioning for the lame man to join hands with him. When he did, Peter *"lifted him up."* The moment he did, the Scripture says, *"immediately his feet and ankle bones received strength."* But he did not stop there; *"leaping up he stood, and walked, and entered with them into the Temple, walking and leaping, and praising God"* (Acts 3:7-8). No wonder!

Three o'clock in the afternoon would forever have a special place in this man's heart. At that moment, he had met Jesus Christ, even though Jesus actually wasn't there. Still, he knew he could not have been healed but that Jesus Christ, present or not, had effected it!

What must the people have thought who brought him to his place of alms-begging each day and who picked him up each night? When they came that night, they undoubtedly went to the same place where they had laid him down early that morning, but he was not there. They were surely puzzled. Where could he have gone? He couldn't walk, so who would bother to take him?

Then they must have seen the commotion. What was going on?

They pushed their way through the crowd, and then they see him.

How could it be? He is not only walking, but he is *"leaping and praising God."*

The man they brought that morning, who they no

doubt had brought many mornings, would not be the same man who would go home with them that night.

How many, down through the centuries, were spiritually lame, despondent, and disconcerted, but then they met Jesus? And they also would never be the same again.

Let the following ever be understood:

This same Jesus is just as alive presently as He was then. He is still healing the spiritually lame!

AUGUST
11

*a*nd saw Heaven opened, and a certain vessel descending unto him, as it had been a great sheet knit at the four corners, and let down to the Earth: Wherein were all manner of fourfooted beasts of the Earth, and wild beasts, and creeping things, and fowls of the air. And there came a Voice to him, Rise, Peter; kill, and eat (Acts 10:11-13).

This great Vision shown to Simon Peter was one of the greatest in human history. All of the different animals represented in the Vision, almost all of them unclean, as represented by the words, *"all manner,"* proclaims the fact that the Gospel of Jesus Christ, afforded by the Cross, was meant to go to all nations of the world. In other words, when Jesus died on the Cross, He died not only for the Jewish people, but actually for the entirety of mankind (Jn. 3:16).

There was to be *"one fold,"* and only one fold. Jesus said, *"And other sheep I have, which are not of this fold* (meaning the Gentiles): *them* (the other nations of the world, the

497

Gentiles) *also I must bring, and they shall hear My voice* (the Church); *and there shall be one fold, and one Shepherd"* (that One Shepherd is the Lord Jesus Christ [Jn. 10:16]).

This great lesson was hard for Peter and the Twelve to learn. But Christ is *"Lord of all"* and the Gospel is for *"whosoever will"* (Acts 10:43).

Peter had proclaimed the election of the Gentiles to Salvation in Acts 2:21, 39, but he was, as we are, so dull and prejudiced that this Vision had to be given to him three times to make him realize the fact (Acts 10:16). As stated, the meaning of all this, as would be obvious, is significant beyond comprehension, because it pertains to the Salvation of the entirety of humanity, at least all who will believe, as afforded by the Cross. The great concept is: *"Whosoever will . . ."* (Rev. 22:17).

Cornelius and his household were the first to come in under the new order. But thank God this great Vision also included you and me! To know that you and I were in this Vision humbles us, or at least it certainly should!

"Come ye sinners, lost and hopeless,
"Jesus' Blood can make you clean,
"For He saved the worst among you,
"When He saved a wretch like me!"
(Gen. 12:3).

AUGUST
12

*a*nd when he had apprehended him, he put him in prison, and delivered him to four quaternions of soldiers to keep him; intending after Easter to bring him forth to the people. And when Herod would have brought him forth, the same night Peter was sleeping between two soldiers, bound with two chains: and the keepers before the door kept the prison (Acts 12:4, 6).

James, the brother of John, had just been killed by the sword, and now Herod would do Peter the same way. So Peter is arrested.

The Romans divided the night into four watches; so sixteen soldiers were appointed to guard Peter — four soldiers for each watch — one at each gate and two chained to the prisoner. These four soldiers were relieved at the end of their respective watches. Peter's release by the Angel must have taken place during the last watch, between 3 a.m. and 6 a.m. Herod intended to execute Peter exactly as he had James.

Evidently, the night in question was immediately

before Peter was to be executed the next morning (Acts 12:6). The Scripture says, *"Peter was sleeping between two soldiers, bound with two chains."*

Could you sleep, knowing that your execution was scheduled for the next morning?

Peter was human like the rest of us, so how could he sleep so soundly on this occasion? The following answers the question.

Just before the Ascension, Jesus had told Peter that he would grow *"old"* (Jn. 21:18). At the time of his arrest, Peter was probably about 25 or 30 years old, at the most. At any rate, he was not *"old."* He knew that Jesus had said that he would grow *"old"*; knowing that fact had not yet been fulfilled, he knew that the Lord would somehow deliver him from this situation. So he slept soundly!

I seriously doubt, however, that Peter realized that his deliverance would be as dramatic as it actually came to be.

Sometime that night, actually not long before daylight, *"the Angel of the Lord came upon him, and a light shined in the prison: and he smote Peter on the side, and raised him up, saying, Arise up quickly. And his chains fell off from his hands"* (Acts 12:7). Evidently, the guards were asleep, and felt and saw nothing.

The Angel took him out of the cell; the door opened, and a guard was standing there, who also saw nothing. When they came to the *"iron gate,"* which was the main gate to the prison, it also opened, even though a guard was standing there, who, again, saw nothing.

When daylight came, Peter was gone, and the soldiers had no explanation. How in the world could this man have escaped them, considering that he was chained to two soldiers? Murderous Herod condemned the soldiers to death, even though they were totally bereft of all knowledge of the situation.

From this, we learn just how true the Lord is to His Word.

The question, *"Why didn't the Lord deliver James as He delivered Peter?"* also looms large. The Holy Spirit gave us no answer for this question. James, in fact, was the first of the original Twelve to die, not counting Judas, who committed suicide. We do know that the Lord easily could have delivered James. But for His Own Personal reasons, He chose not to do so.

This tells us that some Believers, through no fault of their own, are taken early in life; we must understand, however, that, in everything the Lord does, it is always for the good of all concerned.

AUGUST
13

n ow there were in the Church that was at Antioch certain Prophets and Teachers; as Barnabas, and Simeon who was called Niger; and Lucius of Cyrene, and Manaen, which had been brought up with Herod the Tetrarch, and Saul. As they ministered to the Lord, and fasted, the Holy Spirit said, Separate Me Barnabas and Saul (Paul) *for the work whereunto I have called them* (Acts 13:1-2).

Very few recognize the significance of the facts stated in the first four Verses of this Thirteenth Chapter of Acts. This occasion takes place several years, possibly as many as nine, after the conversion of Paul. Even though the Church began, in a sense, with the conversion of Cornelius and his household, all Gentiles, its systemized order began with the sending forth of Paul.

During these intervening years, i.e., from the time Paul was converted until now, the Lord had given him the meaning of the New Covenant, which was, in effect, the meaning of the Cross. Paul gave that to us in his fourteen

502

Epistles. He was called by the Lord to be the Masterbuilder of the Church, which could not be until this great Revelation was given to him (Gal. 1:12).

The Holy Spirit, in this account of the missionary journey, refers to both Paul and Barnabas as Apostles (Acts 14:4, 14).

As it obvious, Paul and Barnabas were not of the original Twelve. The Holy Spirit names as Apostles over twenty individuals in the New Testament. *"Apostle"* is one of the fivefold Ministry callings, and is, in fact, apropos even unto this hour (Eph. 4:11).

Apostles are not elected by popular ballot, neither are they appointed by men. The Office of the Apostle is a Call of God. An Apostle is recognized by the significance of the Message which He proclaims. In other words, the Holy Spirit will place a special and powerful emphasis on a particular Message, which will always be exactly according to the Word of God. With Paul, one might say that he was the Apostle of Grace, or the Apostle of the Cross. That was his emphasis.

Others may have the same emphasis, even as did Barnabas, etc.

Under the Headship of Christ and the Leadership of the Holy Spirit, Apostles set the course for the Church. This is what the Holy Spirit intends. In the Old Testament times, there were no Apostles, because there was no Church. Prophets served in the capacity of leadership for Israel of old.

This great missionary journey, actually the first, was also the beginning of what we refer to as *"Western Civilization."* Through Paul, the Gospel would go west, because the Holy Spirit knew that the reception would be greater in that direction. When you read the account of this first Missionary effort, as recorded in the Thirteenth and Fourteenth Chapters of Acts, you should also read your Salvation into these two Chapters, because the Gospel that Paul and Barnabas gave to the Gentile world ultimately came to you and me.

From this account, we learn that the Holy Spirit, a Person Who *"speaks"* and *"sends,"* was the Director of all proceedings. He was the Source of their Apostolate; He energized them.

Incidentally, the First Miracle recorded on this First Missionary journey was the making blind of one Elymas the Sorcerer, who withstood Paul and Barnabas, *"seeking to turn away the deputy from the faith"* (Acts 13:7-12). Remarkably, this was also the moment chosen by the Holy Spirit to introduce the change of Paul's name from the Hebrew *"Saul"* to the Greek *"Paul."* This tells us that all who reject the Message of Grace, as proclaimed by Paul, which is, in effect, the Message of the Cross, will become spiritually blind!

AUGUST
14

*a*nd certain men which came down from Judaea taught the brethren, and said, Except you be circumcised after the manner of Moses, you cannot be saved. When therefore Paul and Barnabas had no small dissension and disputation with them, they determined that Paul and Barnabas, and certain other of them, should go up to Jerusalem unto the Apostles and Elders about this question (Acts 15:1-2).

Here we find the beginning of the problem with the Judaizers, a problem which would plague Paul throughout his ministry. The Judaizers were Jews, almost all from Jerusalem and Judaea, who had accepted Christ as the Messiah, but who insisted, at the same time, that all Believers, even Gentiles, must also keep the Law. This was Satan's great effort to dilute and ultimately destroy the Gospel. Satan would do this, as he does most of his insidious work, from inside the Church!

Paul had been given the Revelation that the Lord Jesus had fulfilled the Law in every respect. Consequently, for

Believers to attempt to continue to keep the Law, this said, in effect, that what Jesus did at the Cross was insufficient, which, as should be obvious, was an insult of the highest order to the Lord of Glory. However, this problem did not die with the Early Church. It continues unto this hour. It has been the greatest problem that plagues the Church.

Today it's not the Law of Moses which is in question, but laws of one variety or the other made up by religious men. It probably could be said that every single one of us at some time has formulated some laws in our hearts and minds, which, within themselves, may have been valid, but faith and trust placed in those laws, whatever they may have been or may be, will bring no victory.

Every unsaved person in the world is under the Government of Law, whether they realize it or not (Ex., Chpt. 20). I'm speaking of the Law of God, to which they will answer at the Great White Throne Judgment (Rev. 20:11-15), that is, if they do not accept Christ as their Saviour. When the person comes to Christ, we then come from the Government of Law to the Government of Grace (Rom. 6:14).

Unfortunately, most Christians do not understand the Government of Grace as they should, because they do not understand the Cross. It is, in fact, impossible to properly understand Grace if one does not properly understand the Cross. As such, most Christians are trying to live for God under two Governments at the same time, the Government of Law and the Government of Grace. Such is a miserable existence, which Paul himself tried to do for a period of time, because he understood, at that time, neither the Cross nor the Government of Grace.

We find Paul's account of this period in his life in the

Seventh Chapter of Romans, which is also the account, unfortunately, of most modern Christians. According to the instructions given to us by the Apostle, who received them directly by Revelation from the Lord Jesus Christ (Gal. 1:12), the Believer lives under the Government of Grace by understanding that everything we have from the Lord comes to us through the means of the Cross; the Cross of Christ, therefore, is ever to be the Object of our Faith, which then gives the Holy Spirit latitude to work within our lives (Rom. 6:1-4; 8:1-2,11).

That being done on a constant basis, the Holy Spirit will develop His Fruit within our hearts, which will spring forth in our lives, which is the Gospel of Grace. Otherwise, Christ will profit us nothing (Gal. 5:2).

AUGUST

15

*f*or it seemed good to the Holy Spirit, and to us, to lay upon you no greater burden that these necessary things; That you abstain from meats offered to idols, and from blood, and from things strangled, and from fornication: from which if you keep yourselves, you shall do well. Fare ye well (Acts 15:28-29).

The General Council conducted in Jerusalem saw, for the first and only time, all of the original Apostles, along with Paul and Barnabas, gathered together *"for to consider of this matter"* (Acts 15:6). It was conducted at the Church at Jerusalem, which was, in essence, the first Church, and of which James the Lord's brother was the Senior Pastor, so to speak.

Even though we say *"Church,"* they didn't have a building, and for many and obvious reasons. In a sense, the Temple continued to serve as their *"Church"* in Jerusalem. There were probably as many as 20,000-30,000 people who were members of this *"Church,"* virtually all of them Jews.

From the Text, it seems that Peter spoke first, and rightly

so, because he was much better known to all the people; furthermore, even as Peter said, *"You know how that a good while ago* (approximately ten years) *God made choice among us that the Gentiles by my mouth should hear the Word of the Gospel, and believe"* (Acts 15:7). This had to do with Cornelius and his household, all Gentiles.

Then Paul and Barnabas addressed the crowd.

The great question concerned the *"Law"* and *"Grace."* After they come to Christ, is it right to demand of the Gentiles that they also keep the Law?

At this Council, the Holy Spirit made the decision that the Gentiles would not have to keep the Law. In other words, they were saved by trusting Christ and Him alone! There were four requirements for the Gentiles, and all four, in a sense, had to do with the Cross.

They are:

1. *"That you abstain from meats offered to idols"*: These were lambs or heifers which had been offered in sacrifice to idols, a custom which, of course, was nurtured and fostered by Satan to say, in effect, that the sacrifice of Christ on the Cross was of no consequence. After these animals were offered in sacrifice, the carcass was then offered for sale in the meat markets of the city, and whoever purchased this cut of meat was believed to have good luck, etc. As should be obvious, Christians should not be involved in such.

2. *"From blood"*: Under the Law, the Jews were strictly forbidden to eat blood (Lev. 17:14). To be brief, Christ would shed His Life's Blood on the Cross, which meant the pouring out of His Perfect Life, with Faith in that securing Salvation for all who believe.

3. *"From things strangled"*: This referred to the carcass of animals which had not been properly drained of blood; when this meat was eaten, blood would also be imbibed, which is forbidden. Once again, it goes to the Cross.

4. *"And from fornication"*: This spoke, obviously, of immorality; even more so, however, James is using it in the Old Testament sense of being unfaithful to the Lord. When a Believer trusts in anything except Christ and the Cross, he is, in effect, committing spiritual fornication with that thing, whatever it might be. Each Believer is married to Christ. Christ Alone meets our every need, as He Alone can meet our every need (Rom. 7:1-4). Therefore, our Faith is to be exclusively in Him and what He has done for us at the Cross; otherwise, we commit spiritual fornication.

That's the reason it is imperative for every Believer to make Christ and His Cross the exclusive Object of one's Faith, and that alone! There is nothing more important than that!

AUGUST
16

*a**nd a Vision appeared to Paul in the night; there stood a man of Macedonia, and prayed him, saying, Come over into Macedonia, and help us* (Acts 16:9).

Paul now begins his second missionary journey. He will take Silas with him; Timothy will join him at a place called Lystra. It seems that Paul thought he had the mind of the Lord regarding the destination of this journey, but after starting out, he found that he did not. The Scripture says, *"They were forbidden of the Holy Spirit to preach the Word in Asia"* (Acts 16:6). Then they tried another direction, *"But the Spirit suffered them not"* (Acts 16:7).

Even though every missionary journey undertaken by Paul was of the utmost significance, still, this one was more important than ever, because here the Holy Spirit will direct the Gospel westward; the first preaching in this direction took place in Greece. Satan would do everything he could to greatly hinder this effort, as would be obvious, due to the tremendous significance of this development; however, as the Spirit kept leading, Paul and Silas kept following, until ultimately they received the *"Macedonian Call,"* which was one of the most important Calls in history.

Even though the first missionary journey undertaken by Paul was the beginning of this great episode, still, the Holy Spirit now gives special guidance regarding the Gospel and its geographical direction. To be sure, the Lord did not love those in the west more than those in the east; however, by foreknowledge, He knew that those in the west would be more receptive to the Gospel, hence leading in this direction.

When Paul received this Macedonian Call, even as it regards the man in the Vision, we are seeing here the blueprint for that which we refer to as *"Western Civilization."* In that Macedonian Call is every freedom we now enjoy, all the prosperity which we now have, actually that which has made the United States the envy of the world. To the degree that the Western nations have accepted the Gospel, to that degree have they been blessed.

When our leaders speak of extending democracy to other nations of the world, what most do not seem to realize is that there can be no true democracy without acceptance of the Lord Jesus Christ and the Gospel that He affords. So our efforts at trying to democratize Muslim nations, no matter the good intentions, will little work. For it to truthfully work, they would have to forsake the religion of Islam and accept the Lord Jesus Christ, which the far greater majority of them will not do. If any type of democracy is established in Iraq, or any other Muslim country, it will mostly be democracy in name only, without many of the benefits.

Unfortunately, in the United States of America, we are losing sight of that which has made us great; we are gradually becoming *"heathenized"* ourselves. There is, in fact, no longer a separation of Church and State, which is proper, but rather a separation of God and State, which is catastrophic!

The problem?

The problem is the Church! The Church has strayed so far from the True Gospel of Jesus Christ that it any more little persuades and sways Governmental leaders, which it is meant to do.

Peter said, *"For the time is come that judgment must begin at the House of God: and if it first begin at us, what shall the end be of them who obey not the Gospel of God?"* (I Pet. 4:17).

AUGUST
17

*a*nd at midnight Paul and Silas prayed, and sang praises unto God: and the prisoners heard them (Acts 16:25).

A false message has been circulated in the modern Church that if a person is in the very center of the Will of God, there will be no problems. If there are problems, so it is erroneously claimed, that means the person is out of the Will of God. Nothing could be further from the truth!

The more directly that one is in the Will of God, just as Paul and Silas were when they were preaching the Gospel in Philippi, the more that Satan is going to do everything within his power to hinder. An absence of that hindrance tells us that we are not where we ought to be.

A demon-possessed girl was delivered; her masters, who made great sums of money from her fortunetelling, grew incensed and had Paul and Silas arrested (Acts 16:16-21). As a result, the Magistrates of the city commanded that Paul and Silas be beaten, which they were. Under Roman law, scourging was a most brutal and cruel punishment. Many died under this torture. Paul and Silas must have been given superhuman strength to have endured it.

Then they had to suffer the added torture of the stocks in the inner prison, which usually was a noisome and wet dungeon without any light. The stocks frequently were so placed that the unhappy prisoner's shoulders lay on the wet stone floor, with his feet drawn as far apart as possible, fastened high up to the wall. After a short time, the muscles would begin to constrict, causing unbearable pain.

Satan, no doubt, took this opportunity to taunt the two Apostles, telling them that they were out of the Will of God, etc. If their coming to Philippi was the Will of God, why would the Lord allow them to be treated in this manner?

That question has plagued many throughout the centuries. Why did the Lord allow this terrible beating and imprisonment to come to Paul and Silas?

The reasons are known only to the Lord, but He most definitely had His reasons. Had He desired, He easily could have stopped the situation. Paul may have answered this question in the Epistle to the Church at Corinth. Paul said, *"And lest I should be exalted above measure through the abundance of the Revelations, there was given to me a thorn in the flesh, the messenger of Satan to buffet me, lest I should be exalted above measure.*

"For this thing I besought the Lord thrice, that it might depart from me.

"And He said unto me, My Grace is sufficient for you: for My strength is made perfect in weakness. Most gladly therefore

will I rather glory in my infirmities, that the Power of Christ may rest upon me" (II Cor. 12:7-9).

The *"flesh"* is ever prominent in all of us, even in Paul. Certain problems are then allowed by the Lord in order to let us know that in the flesh there is no strength or power, and that we must depend solely upon the Lord. In fact, the greater the Operation of the Holy Spirit within our hearts and lives, the greater, I think, will be these difficulties.

In the midst of it all, the two Apostles began to pray and sing praises unto the Lord. The Greek Text suggests that bursts of song broke out as they prayed from time to time. This tells us that, especially during times of great testing, and whether we feel like it or not, we should simply *"pray and sing praises unto the Lord."* This proclaims faith and trust!

It was midnight. *"Suddenly there was a great earthquake, so that the foundations of the prison were shaken: and immediately all the doors were opened, and everyone's bands were loosed"* (Acts 16:26). Even though it was an earthquake, it was very unnatural in that it seems to only have affected the jail. Further, it caused every door to be opened and even their iron bands to be unloosed, but without destroying the building.

As a result, the jailer was saved and all of his household. Also, a Church was established in Philippi.

The ways of the Lord are not always easy; however, if they are minutely followed, they always are fruitful!

AUGUST
18

*t*hen Paul stood in the midst of Mars' Hill, and said, You men of Athens, I perceive that in all things you are too superstitious. For as I passed by, and beheld your devotions, I found an altar with this inscription, TO THE UNKNOWN GOD. Whom therefore you ignorantly worship, Him declare I unto you (Acts 17:22-23).

When Paul went to Athens, first of all he ministered in the Jewish Synagogue (17:17). Paul reasoned to the Jews that Jesus was the Messiah and proved it from the Scriptures. In the marketplace where great crowds always gathered, he began daily to minister, with a platform, so to speak, for public speaking. Paul took the opportunity to minister the Gospel.

At a point in time, he was opposed by the *"philosophers of the Epicureans, and of the Stoicks, who encountered him"* (Acts 17:18). The Epicureans were those who claimed that pleasure and gratification of the appetites were the only ends in life. The Stoicks taught that man was not to be moved by either joy or grief. These groups challenged Paul's statements about Christ.

However, Paul's arguments were so convincing, so powerful, and so moving that he was invited to speak on Mars' Hill, which was, at certain times, somewhat similar to our Supreme Court. Strangely enough, those who brought Paul to this place labeled what he said as mere babblings, but yet they thought it important enough to be taken to the highest court in Athens.

Even though the Message Paul preached that day at Mars' Hill was phenomenal, to say the least, still, I'm not sure if the great Apostle was pleased with the direction he took. In other words, I wonder if he felt he had missed the Perfect Direction of the Holy Spirit. And what do I mean by that?

When Paul left Athens, even though he had had some small success, I'm sure he had not seen what he would have liked to have seen. He now departs for Corinth. A Church was established there, and many people were saved. After going on to other fields of endeavor, his first recorded Epistle to the Church at Corinth is given to us.

In that Epistle, he said, *"For I determined not to know anything among you, save Jesus Christ and Him Crucified.*

And my speech and my preaching was not with enticing words of man's wisdom, but in demonstration of the Spirit and of power:

That your Faith should not stand in the wisdom of men, but in the Power of God" (I Cor. 2:2, 4-5).

Does this tell us that, reaching back to when Paul left Athens and was on his way to Corinth, he no doubt sought the Lord earnestly about how he could make spiritual inroads into the city of Corinth, one of the most jaded cities in the world? I personally believe at that time the Holy Spirit spoke to the great Apostle's heart and told him, *"Preach the Cross!"* Corinth was an excellent test case. It was simultaneously a city of unbridled vice and a city of philosophy — the two hardest nuts to crack, so to speak.

The Holy Spirit would show Paul that if the preaching of the Cross would work here, it would work anywhere. As stated, he did not preach the Cross at Athens, and the results were meager. He preached the Cross in jaded Corinth, and the results were phenomenal. That's why he also said:

"*But we preach Christ Crucified* (this is the Foundation of the Word of God, and thereby, of Salvation), *unto the Jews a stumblingblock* (the Cross was the stumblingblock), *and unto the Greeks foolishness* (both found it difficult to accept as God a dead Man hanging on a Cross, for such Christ was to them [I Cor. 1:23]).

That is to be the Message of every God-called Preacher. We must preach the Cross, that is, if we are to see anything truly done for the Lord!

AUGUST
19

*a*nd as he reasoned of Righteousness, temperance, and judgment to come, Felix trembled, and answered, Go your way for this time; when I have a convenient season, I will call for you (Acts 24:25).

Felix was the Gentile Governor of Judaea; however, he was married to a Jewess named Drusilla; consequently, he may have had some scant knowledge of Judaism. Even though Felix knows that Paul is innocent of the charges leveled against him, still, he continues to hold him captive, thinking someone will pay a fat bribe to him for Paul's release. That never happened, so he kept Paul a prisoner until another Governor, Festus, took his place, and Paul was eventually sent to Rome.

Not long after Paul was imprisoned in Caesarea, Felix asked to hear him. He was accompanied by his wife. More than likely there also were many others present.

When Paul ministered to this Gentile and all who were there, he dealt with *"Righteousness,"* stating, in essence,

520

that this attribute could only come by and through Christ and what He did for us at the Cross. Then he dealt with *"Temperance,"* which addressed the bondages and vices which affect humanity. Last, he dealt with the *"Judgment,"* which refers to the fact that one day all must stand before God.

The message was telling! The Holy Spirit anointed it greatly and Felix came under great conviction and *"trembled"*!

Evidently, Paul knew nothing about the now so widely acclaimed modern method of preaching to the unsaved, which states that such unsettling subjects should not be approached. And the Holy Spirit also knew nothing about it! Telling some jokes and spreading some religious pablum would have had no spiritual effect on Felix, and neither will it have any spiritual effect on anyone else.

As a result of the new method, Churches today are being filled with people who have never really been Born-Again. Regrettably, under such preaching, they never will be Born-Again. To reach the lost, or even the Believer, for that matter, the Word of God must, in some manner, be proclaimed. The Holy Spirit will not work or function in any other capacity (Acts 2:16-21, 29-38, 42; 8:14).

AUGUST
20

i am debtor both to the Greeks, and to the Barbarians; both to the wise, and to the unwise. So, as much as in me is, I am ready to preach the Gospel to you who are at Rome also (Rom. 1:14-15).

Realizing the Grace of God which had been shown to him, Paul considered himself as a *"debtor"* to all men, regardless of who they might be, meaning that he must do his utmost best to take the Gospel to all concerned. Of course, Paul couldn't reach all people; however, he felt responsible to all, whether he could reach them or not. He had to do his utmost to take this Gospel as far as he could, which he most definitely did.

Every Believer falls into the same category. By the very fact that we are saved, it means that we too are debtors to all of mankind, in that we must do our very best that they hear the good news of the Gospel. Regrettably, most Believers little feel this burden and this concern.

Every Believer can *"pray,"* and every Believer can *"give."*

If all Believers will set themselves to seek the Face of the Lord, through prayer, the Lord can work wonders. In fact, every great Move of God which has ever taken place has been first of all prayed into existence. I speak of intercessory prayer, which, regrettably, is engaged by only a few; however, the privilege is available to all.

Not only should every Believer give, they should also make double certain that what they are supporting is Scriptural. Sadly, the vast majority of money given to that which purports to be of God is anything but! As stewards of what the Lord has placed in our hands, we are responsible for making certain that we are good stewards. The Lord grandly and plainly exampled this by the Parables of the *"Talents"* and *"Pounds"* (Mat. 25:14-30; Lk. 19:12-26).

We have been saved to serve! When a person truly understands what his Salvation actually is, and actually means, when we truly know how privileged we are to be saved, and that the Gospel somehow came to us, then we gladly serve, and serve gladly.

I was born on March 15, 1935 into a home that had never heard the Gospel. My Dad, in fact, had never heard a Gospel Message, had never been in a Church, and had never heard a Gospel Song, until he was 25 years old. My Mother was in the same category. When I look back and think of that, it's almost inconceivable to me that people could live that long and never even hear a Gospel Song. Of course, that was before Television, and even though Radio was the means of communication in those days, there was no Gospel Radio, none whatsoever, where my parents lived.

I know it was all because of God's Grace that the Gospel came to our home, our hearts, and our lives, which changed everything. When my parents found the Lord, our world changed, and changed forever — and a million times for the better, I might quickly add.

That's one of the reasons that Paul said, *"I am a debtor,"* and that's one of the reasons that I say, *"I am a debtor"*!

AUGUST
21

*t*herefore being justified by Faith, we have peace with God through our Lord Jesus Christ *(Rom. 5:1).*

What did Paul mean when he said, "We are justified by Faith"?

First of all, we must look at Faith. The definition of Faith is to simply believe something. In this case, it refers to having Faith in Christ and what Christ has done for us at the Cross. The Faith of which Paul speaks always must be in this capacity. We must ever understand that Christ is the Source, and the Cross is the means. In no way is Christ to be separated from the Cross, or the Cross separated from Christ.

That's the reason the Apostle said, "We preach Christ Crucified" (I Cor. 1:23).

Paul wasn't meaning that Christ is still on a Cross; in fact, Christ is seated by the Right Hand of the Father, meaning that His task of Redemption is complete (Heb. 1:3). Instead, Paul is speaking of the benefits of the Cross, benefits, incidentally, which will never, never end. For this reason, the Holy Spirit through Paul referred to these benefits as *"The Everlasting Covenant"* (Heb. 13:20).

The Believer must understand that every single thing we receive from the Lord, and in every capacity, is made possible solely by the Cross. That is the Gospel. The story of the Bible is the story of Jesus Christ and Him Crucified, and the story of Jesus Christ and Him Crucified is the story of the Bible.

Once Faith is properly understood and established, now we turn to Justification. The Greek word used by Paul is *"dikaioo,"* which means *"to show or regard as innocent."* In layman's terms, it means the following:

1. It means that every sin — past, present, and future — is forgiven.

2. It means that God looks at the one so forgiven as never having committed the sin or sins in question.

3. It means that one is declared innocent, not guilty, and free of all charges, all made possible by Faith in Christ and what He did for us at the Cross.

Justification cannot be earned or purchased, at least not by the individual. It is given freely upon Faith in Christ and His Finished Work.

AUGUST
22

*W*hat shall we say then? Shall we continue in sin, that Grace may abound? God forbid. How shall we, who are dead to sin, live any longer therein? (Rom. 6:1-2).

Some seventeen times the word *"sin"* is mentioned in the Sixth Chapter of Romans. Fifteen of those times the original Text, in other words, as it was originally written by the Apostle Paul, contains what is referred to as the *"definite article."* That is, in these fifteen times, the Text reads *"the sin."* It refers to the sin nature.

Some claim that Believers no longer have a sin nature; however, considering that Paul is writing to Believers here, if that is the case, i.e., if Believers no longer have a sin nature, then the Holy Spirit went to a lot of trouble to explain something that doesn't exist.

No! Every Believer has a sin nature; however, we are supposed to be dead to the sin nature, even though the sin nature is not dead (Rom. 6:11).

In truth, the sin nature is supposed to be dormant in

the heart and life of the Believer; at the time of Salvation, the sin nature is, in fact, rendered dormant. But if the Believer does not know how to maintain a victorious life, sin will be the result, which then brings the sin nature to life, and then such a Believer can find the sin nature ruling and reigning in his life, even as it did before he was saved.

That's why Paul said, *"Let not the sin therefore reign* (rule) *in your mortal body, that you should obey it in the lust thereof"* (Rom. 6:12). The sin nature will reside in us until the Resurrection, but it's not supposed to reign. The manner and way that we can have victory over the sin nature, the only way, in fact, and on a perpetual basis, is that the Cross of Christ ever be the Object of our Faith. That being the case, the Holy Spirit, Who Alone can make us what we ought to be, can effectually work within our hearts and lives, bringing about the Fruit of the Spirit, which develops Christlikeness in our life and living (Rom. 8:1-2,11).

That is the way, and the only way, that the sin nature in the heart and life of the Believer can be subdued and remain subdued.

We find here, graphically so, that *"sin"* is the problem with the Christian. No matter how many claims are made to the contrary, sin is the problem. And there is only one way that victory over sin can be obtained, and that is through Faith in Christ and what Christ has done for us at the Cross.

Man may devise many ways and claim that victory will be the result, but God has only one way, and that is the Way of the Cross!

AUGUST
23

*k*now ye not, that so many of us as were baptized into Jesus Christ were baptized into His Death? Therefore we are buried with Him by baptism into death: but like as Christ was raised up from the dead by the Glory of the Father, even so we also should walk in newness of life (Rom. 6:3-4).

In the First Chapter of Romans, Paul proclaims the entirety of the Gentile world, to a man, as being spiritually lost, despite all their religion. In the Second and Third Chapters of Romans, the Apostle places the Jews in the same category, i.e., all needing a Redeemer. In the Fourth and Fifth Chapters of Romans, the Holy Spirit through the Apostle proclaims the answer to this dilemma, which is *"Justification by Faith."* Paul belabors the issue, telling us, in no uncertain terms, that works cannot attain to Salvation.

Now that Salvation has been established, in the Sixth Chapter of Romans, the Apostle tells the Believer how to live for God. In fact, if the Believer doesn't understand

529

the Sixth Chapter, he simply does not know how to properly live for the Lord, which makes for a miserable situation. The Seventh Chapter of Romans, in fact, tells us of the Believer who tries to live for God without understanding the principles of the Sixth Chapter of Romans.

In the Eighth Chapter of Romans, we are told *"what"* the Holy Spirit can do within our lives, once we understand *"how"* He works, which is found in the Sixth Chapter. The Ninth, Tenth, and Eleventh Chapters of Romans proclaim a dire warning to the Church. If we forsake God's Way of the Cross and resort to works or Law, as did Israel of old, then the Church will be lost, exactly as was Israel.

Chapters 12 through 16 of Romans give us the practical aspects of Christianity, once the Believer knows and understands God's Prescribed Order of Victory. As it regards victory over sin, as is here obvious, Paul takes the Believer directly to the Cross (Rom. 6:3-4).

Jesus Christ came as our Substitute, lived the life, obeyed the Law in every respect, and then went to the Cross in order to address the broken Law, doing so all for us. As stated, He was our Substitute.

When Paul uses the word *"baptize,"* he's not speaking of Water Baptism, but rather our being baptized into the death of Christ. The moment the believing sinner expresses Faith in Christ and accepts Him as Saviour and Lord, in the Mind of God, that person is crucified with Christ, buried with Christ, and raised with Christ. That is the manner of Salvation, and that is also the manner of Sanctification, the latter being what this Sixth Chapter of Romans is all about. This is God's Prescribed Order of Victory!

AUGUST
24

*f*or if we have been planted together in the likeness of His Death, we shall be also in the likeness of His Resurrection (Rom. 6:5).

This Passage is not speaking of the coming Resurrection of Life, but rather the Resurrection of Christ, and our being spiritually resurrected with Him *"in newness of life,"* which takes place at the New Birth. To believe in Christ implies association with Him in His Death and Resurrection.

Almost every Christian has heard the term, *"Resurrection Life,"* and has also no doubt used it. Of course, *"Resurrection Life"* speaks of a life of victory, and perpetual victory, at that, because it is based on the Resurrection of Christ, and solely on that Resurrection.

That is all correct; however, most who use the term fail to understand that having and enjoying Resurrection Life, which the Lord intends for all of us to have, is predicated solely on our understanding that *"we have been planted together in the likeness of His Death."* In other words, Resurrection Life depends completely on the Cross of Christ and our Faith in that Finished Work. The trouble with most Christians is that the object of their faith is the *"Resurrection Life,"* which God can never accept. The Object of our Faith must ever be the Cross of Christ. That being the case, then *"Resurrection Life"* is ours, and is bountiful indeed!

If we abide by the Word of God, we will receive the results of the Word of God. But too many people have been incorrectly taught. While claiming much, they actually have little! The reason always goes back to an improper and incorrect object of faith. The Lord doesn't require much of us, but He most definitely does require that the Object of our Faith ever be Christ and the Cross.

That, in fact, is the key to all blessings, because that is the manner in which the Holy Spirit works.

That, in effect, was what Jesus was talking about when He said, *"If any man thirst, let him come unto Me, and drink,*

"He who believes on Me, as the Scripture has said, out of his innermost being shall flow rivers of Living Water.

"This spoke He of the Spirit, which they who believe on Him should receive . . ." (Jn. 7:37-39).

Christ is the Source of Resurrection Life, while the Cross is the means. The Holy Spirit is the Bearer of that to us, for which Christ has paid such a price.

AUGUST
25

*K*nowing this, that our old man is crucified with Him, that the body of sin might be destroyed, that henceforth we should not serve sin (Rom. 6:6).

As Paul uses the word *"sin"* here, he is actually speaking of *"the sin nature."* He tells us here that when we accepted Christ, *"the body of sin* (sin nature) *might be destroyed, that henceforth we should not serve the sin nature."* The word *"destroyed"* in the Greek is *"kataigeo,"* which means *"to make ineffective."* So, at conversion, the sin nature was not obliterated, but rather was made ineffective.

What is the sin nature?

At the Fall, man's nature became that of sin. In other words, everything that the unredeemed person does is toward sin, and of every description.

The Gospel declares that man is absolutely ruined by sin and wholly unable to restore himself to God's favor by his own ability and strength. A false gospel teaches that man is not wholly ruined, that by self-culture he can merit

533

God's favor and secure his own happiness.

There is only one way that the human being can properly address sin. Pure and simple, he must die. That's why Paul said, *"For he who is dead is freed from sin"* (from domination by the sin nature [Rom. 6:7]). This *"death"* occurs at the Cross of Calvary, hence the Apostle saying, *"our old man is crucified with Him."* The death of which we speak can occur no place else. This is the reason the Cross is so very, very important, actually the only means by which this horrible problem can be properly addressed.

This *"death"* is obtained by the Believer simply evidencing Faith in Christ and what Christ did at the Cross. The *"old man"* then dies, which refers to what we were before Salvation, with a *"new man"* then rising with Christ in *"newness of life."* Unfortunately, unredeemed man tries to address the sin problem in many and varied ways other than the Cross. He tries to address it with education, money, government, etc., all to no avail!

Worse yet, many Believers attempt to do the same thing. They try to address the sin nature, i.e., the problem of sin, by ways other than the Cross. It simply cannot be done. Some try to address the sin nature by denying its existence. Others try to address it by struggling with it on a day-by-day basis, all to no avail.

The sin nature was conquered at the Cross, and it remains conquered, but only as we maintain Faith in Christ and what Christ did at the Cross. We were crucified with Christ, and, in that, the sin nature was made ineffective. We were raised with Christ in newness of life. That position is maintained by continued Faith in Christ and the Cross, and by no other means.

AUGUST
26

*L*ikewise reckon ye also yourselves to be dead indeed unto sin, but alive unto God through Jesus Christ our Lord (Rom. 6:11).

The words, *"believe"* (Rom. 6:8) and *"reckon"* (Rom. 6:11), signify Faith. In fact, the three words, *"believe,"* *"reckon,"* and *"yield"* (Rom. 6:13), express three energies of the Christian mind which secure and make real a life of Scriptural Sanctification. The entirety of the Sixth Chapter of Romans expresses God's manner and way of Sanctification.

The word *"reckon"* in the Greek is *"logizomai,"* which means *"to conclude, impute, number."* Considering all that Paul has thus far said, we are to conclude ourselves, because of what Christ did at the Cross, *"to be dead indeed unto sin,"* in effect, *"dead unto the sin nature."*

As stated, this Verse does not say that the sin nature is dead, but it does say that we are dead unto the sin nature, that is, if we maintain our Faith in that which made us dead, so to speak, which is the Cross of Christ (Rom. 6:6); however, the Holy Spirit through Paul doesn't leave us in this *"dead position,"* but brings us to a new life altogether, totally different than what we once had, which, in effect, was no life at all, and tells us that we are now *"alive unto God through Jesus Christ our Lord."* This means to be *"alive"* to all that God has, which we have through and by what Jesus did at the Cross, all on our behalf.

The Doctrine of Grace, especially that which declares Justification and Sanctification to be by Faith apart from works, excites the enmity of the natural heart, and this enmity expresses itself today in various ways, but mostly by unbelief. So the following question must be asked:

Is the rejection of the Cross a moral problem or a theological problem?

If it was theological, it would mean that the Cross of Christ is too difficult of understanding for one to grasp; however, the very opposite of that is true. The Gospel of the Cross is a principle of such simplicity that even a child can understand it. So we know from that that the problem is not theological.

To be truthful, the problem is *"moral."* That means that the enmity of the natural heart is at work against God's Prescribed Order of Sanctification, and it registers itself, as stated, in the form of unbelief. In other words, it refuses to believe that what Jesus did at the Cross, and that alone, guarantees victory over every perversion, every type of sin, every work of the flesh, and, in fact, everything that is the opposite of the Lord. That's exactly what the Cross does, but most people, even Believers, refuse to express Faith in that Finished Work.

So, as stated, the problem is a *"moral"* problem, rather than a *"theological"* problem.

As a Believer, understanding what Jesus has done for you at the Cross, all you have to do is to reckon yourself, according to that Finished Work, to be dead to the sin nature, and that you are! On the Cross, Jesus died to sin. He has done with it forever. The Believer died in Him, and this great fact, when believed, reckoned to be true, and practically obeyed, becomes a moral experience in the activities of the life of Holiness and Consecration.

AUGUST
27

l et not sin therefore reign in your mortal body, that you should obey it in the lusts thereof. Neither yield ye your members as instruments of unrighteousness unto sin, but yield yourselves unto God, as those who are alive from the dead, and your members as instruments of Righteousness unto God (Rom. 6:12-13).

Sin as a principle of evil dwells in the Christian's mortal body in the sense of the sin nature; but it is not to reign there; it is, in fact, to be dormant. If Sanctification were based upon the principle of law-obedience, i.e., upon works, it would be impossible to escape from the lawful dominion of the sin nature, because a perfect obedience to Divine Law on the part of man is impossible. But being based upon the opposite principle of Grace, liberation from the power and dominion of sin as a Master is secured and may be enjoyed on a constant basis.

No! We are not teaching sinless perfection, because the Bible does not teach such. But we are teaching victory over sin, and in every capacity. Under Law, sin has a dominion, but it has no dominion under Grace. These are two totally independent realms.

The Believer actually has three natures. They are:

1. The Human Nature.
2. The Sin Nature.
3. The Divine Nature (II Pet. 1:4).

The human nature of the Believer is either controlled by the sin nature or by the Divine nature. Within itself, the human body is neutral. It is neither holy nor evil. If the Believer is totally trusting Christ and what Christ did at the Cross, doing so on an unending basis, this means the sin nature is dormant, and the Believer can then yield the members of his physical body as *"instruments of Righteousness unto God."* It's just that simple!

However, if the faith of the Believer is in something other than Christ and the Cross, then the sin nature is in control, and the Believer will be forced, despite all of his efforts otherwise, to yield his *"members as instruments of unrighteousness unto sin."* It comes as a shock to most Believers when they are told that Satan can override their will, that is, if their Faith is in anything except Christ and the Cross.

The reason is simple:

The Holy Spirit is God. As such, He can do anything; however, He will not go against His Own nature. In other words, the Holy Spirit will not force Satan out of the way if our Faith is in anything other than the Cross of Christ (Rom. 8:2).

In the Bible, we aren't told to fight against sin. If we are struggling with sin, this means that our Faith is not

539

properly placed in Christ and His Finished Work. While the Christian experience definitely entails a struggle, the struggle is to be in the arena of Faith. Paul told us to *"fight the good fight of faith"* (I Tim. 6:12).

The disobedience of the First Man, Adam, assured death for all men, and the obedience of the Second Man, the Lord Jesus Christ, secured life for all men, at least all who will believe. That is, all the sons of the First Adam, by reason of their relationship to him and because they possess his sinful nature, stand in death, and all the sons of the Last Adam, in virtue of their relationship to Him, because they possess His Spirit, stand in life.

In that *"Life,"* the Holy Spirit works. Faith alone on our part, which means Faith in Christ and the Cross, guarantees His participation. Only then will the sin nature no longer rule and reign in your mortal body. Without proper Faith in Christ and the Cross, the Believer is forced to *"obey sin in the lusts thereof."* Proper faith guarantees obedience to Righteousness!

AUGUST
28

*f*or sin shall not have dominion over you, for you are not under the Law, but under Grace *(Rom. 6:14).*

As we have stated, the Bible does not teach sinless perfection, but it most definitely does teach that the *"sin nature shall not have dominion over you,"* that is, if the Believer properly abides by God's Prescribed Order of Victory, as given in this Sixth Chapter of Romans. Otherwise, the sin nature most definitely will exercise dominion over you. Regrettably and sadly, that is the condition of most modern Christians, i.e., the sin nature rules and reigns in their lives.

A short time ago, I read a tract written by the great Preacher, Charles Finney. The title of the tract was *"How to have Victory over Sin."* He correctly stated that victory could not be obtained by works or law, and that it must be done by faith; however, he never mentioned the Cross nor the Holy Spirit. In fact, when most of the modern Church attempts to address the problem of sin, they basically do so in the same fashion as Finney.

But to tell a person that the solution is not by Law, but rather by Faith, and to leave it there, is to fail to say enough. It's like a staircase that only goes halfway to the next floor. As would be obvious, halfway is not enough.

If the question is asked, *"Faith in what?"* most presently would answer, *"Faith in God"* or *"Faith in the Word."* However, that which says too much concludes by saying nothing. These are nebulous answers which really do not answer anything.

The only way to have victory over sin is what the Holy Spirit taught us through Paul in this Sixth Chapter of Romans. The first place that the great Apostle took us was straight to the Cross, as outlined in Verses 3 through 5. The Believer is to understand that every single thing he receives comes to him by virtue of what Christ did at the Cross, all on our behalf.

As we have stated innumerable times, Christ is the Source, while the Cross is the means.

With faith properly placed and properly maintained, which means it neither varies nor moves, the Holy Spirit, Who Alone can make us what we ought to be, will then work mightily in our lives, bringing about the desired result (Rom. 8:1-2, 11). This is God's Prescribed Order of Victory over sin. If faithfully followed, which any child can do, *"the sin nature shall not have dominion over you."*

Paul made the statement, *"For you are not under the Law,"* for a specific purpose. Even though Calvary satisfied the demands of the Law in totality, still, most Christians have placed themselves under Law.

Please understand the following:

There are only two places to be, *"Law"* or *"Grace."* If one exhibits faith in anything except Christ and the Cross, then one has put himself under Law, with all of its negative results, whether he understands such or not. If his Faith is in Christ and the Cross, then he's functioning under *"Grace."* Such Faith guarantees an uninterrupted flow, i.e., *"Victory."*

AUGUST
29

*b**ut God be thanked, that you were the servants of sin, but you have obeyed from the heart that form of Doctrine which was delivered you* (Rom. 6:17).

The formula, *"form of doctrine,"* is very important. It declares the Christian Faith to have been once for all delivered to Believers as fixed and complete, therefore, neither needing nor accepting additions.

Into that form, as into a mold, the Believers are poured or *"delivered."* The two sides of that mold being Justification and Sanctification, it was manifest that anyone leading a sinful life had not been poured into the mold. In other words, such a Believer was not subscribing to God's Prescribed Order.

This *"form of doctrine"* is the oldest Doctrine, one might say, in the world today, and ever has been. It was formulated in the Mind of the Godhead even before the foundation of the world (I Pet. 1:18-20). Through foreknowledge, God knew that He would make man and that man would fall. The Godhead then decided that man would be redeemed by God becoming Man, going to the Cross, shedding His Life's Blood, and thereby purchasing man's Redemption.

This means that every single doctrine in the Bible, irrespective as to what it might be, must be built on the foundation of the Cross of Christ; otherwise, it is spurious. All false doctrine, in fact, has its beginning because of either an improper interpretation of the Cross or else outright rebellion against the Cross.

Not only is the Cross the first Doctrine, formulated before the foundation of the world, it was also the first Doctrine proclaimed after the Fall of man. The Lord said to Satan through the serpent, *"And I will put enmity between you and the woman, and between your seed and her Seed; it shall bruise your head, and you shall bruise His heel"* (Gen. 3:15).

The only *"Seed"* that woman has ever had is the Lord Jesus Christ. At Calvary's Cross, He bruised Satan's head, and Satan bruised His heel, referring to the sufferings of the Cross. This is the only *"form of doctrine"* that's been delivered by the Lord regarding victory over the world, the flesh, and the Devil. It is the only one because no other is needed; consequently, if this *"form of doctrine"* is rejected, there is no other, and wreckage is the result. To reject it is to accept the way of Cain. To accept it is to accept the way of Abel.

AUGUST
30

*W*herefore, my Brethren, you also are become dead to the Law by the Body of Christ; that you should be married to another, even to Him Who was raised from the dead, that we should bring forth fruit unto God (Rom. 7:4).

While the Sixth Chapter of Romans reveals the Divine method of Sanctification, the Seventh Chapter sets out its impossibility under the bondage of Law.

The argument here is:

Just as death is the only force that can liberate from the claims of sin, so is it the only force that can liberate from the claims of Law.

Paul pictures a woman being married to a man and then, without Scriptural foundation divorcing him and marrying another. He said, *"She shall be called an adulteress."* The Apostle is not teaching here on the law of divorce and remarriage. He is making a point regarding Victory in Christ.

The Believer is married to Christ. This means that

Christ is our husband. If we are unfaithful to Christ, and we go to Law, which is the only place to go if our faith is not solidly anchored in Christ and the Cross, we are then committing *"spiritual adultery."* We should also realize that if the Believer is living in spiritual adultery, the Holy Spirit simply will not help such a Believer. If He did, He would be condoning this act of rebellion, which He cannot do.

To trust anything other than Christ and the Cross is the highest insult directed at Christ, whether the Believer understands such or not. Sadly, because of not understanding the Cross, almost all modern Believers are living in a state of spiritual adultery. Actually, most Christians have never even heard the term, *"spiritual adultery."*

Paul deals greatly with *"Law"* in this Seventh Chapter. What does Paul mean by *"Law"*?

He is speaking of the Law of Moses, or any type of Law that we devise ourselves, or which is devised by a religious Denomination, etc. In other words, anything in which we place our faith, other than the Cross of Christ, becomes Law. In fact, many of the things in which we place our faith are good things, and, because they are good things, they deceive us.

Look closely at this example:

If a Believer tries to overcome sin by praying an hour each day, while he will definitely be blessed, he will not be delivered from sin.

The reason?

He has just turned prayer into *"Law,"* and the Holy Spirit will not work in that capacity, because such a Believer is committing spiritual adultery.

547

I realize that comes as a shock, especially considering that there is nothing which is greater than a consecrated prayer life, other than our Faith. But it is very easy to turn such into Law; in fact, that's exactly what will happen if the Believer doesn't have his faith anchored solidly in the Cross of Christ. But when a Believer does have his Faith anchored squarely in the Cross of Christ, prayer then becomes the powerful force it is meant to be, because it is engaged in the proper manner.

Spiritual adultery is a position in which no Believer can afford to be. Simple Faith in Christ and the Cross will solve the problem.

AUGUST
31

*W*hat shall we say then? Is the Law sin? God forbid. No, I had not known sin, but by the Law: for I had not known lust, except the Law had said, You shall not covet (Rom. 7:7).

When Paul first came to Christ, not understanding the Message of the Cross, because that word had not yet been given, Paul tried to live for the Lord the only way he knew, which was by the means of trying to keep the Law. Since he had come to Christ, was now Born-Again, even baptized with the Holy Spirit (Acts 9:17), he thought surely he could now keep the Law. But he found that he could not! And neither can you, nor I, nor anyone else, for that matter!

The Law was, and is, God's Standard of Righteousness. It tells us what man ought to do and what man ought to be. Furthermore, as with all Law, the penalty for breaking it is dire indeed! It is death, i.e., *"spiritual death,"* which is separation from God.

The Law was like a mirror into which man looks, and it shows him what he is, which is total depravity, but

549

giving him no power to change what he sees. The Law, in other words, can tell one where one should go, but it doesn't tell him how to get there.

When Jesus came to this world, He was born *"under the Law"* (Gal. 4:4). He came as the *"Last Adam"* and the *"Second Man"* (I Cor. 15:45, 47). As such, He came to address the Law in every respect. In His Life, He kept the Law perfectly, never failing in even one point. He did it all for you and me. But there remained the problem of the broken law, which was the case with every human being. To address that, He had to go to the Cross, and there give His Perfect Body in Sacrifice by the pouring out of His Life's Blood, which satisfied every demand of the broken Law, also satisfying the demands of a thrice-Holy God, which means that God accepted the Sacrifice. This means that the Law of God was now satisfied in every respect.

So, when a person accepts Christ, thereby placing their Faith in Him and what He did at the Cross, that person, in the Eyes of God, becomes a perfect Law-keeper, because the Law has no more claim on Him. Every Believer has died in Christ, and the Law can no longer have a claim on a dead man. The *"old man"* is now dead and a *"new man"* is now risen, all in Christ.

That is the only manner in which one can be free of the demands of the Law; otherwise, every person not availing himself of the Salvation afforded by Christ will one day stand at the Great White Throne Judgment, and will answer to the Law. To be sure, there will be no Redemption there, because there is no Redemption in the Law, because all had broken the Law. All Redemption is solely in Christ and Christ Alone!

SEPTEMBER

1

f or that which I do I allow not: for what I would, that do I not; but what I hate, that do I (Rom. 7:15).

Most Preachers, not understanding the Sixth Chapter of Romans, totally misunderstand this Seventh Chapter, thinking that it is speaking of Paul before his conversion. Nothing could be further from the truth.

The Seventh Chapter of Romans proclaims Paul's efforts at trying to live a victorious life for the Lord after he was saved, baptized with the Holy Spirit, and called to be an Apostle. At that time, he did not understand God's Prescribed Order of Victory, because that particular Truth had not yet been given. In fact, it was given to the Apostle Paul, which he gave to us in these Chapters.

If the great Paul could not live for God outside of Faith in Christ and the Cross, how do you think you can do so?

He tried to live for the Lord, as stated, by trying to keep the Law, because that's all he knew to do. He made the statement, *"For I was alive without the Law once,"* which refers to when he was saved on the road to Damascus. The Law actually had nothing to do with his Salvation, and that's what he means by being *"alive without the Law."*

But after getting saved, he then tried to live for the Lord by Commandments. When he did that, *"sin revived."* This means that the sin nature was now ruling him. Then he said, *"I died,"* not meaning that he physically died, but rather that he failed the Lord (7:9). To be sure, there was nothing wrong with the Commandment, but there was something wrong with Paul. Even though he was Spirit-filled, he still couldn't keep these Commandments, and neither can we!

If we are Spirit-filled, why can't we keep them?

The Holy Spirit will not give power to the flesh. Many people think that when they are baptized with the Spirit, this means that the Lord will give them a greater will-power, a greater spiritual and emotional strength, etc., but He won't! That's not how He works! He works strictly on the order of Faith, and no other way. And when we say *"faith,"* we mean Faith in Christ and what Christ did at the Cross. That being done, the Holy Spirit then works mightily within our lives. Otherwise, He won't!

Christ has already kept the Law and has done so in every respect; He thereby did what we could not do for ourselves.

You see, keeping all of the Law some of the time is not good enough. Likewise, keeping some of the Law all of the time is not good enough. One has to keep all of the Law all of the time, which, of course, is impossible. It is impossible because man, due to the Fall, is born into sin.

This makes it impossible for him to do what he needs to do, at least in that fashion.

Paul was trying so hard and yet failing. And he did not understand why. That's what the word *"allow"* in Verse 15 means; it should have been translated accordingly:

"For that which I do I understand not" (Rom. 7:15).

There are millions of Christians presently who are trying with all of their strength and might to live the life they ought to live, but nevertheless failing, and they simply don't understand why. The very thing they want to do, which is to live a righteous life, they find they cannot do. And that which they don't want to do, which is to fail the Lord by the means of sin, that's what they find themselves doing.

This situation is the result of the Believer attempting to live for the Lord in all the wrong ways. He tries to live for the Lord by keeping Commandments, whatever those Commandments might be. The end result will be failure. In fact, the failure, despite all the efforts otherwise, will become worse and worse.

Once again, the Cross is the only answer!

SEPTEMBER

2

f or I know that in me (that is, in my flesh,) dwells no good thing: for to will is present with me; but how to perform that which is good I find not (Rom. 7:18).

Most Christians think that when a person comes to Christ, the Lord gives them an extra strong willpower. Consequently, they now have, they think, the power to say *"No!"* to sin.

None of that is correct!

It may come as a shock and a surprise to most Christians, but the Devil can easily override the willpower of a person. The only *"willpower"* that the Lord gives a person is the will to say *"Yes!"* to Christ, which is, in fact, very important. This means that the worst sinner in the world, for example, one totally bound by alcohol or drugs, who cannot say *"No!"* to those vices, can, if he so desires, say *"Yes!"* to Christ. It is the same principle with the Believer.

The Lord doesn't really give the Believer the capacity to say *"No!"* to sin, because we are *"dead to sin."* A dead man doesn't say anything. In this *"newness of life,"* however, we are given the capacity to say *"Yes!"* to Christ and His Way, which is the Way of the Cross. That is where the will of man begins and ends.

The Believer does not overcome by willpower; he overcomes by Faith. This means, as we have repeatedly stated, Faith in Christ and the Cross (Gal. 6:14).

If one studies the life of the Apostle Paul, one must come to the conclusion that he was a man with a strong constitution. I personally believe Paul had extremely strong willpower; however, he very clearly states in Romans 7:18 that he had the will to live the life he knew he ought to live, but *"how to perform that which is good he found not."* His willpower, in other words, simply was not good enough. And neither is yours!

Law, as a barrier to the will, excites it; and the consciousness of sin thereby awakened produces in the Presence of God a conscience under sentence of death. Thus, the Commandment ordained unto life becomes, in fact, the instrument of death. *"This do and you shall live"* became death to man because his sinful nature refused to obey; and in so refusing his own conscience, it condemned him to death.

Thus, the Law was holy and each of its Commandments just and good, but it condemned to death all who failed to render to it a perfect obedience, as condemn it must! Such is the effect of Divine Law upon man's carnal nature; the rest of this Seventh Chapter illustrates the doctrine by showing how fruitless is the effort of the *"old man"* to live as the *"new man."* There is simply no such thing as moral evolution, i.e., self cannot control self;

555

the flesh cannot control the flesh.

If the Believer is trying to live for God by any means other than Faith in Christ and the Cross, no matter how hard he tries, he will find himself sinking deeper and deeper into the morass of sin. That means the situation will become worse and worse.

There is no victory in *"trying harder."* There is victory only in Christ and the Cross!

SEPTEMBER

3

*f*or I delight in the Law of God after the inward man: But I see another Law in my members, warring against the Law of my mind, bringing me into captivity to the Law of sin which is in my members (Rom. 7:22-23).

There are several *"laws"* listed here, all designed by God, which will definitely work as they were designed to work. Those laws are:

1. *"The Law of God"*: This is the moral part of the Mosaic Law, in which the inner man delighted, but which, within himself, he was unable to keep. This is, in effect, The Ten Commandments (Ex., Chpt. 20).

2. *"The Law of the mind"*: This is the mind of the redeemed man, which wants to walk in victory. It has the desire and the will; but, within itself, it is insufficient.

3. *"The Law of sin"*: This is the sin nature, which is stronger than the *"Law of the mind,"* and which brings a person into spiritual captivity — captivity, in some way, to sin. The *"Law of the mind"* wants to serve the *"Law of God,"*

but not being strong enough within itself, instead finds the flesh serving *"the Law of sin"* (Rom. 7:25). This is the same as the *"Law of sin and death"* of Romans 8:2.

That's the reason the Apostle said, *"O wretched man that I am! Who shall deliver me from the body of this death?"* (7:24). Regrettably, this is exactly where most Christians are, at least those who sincerely want to live for God.

4. *"The Law of Faith"* (Rom. 3:27): This is the *"law"* designed by God which opens up the next law, which we will momentarily discuss. The *"Law of Faith"* refers strictly to Faith in Christ and His Finished Work.

5. *"The Law of the Spirit of Life in Christ Jesus"*: This is the most powerful law in the universe; it is the only law which is more powerful than the *"Law of sin and death,"* which is the same as the *"Law of sin"* of 7:23.

If the Believer doesn't function according to *"the Law of the Spirit of Life in Christ Jesus,"* he cannot walk in victory, cannot enjoy more abundant life, and he is, in fact, in danger of losing his way with God, even as millions already have.

These are laws which were designed by God; to be sure, these laws will always have the intended effect.

"The Law of sin and death" is the second most powerful law in the universe. It has filled the Earth with graves and has caused untold pain, sickness, suffering, and catastrophe. Unconverted man keeps trying to overcome this law by all type of means, but he cannot. Unfortunately, redeemed man tries to do the same thing. Either through ignorance or unbelief, with the results being the same in either case, far too many Believers attempt to overcome this terrible *"Law of sin and death"* by means other than

"the Law of the Spirit of Life in Christ Jesus" (8:2). It cannot be done, and it is not meant to be done.

We learn just how powerful *"the Law of sin and death"* actually is by understanding the price that had to be paid in order for this law to be overcome. That price was the Cross of Christ! That's the reason that Paul preached the Cross. That's the reason we preach the Cross. There is no other way.

SEPTEMBER

4

*t*here is therefore now no condemnation to them which are in Christ Jesus, who walk not after the flesh, but after the Spirit (Rom. 8:1).

As the subject of the Third and Fourth Chapters of Romans is God declaring how the sinner can be righteous, so the theme of this Chapter is God making the sinner holy. This Chapter opens with *"no condemnation"* and closes with *"no separation."* The subject of Romans 5:12-21 is *"condemnation"* for all who are in Adam; the theme of this Chapter is *"no condemnation"* for all who are in Christ.

The word *"condemnation"* in the Greek is *"katakrima,"* which means *"an adverse sentence, a verdict of guilt."*

Going back to 7:24, an Egyptian punishment at that time was to fasten a criminal to a corpse and leave it attached until death. It was a terrible bond, as would be obvious, and the more so because the man bound knew that the bond would result in death. This was possibly before the Apostle's mind when he wrote 7:24. Such a helpless and hopeless prisoner, held in a bond so loathsome and fatal, would cry out with anguish, *"Who can deliver me from this dead body?"*

This is the moral condition of all who are in Adam.

Christ, in a sense, took this very position at Calvary, and died in consequence. But having atoned for all sin, Satan could not hold Him in the bondage or captivity of death, so He rose from among the dead and ascended above the highest heavens, having, by His Death, destroyed death (Heb. 2:14), abolished sin in the flesh (Heb. 9:26), and exhausted the curse of the Law (Gal. 3:13). The glad tidings of the Gospel consist in the declaration that all who by Faith are in Christ died and rose with Him, and there is consequently no person and no thing that can condemn them. For Christ there is now no condemnation. He suffered its fullness infinitely at Calvary.

But He suffered that condemnation there on behalf of, and for the benefit of, all who believe upon Him. Hence, there is no condemnation for us. We are in a new position entirely beyond and above the reach of everything to which condemnation attaches. Where Christ and all who are in Him now stand there can be no question of sin, of wrath, of condemnation, or of imputation of punishment. All such questions were settled before He ascended thither; and He is on the Throne of God, His Person and Work accepted because these questions were settled.

The glorious truth that liberates the Believer's heart is that he is there in that glory with Christ, where nothing that condemns can reach him.

"Even when we were dead in sins, has quickened us

together with Christ, (by Grace you are saved;)

"And has raised us up together, and made us sit together in Heavenly Places in Christ Jesus" (Eph. 2:5-6).

The Believer is dead to the old life, for he was Crucified with Christ. As a partner with Christ, he, therefore, enjoys all the advantages of the partnership acquired by Christ before he was brought into it. This is not merely an experience, it is a Divine Operation apprehended and enjoyed by Faith.

SEPTEMBER

5

*t*here is therefore now no condemnation to them which are in Christ Jesus, who walk not after the flesh, but after the Spirit (Rom. 8:1).

How does the Believer *"walk after the Spirit"* and *"not after the flesh"*?

Most Believers have it in their mind that *"walking after the Spirit"* (Holy Spirit) is doing spiritual things. It isn't! At least not in that manner.

At a prayer meeting some time ago, I asked those assembled what *"walking after the Spirit"* actually meant. The answers were typical.

One said that it was reading several Chapters of the Bible each day. Another said that is was praying so much each day. Another mentioned witnessing to souls. All of the answers were in that vein.

No! The doing of spiritual things is not what Paul was talking about when he mentioned *"walking after the Spirit."*

So what does it mean?

First of all, the word *"walk"* refers to the manner in which we order our behavior regarding our life and living. To *"walk after the Spirit"* refers to the manner in which this is done.

How is it done?

The *"Spirit,"* of course, is the Holy Spirit. The Passage refers to the manner in which He operates. We find that in the next Verse, Romans 8:2. To be brief, the manner in which the Holy Spirit works concerns the parameters of the Finished Work of Christ. In other words, He works exclusively within the confines of the Cross of Christ. For a person to *"walk after the Spirit,"* that person must therefore exhibit Faith in Christ and the Cross, and do so exclusively. That's what *"walking after the Spirit"* actually means.

Reading one's Bible, prayer, witnessing, and all such like things are, of course, very helpful to the Child of God, and are things in which every true Believer will frequently engage. However, those things should be a result of walking after the Spirit instead of the cause. In fact, they cannot be the cause.

Conversely, if we *"walk after the flesh,"* this means that we are placing our faith in something other than the Cross of Christ. And it really doesn't matter what the other thing might be. In fact, most of the those things other than the Cross in which Believers place their faith are generally good things, and that's what deceives us. They are *"good,"* so we think the doing of them should merit us something with God or else should bring some type of victory.

Let it ever be understood:

The only way the Child of God truly can have victory and walk after the Spirit is to constantly exhibit Faith in Christ and what Christ did at the Cross. But problemati- cally, most Believers are not content to do that; they rather want to do something else — and the something else always constitutes *"walking after the flesh,"* which always brings defeat.

When one truly begins to *"walk after the Spirit,"* doing so on a constant basis, which all can do, then the *"more abundant life"* promised by Christ, definitely given at conversion, will then be totally and completely enjoyed (Jn. 10:10).

SEPTEMBER

6

*f*or the Law of the Spirit of Life in Christ Jesus had made me free from the law of sin and death (Rom. 8:2).

Without a doubt, Romans 8:2 is one of the most important Scriptures in the entirety of the Bible. It sums up all that Paul has been teaching. It tells us how the Holy Spirit works in our lives, and there could be nothing more important than that. Tragically, most Christians just take the Holy Spirit for granted, not really knowing how He works, what He does, and the manner in which He does it. Even though the Holy Spirit will do all He possibly can to help the Believer, still, if we function outside of God's Prescribed Order, which is Christ and the Cross, the help the Holy Spirit gives is greatly curtailed. This spells trouble. But let's see how He works.

First of all, this of which we speak is *"the law,"* a law devised by the Godhead even before the foundation of the world (I Pet. 1:18-20). Being a *"law,"* actually *"the law,"* this means that the Holy Spirit is not going to work outside of the framework of this law. We should understand that.

It is the Holy Spirit Who works in the hearts and lives of Believers, Who Alone can make us what we ought to be. If we try outside of this *"law"* to develop His Fruit, or Christlikeness, Righteousness, Holiness, or Victory of any nature, we are doomed to failure. We need to remember that! He will not differ from this, nor vary from God's Prescribed Order.

He is called *"The Spirit of Life"* because He is the Superintendent of all that Christ did at the Cross. In a sense, the Holy Spirit is a dispenser of this *"Life"* afforded by Christ. In other words, you are not going to get it any other way.

The word *"Life,"* as it is used here, refers to every single thing that Christ did at the Cross. In other words, everything that man lost in the Fall, and we mean everything, was addressed at the Cross, which is all wrapped up in the one word *"Life."* Admittedly, we do not now have everything for which Jesus paid such a price, actually having only the firstfruits, with the balance coming at the Resurrection; still, what we actually do now have in Christ is enough to supply all that we presently need, whatever that might be. This is what *"Life"* in Romans 8:2 actually means.

While all of this *"Life"* comes from Christ as the Source, with the Cross as the Means, still, it is the Holy Spirit Who is the Superintendent of all that Christ has done — the Dispenser, as one might say. It comes from Christ by the means of the Cross and through the Spirit (Jn. 7:37-39).

The phrase, *"In Christ Jesus,"* describes this *"Law"* and the way the Spirit works. Paul uses this phrase, *"in Christ Jesus,"* or one of its derivatives, such as *"in Him,"* etc. over one hundred times in his fourteen Epistles. Without exception, it refers to what Christ did at the Cross, all on our behalf. Paul never uses it in any other fashion. It always refers to the Cross.

For us to be the beneficiary of all that Christ did, through which the Holy Sprit works, all that is demanded of us is that our Faith constantly rest in that Finished Work. This is imperative. When this is done, all that Jesus did will be ours, guaranteed by the Holy Spirit.

"The Law of the Spirit of Life in Christ Jesus," which we hopefully have explained, is the only *"Law"* which can give one victory over *"the law of sin and death."* No matter the effort made, if we try to obtain that victory by any other manner, defeat is sure.

If the Believer faithfully follows this which the Holy Spirit gave to the Apostle Paul, which Paul then gave to us, victory then is guaranteed and *"the sin nature will not have dominion over us"* (Rom. 6:14). But if works of the flesh are prevalent in the Believer's life, that means that he or she is not functioning in *"the Law of the Spirit of Life in Christ Jesus,"* but rather in some law made up by themselves or other men.

In the Lord's Way is *"Life"*! In the Lord's Way alone is *"Life"*!

SEPTEMBER

7

f or to be carnally minded is death; but to be Spiritually minded is life and peace (Rom. 8:6).

What does it mean to be *"carnally minded"*? What does it mean to be *"spiritually minded"*?

To be *"carnally minded"* is <u>not</u> watching too much television, or being too interested in sports, etc., as most Christians think. Actually, those things have absolutely nothing to do with what Paul is addressing here. Being *"carnally minded"* is placing one's faith in something other than Christ and the Cross. That sums up what the Apostle is here saying.

There are two wills contrasted in Verses 5 through 8: the will of the carnal nature and the Will of God. The carnal will, being independent of God's Will, is hostile to it and cannot be otherwise. All who are governed by the carnal will cannot, so long as they are thus governed, please God, let them be ever so religious, moral, cultivated, or noble. It is not that God takes no pleasure in noble actions, but that He cannot take pleasure in and accept worship and meritorious actions designed to purchase His favor which are prompted by the carnal mind. Hence, he rejected Cain's worship and offerings.

All who are controlled by the carnal will set their affections upon gratifying it. The opposite is true in the case of those controlled by the Divine Will. The one control ends in death; the other, in life.

Cain offered a sacrifice which God can never accept, because it was the labor of his own hands. Regrettably, the far greater majority of modern Believers are attempting to do the same. That is what the Holy Spirit is referring to here by being *"carnally minded."* Our Faith must be exclusively in Christ and the Cross, otherwise, it is that which is not of the Lord, no matter how noble or righteous it might, on the surface, seem to be.

Any way other than the Cross leads to failure, sin, disobedience, and spiritual death.

To be *"spiritually minded"* is to follow the pattern laid down by the Lord, which is *"Christ and Him Crucified."* Being *"spiritually minded"* is what one must be to successfully *"walk after the Spirit."*

Let us say it again:

It simply means placing one's Faith exclusively in Christ and the Cross, excluding all else, and not allowing anything to take the place of the Cross.

Modern Christians have some understanding of the Cross regarding Salvation, but almost none as it regards Sanctification. As a result, spiritual failure all too often characterizes most modern Believers, even those who try extra hard not to fail. It is because of a *"carnal mind."* When one is *"spiritually minded,"* he has *"life and peace,"* which is the way it ought to be, and which is the way it can be.

SEPTEMBER

8

*S*o then they who are in the flesh cannot please God (Rom. 8:8).

Paul uses the terms, *"the flesh"* or *"in the flesh,"* quite often. What does he mean?

He is speaking of a person's own natural ability, our natural strength, our own efforts, in other words, what we as a human being can do.

We cannot do anything within our own strength and power that will gain anything with the Lord, no matter how noble our efforts might be. In other words, the Lord cannot accept our efforts, our ability, our personal power, etc. So to have what we must receive from the Lord, that is, if we are to live as we ought to live, then we will have to depend totally, and I mean totally, on Christ and what Christ has done for us at the Cross.

To help us understand it better, anything we try to do, any way we attempt to go, any effort we attempt to make, other than by Faith in Christ and the Cross, is labeled by the Holy Spirit as *"the flesh,"* which is displeasing to God, and which will never bring victory.

Why not?

In the first place, what needs to be done, no matter how strong we are, no matter how courageous we are, no matter our great effort, no matter the willpower, what is needed is beyond the scope of humanity. That being the case, God became Man, and, as the Lord Jesus Christ, did for man what man could not do for himself. The price, to be sure, was high, and we speak of the Cross. But He gladly paid it!

So when we ignore that, we are in essence saying that the Sacrifice of Christ is insufficient, or else it needs something which we can add to it, which is a tremendous insult to Christ, as should be overly obvious. As the Scripture plainly proclaims here, such a direction seriously displeases God.

Many Believers have the erroneous idea that when they are baptized with the Holy Spirit, then the Lord will give them greater willpower, greater fortitude, and greater courage, thus enabling them to say *"No!"* to the world, the flesh, and the Devil.

Let the following ever be understood:

The Holy Spirit will never give victories to the flesh. In other words, He does not strengthen the willpower of the Believer, or our own natural ability, etc. That would only glorify the flesh, which would tend to increase pride in the heart and life of such a person, which the Lord will never do.

The *"power"* He speaks of giving us (Acts 1:8) is His Power manifested in our lives, as we evidence Faith in

Christ and the Cross. Then, and only then, will <u>His</u> Power be manifested. Unfortunately, far too many Christians think that the Holy Spirit makes them stronger. He doesn't!

Concerning this very thing, Paul said, *"When I am weak, then am I strong"* (II Cor. 12:10).

Truly, every Christian is weak; they just won't admit it. When we recognize that we are weak, which means that we can't do what needs to be done, and then we correctly place our Faith in Christ and the Cross, then the Holy Spirit will do for us what only He can do.

SEPTEMBER

9

b*ut if the Spirit of Him Who raised up Jesus from the dead dwell in you, He Who raised up Christ from the dead shall also quicken your mortal bodies by His Spirit who dwells in you* (Rom. 8:11).

Paul is not speaking here of the Resurrection, when the Trump of God shall sound, as most Christians think. He is speaking of Jesus being raised from the dead, and the fact that the same Holy Spirit Who effected this in Christ (raised Him from the dead) also lives within us, i.e., *"dwells in you."* It also means that the same power that was made available to Christ is made available to us in order that we might live the life we ought to live, i.e., *"the Resurrection Life."*

Listen to what the Apostle said:

"He Who raised up Christ from the dead shall also quicken your mortal bodies."

What does he mean by that?

Once again, he is not speaking of the Rapture of the

Church, when our vile bodies will be changed into Glorified Bodies, but rather to our present physical bodies being quickened, i.e., made alive, by the Holy Spirit.

And what does that mean?

Man is created spirit, soul, and body. Of these three, the body is the weak link. Even though sin originates in the heart, i.e., *"the soul and the spirit of the individual,"* still, it manifests itself through the physical body. The physical body of the Believer is neutral. It is not holy or unholy, but only one or the other in the way it is used.

Without the Holy Spirit making alive our mortal bodies, no matter how hard we try, no matter the effort made as Believers, no matter how many Scriptures we quote, etc., sin will manifest itself through the physical body. That's what Paul was talking about when he told us not to yield the members of our body as instruments of unrighteousness unto sin, but rather to yield our members (members of our physical bodies) as instruments of Righteousness unto God (Rom. 6:13).

Two factors are brought to play in order that we may accomplish the yielding to righteousness instead of yielding to sin. First of all, we cannot, as we have already stated, do this thing ourselves. Only the Holy Spirit can do it. To be sure, He most definitely can do whatever it is that needs to be done. For Him to do such, even as we have repeatedly stated, all that is required of us is that our Faith be ever anchored in Christ and what Christ has done at the Cross.

When we do this, and continue to do this, not allowing our faith to be moved elsewhere, then the Holy Spirit will begin to *"quicken our mortal bodies,"* meaning that we will then yield to Righteousness instead of unrighteousness.

This is God's Way, and His only Way.

Unfortunately, almost all of the books and tapes which are now being printed in connection with this very subject are, for all practical purposes, useless!

The reason?

They are telling people how to function outside of God's Prescribed Order, which is Christ and the Cross; they rather emphasize "the flesh," whether they realize such or not.

The path to victory is Christ and the Cross. The only path to victory is Christ and the Cross!

SEPTEMBER
10

*f*or as many as are led by the Spirit of God, they are the sons of God (Rom. 8:14).

The idea of this Verse is that inasmuch as we are sons of God, we can be led by the Spirit of God. Unfortunately, most Believers are not led by the Spirit of God, simply because they don't know how to be led by the Spirit of God. Merely having the Spirit of God, which, within itself, is spectacular, doesn't guarantee His Leading. Sadly, most Christians take the Holy Spirit for granted.

If they are truly Born-Again, they know that the Holy Spirit lives within their hearts and lives, but they hardly understand at all the manner and the way in which He functions within their hearts and lives. Consequently, things are done which greatly hinder Him.

We must remember that all the wonderful things that He can do, which He wants and desires to do, actually which He has been sent by God the Father to do, and which He actively seeks to do, are only potential in nature.

This means that the potential for Him to do all of these great things is there, but that doesn't necessarily mean that they will get done.

As should be obvious, it is a shame to have the Holy Spirit, Who is God, living and residing in our hearts and lives, and have Him strongly desiring to do great things for us, which He can do because He can do anything, but yet not see them done. This is not an isolated problem. It is pandemic in the Christian community; that is, most Christians are only seeing a tiny part of what the Spirit can do within our hearts and lives.

How can the Christian be led by the Spirit of God?

He is led by the Spirit of God in the same manner as his *"walking after the Spirit"* or being *"spiritually minded."*

I keep saying it over and over again, simply because I must say it over and over again:

The Believer simply has to place his Faith exclusively in Christ and the Cross, and keep his Faith in Christ and the Cross, renewing it, in a sense, on a daily basis (Lk. 9:23), which will guarantee our being *"led by the Spirit."* This is the manner, and the only manner, in which one is so led!

This way brings the Fruit of the Spirit, Righteousness, Holiness, Christlikeness, and Victory in every capacity.

The other way, which is the way of the flesh, brings nothing but defeat, sadness, sorrow, and heartache, echoing what Paul said, *"O wretched man that I am! Who shall deliver me from the body of this death?"* (Rom. 7:24).

For you who hold this book in your hands, you who have read these words, there is no more excuse for failure in your life. You now know the way, so walk therein!

SEPTEMBER
11

*a*nd not only they, but ourselves also, which have the *Firstfruits of the Spirit, even we ourselves groan within ourselves, waiting for the Adoption, to wit, the Redemption of our body* (Rom. 8:23).

Several things are said in this Passage, all of extreme significance to the Believer.

First of all, we are told here that we only have the *"Firstfruits of the Spirit,"* which refer to the fact that all that Jesus did at the Cross is not yet available to us. As stated, we only have the *"firstfruits."*

Everything that man lost in the Fall, and everything that Satan did in his revolution against God, which continues unto this hour, all, and without exception, were addressed at the Cross (Eph. 1:10). And, to be sure, what we now have is more than enough to live as we ought to live and be as we ought to be. Of that, one can be doubly certain!

Second, this Passage tells us that the struggle of faith

is ever with us while we wait for the Redemption of the body, i.e., *"the Glorified Body."*

Upon reading the information that Paul gives us regarding victory in Christ and the Cross, many Believers immediately sense in their spirit that this is right. They set out to anchor their Faith exactly as it ought to be anchored, i.e., in Christ and the Cross, and then immediately run into Satan, which oftentimes results in failure. Many then think that the Cross doesn't work.

They have been led to believe that, from the moment they correctly register their Faith, there will never again be another problem. That's not the case at all.

While we may fail, the Cross never fails. This means that if we, in fact, do fail, and, to be sure, every one of us will, at least in one way or the other, this shows that our faith is deficient. It's never really as strong as we think it is. And even when our faith is strong, we may misunderstand the struggle of this conflict.

Let me give you an Old Testament example:

The Lord told Moses that he was to inform Pharaoh that the Children of Israel must be released from Egyptian bondage. Moses obeyed the Lord; however, Pharaoh didn't budge. It didn't matter what the Lord had said. Moses had to appear before Pharaoh seven times demanding the release of the Children of Israel (Ex. 5:1-2).

Just because your Faith is properly anchored doesn't mean the Evil One is going to fold and buckle. Satan will try your Faith, just as Pharaoh tried the Faith of Moses and Aaron.

Second, instead of letting the Children of Israel go, Pharaoh doubled their burden. Heretofore, he supplied the straw, and they made the brick. Now they must supply their own straw and continue to make just as many bricks as always (Ex. 5:4-13).

Once your Faith is properly anchored, Satan may very well double the temptation against you; however, the Lord will only allow that to last for a period of time. Faith must be tested, and great Faith must be tested greatly! If you, dear Reader, fail, as most do, you should ask the Lord to forgive you, get back up, and start back on your course. The difference in now and before is that you are now on the right road. Victory will ultimately be yours. Before, that definitely was not the case!

Because of the extra work load, some Israelites began to turn against Moses and Aaron (Ex. 5:19-23). To be sure, the possibility definitely exists that some of your Christian friends, even your Christian relatives, will turn against you.

Why?

The Message of the Cross exposes the flesh, false doctrine, even everything that opposes Christ; therefore, it arouses the hostility in the natural man — Christian or no! This will be the unkindest cut of all. But, if you stay the course, the course of the Cross, Victory most definitely will be yours — a Victory unparalleled. Moreover, Romans 8:23 also points to the time that is coming, when the struggle will be completely over, and we will be with Christ, with a Glorified Body. That time is closer now than ever!

SEPTEMBER
12

*L*ikewise the Spirit also helps our infirmities: for we know not what we should pray for as we ought: but the Spirit itself (Himself) makes intercession for us with groanings which cannot be uttered. And He Who searches the hearts knows what is the Mind of the Spirit, because He makes intercession for the Saints according to the Will of God (Rom. 8:26-27).

The *"intercession"* the Holy Spirit makes for us is not the same as the intercession made by Christ for us. The intercession made by Christ concerns sin (Heb. 7:25). As someone has well said, *"Were it not for the constant, never-ceasing intercession by Christ, all on our behalf, we wouldn't last out the day."* How true that is!

The type of intercession made for us by the Holy Spirit concerns the help that we need in order to live a holy life, i.e., that which we have been discussing in previous devotions. This involves the manner in which the Holy Spirit works on our behalf. If we go wrong and fail, Christ then serves as our Intercessor, but, at the same time, the Holy

Spirit desires to show us why we failed, which always involves faith improperly placed, which, of course, has to do with the Cross.

The phrase, *"With groanings which cannot be uttered,"* does not refer to the Holy Spirit groaning, but rather to Believers, which pertains to that which comes from the heart and cannot properly be put into words. The overriding goal of the Spirit is to carry out the Will of God in our lives, not our personal will; in other words, the Spirit is not a glorified bellhop, as some have been led to believe.

To have the help of the Holy Spirit is to have the help of God, for the Holy Spirit is God. This means the help we receive is perfect and more than enough. He knows exactly what we need, why we need it, how much of it we need, etc.

The word *"infirmities"* in the Greek is *"astheneia,"* which means *"feebleness of body or mind, frailty, disease, sickness, weakness."* These are things that Believers face constantly. When we try to pray about them, oftentimes we don't really know how to pray. However, if our Faith is properly placed, and we continue to speak of Christ and the Cross, this will give the Holy Spirit latitude to work. To be sure, He will make things right.

As we keep saying, the reason we have so little help from the Holy Spirit is because our faith is improperly placed. That is the sole reason. He will not penalize us for any other situation. If we properly place our Faith in Christ and the Cross, then we will have His full help and His full intercession, and our entire life will function 100 percent better.

SEPTEMBER

13

*a*nd we know that all things work together for good to them who love God, to them who are the called according to His purpose (Rom. 8:28).

This Scripture is, without a doubt, one of the most quoted found in the entirety of the Word of God. It is an astounding Promise! There are, however, some conditions in this Promise, conditions which many Christians overlook. The Promise made here is not a blanket guarantee, as many think; but, if the conditions are met, then most definitely it is a guarantee.

What are those conditions?

First of all, to have all things working together for our good, we have to *"love God."* As Believers, we might automatically think this is a simple requirement. But it's not quite as simple as we would think. That is why Jesus, after His Resurrection and immediately before His Ascension, questioned Peter closely. The questions concerned Peter's love for Christ (Jn. 21:15-17). It is very easy to

584

loudly acclaim how much we love the Lord, but words oftentimes are hollow.

To make a lengthy subject brief, if we really love the Lord as we say we do, we will place our Faith exclusively in Him and what He did for us at the Cross. In a greater manner than anything else, that will show our love and will open the door for the consecration we need to make.

The second requirement is that we function in His Calling for our lives *"according to His Purpose."* So many times, it is *"our purpose"* instead of *"His Purpose"*! Moreover, we cannot know that for which He truly has called us, or what His Purpose is for our lives, unless our Faith is properly anchored in the Cross.

The reason?

When our faith is anchored elsewhere, this means that we are functioning according to the flesh, which harks back to our own personal desires, and not at all what the Lord wants. In fact, faith anchored outside of the Cross can hardly achieve His Purpose at all. Accordingly, we have all kind of things, which are very obvious, not working for the good of Christians.

To have our Faith properly placed doesn't mean that Satan will cease his operation against us; however, it does mean that whatever he tries to do, the Lord will ultimately turn it to our good. We here have His Promise to that effect, and the Lord most definitely keeps His Promises, that is, if we meet His Conditions, which, in fact, can easily be met, if we get *"self"* out of the way.

SEPTEMBER

14

*N*o, in all these things we are more than conquerors through Him Who loved us (Rom. 8:37).

If we follow what the Holy Spirit gave to the Apostle Paul, thereby ordering our lives accordingly, which refers to Faith being properly placed in Christ and the Cross (I Cor. 1:17-18, 23; 2:2; Gal. 6:14), then we are assured of the fact that we are not only *"conquerors,"* but also *"more than conquerors."* We must, however, always remember that it is *"through Him Who loved us."* We cannot be conquerors any other way.

"Through Him" refers exclusively to His atoning Work at the Cross, which totally and completely defeated the Evil One, and did so by atoning for all sin (Col. 2:14-15). *"More than conquerors"* is what the Lord wants His People to be. But this modern generation of Christians represents, I'm afraid, the most defeated generation since the Reformation. Why?

Although more books have been written on faith in

the past several decades than possibly the balance of the Church Age put together, virtually all of these books and tapes are worthless, because they direct the faith of the Believer to something other than Christ and Cross. As a result, *"more than conquerors"* is not what is happening, but rather *"more than conquered."* Satan has not only *"conquered"* this generation of Christians, but even *"more than conquered"* them, making abject slaves of them, which means that the sin nature runs wild.

Let me say it this way:

It is absolutely impossible for the Believer, be he the Pastor of the largest Church in the land or the Evangelist drawing the biggest crowds, to maintain victory over the world, the flesh, and the Devil, if such a Believer doesn't know God's Prescribed Order of Victory.

That Prescribed Order is:

1. The Cross of Christ: Everything we receive from the Lord, irrespective as to what it is, comes to us strictly from Christ as the Source and the Cross as the means.

2. Our Faith: Every single Believer is to place his Faith exclusively in Christ and what Christ did at the Cross, never separating the two. And when we speak of the Cross, we are speaking of the benefits which come from that Finished Work, and which will never cease.

3. The Holy Spirit: Once our Faith is properly placed, the Holy Spirit, Who works exclusively within the parameters of the Finished Work of Christ, will then make of us *"more than conquerors."*

This is God's Way. This is God's only Way, because no other way is needed (Gen. 3:15; Lk. 9:23; Rom. 6:1-14; Gal. 6:14; I Cor. 1:17-18; 2:2).

SEPTEMBER
15

*W*ho are Israelites; to whom pertain the Adoption, and the glory, and the Covenants, and the giving of the Law, and the service of God, and the Promises; Whose are the fathers, and of whom as concerning the flesh Christ came, Who is over all, God blessed forever. Amen (Rom. 9:4-5).

The Apostle Paul was accused of being disloyal to Israel and to the Promises made to it through the fathers. The Doctrine of Justification by Faith, apart from works, common to all men, whether Hebrews or not, seemed to set aside those Promises. The problem, therefore, was to reconcile the Grace of God in Justification with the special privileges granted to Israel. The resolution of the problem is found in the Doctrine of the Cross, and the Cross alone!

The Apostle begins by affirming his deep love for Israel. Far from despising them, he loved them as much as Moses did. He points out that all the privileges belong to them, and argues that the sovereignty of God admits the Gentiles to these privileges, thereby enriching

Israel's glories instead of nullifying them.

This section, Chapters 9 through 11 of Romans, begins with Paul's sorrow over Israel's failure (9:1-5), and it closes with Paul's joy over Israel's future (11:33-36). The main reason, however, for these three Chapters is not to prophetically analyze Israel, although a prophetical analysis is readily given. The reason is something else altogether, which we will deal with in the next devotion.

Dealing first of all with the Prophetical analysis given in Chapters 9 through 11, the Apostle, by the Holy Spirit, reiterates the Prophecies of old by predicting Israel's Restoration. He said, *"For I would not, Brethren, that you should be ignorant of this mystery* (what has happened to Israel), *lest you should be wise in your own conceits* (the Gentiles were not pulled in because of any merit or righteousness on their part, but strictly because of the Grace of God); *that blindness in part is happened to Israel* (Israel is the *"mystery"* of which Paul speaks), *until the fullness of the Gentiles be come in* (refers to the Church; in fact, the Church Age is even now coming to a close).

"And so all Israel shall be saved (when the Church Age ends and the Second Coming commences, then Israel will accept Christ and be saved): *as it is written* (Isa. 27:9; 59:20-21), *There shall come out of Sion the Deliverer* (Jesus Christ will be the Deliverer), *and shall turn away ungodliness from Jacob* (Christ will deliver Israel from the Antichrist, and, more importantly, will deliver them from their sins):

"For this is My Covenant unto them (a Promise), *when I shall take away their sins"* (as stated, it will be done at the Second Coming [Zech. 13:1]) Rom. 11:25-27.

Since 1948, when Israel once again became a nation, all the events up until now, have to do with the fulfillment of these things here discussed by Paul, which will continue until the Second Coming, when Israel will accept Christ. We are, therefore, coming down to the end of the Age.

SEPTEMBER
16

*b*rethren, my heart's desire and prayer to God for Israel is, that they might be saved. For I bear them record that they have a zeal of God, but not according to knowledge. For they being ignorant of God's Righteousness, and going about to establish their own righteousness, have not submitted themselves unto the Righteousness of God (Rom. 10:1-3).

The main purpose of the Holy Spirit giving us, through Paul, Chapters 9 through 11 of Romans was not, as stated, for Prophetical analysis, even though that, in measure, was given, but rather to warn the Church. If the Church follows in Israel's footsteps by being ignorant of God's Righteousness or by refusing God's Righteousness, attempting, as Israel, to establish its own righteousness, the Church will be cut off just as Israel was cut off.

Concerning this, Paul said, "For if God spared not the natural branches (Israel), take heed lest He also spare not you (refers to the Church, as is obvious). Behold, therefore the goodness and severity of God (don't mistake the

Goodness of God for license): *on them which fell, severity* (speaks of Judgment which came on Israel, God's chosen People); *but toward you, goodness, if you continue in His Goodness* (proclaims the conditions; the continuing of that *"Goodness"* pertains to continued Faith in Christ and the Cross): *otherwise you also shall be cut off"* (Rom. 11:21-22).

"God's Righteousness" is that which is afforded by Jesus Christ, gained by and through the Cross. The only way that God's Righteousness can be given to anyone is by virtue of the Cross, which demands Faith on the part of the recipient. If one attempts to gain righteousness by any other manner, the Lord refers to it as *"self-righteousness,"* and it is unacceptable — totally unacceptable!

I ask the following question:

How much is the modern Church preaching the Cross?

The answer screams back at us, *"Precious little!"*

The Church has already apostatized. The Church Age opened with Christ standing in the midst of the candlesticks, in which the candlesticks represent the Church (Rev. 1:12-13). At the close of the Church Age, which pertains to the present time, we no longer find Christ in the midst of the Church, but rather outside, knocking on the door, trying to get it (Rev. 3:17-20). The Lord is, in fact, no longer dealing with the institutionalized Church as a whole, but rather with individuals only.

To be sure, the Lord has always dealt with individuals, but now it is <u>only</u> individuals.

"If any man hear My Voice, and open the door, I will come in to him, and will sup with him, and he with Me" (Rev. 3:20).

So, who presently is saved?

It is the same now as it was with Israel of old.

Paul said, *"Even so then at this present time* (Paul's day) *also there is a Remnant according to the election of Grace* (definitely speaks of Predestination, but not as many think; it is the *"Remnant"* that is elected or predestined, not who will be in the Remnant).

"And if by Grace (the Goodness of God, all made possible by the Cross), *then is it no more of works* (no one can point to their works as grounds for Salvation): *otherwise Grace is no more Grace* (if works are mixed with Grace, they nullify Grace). *But if it be of works, then is it no more Grace* (works can never produce Grace): *otherwise work is no more work"* (for example, Water Baptism, if acted upon wrongly, nullifies its true meaning; this also holds true for all other great Ordinances of the Lord) (Rom. 11:5-6).

As there was a *"Remnant"* in Israel who were saved, meaning that most were lost, likewise, there also is a *"Remnant"* in the modern Church who are saved, but only a Remnant. Israel had rejected much of that which was of the Lord, but when they rejected the Cross, there was nothing left. They were cut off. The modern Church has done the same thing. It has rejected much which is of the Lord, but now it is rejecting the Cross. As with Israel, if the Cross is rejected, that means the Righteousness of God is rejected, and that means the Church is also cut off — except for the *"Remnant."*

Are you in the Remnant?

The only way that anyone can be in the Remnant is by accepting Christ and what Christ did at the Cross. There is no other way!

SEPTEMBER
17

i *beseech you therefore, Brethren, by the Mercies of God,
that you present your bodies a Living Sacrifice, holy, acceptable unto God, which is your reasonable service. And be not
conformed to this world: but be ye transformed by the renewing of your mind, that you may prove what is that good, and
acceptable, and perfect, Will of God* (Rom. 12:1-2).

The first evidence of real Christian life is consecration to God and transformation from the world. This is
not an outside mechanical action, but an inward perpetual renewing of the mind, a seeking for, the doing of,
the Will of God.

In this consecration, the Holy Spirit through Paul demands of the Believer that we *"present our bodies a living
sacrifice, holy, acceptable unto God."* Then he tells us that
this is our *"reasonable service."*

How is this to be done?

Whenever the word *"sacrifice"* is mentioned in the Bible,
as it refers to the Lord, always, and without exception, it

goes back to the Cross. The only way that one can present one's physical body as a *"living sacrifice, holy, acceptable unto God,"* which, incidentally, is the only thing acceptable to God, is, as we have repeatedly stated, by the Believer placing his Faith exclusively in Christ and His Finished Work. The Holy Spirit will then do that which is necessary in the heart and life of such a Believer, which will make the Believer what he ought to be.

If anything else is presented to God, and I speak of any manner or way other than the Cross, it is totally unacceptable to God.

"So then they who are in the flesh cannot please God" (Rom. 8:8).

When the Believer attempts to function outside of the Cross, the situation becomes impossible. Sin and failure are the constant results, no matter how hard one may try otherwise. However, when the Believer places his Faith exclusively in Christ and His Finished Work, i.e., *"the Cross,"* the Holy Spirit then does for us what we cannot do for ourselves, and the situation then becomes easy. In other words, that which the Lord requires becomes a *"reasonable service."*

That's what Jesus was talking about when He said, *"Come unto Me, all ye who labor and are heavy laden, and I will give you rest.*

"Take My yoke upon you (the *"yoke"* of the *"Cross"* [Lk. 9:23]), *and learn of Me* (learn of His Sacrifice [Rom. 6:3-5]); *for I am meek and lowly in heart: and you shall find rest unto your souls* (the soul can find rest only in the Cross).

"For My yoke is easy, and My burden is light" (what He requires of us is very little, just to have Faith in Him, and

His Sacrificial Atoning Work [Mat. 11:28-30]).

Then, and only then, can such a Believer present his physical body as *"a living sacrifice, holy, acceptable unto God."* He will then find that what God demands is a *"reasonable service."*

SEPTEMBER
18

*f*or Christ sent me not to baptize, but to Preach the Gospel: not with wisdom of words, lest the Cross of Christ should be made of none effect (I Cor. 1:17).

Several things are said in this very informative Passage. They are as follows:

1. *"For Christ sent me not to baptize"*: We learn here that Water Baptism is not to have the emphasis regarding the Gospel, and neither should any other Church Ordinance. The Cross of Christ is to have the emphasis.

Paul is not demeaning Water Baptism, but only requiring that it be placed in its proper perspective. It should be obvious to all that Water Baptism, as important as it is in its own way, is not essential to Salvation. If it is essential, then the Apostle thanked God that he saw so few saved. Nor is it essential to obedience, even as others claim, for, in that case, the Apostle thanked God that he had made so few obedient (I Cor. 1:14-16).

2. *"But to Preach the Gospel"*: In this particular Verse,

we are emphatically told what the Gospel of Jesus Christ is. In brief, the Gospel is *"the Cross of Christ."* In other words, the Cross must be the foundation of all we believe, teach, and practice. If it is not, then whatever it is we are proclaiming, is, pure and simple, not the Gospel. This is extremely important, as should be overly obvious.

If our Message is right, we will get the results that a correct Message brings forth. If the Message is incorrect, there will be no favorable results, because there can be no favorable results. The entirety of the Christian Faith rests on the correct Message. If that Message is corrupted, diluted, or perverted in any way, this means that it is no longer the Gospel of Jesus Christ, but something else entirely.

The Message must be *"Jesus Christ and Him Crucified."* This is where the emphasis must be, and in every capacity.

3. *"Not with wisdom of words"*: Paul here plainly says that intellectualism is not the Gospel. This means that humanistic psychology is not the Gospel. Once again, the Gospel is, and must be, the Cross of Christ. Preachers of the Gospel must *"preach the Cross."*

4. *"Lest the Cross of Christ should be made of none effect"*: This tells us, in no uncertain terms, that the Cross of Christ must always be the emphasis of the Message. If it isn't, all that Christ did will be to no avail.

This coming Sunday morning, how many Preachers are making the Cross of Christ of none effect, because they are preaching a false message?

Of course, only the Lord knows the answer to that;

sadly, however, most fall into that category. This means that few people are truly being saved. Few are baptized with the Holy Spirit. Few are delivered, if any. As should be obvious, we should be very, very careful that we do nothing that makes *"the Cross of Christ of none effect."*

SEPTEMBER
19

*f*or the Preaching of the Cross is to them who perish foolishness; but unto us which are saved it is the Power of God (I Cor. 1:18).

How is the Cross the Power of God? That is the great question of this Text.

First of all, the statement in this Bible Text tells us that outside the *"preaching of the Cross"* there is no *"Power of God."*

Sin is a frightful business! Its bondage is so severe that man, with his ability, even religious man, holds no answer. In other words, there is no remedy for sin as it regards the intellectualism of man, the ability of man, or anything that man has. Sin is so powerful, so destructive, and so perverted that God had to become Man and had to go to the Cross in order that this most horrifying malady could be properly addressed. Otherwise, the human race was doomed!

Therefore, at the very beginning, we have to learn just

how bad the problem actually is. That, within itself, is a problem. Mankind doesn't admit how bad sin is, and the Church, by its actions, shows that it little understands the potency of sin. If it did, it would hardly try to adopt the bankrupt ways of the world in order to address this malady of darkness.

As it regards *"power,"* which is an absolute must if people are to be delivered, we must come to the conclusion that there is no power in a wooden cross. Likewise, there was really not any power in the death of Christ. Paul said that Jesus was *"Crucified through weakness"* (II Cor. 13:4). However, it must be understood that this *"weakness"* was contrived. In other words, He purposely did not use His Power to extricate Himself from the Cross. Had He done so, man could not have been redeemed. Furthermore, there certainly is no power in death itself, as would be overly obvious.

So, how does the preaching of the Cross bring about *"the Power of God"*?

It is not so much what happened at the Cross which brings about power, but rather what the death of Christ on the Cross made possible.

When Jesus died, He atoned for all sin — past, present, and future — at least for all who will believe (Jn. 3:16). Satan's power over humanity is sin; with all sin atoned, however, Satan loses his legal right to hold man in bondage. And yet, Satan continues to hold untold millions in bondage. So, how do we reconcile this?

Those who are unconverted have not availed themselves of what Jesus did at the Cross, so Satan has a legal right to keep them in bondage. Millions of Christians

601

also fall into the same category. They also have not availed themselves of what Jesus did at the Cross. So, in some way, Satan also holds these also in bondage.

That's why Paul said, "*Stand fast therefore in the liberty wherewith Christ has made us free, and be not entangled again with the yoke of bondage*" (Gal. 5:1). I remind the Reader that Paul here is speaking to Believers.

When Jesus atoned for all sin, this means that the sin debt was paid, at least for those who will believe, which then gives the Holy Spirit the latitude to work powerfully within our lives. The power is in the Holy Spirit, Who manifests such on our behalf, at least if our Faith is correctly placed in Christ and the Cross. The Cross is what afforded this.

Whenever we preach the Cross, and when individuals believe what we preach, the Holy Spirit can then exercise His Almighty Power on their behalf, for He is God; then sin, in all of its forms, can be overcome; then every bondage can be broken.

That's what the *"preaching of the Cross"* will do!

SEPTEMBER

20

*b*ut we Preach Christ Crucified, unto the Jews a stumblingblock, and unto the Greeks foolishness: But unto them which are called, both Jews and Greeks (Gentiles), Christ the Power of God, and the Wisdom of God (I Cor. 1:23-24).

The story of the Bible is the story of Jesus Christ and Him Crucified. Every Sacrifice in the Bible points toward that coming event. The entirety of the Tabernacle and Temple, with all of its furnishings, ceremonies, and rituals, all and without exception, point to Christ in either His Atoning, Mediatorial, or Intercessory Work. In fact, the entirety of the Law pointed to Christ in some manner.

That's why Paul said, "We preach Christ Crucified."

He didn't merely say, "We preach Christ," but rather "We preach Christ Crucified."

Many presently are preaching Christ, but, within itself, that is not enough.

Why isn't it enough?

The Virgin Birth of Christ was an absolute necessity;

however, had it stopped there, not one single soul would have been redeemed. The Perfect Life of Christ was an absolute necessity, but had it stopped there, not one single soul would have been redeemed. The healings and miracles were an absolute necessity, but had it stopped there, not one soul would have been redeemed.

Jesus had to go to the Cross. The Cross was ever His goal. Some 750 years before the fact, Christ said, *"I gave My back to the smiters, and My cheeks to them who plucked off the hair: I hid not My face from shame and spitting.*

"For the Lord GOD will help Me; therefore shall I not be confounded: therefore have I set My face like a flint, and I know that I shall not be ashamed" (Isa. 50:6-7). His Face was set like flint for the Cross, meaning that He would not be deterred.

The preaching of Christ Crucified is the Doctrine of the Atonement. It is the very heart of the Gospel. Remove that and there is no Gospel, but merely the ramblings of demented minds.

Why is Christ Crucified a stumblingblock to the Jews?

The Jews knew that anyone who was hung on a tree for committing a dastardly crime was cursed by God (Deut. 21:22-23). Jesus was hung on a Cross. So in the mind of the Jews, He was cursed by God. Consequently, He could not be the Messiah, or so they thought. For how could one who was cursed by God be the Messiah?

Christ was, however, not cursed by God, but rather was made a curse, which is altogether different (Gal. 3:13). He had to be *"made a curse"* because He had committed no crime or sin of any nature — ever! The reason His death had to be on the Cross is because He had to pay for the very worst sins that could ever be imagined; He therefore had to die even as the worst sinner would die, but not because of any sin that He Himself had committed, because, as stated, He never committed any.

In effect, He actually became a *"Sin Offering."* But all of this was a stumblingblock to the Jews.

Regarding the Greeks, i.e., *"Gentiles,"* the idea of a naked man hanging on a wooden gibbet, thereby redeeming the entirety of mankind, was, in their thinking, *"foolishness."* Those problems remain even unto this hour! But in spite of all that, if *"Christ Crucified"* is faithfully preached, whether to Jew or Gentile, to those who accept Christ, He becomes *"the Power of God, and the Wisdom of God."*

No other Message will bring about these twin attributes. We must *"preach Christ Crucified,"* i.e., *"Christ Crucified"* must be the underlying foundation of all that we believe and preach.

SEPTEMBER
21

*a*nd I, Brethren, when I came to you, came not with excellency of speech or of wisdom, declaring unto you the Testimony of God. For I determined not to know anything among you, save Jesus Christ, and Him Crucified (I Cor. 2:1-2).

Concerning Paul's statement, Williams says, "As today, so in Paul's day, people demanded that the Gospel should be preached in 'terms of modern thought' embellished with scholastic learning, convincing logic, forensic reasoning and cultured eloquence. The Apostle refused, declared such culture to be the wisdom of this world, and said that preaching according to the Divine Wisdom was preaching in the Power of the Holy Spirit, and that that was the only power which effected the moral result of the new birth."

So the theme of the preaching of the Apostle, which also should be our theme — which must be our theme — was the Divine Person and atoning Work of the great God and Saviour Jesus Christ.

I think Paul definitely could have been labeled an

"intellectual." He was one of the most educated men used by the Holy Spirit in the writing of the Scriptures. However, he purposely never used any of that particular learning, rather concentrating on one aspect, which from him we learn is the very heart of the Gospel — *"Jesus Christ and Him Crucified."*

Changed lives are to be the end result of the Gospel. That refers to the entire gamut of society, even to the worst cases of bondage. Every single person in history who has ever been changed for the good, that change has been effected by the Lord Jesus Christ, and only by the Lord Jesus Christ. Millions down through the ages can declare that testimony.

But Paul proclaims here that that which makes the work of Regeneration, the work of change brought about in the hearts and lives of individuals, is the Cross of Christ. As we keep saying, and even as Paul proclaims here, Christ and His Cross must never be separated. By that we speak of the benefits of what He did.

As we have stated many times:

Jesus Christ is the Source, and the Cross is the means, by which all these things are done.

The word *"determined"* lends credence to the idea that Paul was tempted to go in other directions; however, the Holy Spirit insisted that if the purpose of the Gospel is to be realized, then the theme must always be *"Jesus Christ and Him Crucified."* That, and that alone, is the answer for hurting, dying, sin-benighted humanity. There is no other solution for man's dilemma, even as there needs be no other solution.

SEPTEMBER
22

b *ut the natural man receives not the things of the Spirit of God: for they are foolishness unto him: neither can he know them, because they are spiritually discerned* (I Cor. 2:14).

The true Christian life is unintelligible to human wisdom, just as God's Mind and Ways are beyond natural wisdom.

The Scripture declares that all unsaved individuals are *"dead in trespasses and sins"* (Eph. 2:1). And *"dead"* is *"dead"*! This means that the unconverted individual is totally depraved, has no true knowledge of God, has no true understanding of God, has no true understanding of the things of God, etc. The unconverted man is dead to God in every respect.

That's why it is foolishness to appeal to the lost by the means of intellectualism. No matter how much one tries to explain something to a dead person, such explanation obviously is lost. How can a dead person understand anything concerning that to which he or she is dead?

For a person to be saved, the Word of God must be ministered in some way to such a heart and life. It may be in the form of preaching, or the words which are Scriptural in a song brought to the heart of the person, or even a Scripture learned as a child brought to the heart of the individual. The point I am making is that, in some way, the Word of God must be tendered toward the lost soul, that is, if the individual is to be saved.

While the unredeemed person doesn't understand the Word, and cannot understand the Word, still, the Word forms a basis on which the Holy Spirit works, without which He will not work. As the Word in some way goes forth, and as the Holy Spirit quickens it to the heart, the person is brought under conviction, and the one thing they do then know is that they are lost. In other words, they are convicted of their lost condition.

There is a pull generated then by the Holy Spirit to bring that person to an acceptance of Christ, Who Alone can meet and change the condition of the heart. If such a person then believes in their heart on Christ, that person is then Born-Again — instantly Born-Again, we might quickly add.

So, understanding the condition of the lost soul and how the Holy Spirit works, Preachers should realize that if they fail to preach Jesus Christ and Him Crucified, if they fail to make that the foundation of the presented Gospel, there will be no spiritual results.

The Word is clear. The Message is clear. There is no reason that Preachers of the Gospel should take any other tack than that laid down by the Apostle Paul. *"Excellency of speech or of wisdom"* will serve little purpose. The Message must be *"Jesus Christ and Him Crucified."*

SEPTEMBER
23

*k*now ye not that you are the Temple of God, and that the Spirit of God dwells in you? (I Cor. 3:16).

It is the Holy Spirit, the Third Person of the Trinity, Who has always carried out the Work of God on Earth. In fact, the Word of God begins by telling us that *"the Spirit of God moved upon the face of the waters"* (Gen. 1:2). As someone has well said, *"The Moving of the Spirit is the beginning of life, and without a Moving of the Spirit, there is no life."*

Regarding the Godhead, the only thing the Spirit of God didn't do on this Earth was the great Redemption process of Christ in coming to this world and dying on a Cross. But yet, the Holy Spirit most definitely superintended that great Work, the greatest Work of the ages, from beginning to end. The Holy Spirit even told Jesus when He could die.

Paul wrote, *"How much more shall the Blood of Christ, Who through the Eternal Spirit offered Himself without spot to God, purge your conscience from dead works to serve the*

Living God?" (Heb. 9:14).

It is the Holy Spirit Who makes Christianity different than any religion in the world. Nothing can compare with Bible Christianity.

Once I asked a Muslim why my Telecast was not allowed to air in Muslim countries, adding that Muslims could be on Radio or Television all over the United States if they wanted to be. He passed it off as just being their law, etc. But the real reason is that Islam cannot compete with Bible Christianity, and neither can any other religion.

Tragically, however, much of modern Christianity is corrupt, which means there is no Moving or Operation of the Holy Spirit. As such, the Church becomes ineffective. For the Church to be effective, for our lives to be effective, there must be a Moving and Operation of the Holy Spirit in the Church. This is absolutely indispensable!

When the Tabernacle was constructed, almost immediately after the Law was given by God, the Lord took up residence in the Tabernacle, actually residing between the Mercy Seat and the Cherubim (Num. 7:8-9; I Sam. 4:4). When Christ came, the Holy Spirit dwelt in Christ to a degree unknown by others (Lk. 3:22; 4:18-19; Ps. 45:7).

But the advent of the Cross, which atoned for all sin, satisfied the sin debt owed by all people. So now, upon confession of Faith in Christ, i.e., trusting in what He did for us at the Cross, the Holy Spirit comes into the heart and life of the Believer to abide permanently, as Paul records here.

Jesus actually had said, *"And I will pray the Father, and He will give you another Comforter ('parakletos,' which means 'one called to the side of another to help'), that He may abide with you forever* (before the Cross, the Holy Spirit could only help a few individuals, and then only for a period of time; since the Cross, He lives in the hearts and lives of all Believers, and does so forever);

"Even the Spirit of Truth (the Greek says, 'The Spirit of The Truth,' which refers to the Word of God; actually He does far more than merely superintend the attribute of Truth, as Christ *'is Truth'* [I Jn. 5:6]); *Whom the world cannot receive* (the Holy Spirit cannot come into the heart of the unbeliever until that person makes Christ his or her Saviour; then He comes in), *because it sees Him not, neither knows Him* (refers to the fact that only Born-Again Believers can understand the Holy Spirit and know Him): *but you know Him* (would have been better translated, 'but you shall get to know Him'); *for He dwells with you* (before the Cross), *and shall be in you"* (which would take place on the Day of Pentecost and thereafter, because the sin debt has been forever paid by Christ on the Cross, changing the disposition of everything) (Jn. 14:16-17).

However, it's not finished yet!

The ultimate desire, that, in fact, which will be the ultimate conclusion, is when God changes His Headquarters from planet Heaven to planet Earth, which the last two Chapters of Revelation proclaim. Then everything will be as it ought to be.

John said, *"And I heard a great Voice out of Heaven saying* (according to the best manuscripts, the Voice now heard was heard *"out of the Throne"*), *Behold, the Tabernacle of God is with men, and He will dwell with them, and they shall be His people, and God Himself shall be with them, and be their God* (finally proclaims that which God intended from the beginning).

"*And God shall wipe away all tears from their eyes* (actually says "*every teardrop*" in the Greek, referring to tears of sorrow); *and there shall be no more death, neither sorrow, nor crying, neither shall there be any more pain* (addresses sin and all its results): *for the former things are passed away*" (refers to the entire effect of the Fall) (Rev. 21:3-4).

SEPTEMBER
24

f or I received of the Lord that which also I delivered unto you, That the Lord Jesus the same night in which He was betrayed took bread: And when He had given thanks, He broke it, and said, Take, eat: this is My Body, which is broken for you: this do in remembrance of Me. After the same manner also He took the cup, when He had supped, saying, This cup is the New Testament in My Blood: this do ye, as oft as you drink it, in remembrance of Me (I Cor. 11:23-25).

In brief, this which Paul here gives us is a description of the New Covenant. It is what we refer to as *"The Lord's Supper."*

Within itself, it has no Salvation, as should be obvious; however, that which it represents, the Atoning Work of Christ carried out on the Cross, when coupled with Faith properly registered in Christ, definitely does bring Salvation (Rom. 10:8-9, 13).

There are many who claim that Salvation is in the Resurrection, etc. That is decidedly incorrect. Of course, the Resurrection is of immense significance, but the emphasis must always be placed on the Cross. Every part of the Lord's Supper directs one to the Cross, and the Cross alone!

The *"Body"* of Christ, which was prepared especially for Him, was done so for one purpose. The Scripture says, *"Wherefore when He* (the Lord Jesus Christ) *comes into the world* (presents Christ coming as the Saviour, Who undertakes in Grace to meet every claim the Throne of God has against penitent sinners), *He said* (Ps. 40:6), *Sacrifice and Offering You would not* (refers to the fact that He would pay for sin, but not with animal sacrifices), *but a Body have You prepared Me"* (God became Man with the full intention that His Perfect Physical Body was to be offered up in Sacrifice on the Cross, which it was; the Cross was ever His destination) (Heb. 10:5).

The *"cup"* represented His shed Blood, testifying to the fact that the *"New Testament"* (New Covenant) is in the giving of His Life, which spoke of His shed Blood. His Blood was pure, untainted, unsullied, unspoiled by sin in any way, for He never sinned. Satan had no claim on Him whatsoever; therefore, when He went to the Cross, He did so with a Perfect Body, and He gave that Perfect Body in Sacrifice, and did so by the pouring out of His Blood, which poured out His Life.

Both cases, the broken bread, which symbolized His broken Body, and the shed Blood, which symbolized His poured out Life, are ever to be held in remembrance. That's the reason that Paul said, *"We preach Christ Crucified"* (I Cor. 1:23). The Lord's Supper is a symbolism of the New Covenant, meant to represent that Finished Work,

615

which means that every time we partake of the "*Supper*," it is once again to make afresh the great price paid by the Lord Jesus for our Salvation.

The Lord's Supper, in other words, proclaims the fact that the Cross is the centerpiece, the very foundation, of Salvation.

SEPTEMBER

25

*f*or as often as you eat this bread, and drink this cup, you do show the Lord's death till He come. Wherefore whosoever shall eat this bread, and drink this cup of the Lord, unworthily, shall be guilty of the Body and Blood of the Lord. But let a man examine himself, and so let him eat of that bread, and drink of that cup. For he who eats and drinks unworthily, eats and drinks damnation to himself, not discerning the Lord's Body. For this cause many are weak and sickly among you, and many sleep (I Cor. 11:26-30).

The above Scriptures are of immense significance to every Believer, and should be minutely understood. In fact, not properly understanding them causes many Christians to be sick, even *"many"* to die prematurely. They don't lose their soul, but their lives are cut short, which is extremely detrimental, not only to families, but also to the Work of God.

So what is the Holy Spirit through Paul saying here?

1. First of all, even though we aren't told how often

we should partake of the Lord's Supper, the Holy Spirit does say, *"As often as you eat this bread, and drink this cup,"* specifying something significant. What is so significant is that we understand that the Lord's Supper is meant to portray *"the Lord's death till He come."* This refers not only to the fact of His Death, but also to the manner in which He died. We are ever to keep the Cross before us.

2. It is possible, and said so by the Holy Spirit, to eat the bread and drink the cup of the Lord, *"unworthily."* When that happens, we become *"guilty of the Body and Blood of the Lord."*

What does that mean?

The Lord does not demand sinless perfection for one to partake of the *"Supper."* However, He does demand that our Faith be exclusively in Christ and the Cross, as evidenced in Verse 26. If we make anything else the object of our faith, we are eating and drinking unworthily, and the results will not be good. This is, in fact, the reason that so many Christians are sick, even the reason why many Christians die prematurely.

Understanding that, I'm sure we see how important all of this actually is.

3. Before taking the *"Supper,"* every Believer should *"examine himself"* as to whether his faith is properly placed in Christ and the Cross. The idea is this:

If anyone has it in their mind that belonging to a certain Church or Denomination denotes some type of spirituality, then their faith is not properly placed in Christ and the Cross. If one believes that Salvation comes in any manner except by simple Faith in Christ and the Cross, then that person is *"guilty of the Body and Blood of the Lord."*

That person had best not partake of the *"Supper."*

4. If a Believer eats and drinks unworthily, which means their faith is placed in something other than Christ and the Cross, such a Believer is actually *"eating and drinking damnation to himself,"* because he is *"not discerning the Lord's Body."*

We *"discern the Lord's Body"* by understanding what the broken bread means and what the cup means. They refer, respectively, to His broken Body and His shed Blood, which both refer to the Cross.

There will be millions of Christians this Sunday morning who will take the Lord's Supper, whose faith is not properly placed in Christ and the Cross, but something else altogether. If they are true Believers, such action will cause many to be sick, and even to die prematurely. These misfortunes may be ascribed to something else, but if the truth be known, they occurred because of *"not discerning the Lord's Body."*

Simple Faith in Christ and what He did at the Cross addresses this perfectly and stops the sickness and the premature death.

It's obvious we should realize how important all of this actually is.

SEPTEMBER
26

n *ow concerning Spiritual Gifts, Brethren, I would not have you ignorant* (I Cor. 12:1).

There are nine Gifts of the Spirit listed here by the Apostle Paul. For one or more of these Gifts to be resident in the heart and life of the Believer, one must be baptized with the Holy Spirit, with the evidence of speaking with other Tongues (Acts 2:4). All Believers who are Spirit-filled should *"covet earnestly the best Gifts"* (I Cor. 12:31). This speaks of that which the Holy Spirit wants a particular Believer to have.

Every Spirit-filled Believer probably has one or more Gifts of the Spirit, but needs instructions to know how those Gifts are developed.

In brief, the following, hopefully, will present some understanding of the Gifts.

1. *"The Word of Wisdom"*: This pertains to people, places, and things, as they relate to the future. The Holy Spirit will not give total information concerning

the subject, but rather only a *"word."*

2. *"The Word of Knowledge"*: This concerns people, places, and things, as they regard the present or the past. Once again, total knowledge will not be given, but rather just a *"word."*

3. *"Faith"*: This could be translated *"Faithfulness."* This Gift probably works in tandem with any of the other Gifts, because faith is required regarding anything done for the Lord.

Several of the Gifts work in tandem, meaning if a person has one, he probably also has the other.

4. *"Gifts of Healings"*: While any Believer can, and should, pray for the sick in the Name of Jesus, there are those who have this special Gift, and who obviously will see more people healed.

5. *"The Working of Miracles"*: This Gift constitutes a suspension of natural laws in some manner or way.

6. *"Prophecy"*: This Gift is not so much in the realm of foretelling as it is in forthtelling. It is mostly for *"edification, exhortation, and comfort"* (I Cor. 14:3).

7. *"Discerning of spirits"*: This is <u>not</u> the gift of discernment, as some think, but rather the discerning of spirits, which pertain to evils spirits, even Angels, and, at times, even human spirits. The person with such a Gift understands more readily the type of spirit in operation and its purpose. Oftentimes, this Gift works in tandem with the *"Word of Knowledge"* and even *"Gifts of Healings."*

8. *"Kinds of Tongues"*: This does not pertain to one's prayer language of worship, but rather to utterances given in a public assembly, which are meant for interpretation. (Tongues, which every Spirit-baptized person has, and

which are used for prayer and worship, do not fall into this category. In other words, no interpretation is required.)

9. *"Interpretation of Tongues"*: At times, the person with the Gift of Tongues, referring to this Gift of the Spirit, will also have the Gift of *"Interpretation of Tongues."* But at other times, one person will exercise the Gift of Tongues and another person will exercise the Gift of *"Interpretation of Tongues."*

In every Church, there should be some Believers who have these Gifts, and their operation (done in order, of course) should be encouraged.

SEPTEMBER
27

*t*hough I speak with the tongues of men and of Angels, and have not charity (love), I am become as a sounding brass, or a tinkling cymbol (I Cor. 13:1).

In the Twelfth Chapter of I Corinthians, the Gifts of the Spirit are listed, while in the Fourteenth Chapter of I Corinthians, the three vocal Gifts of Prophecy, Tongues, and Interpretation of Tongues are regulated, so to speak. Between these two Chapters is the Chapter on love, exactly where Holy Spirit wanted it to be placed.

Paul is not demeaning tongues here, as some claim, but is merely stating the fact that irrespective of how many Gifts one might have, or however one is used by the Lord in other ways, still, love must be present, or else the other things will ultimately be invalidated.

Incidentally, the word *"charity,"* as used here, should have been translated *"love,"* because the Greek word *"agape"* used here means *"love,"* i.e., *"the God-kind of love."*

One cannot develop love in one's heart by the means

of the flesh. It has to be developed by the Holy Spirit. Love is actually one of the Fruit of the Spirit (Gal. 5:22-23).

Due to the fact that the Holy Spirit works exclusively in the heart and life of the Believer by and through the parameters of the Finished Work of Christ (Rom. 8:2), such demands that the Believer also have his Faith exclusively in Christ and the Cross. The very epitome of the Cross is *"love."*

"For God so loved the world, that He gave . . ." (Jn. 3:16).

There is no greater expression of love than the Cross of Christ.

So, when the Believer has his Faith anchored solely in Christ and the Cross, then the Holy Spirit can begin to work within such a heart and life, developing this Fruit, which is the only way it can be done. Unfortunately, many Believers read this Thirteenth Chapter of I Corinthians and conclude that they *"need more love."* While that is certainly true of all of us, for one to set about to try to bring it to pass within one's own machinations, such cannot be.

The Believer doesn't have to fret himself about this wonderful ingredient of love, or any of the Fruit of the Spirit, for that matter, providing the Believer has his faith properly placed. Properly placed, such faith will guarantee the work of the Holy Spirit in the heart and life of such a person, and these things will automatically be developed.

Believers must learn that anything pertaining to the Lord can never be developed by the flesh, i.e., *"our own ability, strength, and power."* Anything and everything which pertains to the Lord can only be developed by the Holy Spirit, including *"love."*

SEPTEMBER

28

i thank my God, I speak with Tongues more than you all (I Cor. 14:18).

In this Chapter, the Holy Spirit through Paul regulates, of a sort, the vocal Gifts of Prophecy, Tongues, and Interpretation of Tongues; the greatest degree of instruction is given regarding the Gift of Tongues.

Let us say first that it is the Gift of Tongues, i.e., one of the nine Gifts of the Spirit, and which is meant to be interpreted, which is mostly addressed. Tongues as a prayer language and as an instrument of worship, which every Spirit-filled Believer has and should use constantly, are not the topic of discussion here, except only in passing.

So what is the Apostle saying regarding the Gift of Tongues?

1. When it is time to give truth to the public, it would do no good to get up and speak in tongues, for no one would know what you were talking about. When it's time for the Word to be preached, Paul says, *"Five words with*

625

my understanding" is of more value than *"ten thousand words in an unknown Tongue,"* which no one can understand (I Cor. 14:6-11, 19).

2. Those to whom the Lord has blessed with *"Spiritual Gifts"* should *"seek that you may excel to the edifying of the Church"* (I Cor. 14:12). These Gifts are not for personal edification, but rather for the edifying of the entirety of the Body of Christ; consequently, this should ever be kept in view, meaning an individual should never stand out or show out, but seek to be used to bless the entirety of the congregation.

When an utterance in tongues is properly given in the Church, and it is interpreted, the Holy Spirit will always use such to *"edify, exhort, and comfort"* the entirety of the congregation.

Many times I have personally been strengthened and blessed by an utterance in Tongues, as the interpretation came forth! And so have millions!

3. If Lord has given a person the *"Gift of Tongues,"* that person should pray that the Lord will also give him the Gift of *"Interpretation of Tongues."* And if the Lord spelled it out as He did in this fashion, it should be obvious that this is a prayer that He definitely will answer, that is, if the person is sincere before the Lord, and seeks to edify the entirety of the Body of Christ instead of edifying only himself.

4. Paul tells us that it is proper to pray in Tongues along with praying in our regular language. The same can be said for singing (I Cor. 14:15). Some have claimed that their praying in the Spirit should also be interpreted. I see nothing in the Scriptures which validates such a

conclusion. Paul certainly does not give credence to such here. Furthermore, if one attempts to interpret one's own tongue while praying in private, there is no place for such to be judged; therefore, checks and balances provided by the Holy Spirit cannot be put into play (I Cor. 14:29).

5. In the company of unbelievers, if one is asked to pray, it would not be wise, for all the obvious reasons, to pray in Tongues (I Cor. 14:16-17).

6. Paul said, *"I thank my God I speak with Tongues more than you all,"* which proves that he was not ridiculing tongues, but, by the Holy Spirit, was regulating them. The Apostle also was not speaking of his linguistic abilities, but rather of the subject at hand (I Cor. 14:18).

7. The Apostle quotes the Prophet Isaiah, demonstrating that Tongues did not break upon the Church unannounced. Tongues had been predicted approximately 750 years earlier (I Cor. 14:21; Isa. 28:11).

8. We are told that *"Tongues are for a sign, not to them who believe, but to them who believe not"* (I Cor. 14:22).

What did Paul mean by that?

He is saying that these Gifts breaking forth upon the world, especially in the latter days, serve as a sign to an unbelieving world that time has about run out. In other words, the Church Age is about to end, and the great Prophecies of Daniel and John are about to be fulfilled.

9. Paul regulates the number of Messages or utterances which are to be given and meant to be interpreted. There should be no more than two or three, *"and that by course,"* meaning at the proper time.

If the person doing the speaking doesn't have the Gift of Interpretation of Tongues, and there is no other

Interpreter in the service, then the individual should *"keep silent"* (I Cor. 14:27-28).

10. The Holy Spirit through the Apostle says that no Believer should claim that he had to speak out in Church, and that he had no choice, thereby interrupting what the Lord was doing, as many have done.

The reason?

"The spirits of the Prophets are subject to the Prophets," which means that the Holy Spirit will never override a person's spirit to force him to do something.

So, if someone claims they had to do such, it means they were operating in the flesh, and not according to the Holy Spirit. Plainly and clearly, the Apostle says, *"God is not the Author of confusion"* (I Cor. 14:32-33).

The Holy Spirit will never interrupt Himself. If He is anointing the Preacher to preach, He will not, at the same time, anoint someone to blurt out a message in Tongues, thereby interrupting what He is anointing someone else to do. As stated, the Lord doesn't cause confusion.

Many people sense the Presence of God as the Spirit of God is moving; because of that, they think they have to give an utterance in tongues.

But let us say it again:

The Holy Spirit will never interrupt Himself. The Holy Spirit also will never override the spirit of the individual, forcing that person to do anything. The Holy Spirit doesn't work that way.

If a person makes a mistake, honestly believing they should have given a message in tongues and didn't, they should not be discouraged, for the Holy Spirit will provide another opportunity.

11. In I Corinthians 14:34, the Holy Spirit through Paul is not saying that it's wrong for a woman to say something in Church, or to give an utterance in tongues, as some have claimed, etc. The following is actually what Paul is addressing.

In those days, when people gathered together for Church, wherever it was, the men sat on one side, and the women sat on the other. At times, women were calling out to their husbands across the way, asking what certain things meant. As one can easily imagine, this was causing confusion and disorder. The Apostle is merely saying, *"If they will learn anything, let them ask their husbands at home."*

The Holy Spirit through the Prophet Joel, and quoted by Simon Peter, plainly stated, *"And it shall come to pass in the last days, saith God, I will pour out of My Spirit upon all flesh: and your sons and your daughters shall Prophesy . . . and on My servants and on My handmaidens I will pour out in those days of My Spirit; and they shall Prophesy"* (Acts 2:17-19). This includes women.

12. The Holy Spirit through Paul is here regulating the vocal Gifts. He is quick to say, when closing this section, *"Forbid not to speak with Tongues"* (I Cor. 14:39). His final word then is, *"Let all things be done decently and in order,"* which is what this Chapter is all about (I Cor. 14:40).

SEPTEMBER
29

*b*ehold, I show you a mystery; We shall not all sleep, but we shall all be changed, In a moment, in the twinkling of an eye, at the last trump: for the trumpet shall sound, and the dead shall be raised incorruptible, and we shall be changed. For this corruptible must put on incorruption, and this mortal must put on immortality (I Cor. 15:51-53).

In this Fifteenth Chapter of I Corinthians, the Apostle proclaims in detail the certitude of the Resurrection.

The question may be asked, *"What is the Gospel?"* The answer is found in Verses 3 and 4 of this Fifteenth Chapter of I Corinthians. It is the Atonement and the Resurrection of the Lord Jesus Christ. These Doctrines are the two great foundation stones of the Gospel. If either of them be denied, then the Gospel ceases to exist. For if Christ did not die as an atoning Sacrifice for sins, then sin has never been put away, nor God's eternal claims satisfied, and there is consequently no deliverance from its power and doom. And if the Resurrection be denied, then Christ failed to accomplish what He purposed to perform, for He came to put away sin by the sacrifice of Himself as a Sin Offering (Heb. 9:26).

These two great foundation Doctrines are based upon the Scriptures of the Old Testament; those writings being from God, their Testimony silenced all discussion and controversy. The Apostle proclaims the fact that the Scriptures and more than 500 human witnesses established the Resurrection. But he subordinates human testimony to the witness of the Bible. The latter was conclusive because it was Divinely inspired.

Much modern religious teaching reverses this order. It puts human testimony first and Bible testimony second, if at all, and for two reasons — to gratify man's high opinion of himself and to belittle God's Word.

For the benefit of the Bible student, the *"Rapture"* and the *"Resurrection"* are one and the same. They are just two names for the same glorious act. In I Thessalonians 4:13-18, the Holy Spirit through Paul states the <u>fact</u> or certitude of the Rapture or Resurrection. In I Corinthians, Chapter 15, he gives <u>details</u> as it regards this coming momentous event. The former states that it will happen; the latter states how it will happen.

Incidentally, I Thessalonians is probably the first Epistle written by Paul. It was probably written in A.D. 54. I Corinthians was written approximately five years later, in A.D. 59.

First of all, the Apostle proclaims the fact that if Christ did not actually rise from the dead, then *"preaching and faith"* are vain, i.e., *"useless."* And if Christ did not actually rise from the dead, then there is no such thing as sins being washed and cleansed. In other words, all are still in their sins. Further, if Christ did not rise from the dead, then every Believer who trusted Him and has died has *"perished."*

However, the great Apostle then dogmatically says, *"But now is Christ risen from the dead."* Christ having risen from the dead guarantees the Resurrection of all Saints (I Cor. 15:20). Some were belittling this great Doctrine, asking *"How are the dead raised up? With what body do they come?"*

The human body, after death, quickly goes back to dust. So the detractors, with sarcasm, were ridiculing the Doctrine of the Resurrection. Paul quickly answered by saying, *"You fool . . . God gives it a body as it has pleased Him, and to every seed his own body"* (I Cor. 15:35-36, 38).

This latter phrase tells us that the colors will remain the same in the Resurrection: black, white, red, yellow, and brown. The Glorified Body will also come in the male and female varieties. However, babies, although retaining their gender, will not remain babies, but, at some point in time, whether instantly or gradually, will develop into full maturity — *"God gives it a body"* (I Cor. 15:38).

At the Resurrection, the glory of some Saints will be greater than others because of their consecration and work for the Lord (I Cor. 15:41-42). And the Glorified Body will have no sin nature; considering other things, it will be impossible to sin (I Cor. 15: 53-54).

The coming Resurrection, or Rapture, will be one of the most cataclysmic events the world has ever known. It most certainly will take place, and it's going to happen very soon.

SEPTEMBER

30

*f**or we must all appear before the Judgment Seat of Christ; that every one may receive the things done in his body, according to that he has done, whether it be good or bad* (II Cor. 5:10).

The Apostle is speaking here to Believers. All Believers must appear before the Judgment Seat of Christ, where our work — but not our sins, for they were eternally abolished at Calvary — will be tested; if found incorruptible, with *"gold, silver, and precious stones"* serving as examples (I Cor. 3:12), it will be declared *"good,"* but, if found to be corruptible, with *"wood, hay, and stubble"* serving as examples, it will be declared *"worthless."*

The *"work"* or *"works"* of every single Believer who has ever lived will be judged first of all by the Lord Jesus Christ, Whose Judgment is Perfect, as would be understood. He will judge not only the action of our works, but also our motives, which are, in fact, the most important. For every individual, rewards will be given or withheld according to the perfect judgment of Christ.

More than anything else, however, Judgment by the Saviour is going to be based on the foundation of the Gospel, of which Paul was the Masterbuilder, appointed such by the Holy Spirit (I Cor. 3:10-15). That *"foundation"* is the Cross of Christ, which was actually formulated in the Mind of God before the foundation of the world (I Pet. 1:18-20).

So if anything is built on that foundation of the Cross, it must be compatible with the Cross or else it's unacceptable. On this basis, the greatest degree of judgment will be rendered — the standard of Faith regarding the Cross of Christ.

OCTOBER

1

m *oreover, Brethren, we do you to witness of the Grace of God bestowed on the Churches of Macedonia; How that in a great trial of affliction the abundance of their joy in their deep poverty abounded to the riches of their liberality. For to their power, I bear record, yea, and beyond their power they were willing of themselves; Praying us with much intreaty that we would receive the gift, and take upon us the fellowship of the ministering to the Saints. And this they did, not as we hoped, but first gave their own selves to the Lord, and unto us by the Will of God (II Cor. 8:1-5).*

In Chapters Eight and Nine of II Corinthians, the Apostle Paul gives the greatest dissertation on giving found anywhere in the Word of God. Ironically, the Holy Spirit chose the poorest Churches to serve as examples — the Churches in Macedonia.

Some years before, because of some type of insurrection, the Roman army had gone through this area and denuded it, which greatly impoverished the area and the people. Of course, God's People also were greatly affected in an adverse way. The Apostle Paul likened their situation to *"deep poverty,"* which means they were doing the best they could to keep the proverbial body and soul together.

The Apostle was taking up an offering among all the Churches, including the Churches of Macedonia, in order to help the Christian Jews in Jerusalem, who were being greatly persecuted for their stand for Christ. Thousands had lost their jobs, because they were excommunicated from the Synagogue immediately upon their acceptance of Christ, which meant they lost everything. The Apostle, therefore, receives an offering to hopefully alleviate somewhat the situation.

He had thought that possibly the people of the Churches of Macedonia could give a small amount, but, due to their *"deep poverty,"* they would not be able to do very much. But they gave far more than he could ever think of expecting, so much so that he didn't even want to receive it. But they insisted that he do so.

That which prompted them to conduct themselves as they did was that they *"first gave their own selves to the Lord"*; then they gave themselves to *"Paul by the Will of God."* In other words, they believed what the Apostle said about the need in Jerusalem, and they determined to do what they could, even beyond what it was believed they could do.

So the Holy Spirit uses these Churches, the poorest possibly in the Roman Empire of that day, to serve as an example. If they could do what they did, well then others could do even much more.

"But this I say, he who sows sparingly shall reap also sparingly; and he who sows bountifully shall reap also bountifully" (II Cor. 9:6).

I believe Paul had in mind the Churches of Macedonia when he wrote this Verse. Every evidence is that the Lord saw to it that the people in the Churches in Macedonia who had sowed bountifully now would reap bountifully. How the Lord did it, the Apostle didn't say.

Paul said we should give to *"prove the sincerity of our love"* (II Cor. 8:8). If we say we love the Lord, we will give to support His Work. It's just that simple! The opportunity and privilege of giving to the Work of the Lord is a privilege indeed! Truly, one cannot out-give God. Every true Christian will give liberally to the Work of the Lord.

In the entire two Chapters of this dissertation, the Holy Spirit through the Apostle did not mention tithing one single time.

Why not?

These two Chapters present the idea that the Believer not be hidebound by ten percent. The Bible definitely teaches that ten percent should serve as a base or foundation of our giving; still, the Holy Spirit wants us to know that everything we Believers have, which, incidentally, has been given to us by the Lord, belongs, in turn, to the Lord. We are to be at His beck and call! The Lord may want some to give ten percent, and He may want far more than that from others. And He no doubt does!

So if tithing had been addressed, many Christians would have missed the whole point of the dissertation. We are to be led by the Holy Spirit in our giving, and the

Holy Spirit will never lead us wrong.

I like what one of my Evangelist friends said. Some Christians had remarked to him that the Lord had never spoken to them about anything. He replied, *"Just ask the Lord what He wants you to give to His Work. You'll find out that He'll speak to you instantly."* My friend is right!

If we truly love the Lord, we are going to be very generous with our giving to Him, always realizing that the Lord is the One Who has sent every Blessing that has come our way. We are not our own, we have been bought with a price.

In closing, it is imperative that we know where our money goes and what it does. It's not enough to just give. Believers are to be good stewards, understanding that what we give will turn into souls. Sadly, most giving to what purports to be the Work of the Lord is anything but. Too much of it goes to line the Preacher's pockets, or else is wasted on frivolous projects that have nothing to do with the true Work of God.

The Believer should not only ask the Lord how much to give, but also to whom it should be given! Both are equally important!

OCTOBER
2

f or though we walk in the flesh, we do not war after the flesh: (For the weapons of our warfare are not carnal, but mighty through God to the pulling down of strongholds;) Casting down imaginations, and every high thing that exalts itself against the Knowledge of God, and bringing into captivity every thought to the obedience to Christ (II Cor. 10:3-5).

Paul deals here with spiritual warfare, which every Believer must engage more or less.

In the last few years, I have observed all type of ridiculous proposals regarding *"spiritual warfare."* Without enumerating them, every last one was of the flesh and, therefore, useless as it regards the situation.

I remember, some years ago, watching a particular Preacher over Television, whom the Lord definitely was using; however, he knew absolutely nothing about the Cross and precious little about the Holy Spirit, at least as it regards spiritual warfare.

Without going into any detail, his claim to victory

was being militant against the Devil, which meant screaming at him and conjuring up all type of physical contortions.

Observing that situation, I remember telling one of my associates that our dear brother was in for some hard days. Tragically and regrettably, that's exactly what happened. He lost his family, his Ministry, perhaps for many reasons, but the major reason was that he was trying to live this life, even as the majority of the modern Church, in all the wrong ways.

What are the *"weapons of our warfare"*?

First of all, Paul says they aren't *"carnal,"* which means they aren't anything we think up; irrespective as to how religious it might be, the Lord judges such as being *"carnal,"* which means unacceptable. This takes in the *"family curse"* theme, *"generational curses,"* *"Purpose Driven Life"* doctrine, *"Government of Twelve"* teaching, *"the confession principle,"* *"Denominationalism,"* etc. All of these things are *"carnal,"* meaning that they were conjured up out of people's minds, or were generated by *"angels of light"* (II Cor. 11:13-15).

The weapons of our warfare are Faith in Christ and what He did for us at the Cross, and that exclusively. Of course, that includes the Word of God, which proclaims the Cross as the means by which the Holy Spirit carries out His Work (Rom. 6:1-14; 8:1-2, 11). Once our faith is properly placed in the Finished Work of Christ, the Holy Spirit, Who Alone can carry forth this conflict to total victory, will then work mightily on our behalf. All that is required of us is Faith, but Faith in the proper Object, which must be ever the Cross of Christ (I Cor. 1:17-18; 2:2).

This which I have just stipulated is *"mighty through God to the pulling down of strongholds,"* which is God's Way. To be sure, the Evil One will try to erect spiritual strongholds of evil in our lives, designed to destroy us, and he succeeds with many Christians. But if we function according to the Word of God, total victory will be ours.

OCTOBER
3

*b**ut I fear, lest by any means, as the serpent beguiled
Eve through his subtilty, so your minds should be corrupted
from the simplicity that is in Christ. For if he who comes
preaches another Jesus, whom we have not preached, or if you
receive another spirit, which you have not received, or another gospel, which you have not accepted, you might well bear
with him (II Cor. 11:3-4).*

The Gospel of Christ, i.e., *"the Message of the Cross,"* is
very simple and easy to understand. In fact, a little child
can understand it. It is *"Jesus Christ and Him Crucified,"*
and our Faith in that Finished Work. But Satan seeks to
pervert the Gospel by introducing his wares, which he always does through the Church. In other words, religious
men come up with all types of attractive schemes, which
seem right to the carnal mind, but which, in fact, are very
wrong. They are wrong because they do not make Christ
and the Cross the central theme of their belief system.

The problem in Paul's day, i.e., the method Satan

was using, concerned Jewish Preachers from Jerusalem or Judaea who claimed Christ as the Messiah, but who also claimed that the Gentiles had to also keep the Law of Moses, that is, if they were to be saved (Acts 15:1).

Their gospel would not win souls, as no false gospel will win souls, so they had to parasite off the Churches which Paul had planted. They tried to turn these converts, whether in the Church at Corinth, Ephesus, or Galatia, etc. They wanted to turn them from Grace to Law.

So Paul's statement is according to the following:

Unless the Message is *"Jesus Christ and Him Crucified,"* then whatever is being preached is, pure and simple, *"another Jesus."* It is produced by *"another spirit"*; the end result is *"another gospel,"* which will help no one. In fact, it will greatly hurt and hinder, as should be obvious.

Tragically and sadly, most of that which is presently being preached in the Churches in America, in fact, all over the world, is *"another Jesus."* I say that simply because I also know that the Cross is little preached. It is alluded to at times regarding Salvation, and there are certainly some who strongly uphold the great Salvation Message that *"Jesus died for us."* But most know absolutely nothing about the Cross of Christ as it regards Sanctification. In other words, to tell someone how to live for God, they will propose things which aren't Scriptural, and which fall out to *"another Jesus."*

That's the reason the Apostle said that we must *"examine ourselves, whether we be in the Faith"* (II Cor. 13:5).

643

OCTOBER
4

f or such are false apostles, deceitful workers, transforming themselves into the Apostles of Christ. And no marvel; for Satan himself is transformed into an angel of light. Therefore, it is no great thing if his ministers also be transformed as the ministers of righteousness; whose end shall be according to their works (II Cor. 11:13-15).

In these Passages, Paul warns of false leaders.

It may be gathered from the statements given by the Apostle that these false apostles were Hebrews (11:22); that they were of commanding presence and gifted with eloquence (10:10); that they were highly cultivated (10:5); that they had attractive personalities, for they had a large following, it seems, in the Church (11:18); and that they announced an *"ethical gospel"* (11:15).

As stated, these men preached Christ as the Messiah, but the Cross had no meaning to them. So the gospel they preached was not a true Gospel, and would not effect any type of true Biblical results.

644

I might hurriedly ask the question, *"If that yardstick is applied presently, the yardstick of the Cross, where does that leave the modern Church?"*

If Christian Television serves as any type of barometer, most Preachers presently fall into the category of these *"false apostles,"* as described by Paul.

Satan doesn't try to deny the Gospel, for, in fact, he can't! Therefore, he seeks to corrupt it, and does so by presenting something else, and it doesn't really matter too much what the *"something else"* is. In the corrupting of the Gospel, what he presents sounds so right that the Holy Spirit through Paul referred to Satan as an *"angel of light."* That means that what he presents looks genuine, sounds genuine, and, of course, is claimed to be genuine.

But always remember the following:

The yardstick always is *"The Cross of Christ."* That, and that alone, is the measuring line. If Preachers aren't preaching the Cross regarding Salvation and Sanctification, which refers to the Scriptural fact that the Cross is to be the foundation of all things, then whatever it is they are preaching is not the Gospel. According to II Corinthians 11:15, this means that such Preachers are *"Satan's ministers."*

Paul is actually saying that every single Believer must investigate thoroughly what is being preached by the Preacher they are following!

OCTOBER

5

*a*nd lest I should be exalted above measure through the abundance of the Revelations, there was given to me a thorn in the flesh, the messenger of Satan to buffet me, lest I should be exalted above measure. For this thing I besought the Lord thrice, that it might depart from me. And He said unto me, My Grace is sufficient for you: for My strength is made perfect in weakness. Most gladly therefore will I rather glory in my infirmities that the power of Christ may rest upon me (II Cor. 12:7-9).

Most Preachers boast of their strength, but Paul boasted of his weakness.

Paul recognized himself as an earthen vessel; as such, he also realized that nothing could amend the carnal nature, not even the great revelations and visions which had been given to him by the Lord. So, to save him from failure and even falling, he was impaled upon a stake, so to speak.

Whatever that thorn in the flesh was, the Holy Spirit

did not see fit to reveal that to us, but what is necessary to learn from this experience is the moral purpose of that thorn in saving the Apostle from destruction. To have all the revelations and visions which Paul had, being given, in effect, the meaning of the New Covenant, actually being appointed by the Lord as the Masterbuilder of the Church, all can minister unto pride, if one is not very careful. Such can easily be a subject of carnal boasting.

We must come, therefore, to the conclusion that whatever the thorn in the flesh was, the Lord knew that Paul needed such, and if Paul needed such, what about us? It must be remembered that this *"thorn in the flesh"* was given by God, but yet was a *"messenger of Satan"* sent to buffet Paul, and to do so continually.

"Prevention" and *"humiliation"* are both Divine instruments. Paul was saved from failing, and possibly even from falling, by prevention; Peter was permitted to fail, thereby, greatly humiliated. There was, however, no difference between Paul and Peter; they were both indwelt, as all Believers are, by a corrupt nature incapable of amendment, at least by human instrumentation.

This is one of the most bitter and humbling lessons for the human heart. It is painful but necessary for the Believer to have an experiential sense of the principle of evil which indwells him, and we speak of the Sin Nature. But a greater power also inhabits the temple of the Believer's heart and body, and its victorious warfare is a profitable exercise for the heart.

If the Apostle Paul needed so humbling and painful an experience of what the carnal nature is, it is evident that all Christians need it; and it is plain that whatever

647

weakens, belittles, and humiliates that proud and will-ful nature should be regarded by the Believer as most worthful.

The distinction between the *"sinless nature"* of Christ and the *"sinful nature"* of Paul, in fact, of all Believers, is seen in that Christ needed no stake in His Flesh on de-scending from the Mount of Transfiguration. Facing Sa-tan at the foot of the Mount, He was the same Person Who shone in the Glory of God on the top of the Mount. The scenes were different, but He was alike Perfect in both. All was Perfection and Evenness in Him — symbolized in the Old Testament by the fine flour of the Meal Offering. What is the moral of all of this?

The Grace of God was *"sufficient,"* irrespective of the *"thorn."* Every time that Paul received a buffet, there was a sufficiency of Grace immediately given to meet the blow — not a moment too soon, not a moment too late, not too little, and not too much.

The lesson of all of this is that the higher the Christian experience, the sharper must be the *"thorn,"* and for all the obvious reasons.

<u>OCTOBER</u>
6

*e*xamine yourselves, whether you be in the Faith; prove your own selves. Know ye not your own selves, how that Jesus Christ is in you, except you be reprobates? (II Cor. 13:5).

Self-examination, according to the measuring rod of the Cross, is here demanded. *"The Faith"* is the Cross, i.e., *"Jesus Christ and Him Crucified."*

If the Holy Spirit had the Apostle Paul to place this in the Word of God, that we should examine ourselves, then we should realize just how important all of this is.

What is actually at stake?

The single most important thing in the world is at stake, your eternal soul. There is nothing more important than that! That's why the Holy Spirit also had Peter to say, *"Wherefore the rather, Brethren, give diligence to make your calling and election sure: for if you do these things, you shall never fall"* (II Pet. 1:10).

"Deception" is one of Satan's greatest weapons. It was the weapon with which he caused Eve to fall, and,

649

thereby, Adam also, which doomed the entire human race. Inasmuch as deception was the primary weapon of Satan's effort, this means that the human race is plagued with deception, meaning that it is so easy for human beings to be deceived — even Believers!

When Paul uses the term *"the Faith,"* he is not speaking of faith in general, but rather the very embodiment of Christianity, which is referred to as *"The Faith."* It answers to the statement of *"Jesus Christ and Him Crucified."* As stated, this means that the Cross of Christ is the yardstick, the measuring rod, the plumb line. Everything is to be measured by that yardstick, and by that alone, which, in effect, is the Word of God (Jn. 1:1, 14, 29; I Cor. 1:17-18, 23; Gal. 6:14).

This is the alarming thing about the modern gospel, which is not the Gospel of the Cross of Christ, but something else altogether, and is accepted by millions. As an example, look at the Purpose Driven Life scheme. At the time of this writing, the book, *"The Purpose Driven Life,"* has sold over 30 million copies. It is being adopted by virtually every Church Denomination, and even by the business world. This widespread acceptance should be a warning sign. To be sure, and as is obvious, the Cross of Christ doesn't have that type of appeal. In fact, the Cross of Christ has little appeal at all!

There is no *"Cross"* in the Purpose Driven Life doctrine, and, for that reason alone, it is basely wrong! To be sure, the Cross of Christ, which is *"The Faith,"* is not attractive at all to the world, and, regrettably, not attractive at all to the Church. But it happens to be *"The Way,"* in fact, the only way!

So, whenever Satan's wares are looked at closely, even though he may put a different face on his efforts from time to time, still, when the face is pulled off, it is the same old spirit of deception — a *"Cross-less"* Christ, a *"Cross-less"* gospel!

Every Believer had better do exactly what the Apostle said, *"Examine yourselves, whether you be in the faith."* Apply the measuring rod of the Cross to your belief system. If it doesn't measure up, abandon that which you have previously accepted. Then deny all of these false ways (deny yourselves) and take up the Cross daily, and follow Christ (Lk. 9:23).

OCTOBER

7

i marvel that you are so soon removed from Him Who called you into the Grace of Christ unto another gospel: Which is not another; but there be some who trouble you, and would pervert the Gospel of Christ (Gal. 1:6-7).

God, in His Love, has given man the Gospel and suited it to his needs. Satan, in opposition, degrades it to the level of man's corrupt nature and proud will, and fashions it into a religion that suits man, as man, in the flesh.

The Gospel of Jesus Christ condemns man, as man, to death, and so puts an end to him and all his religion, and it reveals a *"new man"* born of the spirit and not of nature. The impotency of man to serve, please, and obey God was made manifest under the Law. Satan's aim during the present day of Grace is to unite the religion of the flesh with that of the Spirit; and the impossibility and wickedness of that union are plainly set out in the Epistle to the Galatians.

Christ gave Himself up as a Sin Offering in order to take His People out of the world (Gal. 1:4). In His Cross, man, his religion, and the world are judged. Every effort of man, therefore, as a man and by natural birth, to make himself religiously acceptable to God is rebellion, which is the greatest sin of man. In fact, that effort is no more than the energy of the *"evil world,"* out of which Christ redeems.

Paul was the founder of the Churches in Galatia; however, after he left, called by the Lord to other fields of endeavor, certain false teachers had interjected themselves into these Churches to attack both the Doctrine and the person of the Apostle, and did so by introducing a gospel of *"works."*

In the writing of this Epistle to the Galatians, the Apostle Paul offered no commendation at the opening of this Epistle, as he did others, but at once an abrupt exclamation of amazement. How could these converts to the Lord, in fact, Paul's converts, so quickly turn to a perverted gospel? As we have stated, it is not Satan's aim to deny the Gospel, for that he cannot do, so he tries to corrupt it.

Anything other than the Message of the Cross, pure and simple, is *"another gospel,"* which, in fact, is *"not another,"* at least that will help anyone. Anything other than the Gospel of Jesus Christ and Him Crucified is a *"perversion of the Gospel of Christ."* And, to be certain, a *"perverted gospel"* will not save, will not heal, will not deliver, and will not bring about any positive results whatsoever. In truth, it will push the person deeper into bondage and deception. There is no deliverance in a perverted gospel;

there is no power in a perverted gospel; there is no Salvation in a perverted gospel! The only thing there is in a perverted gospel is *"trouble,"* hence, the Apostle saying, *"there be some who trouble you."* To be sure, it's *"trouble"* with a capital *"T."*

It is my belief that the Church presently is in worse spiritual condition than at any time since the Reformation. To be sure, it is richer than ever, and with greater numbers of people; however, Jesus said, *"And knowest not, that you are wretched, and miserable, and poor, and blind, and naked"* (Rev. 3:17).

Any gospel, so-called, which doesn't have the Cross of Christ as its foundation, and its only foundation, is, pure and simple, a *"perverted gospel."* And the world is rife with such presently!

At approximately the turn of the Twentieth Century, the great *"latter rain"* outpouring of the Holy Spirit began. The *"former rain"* took place during the time of the Early Church, as recorded in the Book of Acts. Both were prophesied by Joel (Joel 2:23). Most, if not all, of the mainline Denominations rejected this latter rain outpouring. As a result, some of them attempted to preach the Cross without the Holy Spirit, which presented a *"perverted gospel,"* which the Lord could never accept. As a result, they are no longer preaching the Cross or the Holy Spirit.

The Full Gospel Churches, which were born out of this great latter rain outpouring, tried to preach the Holy Spirit without the Cross. As the former would not suffice, neither would the latter. Now, most Full Gospel Churches, so-called, are not preaching either. The Message of the Cross of Christ and the Holy Spirit are so intertwined that it is impossible to separate the two (Rev. 5:6; Jn. 7:37-39).

Tragically, all of this means that what is being presently presented, with some few exceptions, is little more than a *"perverted gospel."* Jesus predicted this by saying, *"Nevertheless, when the Son of Man comes, shall He find faith on the Earth?"* (Lk. 18:8). In the original Greek Text, this reads, *"Shall He find The Faith upon the Earth?"* He is speaking of the same Faith which the Apostle Paul addressed in II Corinthians 13:5. It pertains solely to the Message of the Cross.

The question must be asked:

Are you in *"The Faith,"* or have you accepted *"another gospel"*?

655

OCTOBER
8

*b*ut though we, or an Angel from Heaven, preach any other gospel unto you than that which we have preached unto you, let him be accursed. As we said before, so say I now again, If any man preach any other gospel unto you than that you have received, let him be accursed (Gal. 1:8-9).

The word *"accursed"* in the Greek is *"anathema,"* which means *"a person or thing devoted to destruction because it is hateful to God."* In a spiritual sense, it denotes one who is alienated from God by sin — the sin of rebellion against God's Way, which is *"Jesus Christ and Him Crucified."* Other than blaspheming the Holy Spirit, this sin of rebellion is the worst sin one can commit. It is especially grievous when it involves Preachers, for, it is to Preachers that these words are directed.

In the words, *"any other gospel,"* we have in the original Text the idea, as before, that *"the other gospel"* was a message that went beyond that preached by Paul. It was not so much a perversion of Paul's Gospel, but a message that was diametrically opposed to it. In character it was of an opposite nature to Paul's Message.

When Paul uses the phrase, *"Preach any other gospel unto you than that which we have preached unto you,"* he was not using terminology of ego. It was to Paul that the great Revelation of the Gospel of Grace was given. He said, *"For I neither received it of man, neither was I taught it, but by the Revelation of Jesus Christ"* (Gal. 1:12). The reason his statements were so harsh was because he knew that any gospel *"other than the message of the Cross"* was fundamentally wrong! As such, if these wrong messages were followed, these perverted gospels, they would lead to destruction. One cannot have it both ways.

Jesus said, *"I am the Way, the Truth, and the Life"* (Jn. 14:6).

This means that Jesus and what He did at the Cross is the only answer for hurting humanity. As we've said before, we say again:

1. The only way to the Father is through Jesus Christ (Jn. 14:6).

2. The only way to Jesus is through the Cross (Lk. 9:23).

3. The only way to the Cross is by a denial of self, i.e., self's ability, which spawns self-efforts (Lk. 9:23).

Judaizers were Jews from Jerusalem and Judaea who accepted Jesus as the Messiah, but did not accept the Cross. These Judaizers were coming into the Churches in Galatia and preaching *"another gospel,"* which was the gospel of *"law"* and *"works."* Paul preached that works and the Law had no place in Christianity; by Law, he was speaking of the Law of Moses, which had been fulfilled in Christ. The way to Salvation and the way to Sanctification were solely through Faith in Christ and what Christ did at the Cross. If "*works*" entered into this, it perverted the message, and that's exactly what these Judaizers were doing.

So the Holy Spirit through the Apostle said that all who preach "*another gospel*" would be excommunicated, cursed, cast out, etc. In closing, I ask the following question:

Where does that put most modern Preachers?

OCTOBER
9

*b*ut when Peter was come to Antioch, I withstood him to the face, because he was to be blamed. For before that certain came from James, he did eat with the Gentiles: but when they were come, he withdrew and separated himself, fearing them which were of the circumcision. And the other Jews dissembled likewise with him; insomuch that Barnabas also was carried away with their dissimulation (Gal. 2:11-13).

What had Peter done here that was so wrong?

Due to what Christ did at the Cross, the Mosaic Legislation had been fulfilled and set aside. In fact, the Lord had given Peter a Vision showing him all of this while he was at the home of Simon the Tanner, after which Peter was willing to go to the home of Cornelius, a Gentile, and preach the Gospel to him and his house (Acts, Chpt. 10).

So when Peter came to the Church at Antioch, he acknowledged no difference between Gentiles and Jews regarding the Gospel, which is the way he should have conducted himself. But certain Jewish Preachers had come from Jerusalem, actually sent by James, who, even though they are not identified, evidently were men of distinction. These individuals saw Peter eating with the Gentiles, which was opposed by Mosaic Law. They contended that he was going against Levitical Legislation. They brought pressure to bear upon Peter, and he discontinued his practice of eating with the Gentiles. This caused the Jews in the Church at Antioch, even including Barnabas, to cease eating with the Gentiles, meaning to have fellowship with them, and brought about a division in the Church. Peter, being the senior Apostle, was the leader in this.

Paul, therefore, in resisting Peter, thus showed that he not only refused to take orders from the Jerusalem Apostles, whoever these might have been, but, on the other hand, felt that his Apostolic position gave him the right to stand openly against them in matters of wrong conduct, which it most definitely did. Even though Peter was older than Paul, Paul felt he had no choice. If this position was allowed to continue in the Church in Antioch, it would wreck the Gospel of Grace, which means it would destroy the Message of the Cross, that for which Jesus died. Paul could not keep silent, but was forced to rebuke Peter.

Most may look at this and not realize how serious the offense actually was. It was, in fact, an attack by Satan of the highest order. If Paul had not rebuked Peter publicly (Peter evidently backed off), the entire Message of Grace could have been compromised, and most likely would have been!

As we have repeatedly said, Satan carries on his

greatest work, not from outside the Church, but from inside the Church.

Referring again to Peter, the Text says, *"And the other Jews dissembled likewise with him."* The word *"dissembled"* in the Greek is *"hupokrinomai,"* which actually means *"hypocrite."* By characterizing their actions as hypocrisy, Paul implied that there had been no real change of conviction on the part of Peter and the other Jews. They knew what the Gospel of Grace was; and, in their hearts they had not retreated from this conviction; however, to do what they did because of *"fear"* made the matter even worse (2:12).

All of this tells us that we must stand for the Message of the Cross at all costs. Those who preach another message must be withstood, even publicly, even as Paul did Peter. I am certain that Paul took no delight whatsoever in this; however, had Paul not stood up that particular day at Antioch, quite possibly we would not have the Gospel presently.

Every Preacher should ask himself, *"Am I standing up for the Gospel, as did Paul?"*

OCTOBER
10

*k*nowing *that a man is not justified by the works of the Law, but by the Faith of Jesus Christ, even we have believed in Jesus Christ, that we might be justified by the Faith of Christ, and not by the works of the Law: for by the works of the Law shall no flesh be justified* (Gal. 2:16).

The statement that Paul makes here is exactly what he told Peter and Barnabas that day, along with the Jewish Preachers who had been sent from Jerusalem by James, and all the other Jews in the Church at Antioch. It seems that the Church at Antioch was pretty well divided between Jews and Gentiles, all having accepted Christ, which was the Message of the Cross.

Paul's standing up to Peter, as is recorded in Galatians 2:11-14, no doubt saved the Church at Antioch and possibly the entire Work of God. Paul now makes a bold statement about what Salvation and Sanctification really are. He emphatically states that *"a man is not justified by the works of the Law, but by the Faith of Jesus*

Christ," which automatically places every Believer in one of two categories.

The True Way is *"the Faith of Jesus Christ,"* which refers to what Christ did at the Cross. But if a person doesn't accept that wholeheartedly, then they are trying to justify themselves by *"works of the Law,"* whether they understand such or not.

Every person in the world, in fact, is either under *"law"* or *"Grace."* All unbelievers are under Law, even though they do not understand such. Unless they come to Christ, they will be judged by that Law, and we speak of the moral law, as outlined in Exodus, Chapter 20.

When the person comes to Christ, the broken law of which all are guilty is set aside as paid in full, done so by what Christ did at the Cross (Col. 2:14-15). Now the Believer has the privilege of living under *"Grace"* (Rom. 6:14). However, the Believer must also understand the Cross as it refers to Sanctification, meaning that we live a sanctified life strictly by Faith in Christ and what He did for us at the Cross, which then gives the Holy Spirit the latitude to work within our lives, bringing about His Fruit (Gal. 5:22-23).

However, most Christians don't understand Grace, which means they don't understand the Cross, so they try to live this life *"by works of the Law,"* whether they understand such or not. If the Believer doesn't understand the Cross, then there is nowhere else to be but *"Law,"* which is going to bring tremendous trouble, as described in the Seventh Chapter of Romans.

The argument of Verse 16 is: Man is guilty and needs a spotless Righteousness. This Righteousness cannot be obtained through law-keeping, but only through Christ and what He did for us at the Cross and our Faith in that Finished Work.

The entirety of the Book of Galatians deals with the Sanctification of the Saint. It is through Christ and what He did at the Cross — and through that alone! The Church basically has three problems. They are:

1. Antinomianism: The word means *"anti-law."* This describes those who claimed that inasmuch as Grace was greater than sin, then it didn't really matter how much they sinned. Paul answered that by saying, *"God forbid. How shall we, who are dead to sin, live any longer therein?"* (Rom. 6:2).

2. Legalism: This refers to Salvation by works, which actually is impossible (Rom., Chpts. 4-5).

3. Galatianism: This was the problem with the Galatians and is still the problem with most presently. This is, in fact, the most severe problem in the Church and always has been. It pertains to Believers who are saved by Faith, but try to bring about Sanctification by *"self."*

As Salvation comes by Faith in Christ and what Christ did at the Cross, likewise, Sanctification comes by Faith in Christ and what He did at the Cross. The Cross is the only way!

OCTOBER
11

i *am crucified with Christ: nevertheless I live; yet not I, but Christ lives in me: and the life which I now live in the flesh I live by the Faith of the Son of God, Who loved me, and gave Himself for me* (Gal. 2:20).

The verb *"crucified"* is in the perfect tense, which speaks of a past completed action having present results. Paul uses it to show that his identification with Christ at the Cross was a past fact, and that the spiritual benefits that have come to him through his identification are present realities with him. By this statement, he also shows how he died to the Law, namely by dying with Christ, Who died under its penalty (Rom. 6:3-5). The Law's demands were satisfied and, therefore, have no more hold on Paul, or any Believer, at least one whose Faith is exclusively in Christ and what Christ did at the Cross.

But to Paul being thus crucified with Christ also meant death to self. When Paul died with Christ, it was the Pharisee Saul who died. As far as he was concerned, what he was and did up to that time had passed away. Saul was buried, and the old life with him. The dominating control of the Adamic nature had its power over him broken.

Consequently, it is no longer a self-centered life that he lives, but a Christ-centered one. His new life is a Person, the Lord Jesus, through the Person of the Holy Spirit, living in Paul. And through the Ministry of the Holy Spirit, the Lord Jesus is manifest in his life. The new life is no longer, like the former one, dependent upon the ineffectual efforts of a man attempting to draw near to God by his own works. The new life is a Person, namely Christ, within a person, living out His Life in that person. Instead of attempting to live his life in obedience to a set of rules in the form of the legal enactments of the Mosaic Law, Paul now yields to the indwelling Holy Spirit and cooperates with Him in the production of a life pleasing to God, energized by the Divine Life resident in him through the regenerating work of the Spirit, all made possible by the Cross (Wuest).

However, man, even believing man, somewhat balks at this position given here by the Holy Spirit through Paul. Man likes to have some credit and some position. He likes that which he can see and handle. He refuses to be treated as vile and incapable of good, and is angered that he and his religious efforts should be condemned to annihilation.

Oh yes! He will willingly practice efforts to annihilate himself; for that ministers to his own importance; but to accept the absolute judgment of death upon his nature, his religious energies, and his moral virtues, and to be commanded to be silent, and, as a dead sinner, to trust the life-giving Saviour, finding in Him all that is needful for Righteousness and worship, is distasteful and repelling, hence, the offense of the Cross. But this is the Doctrine of the Twentieth Verse.

When Paul mentioned *"living by the Faith of the Son of God,"* he is once again taking the Believer to the Cross. With the first phrase, *"I am crucified with Christ,"* he takes the Believer to Romans 6:3-5. There the Believer was baptized into the death of Christ, buried with Him by baptism into death, and raised with Him in newness of life. No! This is not speaking of Water Baptism, but the Crucifixion of Christ. The Believer gains this place and position in Christ by simply having Faith in Christ and what Christ did at the Cross.

OCTOBER
12

i do not frustrate the Grace of God: for if Righteousness come by the Law, then Christ is dead in vain (Gal. 2:21).

Many Believers think that because we are now living in the Dispensation of Grace, then Grace is an automatic thing. It isn't! As the Holy Spirit through the Apostle here boldly proclaims, it is most definitely possible to *"frustrate* (throw away) *the Grace of God,"* which means to stop its action in our life.

The Grace of God is simply the Goodness of God extended to undeserving Believers. Christ is its Source, and the Cross is its means. It is superintended, totally and completely, by the Holy Spirit.

The word *"frustrate"* is from the Greek word *"athetio,"* which means *"to do away with something laid down, presented, or established; to act towards anything as though it were annulled, to thwart the efficacy of anything, to nullify, to make void."*

The idea is this:

668

When a Believer attempts to live for the Lord by means of works, of adhering to law, indeed of any form, which means he is not living by Faith, Faith in Christ and the Cross, then such a Believer is *"frustrating the Grace of God."* In other words, he stops its flow, without which no Believer can successfully live for the Lord.

The Holy Spirit bluntly says through the Apostle that *"Righteousness"* cannot come by the Law. In other words, it is impossible.

What did the Apostle mean by that?

Most modern Christians dismiss this Passage, thinking that because we are now living in the Dispensation of Grace, then Law is no longer a problem. But I would remind the Reader that Paul was living in the Day of Grace, and yet the Holy Spirit knew it was necessary to give this admonition.

Why?

When Paul spoke of *"Law,"* he was either speaking of the Law of Moses or else any type of law devised by anyone, which purports to help one live for God. And that is the problem of the modern Church! It is not so much the Law of Moses that is presently the problem, but rather laws made up by Churches or individuals. If it's not Faith in Christ and the Cross, and that alone, then, in some way, it's Law. That being the case, all Righteousness is stopped, because no Righteousness can come by law, whether God-devised or man-devised. If it can, then Jesus didn't need to come down here and die on a Cross.

So, we are told in this one Verse of Scripture that it is *"Jesus Christ and Him Crucified,"* or it is nothing!

OCTOBER
13

O *foolish Galatians, who has bewitched you, that you should not obey the truth, before whose eyes Jesus Christ has been evidently set forth, crucified among you?* (Gal. 3:1).

The phrase, *"O foolish Galatians,"* is an expression of surprise mingled with indignation. The word *"foolish"* is from the Greek word *"anoetos,"* which means *"stupidity that arises from deadness and impotence of intellect."* In other words, he was telling them, *"You know better than to throw over the Gospel of Grace, which you have been taught and which you received, for this perverted gospel."*

The word *"bewitched"* is from the Greek *"baskaino,"* and refers, in a sense, to being hypnotized. It's the same as a snake transfixing a rodent with its eyes, and the rodent looking into the snake's eyes, unable to move. It refers to a *"power of evil."* In other words, the unscriptural message being preached by the Judaizers, which repudiated the Cross, had a bewitching effect to it, because of the power of the Devil.

That is the reason that Believers accept the false messages of the *"Word of Faith"* doctrine, the *"Government of Twelve"* doctrine, the *"Purpose Driven Life"* doctrine, etc.

There is, however, one difference, in then and now:

The Galatians had had Paul as their teacher originally; therefore, they had most definitely been brought in correctly. So they were leaving, or at least some of them were, the Message of the Cross for a perverted message, which causes the Apostle to refer to them as *"fools."* Presently, most modern Believers have absolutely no knowledge regarding the Cross and Sanctification. They have heard messages only on the Cross as it regards Salvation.

In fact, one of the favorite sayings among Believers who are truly Born-Again, and rightly so, is, *"Jesus died for me."* Beyond that, however, they have no idea how the Cross plays into their daily living. As a result, they are perfect targets for false doctrine, i.e., *"the bewitched eye."* Continuing to speak of the modern Church, even when the Cross is preached to them, it is little received by most, hence, Jesus saying, *"Because straight is the gate, and narrow is the way, which leads unto life, and few there be who find it"* (Mat. 7:14).

Just the other day over the SonLife Radio Network, a dear Brother who is a member of Family Worship Center gave his testimony. He had been brought out of the *"Government of Twelve"* doctrine. He mentioned that he and his wife had recently listened to some of the tapes of the things demanded of them while they were in that particular doctrine. He exclaimed how ridiculous some of the demands were that were placed on them — demands which were totally unscriptural. His summation was, *"How stupid we*

671

were to have put up with that for even one hour!"

Is the Holy Spirit through Paul also saying to many today, *"O foolish Believers. . . ."*

To the Galatians, Paul preached Christ and Him Crucified so powerfully, so strongly, under such an anointing, that it was like Jesus had been *"crucified among you."*

Over the SonLife Radio Network, owned by Jimmy Swaggart Ministries, the Lord has strongly demanded that I teach the Cross until He tells me to do otherwise. And that we shall do!

OCTOBER
14

*t*his only would I learn of you, did you receive the Spirit by the works of the Law, or by the hearing of Faith? Are you so foolish? Having begun in the Spirit, are you now made perfect by the flesh? (Gal. 3:2-3).

There are two methods proposed here: One is man's way; the other, God's Way. Man's way is the activity of law and works; God's Way is the hearing of the Gospel and believing it. These two methods are opposed; and the answer to the question of Galatians 3:2 is that the Spirit is not received by legal works of any nature, but by listening faith, so to speak. In fact, *"works"* and *"faith"* are the keywords of Galatians 3:1-14. These two words set forth the opposing principles of Salvation by merit and Salvation by Grace.

In Galatians 3:3, the Apostle asks the question, *"Are you to such a degree rational? Having begun your Christian life in dependence upon the indwelling Spirit, are you now being brought on to the state of spiritual maturity by means*

673

of self-effort?"

The words, *"made perfect,"* are from the Greek *"epiteleo,"* which means *"to bring something to the place where it is complete."*

In preaching a message of law-obedience, the Judaizers caused the Galatian Christians to abandon the position of Grace and to put themselves in the sphere of law, both of the Judaizers' system of legalism and that of the Old Testament economy. Regrettably, this is the type of message, i.e., law-obedience, that is mostly being preached today.

In the Old Testament Mosaic Law, there was no provision for an indwelling Spirit Who would sanctify the Believer as that Believer trusted Christ and what He did at the Cross. As a result, the Galatians were turning away from the teaching and the reality of the Ministry of the Holy Spirit in the life of the Believer in this dispensation of Grace, Who works exclusively within the parameters of the Finished Work of Christ; instead, they were starting to depend upon self effort in an attempt to obey an outward legalistic system of works.

Thus, these Christians who had begun their Christian lives in dependence upon the Holy Spirit now were depending upon self effort to continue in them the work of Sanctification which the Holy Spirit had begun. In answer to that, Paul says, *"How foolish to think that you can bring yourselves by this manner to a state of spiritual maturity in your Christian lives. That is the work of the Spirit, which He carries out in your life solely by your Faith evidenced in Christ and the Cross. Only He can do that for you."*

To make the idea, hopefully, simpler, consider this:

Believers are saved by Faith, which refers to Faith in Christ and what Christ did at the Cross. That alone is the basis of one's Salvation. Nothing else must be interjected into that Finished Work. Further, Believers are sanctified, which refers to living a Godly, Holy life, solely by maintaining their Faith in Christ and the Cross, which then allows the Holy Spirit to perform His Work of Christlikeness and His Fruit within our lives (Gal. 5:22-23).

The Apostle asks, *"Are you so foolish? You began in the Spirit, which came to you simply by Faith in Christ, and now do you think that you can come to maturity by 'the flesh'?"* The answer is a resounding *"No!"*

OCTOBER
15

*C*hrist has redeemed us from the curse of the Law, being made a curse for us: for it is written, Cursed is everyone who hangs on a tree: That the Blessing of Abraham might come on the Gentiles through Jesus Christ; that we might receive the Promise of the Spirit through Faith (Gal. 3:13-14).

The Law assured Righteousness to all who perfectly obeyed it (Gal. 3:10), but condemned to death all who failed to give it that perfect obedience. Such an obedience was impossible to man, for he is morally imperfect, and moral imperfection cannot possibly render moral perfection. Christ redeemed the Believer from that doom because He suffered it Himself on the Believer's behalf; and thus at Calvary affirmed the authority of that Law and vindicated its justice and goodness.

The Law has nothing to do with Faith (Gal. 3:12), for it teaches that he who practices its requirements lives by doing them. Christ in His Life perfectly obeyed all its commands, and in His Death discharged all its claims;

676

and the merits of both His Life and Death are credited to the Believer in Him as though the Believer himself had performed them.

The word *"redeemed"* in the Greek is *"exagorazo,"* which means *"to redeem from slavery, to purchase from off the auction block."* It carries the idea that such deliverance involves cost of some kind, effort, suffering, or loss to the one who effects the deliverance. It conveys the figure of a ransom. Men needed a ransom, for the law had left them prisoners under sentence of death. In fact, there are three Greek words for *"redeemed"* or *"redemption."* They are:

1. *"Agorazo"*: This word means *"to purchase from the slave market"* (I Cor. 6:20).

2. *"Exagorazo"*: This words means *"to purchase out of the slave market, never to be put up for sale again in any slave market,"* which is the word of our present Text.

3. *"Lutroo"*: This root means *"ransom money used to liberate a slave."* The idea is, *"such a price has been paid that demons, devils, angels, Heaven, or Hell will never be able to say in eternity future that the price was insufficient"* (I Pet. 1:18; Tit. 2:14).

The *"curse of the law"* is that which the legalistic passages of the Mosaic Law pronounced upon those who did not perfectly obey its demands. The Law pronounced a blessing and a curse. But the blessing proved barren, for the Law made no allowance for human sin and frailty. The curse, which involved the wrath of a righteous God, brought condemnation upon the offender. From this hopeless state of condemnation in which the sinner was not only helpless to redeem himself, but helpless to satisfy the just demands of the law and thus find acceptance with

God, Christ redeemed us by satisfying the just demands of the law which we broke, paying the penalty in our stead, leaving a Holy God free to bestow mercy on the basis of justice satisfied (Wuest).

Christ was *"made a curse,"* which means that He was not actually cursed by God.

The phrase, *"Cursed is everyone who hangs on a tree,"* is taken from Deuteronomy 21:23. Any Jew who committed a heinous crime was first stoned to death and then hung upon a tree as a sign that he was cursed by God. When Jesus died on the Cross, He had to atone for the worst sins that could be imagined — in fact, all sin, and even the cause of sin. Inasmuch as He Himself had never sinned, and He, therefore, could not be cursed by God in that capacity, He had to be made a curse, which He was, as a Substitute on our part. It was the curse of the Mosaic Law that descended on Christ, subjecting Him to the death of a malefactor. The death of Jesus satisfied the legal demands of the Law, and, as our Substitute, when we identify with Him in His Death, in which He paid our penalty, the curse of the Law is likewise removed from us; consequently, the Cross of Christ is where our Redemption took place, and did so in totality (Col. 2:14-15).

Due to the curse being lifted on all Believers, the *"Blessing of Abraham,"* which is *"Justification by Faith,"* is given to all who believe, which includes the reception of the Holy Spirit, all through Faith — Faith in the Cross of Christ.

OCTOBER
16

*b*ut now, after that you have known God, or rather are known of God, how do you turn again to the weak and beggarly elements, whereunto you desire again to be in bondage? (Gal. 4:9).

The Galatians, who had been saved by Grace, were in the act of turning away from Grace to Law, which occasioned Paul to write this letter. Judaizers (Jews who accepted Christ as the Messiah, but claimed that it was still necessary to keep the Law of Moses, which denied the Cross) were making headway in corrupting the Gospel.

The question, *"How is it possible that you are turning back again to the weak and beggarly rudimentary things to which you desire to be in bondage again?"*, is a rhetorical question, the purpose of which is to show the absurdity of their actions. It also calls the attention of the Galatians to the ineffectiveness and poverty of their old religion system, which actually was paganism, contrasted to the power and richness of the Gospel. Paul is, in effect, dealing with two situations: a perverted form of Judaism to which they were turning, and also to pagan religions. Both were legalistic in character, and were without a dynamic to make actual the realization of ethical principles in the life.

The Apostle puts Judaism and paganism into the same category, even though Judaism was lightyears ahead of paganism. Although the Mosaic Law was originally given by God, still, it was totally and completely fulfilled in Christ. To go to that now, by either Gentiles or Jews, is, in Paul's thinking, no different than going back into unconverted heathenism.

In fact, in Verses 8 and 10, idolatry (paganism) and ritualism (Judaism) are united and presented as having the same source and operating upon the same principle. Man misuses God's Gifts and corrupts His Truths. The Law, which taught man that he was a sinner and needed Righteousness, was used by man as an instrument to establish his own righteousness through a carnal observance of its outward requirements. On the other hand, the idolater (Gentile) similarly debased conscience and became the willing slave to gods who only existed in his imagination.

The time of the Law consisted of symbols and examples, i.e., "*shadows*" used by God to teach His ancient People of the realities which they would find only in Christ, and only thus did these things have any value. He knew how to employ these figures in connection with a Law that tested man in the flesh and that demonstrated man's inability to serve God. To go back, therefore, to these shadows made for man in the flesh, now that God had proved the impossibility of man by them acquiring merit before Him, and now that the substance of the shadow was come, was to go back to the position of men in the flesh, and, as men in the flesh, to seek a carnal righteousness, which, of course, was, and is, impossible. In fact, it was actually going back to the principles of idolatry. As a result, it greatly perplexed the Apostle that the Galatian Believers should wish to go back to paganism; for that, in effect, would be the import of their action if they went into Judaism under the guidance of these false teachers.

Let the Reader understand:

The problem presently is identical as that then. Any Believer who tries to live for God by any means other than by simple Faith in Christ and the Cross is doing exactly what some of the Galatians were doing. Such a Believer is accepting something that not only will not bring freedom, but which will thrust one into bondage. There is no *"freedom"* in anything except Christ and Him Crucified.

Let it also be understood:

The *"bondage"* addressed here refers to bondage to the Sin Nature. That's the reason we speak so strongly against the *"Purpose Driven Life"* doctrine, the *"Government of Twelve"* doctrine, the *"Word of Faith"* doctrine, etc. These systems do not look exclusively to Christ and the Cross, but rather to legalistic demands formulated by men. The only answer is the Cross of Christ!

OCTOBER
17

*b*ut as then he who was born after the flesh persecuted
him who was born after the Spirit, even so it is now. Nevertheless what says the Scripture? Cast out the bondwoman and her
son: for the son of the bondwoman shall not be heir with the
son of the freewoman (Gal. 4:29-30).

The Law and the Gospel cannot coexist. The Law must
disappear before the Gospel. When Paul mentions "*Law,*"
he is speaking not only of the Law of Moses, but any type
of law which is conjured up by man, supposedly to help
one live for God.

Concerning these things, Lightfoot says, "*It is scarcely
possible to estimate the strength of conviction and depth of
prophetic insight which this declaration given by Paul implies. The Apostle thus confidently sounds the death-knell of
Judaism at a time when approximately one-half of Christendom
clung to the Mosaic Law with a jealous affection little short of
frenzy, and while the Judaic party seemed to be growing in
influence, and was strong enough even in the Gentile Churches*

of Paul's own founding to undermine his influence and endanger his life."

What Paul gave was, nevertheless, the Word of God, and ultimately it overcame the Judaism problem; however, the problem of *"law"* did not abate but, in fact, continued to weaken the true Gospel, even as it does presently. Virtually the entirety of the modern Church, sadly, has presently opted for law instead of Grace; the latter can come only by and through the Cross. Of course, they do not think of such as law, but that's what it is. As a result, those who are law-followers will persecute those who are of true Faith.

Paul's statement, *"He who was born after the flesh persecuted him who was born after the Spirit"* refers back to Isaac and Ishmael. Ishmael was a work of the flesh, in other words, the product of Abraham's and Sarah's scheming. Isaac was totally a work of the Holy Spirit. He was born when Abraham was 100 years old and Sarah was 90, which proclaims the fact that his birth was miraculous.

The effect of the birth of Isaac was to make manifest the character of Ishmael. Ishmael hated Isaac, and so did Ishmael's mother Hagar. Prompted by her, he sought to murder Isaac, which is what the word *"persecuted"* (Vs. 29) means. He and his mother were justly expelled. Both merited the severer sentence of death. Thus, the birth of Isaac, which filled Sarah's heart with joy, filled Hagar's with murder.

Isaac and Ishmael symbolize the new and the old nature in the Believer. Hagar and Sarah typify the two Covenants of works and Grace, of bondage and Liberty. The birth of the new nature demands the expulsion of the old. It is impossible to improve the old nature. The

683

"*bondwoman and her son*" must go!

In the Eighth Chapter of Romans, the Holy Spirit says that "*it is enmity against God, that is not subject to the Law of God, neither indeed can be.*" If, therefore, it (we continue to speak of the old nature) cannot be subject to the Law of God, how can it be improved? How foolish, therefore, appears the doctrine of moral evolution! The Divine way of Holiness is to "*put off the old man,*" just as Abraham "*put off Ishmael.*" Man's way of holiness is to improve the "*old man,*" that is, to improve Ishmael. The effort is both foolish and hopeless. Of course, the casting out of Ishmael was "*very grievous in Abraham's sight,*" because it always foments a struggle to cast out these elements of bondage, that is, salvation by works. For legalism is dear to the heart, just as Ishmael was to Abraham the fair fruit of his own energy and planning.

Paul states to the Galatians that Hagar, the bondwoman, represents the Covenant of the Law, and that her son represents all who are of "*works of law,*" that is, all who seek Righteousness on the principle of works of righteousness. But the bondwoman cannot bring forth the free man!

The Son Alone makes free, and He makes free indeed! Sarah, the free woman, symbolizes the Covenant of Grace and Liberty. And so the Apostle says, "*We are not children of the bondwoman, but of the free*" (Gal. 4:31).

This means that no vestige of law can be left in the heart and life of the Believer. Everything must be in Christ and His Cross. The object of faith must be transferred from all works of the law, from all efforts of the law, even from everything which only hints toward law, and placed exclusively in Christ and what He did at the Cross (Gal. 6:14).

OCTOBER
18

S tand fast therefore in the liberty wherewith Christ has made us free, and be not entangled again with the yoke of bondage (Gal. 5:1).

The teaching that Paul gives in this Verse is that Christ died on the Cross to give us the advantage of having Spiritual Liberty and freedom. This Liberty consists of freedom from law of any type. Under law (law of any type), the individual who subscribes to such has no more liberty than a child under a guardian. The child has no freedom of action, no right of self-determination. He must move within a set of rules prescribed by his guardian. He is not old enough to act alone. He must always act under the restrictions of his guardian.

So it is with a person under the Law.

Here were these Galatian Christians, free from the Law, having been placed in the family of God as adult sons, indwelt by the Holy Spirit, Who would enable them to act out in their experience that maturity of Christian

685

Life in which they were now placed, now putting on the straightjacket of the Law, cramping their experience, stultifying their actions, therefore, depriving themselves of the Power of the Holy Spirit. They were like adults putting themselves under rules made for children.

The word *"liberty,"* as used here by Paul, does not refer to the kind of life a person lives, neither does it have reference to his words and actions, but it has to do with the method by which he lives that life. The subscribers to law must live their lives by dependence upon self-effort in an attempt to obey the law. As such, they come under bondage.

The word *"entangled"* is from the Greek *"enecho,"* which means *"to be held within, to be ensnared."* It is like a net thrown over someone, and them unable to free themselves. The Galatian Christians, having escaped from the slavery of heathenism, were in danger of becoming entangled in the meshes of legalistic Judaism. And so it is with modern Believers who have been brought out of the system of the world, which definitely imprisons an individual, who are trading the liberty they have in Christ for laws of religion. Such will never lead to victory, as such cannot lead to victory. Freedom is found only in Christ and what He did at the Cross. Tragically, most modern Believers don't know that, so they formulate laws in their efforts to live for God, which are works of the flesh, which can never be accepted by the Lord (Rom. 8:8).

OCTOBER
19

*b*ehold, I Paul say unto you, that if you be Circumcised, Christ shall profit you nothing (Gal. 5:2).

When Paul uses here the term, *"Christ shall profit you nothing,"* he is speaking to Believers. He is not speaking here of their *"standing in Grace"* as justified Believers. He is speaking of the method of living the Christian Life and of growth in that Life. Thus, if the Galatians submit to Circumcision (this word *"circumcision"* is a catch-all phrase for any type of law), they are putting themselves under law, and are depriving themselves of the Ministry of the Holy Spirit, which Christ made possible through His Death and Resurrection, a Ministry which was not provided for under Law.

In the Old Testament dispensation, the Spirit came upon Believers, sometimes even <u>in</u> Believers, in order that they might perform a certain service for God, and then left them when that service was accomplished. He did not indwell them for purposes of Sanctification.

Because of the Cross and what was effected there by Christ, the Holy Spirit now lives permanently in the hearts and lives of all Believers; however, for the Holy Spirit to accomplish in us His desired Purpose, which is to bring us to Christlikeness and victory over all dominion of sin, He requires of us that our Faith be placed in Christ and the Cross, and maintained in Christ and the Cross (Rom. 8:1-2, 11; I Cor. 1:17-18, 23; 2:2).

The statement given here by the Apostle is blunt and to the point. He minces no words. If the Believer subscribes to laws in any capacity, whether the laws are made up by his Church, his Denomination, Preachers, or even himself, what Christ did at the Cross will be of no profit for such an individual. Although the Holy Spirit continues to reside in the Believer, He simply will not help him.

The reason?

Such a Believer is committing "*spiritual adultery*" (Rom. 7:1-4). The Holy Spirit is certainly not going to help a person commit spiritual adultery. So such a Believer, which characterizes almost all of the modern Church, simply cannot successfully live for the Lord. He can be saved, but the joy of serving Christ is lost on such a person, and for all the obvious, Scriptural reasons.

Tragically, most modern Believers do not think of what they are doing as "*law,*" because it is all so very religious. However, I remind the Reader that everything Satan does in this capacity is religious, just as it was in Paul's day.

The only way that one can successfully live the Christian Life, with all of its attendant joy, i.e., "*more abundant life,"* is by placing his Faith absolutely and completely in Christ and the Finished Work of Christ, which, of course, is the Cross. Then the Holy Spirit will work mightily on behalf of such a one, bringing about His desired effect of Sanctification.

OCTOBER

20

*C*hrist is become of no effect unto you, whosoever of you
are justified by the Law; you are fallen from Grace (Gal. 5:4).

The idea of this Verse is that the Galatian Christians,
by putting themselves under Law, have put themselves in a
place where they have ceased to be in that relation to Christ
where they could derive the spiritual benefits from Him
which would enable them to live a life pleasing to Him,
namely, through the Ministry of the Holy Spirit. In depriving themselves of the Ministry of the Holy Spirit in the
living of the Christian Life, they have *"fallen from Grace."*

To *"fall from Grace"* refers to the Believer placing his
faith in something other than Christ and the Cross. It
really doesn't matter what the *"other"* is. The person has
placed himself in a position where the Holy Spirit cannot work satisfactorily in their life; therefore, the flow of
Grace stops.

Grace is the Goodness of God extended to undeserving Believers. It is superintended by the Holy Spirit. It is

the Holy Spirit Who makes all of these good things possible in our hearts and lives, but the Source is Christ and the means is the Cross.

Most Christians think that *"falling from Grace"* refers to one committing a great sin. That is correct, but not as they think! It is a great sin for any Believer to forsake Christ and what He has done for us at the Cross, thereby placing his faith in something else. Considering the price that Jesus paid at the Cross, one certainly can realize what an insult such action is.

I once heard two Preachers on Television discussing another person who had grievously failed the Lord by committing an appalling sin of the flesh. They concluded that the commission of this grievous sin constituted *"falling from Grace."*

No! It didn't. No! It doesn't.

While sin is a most horrible and terrible thing, and will always have dire consequences, the person who does such is the one who desperately needs the Grace of God, and, if proper Faith in Christ and the Cross is evidenced, he will always be the beneficiary of such Grace (I Jn. 1:9). Those two Preachers, actually, were the ones who had *"fallen from Grace,"* because neither one of them pointed to the Cross of Christ as the Object of Faith, but rather to works of many and varied kinds. Tragically, due to the fact that the Cross has been so little preached in the last several decades, most in the modern Church belong to the same category.

Every single Believer on the face of the Earth must have a continued, uninterrupted flow of the Grace of God, i.e., *"the Goodness of God,"* in order to live a victorious life.

Without it, it simply cannot be done. To have that uninterrupted flow, all one has to do is to simply place his Faith exclusively in Christ and the Cross (Rom. 6:1-14). This will not guarantee that such a Believer will never again fail, but it does guarantee that such a Believer is on the right path, and will ultimately come out to a total and complete place and position in Christ to where sin no longer has dominion over such a person (Rom. 6:14).

OCTOBER
21

*a*nd I, Brethren, if I yet preach Circumcision, why do I yet suffer persecution? Then is the offense of the Cross ceased (Gal. 5:11).

The doctrine of the Atonement is offensive to the self-righteous mind, for it declares that man is morally lost, wicked and hopeless, helpless and dead, and that he can only be recovered by being re-created. This re-creation takes place when he believes upon Christ as an atoning Saviour. Man denies that he is altogether lost, and he claims that he can add something to the Sacrifice that Christ infinitely accomplished for him at Calvary. Such an addition destroys the Gospel, for it denies the infinite perfection of Christ's Sacrifice. If that Sacrifice is infinite, then there is no room for human additions to it in order to add to its perfection.

To preach Christ and good works — proudly named *"the ethical gospel,"* or some such like — does not involve persecution; but to preach the true Gospel always involves

693

persecution.

What is the offense of the Cross?

Why is the Cross an offense?

The *"offense of the Cross"* is the fact that God demands that there is only one way to Justification and Sanctification, and that is the Cross. That puts to death every effort of man — above all, his religious efforts. This is offensive to the flesh, offensive to the carnal nature, and it arouses enmity against those who place their Faith totally and completely in Christ and the Cross. As we have previously stated, Abraham did not want to give up Ishmael, but the Cross demands it.

The answers to both questions, i.e., *"What is the offense of the Cross?"* and *"Why is the Cross an offense?"* are very similar.

The Cross of Christ, and one's total Faith placed in that Finished Work, must, of necessity, eliminate all self-righteousness. As Ishmael was dear to the heart of Abraham, our self-efforts are also dear to us. The Cross of Christ offends all religion, all self-effort, all works, and all self-righteousness. These things must be cast out, even as the bondwoman and her son were cast out by Abraham (Gal. 4:29-30).

There is no room for both the *"Cross"* and the *"flesh."* One or the other must go! The Cross is always an offense to self-righteousness, because it exposes it for what it really is — the flesh, which God can never accept. The Lord can only accept the Righteousness of Christ.

OCTOBER
22

f or, Brethren, you have been called unto liberty; only use not liberty for an occasion to the flesh, for by love serve one another (Gal. 5:13).

The Gospel does not liberate a man to a life of laziness and self-indulgence, but to an unceasing Ministry of loving service to humanity.

By the use of the word *"liberty,"* Paul here reaches back to all that has preceded it, summing up the whole preceding argument for Christian liberty, and looking ahead to what follows in that it introduces a wholly new aspect of the matter of Christian liberty, namely, the danger of abusing it.

To those who have been accustomed to regard law as the only controlling factor that stands in the way of self-indulgence and a free reign in sin, and to those who have not been accustomed to a high standard of ethics, the teaching of Christian liberty might easily mean that there is nothing to stand in the way of the unrestrained indulgence of one's own impulses. During his Ministry, Paul often had his hearers react in this way to his teaching of Grace.

The questions in Romans 6:1 and 6:15, *"Shall we continue in sin, that Grace may abound?"* and *"Shall we sin, because we are not under the Law, but under Grace?"* were asked by someone who did not understand Grace. Paul answers these questions in the Sixth Chapter of Romans. He shows that the control of the sinful nature over the individual is broken the moment he believes, and the Divine Nature is then imparted; the Believer, therefore, hates sin and loves the right, and he has both the desire and the power to keep from sinning and to do God's Will.

In the Epistle to the Galatians, Paul shows that the Believer has come out from under whatever control Divine Law had over him, and in Salvation has been placed under a superior control, that of the indwelling Holy Spirit, Who exercises a stricter supervision over the Believer than Law ever did over the unbeliever, Whose restraining power is far more effective than the Law's restraining power ever was, and Who gives the Believer both the desire and power to choose the right, a thing which Law never was able to do.

The Believer has, therefore, passed out of one control into another, from the control of a mere system of legal enactments into the control of a Person, God the Holy Spirit. When God abrogated the Law at the Cross, He knew what He was doing. He did not leave the world without a restraining hand.

He ran this world for 2,500 years before the Mosaic Law was enacted. He can run it again without the Mosaic Law. He does not need the help of legalistic Teachers and

Preachers in the Church who think they are helping Him control this world, who control Believers by imposing Law on Grace. Indeed, it is the general ignorance and lack of recognition of the Ministry of the Holy Spirit that is responsible for the tendency in the Church to add Law to Grace.

There is a recognition of the fact that the flesh is still with the Christian even though its power over him is broken, and consequently a feeling that even the Child of God stills needs a restraint put upon him. This is as it should be. But the mistake that so often is made is that the Mosaic Law, or laws devised by men, are substituted for the restraint of the Holy Spirit, always with disastrous results.

Not only does the Law (whatever kind) not restrain evil, but, on the other hand, it brings out evil in the life, because the fallen nature rebels against it (Rom. 7:7-13), and the latter is thus incited to evil. The Holy Spirit, on the other hand, is the Great Restrainer of evil, and He most definitely will do so if the Believer will properly place his Faith in Christ and the Cross and keep his Faith in that Finished Work.

No Preacher ever enables Christians to whom he ministers to live a better Christian Life by putting them under the Ten Words from Sinai and by letting them smell the brimstone of the Lake of Fire. A policeman on the street corner is a far more efficient deterrent of lawbreaking than any number of city ordinances placarded for public notice. To acquaint the Saint with the Ministry of the indwelling Holy Spirit, telling the Saint how He works, is far more productive of victory over sin than the imposition of the Law. The controlling Ministry of the Holy Spirit is the secret of Holy Living, and the only secret for Holy Living. This is the Power of which Paul spoke, and the Power we must have to live a victorious life, which is invested in the preaching of the Cross (I Cor. 1:18).

(Most of the above material on *"liberty"* was derived from the teaching of Kenneth Wuest.)

OCTOBER
23

t his I say then, Walk in the Spirit, and you shall not fulfill the lust of the flesh. For the flesh lusts against the Spirit, and the Spirit against the flesh: and these are contrary the one to the other: so that you cannot do the things that you would. But if you be led of the Spirit, you are not under the Law (Gal. 5:16-18).

The word *"Walk,"* as used here, refers to the act of conducting one's self, or ordering one's manner of life or behavior.

The word *"lust"* refers to a strong desire, impulse, or passion, the context indicating whether it is a good or an evil one.

The word *"flesh"* refers here to the totally depraved nature of the person, the power of which is broken when the Believer is saved.

Therefore, the *"lust of the flesh"* refers to the evil desires, impulses, and passions that are constantly arising from the Sin Nature, as smoke rises from a chimney. The

Sin Nature is not eradicated, as some teach! However, its power over the Believer was broken when the Believer was saved, and the Believer need not obey it, at least if the Believer understands God's Prescribed Order of Victory. But the Sin Nature remains in the Believer, constantly attempting to control the Believer, as it did before Salvation wrought its work in his being.

In these statements made by Paul, we notice that he puts upon the *"Believer"* the responsibility of refusing to obey the behests of the evil nature by conducting himself in the Power of the Holy Spirit and under His control. The will of the person has been liberated from enslavement to sin, which was his experience before Salvation, and is free now to choose to do the right thing. The Holy Spirit has been given to the Believer as the Agent to counteract the evil nature.

So how does the Holy Spirit work?

Is His Work in our lives automatic?

Is there any responsibility on the part of the Believer toward what the Spirit does?

These are just a few of the questions that characterize this subject.

The Holy Spirit, Who resides in the heart and life of every Believer (I Cor. 3:16), doesn't require much of us, but He does require one thing. He requires Faith! However, the Faith which He requires must be placed in the correct object. That correct Object is always Christ and the Cross. It was at the Cross where the Lord Jesus atoned for all sin; consequently, the power of sin was broken, which means that Satan there lost his right to hold man in captivity and bondage.

700

If Satan holds man in bondage (and, regrettably, he does so with most of the world, and even most of the Church), it is simply because that man does not take advantage of what the Lord did for him at the Cross. The sinner can come out from under the bondage of Satan, if the sinner will only accept Christ.

The Believer can stay free of bondage, never allowing the Sin Nature to rule in his life, providing he maintains Faith in Christ and the Cross, which then gives the Holy Spirit liberty to work (Rom. 8:1-2, 11). Only then can the Believer successfully *"walk in the Spirit."* Only then is he in a position where he will no longer *"fulfill the lust of the flesh."*

OCTOBER
24

*n*ow the works of the flesh are manifest, which are these; Adultery, fornication, uncleanness, lasciviousness, Idolatry, witchcraft, hatred, variance, emulations, wrath, strife, seditions, heresies, Envyings, murders, drunkenness, revellings, and such like: of the which I tell you before, as I have also told you in time past, that they which do such things shall not inherit the Kingdom of God (Gal. 5:19-21).

The manner and way that one can tell if one is truly following Christ, and, by that, we refer to placing one's Faith in Christ and the Cross, and maintaining his Faith in that manner, is that the *"works of the flesh"* are no longer in our life. The only way, and we mean the only way, that the Believer is going to be free from the *"works of the flesh"* is by the method which we have just mentioned: Faith in Christ and the Cross. If one resorts to Law in any measure, to self-effort regarding rules and regulations, etc., such a Believer is going to fail the Lord. The Holy Spirit simply will not help such a Believer.

As we have previously stated, the reason the Holy Spirit will not help is that such a person is committing *"spiritual adultery,"* and the Holy Spirit will have no part of that, as should be obvious.

Let us say it in another way:

There is only one way for victory over *"works of the flesh,"* and that is by the Power of the Holy Spirit, Who performs His Work exclusively within the parameters of the Finished Work of Christ. In other words, what the Holy Spirit does in our lives constitutes a legal work. That's why Paul said, *"For the Law of the Spirit of Life in Christ Jesus has made me free from the Law of sin and death"* (Rom. 8:2).

As we have also previously stated, victory over the *"Law of sin and death,"* which characterizes *"works of the flesh,"* can only be brought about through *"the Law of the Spirit of Life in Christ Jesus,"* which is the most powerful Law on the face of the Earth, but yet the only Law that is more powerful than the *"Law of sin and death."*

We should look very thoughtfully at this list of *"works of the flesh"* (Gal. 5:19-21). While all of us might concur to the wickedness of the first four, we very little think of *"idolatry,"* *"witchcraft,"* *"hatred,"* *"heresies,"* etc.

Please, however, note carefully:

Every single Preacher in the world who is preaching something other than Christ and the Cross is preaching *"heresy,"* which is a *"work of the flesh."* Furthermore, anything that we place as a substitute for Christ and the Cross is judged by God as *"idolatry."*

Paul tells us here that if we refuse God's Way, which is the Way of the Cross, which means that these *"works of the flesh"* are going to run unchecked within our lives, even growing steadily worse, the end result can most definitely be the loss of the soul. So God's Way of the Cross is not one option among several. It is the only option!

OCTOBER

25

*b*ut the Fruit of the Spirit is love, joy, peace, longsuffering, gentleness, goodness, Faith, Meekness, temperance: against such there is no Law (Gal. 5:22-23).

Paul places the *"Fruit of the Spirit"* in juxtaposition to the *"works of the flesh."*

The word *"Fruit"* is singular, a fact which serves to show that all of the elements of character spoken of in these Verses are a unity, making for a well-rounded and complete Christian Life. All the *"Fruit"* grows uniformly, which means that the growth rate is the same for all, i.e., whatever growth there is of the *"Fruit"* in one's life, it is the same across the board. One cannot have more *"love"* than one has *"faith,"* etc.

Also, this is the *"Fruit of the Spirit,"* which means it's not the fruit of someone else, or even one's self. This means that development and growth rate are brought about exclusively by the Holy Spirit.

So, how is the development and the growth rate of

the *"Fruit of the Spirit"* brought about in the heart and life of the Believer?

Only one way, which refers, once again, to our Faith in Christ and what He did at the Cross! As I have been continually saying, this gives the Holy Spirit latitude to work within our lives. This alone gives Him such latitude. He will work in no other manner!

In 1997, the Lord began to open up to me the Revelation of the Cross. He first showed me the cause of problems, which is the fact of the Sin Nature and it not being properly addressed by the Believer. The Lord then told me the solution for the Sin Nature, which is the Cross of Christ, and the Cross of Christ alone. Then He showed me the manner in which the Holy Spirit works in all of this, which I had never seen anywhere else until the Lord revealed it to me from Paul's writings. I speak of Romans 8:2.

Unfortunately, all type of schemes, programs, self-efforts, and unscriptural doctrines are being projected as a means of Spiritual Growth.

Let us say it again:

If it's not Christ and the Cross, the Holy Spirit simply will not work, which means there is no development or growth of the Fruit of the Spirit. The Cross is the means by which everything comes to us from the Lord, and Christ is always the Source (Jn. 14:6).

OCTOBER
26

*a*nd they who are Christ's have crucified the flesh with the affections and lusts. If we live in the Spirit, let us also walk in the Spirit (Gal. 5:24-25).

How does one crucify the flesh?

We should notice that Paul uses the term *"crucified,"* which is in the past tense. The Apostle does this because every single Believer crucified the flesh when he came to Christ. That's what Romans 6:3-5 means. When the believing sinner comes to Christ, he is first of all baptized into the death of Christ, then buried with Him by Baptism into death, and then raised with Him in newness of life. This is what Paul is referring to.

At that time, every single sin in the heart and live of the Christian is defeated, and the Sin Nature is made ineffective (Rom. 6:6). But if the new Believer then transfers his Faith from the Cross of Christ, which is the way he came into Redemption, to other things, then the Sin Nature comes to life, and the person is once again ruled

707

by that evil nature (Rom. 6:13), all because his faith has been transferred to something other than the Cross.

The Believer must understand that the only way *"the flesh with the affections and lusts"* can be overcome is by trusting Christ and what Christ did at the Cross. This is what Paul means by the word *"crucified."*

Now that the believing sinner has come to Christ, he *"lives in the Spirit,"* meaning that everything he has from the Lord is imparted to him by the Holy Spirit, Who — as we have been saying over and over again — works exclusively within the parameters of the Christ and the Cross (Rom. 8:2). In view of the fact that every one of us who is a Believer has this Divine Life operating within us, we then should *"walk in the Spirit,"* which refers to the manner in which we conduct our life or our lifestyle.

The word *"walk"* is from the Greek *"stoicheo,"* which means *"to walk in a straight line, to conduct one's self rightly."*

Thus, the exhortation to the Galatian Believers, who have Divine Life resident in their beings, is to conduct themselves under the guidance, impulses, and energy of that life. Here we have the possibility of a total victory over the world, the flesh, and the Devil. Consequently, the responsibility of the Saint is to desire to live a Christlike life, and to depend upon the Holy Spirit for the power to live that life, which we obtain by registering our Faith exclusively in Christ and the Cross. Fulfilling this will bring all the infinite resources of Grace to the aid of the Saint and put in operation all the activities of the Holy Spirit, all on our behalf.

Without one's Faith registered and anchored in Christ and the Cross, and remaining in Christ and the Cross, it is literally impossible to *"walk in the Spirit."* As a result, the Sin Nature will begin to rear its ugly head, with unholy *"affections and lusts"* becoming predominant in the life of the Believer. It doesn't really matter who the Believer is, whether the Pastor of the largest Church in the country, or the Evangelist drawing the largest crowds. The Lord has one way of victory, and one way alone, because that is all that is needed.

As we have said in Devotion after Devotion, that one way is *"Christ and the Cross."* That's why Paul also said, *"Christ sent me not to baptize, but to preach the Gospel: not with wisdom of words, lest the Cross of Christ be made of none effect"* (I Cor. 1:17). Paul wasn't demeaning Water Baptism, only that the theme of our Faith must be *"Christ and Him Crucified."*

OCTOBER

27

*b*rethren, if a man be overtaken in a fault, you which are spiritual, restore such an one in the spirit of meekness; considering yourself, lest you also be tempted (Gal. 6:1).

Because the Galatians, at least some of them, were listening to the Judaizers, which means they were forsaking the Cross and going into Law, they had started to observe sin breaking out in their lives, i.e., *"the works of the flesh."*

The word *"overtaken,"* as it is used here, refers to a person doing all that he can do to escape sin, but nevertheless falling into sin. It happens because the Believer has forsaken the Cross and has gone into Law. Despite all of such a Believer's efforts, the end result, every single time, will be sin. Moreover, if the problem is not corrected, the sin will get worse and worse, despite all the individual's efforts otherwise!

The word *"fault"* speaks of a moral lapse, which means a sin of some magnitude.

The word *"spiritual"* has to do with the realm of the Holy Spirit; consequently, we will learn something here.

The only Believers whom the Holy Spirit judges as truly *"spiritual"* are those who have their Faith anchored solidly in Christ and the Cross, which refers back to Galatians 5:24. Otherwise, though the person may be saved, may even be a Preacher of the Gospel, still, there is no spirituality!

The word *"restore"* is from the Greek *"katartizo,"* which means *"to repair, to restore to a former good condition, to prepare, to fit out, to equip."* It is used of reconciling factions, of setting bones, of putting a dislocated limb into place, of mending nets, or of supplying an army with provisions. It is used by Paul in a metaphorical sense of setting a person to rights, bringing him into line.

So, how is the *"restoration"* to be effected?

The one who is *"spiritual"* is to inform the one who has failed that the reason he has failed is because his Faith has been transferred from Christ and the Cross to something else, and it really doesn't matter what the something else is. Such a Believer is then to be encouraged to put his Faith where it ought to be, namely, in Christ and the Cross, which will then guarantee victory (Rom. 6:1-14).

This is to be done *"in the spirit of meekness,"* meaning that the failed one is not to be lorded over, or subjected to further punishment. The fact of sin is punishment enough! Moreover, only one who truly is *"spiritual"* can deal with such a person with a *"meek spirit."* He can do so because he knows that his victory is not because of any greatness on his part, but solely because of what Christ did at the Cross and his Faith in that Finished

711

Work. Such a *"spiritual"* person knows and understands sin, why it occurs, and how it was defeated at the Cross, which tends to humble one — and greatly so!

Outside of the Believer understanding Christ and the Cross and there placing his Faith, there is no such thing as humility. The Cross alone produces *"meekness."* When one properly understands the Cross of Christ, one then properly understands himself, what sin is, and, above all, what Christ has done to address this terrible problem.

There are three things the Believer should know:

1. Who and what he is;
2. What sin actually is; and,
3. What Christ has done for us at the Cross.

The third is the most important!

OCTOBER
28

*b*ut God forbid that I should glory, save in the Cross of
our Lord Jesus Christ, by Whom the world is crucified unto me,
and I unto the world (Gal. 6:14).

In Verses 12 through 15, Paul sums up all the import
of his Letter.

Those who desire to display their zeal for outward
ceremonies sought to make them necessary to Salvation,
but their real object was to please self and escape persecution. They gloried in these ceremonies applied to
men's bodies.

On the contrary, the Apostle gloried in the Cross,
upon which the religious world of sacraments, shadows, outward ceremonies, and good works had been
crucified, a Cross upon which he himself by Faith had
been crucified, so that he was dead to them, and they
were dead to him.

Outward physical sacraments, good works, and ceremonies are unimportant. What is important is the New

Birth, and the victory and life that it brings, or at least which it will bring if the Believer steadfastly looks to Christ and the Cross. Most certainly the irreligious world has been judged and ended in the Cross of Christ, but so also has the religious world; and it is the abolition of that world which is the subject of this Epistle.

If Paul gloried in anything physical, it was not in the sign of circumcision, but in the marks of man's brutality, which, in the triumph of faith, he called *"the marks of the Lord Jesus"* (6:17). The whole thing is summed up in the fact that, in contrast to the Judaizers who gloried in human attainment and self-effort as a means of Salvation, Paul boasted in the Cross of Christ.

The world of which Paul here speaks is the world Paul knew before he was saved, the world of Philippians 3:4-6, his Hebrew ancestry, his Pharisaic traditions, his zeal for the Law, in short, the world in which he had lived. To all this was he now dead. He had been separated from it by the Cross of the Lord Jesus. It had no more appeal to him, nor influence upon him.

In Galatians 6:15, Paul gives his reason for glorying in the Cross:

While circumcision is of no avail to the Jew, nor the lack of circumcision of any avail to the Gentile, yet the Cross has power to make both a believing Jew and a believing Gentile a new creation, which results in a radical transformation of character. The Cross, in fact, carries the only power which can effect such a transformation.

OCTOBER

29

*b*ut now in Christ Jesus you who sometimes were far off are made near by the Blood of Christ. For He is our peace, Who has made both one, and has broken down the middle wall of partition between us (Eph. 2:13-14).

When Paul speaks of *"the Gospel,"* *"the Word,"* *"the Blood,"* *"Redemption,"* *"Salvation,"* *"The Faith,"* etc., he is actually referring to the Cross, which stands for all of these things, and even many things we have not named here.

The Cross, typified in Verse 13 by *"the Blood of Christ,"* paid the price for man's Redemption, and we speak of the entirety of mankind (Jn. 3:16), and, in so doing, made both Jews and Gentiles one.

The difference between Jews and Gentiles, at least in physical form, was probably evidenced more than anything else by *"the middle wall of partition"* that separated the Court of the Gentiles from the Court of Women, which stood before the Temple. This wall, which was approximately four feet high, represented the whole Mosaic

715

economy, which separated Jew and Gentile.

As far as the Lord was concerned, the Jews were near because of the Abrahamic Covenant, and the Gentiles were far off. The Gentiles were not included in the Abrahamic Covenant, at least not during the time of the Law. They could be saved, but only by becoming a proselyte Jew.

When Jesus died on the Cross, thereby shedding His Precious Blood, which referred to the pouring out of His Life, which served as the great Sacrifice for sin, which God accepted, this satisfied the Law and all its requirements, which, thereby, made it possible for both Jews and Gentiles to come even closer.

As a result of what the Lord did at the Cross, He established *"Peace,"* which eliminates all condemnation and guilt. To *"make peace"* means, therefore, *"to join together that which is separated."* Jews and Gentiles, by God's act of selecting the Jewish nation to be the channel through which He would bring Salvation to the lost, had been separated. Now, in the Blood of Christ, they, in the Church, had been joined. This is the peace spoken of here.

The word chosen by the Holy Spirit to emphasize *"peace"* actually means, *"He, and no other."* This suggests that not only *"He Alone,"* but *"He, in His Own Person,"* made peace. It is not only that peace was made by Christ and ranks as His achievement, but that it is so identified with Him that, were He away, it also would fail — so dependent upon Him that, apart from Him, we cannot have it.

All of this was achieved by the Cross. For us to receive all that was achieved, because it was all done for us, we only have to express Faith in Christ and His Finished Work (Rom. 6:11).

OCTOBER
30

*a*nd that He might reconcile both unto God in one body by the Cross, having slain the enmity thereby: And came and preached peace to you which were afar off, and to them who were nigh. For through Him we both have access by one Spirit unto the Father (Eph. 2:16-18).

Through the Cross, both Jews and Gentiles are reconciled in one body to God. A part of the work of the Cross was to bring the two long-sundered and antagonistic parties together as one whole, one great body, into right relation to God. The words, *"having slain the enmity thereby,"* here refers to the enmity that is between the sinner and God.

The word *"preached,"* as used here, refers *"to bringing good news."* It is the good news of the Cross, and, more particularly, what the Cross has afforded. The Cross opened up the way to the Father.

Please note that the Trinity is here expressed in Verse 18. God the Son provides the way into the Father's Presence through the Blood of His Cross. God the Holy Spirit conducts the Saint in and presents him. God the Father is the One into Whose Presence the Believer is brought (Wuest).

However, let it also be understood: It is the Holy Spirit Who gives access to the Believer regarding the Father, which pertains to the Throne of God. The fact that He can allow access means that He also can bar access, which He most definitely will, if the Believer tries to come any way other than by Faith in *"the Blood of Christ,"* i.e., *"the Cross."* Seeing it in that perspective puts a new light on the subject. If the Cross and our Faith in that Finished Work is the password, so to speak, and if the Cross is ignored or repudiated, then such a person will be barred from access to anything and everything pertaining to God. This presents itself as an extremely serious matter.

I do hope the Reader can now see the tremendous, even outsized, significance of the Cross in all that pertains to God and His dealings with us. To fail to see this is to fail!

OCTOBER

31

*W*herefore He said, When He ascended up on high, He led captivity captive, and gave Gifts unto men. (Now that He ascended, what is it but that He also descended first into the lower parts of the Earth? He Who descended is the same also Who ascended up far above all Heavens, that He might fill all things) (Eph. 4:8-10).

These Passages speak of Christ descending down into the *"lower parts of the Earth,"* which refer to Paradise, and then ascending to Heaven.

The idea is this:

Before the Cross, which paid the terrible debt of sin, and which satisfied the demands of a thrice-Holy God, all Believers who died went down into Paradise, which was next door, so to speak, to the burning side of Hell. Only a great gulf separated the burning side from the Paradise side (Lk. 16:26).

These individuals, which probably numbered many, many thousands, could not be taken to Heaven upon

719

death (their soul and spirit), because the blood of bulls and goats was insufficient to satisfy the sin debt (Heb. 10:4). These individual, although saved, were still captives of Satan, hence, the phrase, *"He (Jesus) led captivity captive."* This means that all of these people who had been captives of Satan, even though they were in Paradise, were now made captives of the Lord Jesus Christ once the sin debt was paid. After Jesus died on the Cross, He first of all went down into Paradise to deliver these individuals, whose very Salvation depended on the Cross. With the Cross now an accomplished fact, Satan had no more claim on them, no legal right to hold them any longer, so Jesus made them His captives and took them with Him to Heaven.

Since the sin debt has been paid at the Cross of Calvary, now when a Believer dies, the soul and the spirit of such a person instantly go to be with the Lord in Heaven. It's been that way ever since the Cross. The sin debt has been paid, so Satan has no more claim (Phil. 1:23).

Furthermore, when Jesus went down into Paradise, which was in the heart of the Earth, and liberated those souls, He didn't go down defeated, as some claim, but rather as a Conqueror. The price had been paid, the victory had been won, and, due to the fact that every single sin was atoned — past, present, and future, at least for all who will believe — the Resurrection was now a given. In other words, there was no doubt that He would be raised from the dead.

The Scripture says that the *"wages of sin is death"* (Rom. 6:23). If even one single sin had remained unatoned, Jesus could not have risen from the dead. But due to the fact that all sin was atoned, the Resurrection was guaranteed. That's why He constantly told His Disciples, *"The Son of Man must suffer many things, and be rejected of the Elders, and of the Chief Priests and Scribes, and be killed, and after three days rise again"* (Mk. 8:31; Mat. 16:21; 17:22; Lk. 9:22). In all these accounts, He plainly told them, *"After three days I will rise again."*

The descent of Christ into Paradise, where He delivered all the Old Testament Saints, and His ascent into Heaven, all as a victorious Conqueror, were all made possible, totally and completely, by the Cross.

NOVEMBER

1

*f*inally, my Brethren, be strong in the Lord, and in the power of His Might. Put on the whole armor of God, that you may be able to stand against the wiles of the Devil. For we wrestle not against flesh and blood, but against principalities, against powers, against the rulers of the darkness of this world, against spiritual wickedness in high places (Eph. 6:10-12).

The above Passages, linked with Verses 13 through 18, present the Believer's armor and resources.

First of all, the armor addressed is the *"armor of God,"* which means that it is not of any human instrumentation or ability. Moreover, all of this armor is to be used, and not just some.

In the word *"wrestle,"* Paul uses a Greek athletic term. It refers to a contest between two in which each endeavors to throw the other, and which is decided when the victor is able to press and hold down his prostrate antagonist, namely, hold him down with his hand upon his neck. When we consider that the loser in a Greek wrestling contest had his eyes gouged out, resulting in blindness for the rest of his days, we understand the seriousness of the conflict.

To be sure, the Christian's wrestling against the powers of darkness is no less desperate and fateful. In other words, the very soul of the Believer is at stake regarding the outcome of this contest.

"Our wrestling is not against flesh and blood." It is against the powers of darkness.

The *"principalities and powers"* constitute the demons of Satan, which fill the air around the Earth.

The *"rulers of the darkness of this world"* constitute fallen angels.

The *"spiritual wickedness in high places"* pertains to the highest rank of fallen angels, all laboring under Satan, attempting to greatly hinder, even destroy, the Child of God.

First, let it be understood: No Believer can be demon-possessed. Believers, to be sure, can be demon-oppressed, but never demon-possessed. Many Believers may think they are demon-possessed, because their faith is in something other than the Cross, which means that despite all of their efforts, they cannot get victory over particular *"works of the flesh."* In other words, the Sin Nature is ruling such a Believer.

So when some Preacher tells them they are demon-possessed, that they need to have certain demons cast out in order to be free, many, out of desperation, believe this lie. However, it doesn't matter what Preacher prays for them, or what type of manifestation they may experience, until they learn the Truth of the Cross, they will know no freedom.

Jesus said, *"You shall know the Truth, and the Truth shall make you free"* (Jn. 8:32).

The Believer's recourse, his only recourse, and the only recourse needed, is Faith in Christ and what Christ did at the Cross. Then the Holy Spirit will subdue the Sin Nature and the problem will go away. Because of many factors, it may take some time, but ultimately it will leave. The Believer who makes Christ and the Cross the total Object of his Faith will ultimately come to the place that "*sin shall no longer have dominion over you*" (Rom. 6:14).

The phrase in Ephesians, Chapter 6, Verse 13 that says, "*And having done all, to stand,*" actually means that the Believer is to serve notice on Satan that he cannot have anything that belongs to the Child of God. It is not the Will of God for the Believer to live in a state of defeat. The Cross of Christ has answered the problem of sin, and in every capacity. It only remains for the Believer to exercise his Faith in that Finished Work.

The first thing the Believer is to do is to "*gird his loins about with Truth.*" This speaks of the Truth which sets one free, which is the Message of the Cross (I Cor. 1:17-18).

The next thing the Believer is to do is to put on the "*Breastplate of Righteousness.*" This is the Righteousness that is afforded by Christ; the Cross is the means of such Righteousness being given to us. This is the only way that Righteousness can be afforded (Rom. 4:3).

Next, the feet of the Believer is to be shod with the "*preparation of the Gospel of Peace.*" This is the "*peace*" that is afforded strictly by the Cross, and the Cross alone.

"*The shield of faith*" consists, once again, of Faith in Christ and what He has done at the Cross. This is the only type of Faith that God will recognize.

Regrettably, so many Believers have their spiritual loins

girded with something other than the Truth, their Breast-plates are something other than the true Righteousness of Christ, and their feet are shod with something which is not exactly the *"Gospel of Peace."* The *"faith"* that most have, although it is *"faith,"* is not Faith in Christ and the Cross; consequently, it will quench no *"fiery darts of the wicked."*

Last of all regarding the armor, the Believer is to *"take the helmet of Salvation,"* which again is afforded by the Cross, and *"the Sword of the Spirit, which is the Word of God,"* which, once again, is the portrayal of the Cross. In fact, the entirety of the Bible is the story of Jesus Christ and Him Crucified.

With all of this, and according to 6:18, the Believer is to *"pray"* and *"watch."*

While Paul had a Roman soldier in mind on which he bases his illustration, still, trying to explain what the Roman soldier wears is of no consequence to the Believer. We are to know and understand what Paul is saying beyond the illustration. Once again, he leads the Believer to the Cross, which affords all of these things, and which alone affords all of these things. Regrettably, when most Preachers attempt to explain the *"whole armor of God,"* they ignore the Cross altogether, which means that their explanation is of no value.

The whole thing consists of the Believer understanding that everything he receives from the Lord, all of his Salvation and protection, come exclusively through Christ and what Christ did at the Cross. Our Faith in that Finished Work gives the Holy Spirit great latitude in our lives, bringing about the desired results, which only He can do! (Rom. 8:2)

725

NOVEMBER

2

*b*ut what things were gain to me, those I counted loss for
Christ. Yea doubtless, and I count all things but loss for the
excellency of the knowledge of Christ Jesus, my Lord: for Whom
I have suffered the loss of all things, and do count them but
dung, that I may win Christ (Phil. 3:7-8).

What the Apostle is saying here is dramatic, to say the
least. It was not sins that Paul surrendered in order to
win Christ, but righteousness: his own personal righteousness. This is a tremendous truth. Christ died not
only to expiate and abolish our sins, but also to expiate
and abolish our righteousnesses.

As an Old Testament example, the great Patriarch Job
had to discover the *"worthlessness of self,"* and then the
"worthfulness of Christ." And to be sure, the latter cannot
be reached until the former be passed through. As Job
had to learn that, so did Paul, and so do we.

First of all, to fully *"win Christ,"* one has to suffer the
loss of all things. By that, we are referring to all the

726

things that make one righteous, or so one thinks, other than Christ and Him Crucified. This refers to place, position, status, works, Church association, religious activity, good deeds, etc. While some of these things may need to be continued, they must be continued, if at all, with the understanding that the doing of them earns us nothing with the Lord.

When Jesus died on the Cross, He died not only to save us from sin, but also to save us from "*self.*" The latter just might be the most difficult!

This doesn't mean that a person ceases to be a "*self*" when one comes to Christ, but rather that "*self*" is properly hidden in Christ. This is what Jesus was talking about when He said, *"At that day, you shall know that I am in My Father, and you in Me, and I in you"* (Jn. 14:20).

This is also what He meant when He said, *"If any man will come after Me* (the criteria for Discipleship), *let him deny himself* (not asceticism, as many think, but rather that one denies one's own willpower, self-will, strength, and ability, depending totally on Christ), *and take up his Cross* (the benefits of the Cross, looking exclusively to what Jesus did there to meet our every need) *daily* (this is so important, our looking to the Cross, that we must renew our Faith in what Christ has done for us, even on a daily basis, for Satan will ever try to move us away from the Cross as the Object of our Faith, which always spells disaster), *and follow Me* (Christ can be followed only by the Believer looking to the Cross, understanding what is accomplished, and by that means alone) (Mat. 16:24; Rom. 6:3-5, 11, 14; 8:1-2, 11; I Cor. 1:17-18, 21, 23; 2:2; Gal. 6:14; Col. 2:14-15).

"For whosoever will save his life shall lose it (try to live one's life outside of Christ and the Cross): *but whosoever will lose his life for My sake, the same shall save it*" (when we place our Faith entirely in Christ and the Cross, looking exclusively to Him, we have just found *"more abundant life"* [Jn. 10:10]) (Mat. 16:25).

Most Believers, sadly, never truly follow Christ, simply because they do not desire to obey what He demands. As a result, they never really fully have all that He desires to give. That loss is the greatest loss of all!

NOVEMBER

3

*a*nd be found in Him, not having my own Righteousness, which is of the Law, but that which is through the Faith of Christ, the Righteousness which is of God by Faith (Phil. 3:9).

A great truth here is given to us, at least if we understand what the great Apostle is saying.

He is saying that it was not sins that he had to surrender to win Christ, even though that definitely was done, but rather his own personal righteousnesses. Christ died not only to expatiate and abolish our sins, but also to expatiate and abolish our righteousnesses.

The Righteousness which is from God is offered to the sinner in Christ, and secured by him by Faith, as opposed to works.

Let us explain it:

An excellent Old Testament example is the Patriarch Job. He had to discover the worthlessness of self, as stated, before he could discover the worthfulness of Christ. Before the latter could be reached, the former had to be first

729

passed through. Man's problem, whoever he might be, is that he tries to make his own righteousness. Unfortunately, when we come to Christ, the effort doesn't stop; it mostly continues.

It is hard for the unconverted man to admit what he really is: a worthless sinner. Because he does some good things, or doesn't do some bad things, he likes to think of himself as *"good."* The reason most never come to Christ is that before one can come to Christ, he must admit that he is a worthless sinner. But if he does admit he is a worthless sinner and comes to Christ, a perfect, spotless Righteousness, found only in Christ, and our acceptance of Him, is afforded such a person. It is called *"imputed righteousness,"* meaning that it is imputed by the Lord to the believing sinner, and done so freely.

But yet, the problem doesn't cease with the unsaved. All too often, after coming to Christ, and not being properly taught, the Believer tries once again to establish his own righteousness by doing certain things, or not doing certain things. He will have no more success than the unbelieving sinner has in trying to be saved by his own means and ways.

Because of a lack of proper teaching, almost all Christians presently are trying to develop their own righteousness. Many of them will tell the unsaved soul that it's impossible to come to Christ unless they accept Him fully, not at all depending on their own good works, etc. And then they will turn right around and do the very thing they told the sinner he cannot do. They will try to gain victory over sin by law, by self-will, by works of righteousness, etc.

However, the Apostle is here saying that whatever righteousness we think we have, whatever we think we have gained by our own efforts, will never be recognized by God. That which is recognized by the Lord is that which we obtain *"through the Faith of Christ."* This refers to what Jesus did at the Cross and our Faith and confidence totally and completely in that, and that alone! That is *"the Faith of Christ."* That being done, we will obtain *"the Righteousness which is of God by Faith,"* which will then give the Holy Spirit latitude to work in our lives, and thereby give us victory over sin and all the works of the flesh.

In this Ninth Verse is found the reason that Believers cannot get victory over sin. They are trying to gain a position by law which God will never accept. They don't think of it as such, but that is what is actually happening. The only faith the Lord will recognize is Faith in Christ and what Christ did at the Cross. Everything else is unacceptable!

NOVEMBER

4

*t*hat I may know Him, and the Power of His Resurrection, and the fellowship of His Sufferings, being made conformable unto His Death (Phil. 3:10).

When the Apostle said, "*That I may know Him*," he was speaking of knowing Christ in a particular way, which is outlined in the balance of the Scripture. That which the Apostle desired to know, and that which we also must desire to know, is the following:

1. "*The Power of His Resurrection*": Paul is not speaking of the coming Resurrection of Life, but rather the Resurrection of Christ, which refers to every Believer being resurrected with Him, and resurrected to a "*new life*" (Rom. 6:4). This is true Resurrection Life, which gives the Believer a power that is absolutely undeniable. However, Resurrection Power to live a Resurrection Life can only come about by following the admonition of the next two points.

2. "*The fellowship of His Sufferings*": Whenever Jesus

died on the Cross, in the Mind of God, every person who exhibits Faith in Christ and what He did in the Sacrifice of Himself is baptized into His Death. In effect, Jesus did it all for us. Our identification with Him as our Substitute gives us all that for which He died. We were buried with Him by Baptism into death, which means that all of the old life was buried once and for all with Him, never to plague us again. We were then raised with Him in newness of life.

Consequently, when Paul speaks of *"the fellowship of His Sufferings,"* he is meaning that we are meant to reap the benefits of all that for which he paid such a great price. He suffered terribly to give us what we have. For us not to have all that for which He suffered is, in a sense, an insult thrown in His Face.

3. *"Being made conformable unto His Death"*: The Cross is the great pivot point of the Plan of God. It was planned by the Godhead from before the foundation of the world (I Pet. 1:18-20). When we *"conform unto His Death,"* we, in effect, are basing our lives strictly and totally on what He did for us at the Cross, which is the intention here of the Holy Spirit. In this one Verse of Scripture, we have the means given to us by which we can live a victorious life: victorious over the world, the flesh, and the Devil. This is, in fact, the only way it can be carried out.

When we enter into the *"fellowship of His Sufferings,"* when we are *"made conformable unto His Death,"* which refer simply to Faith in Christ and what He did at the Cross, all on our behalf, then we will know *"Resurrection Life"* (Rom. 6:5).

NOVEMBER
5

*b*rethren, be followers together of me, and mark them which walk so as you have us for an example. (For many walk, of whom I have told you often, and now tell you even weeping, that they are the enemies of the Cross of Christ: Whose end is destruction, whose God is their belly, and whose glory is in their shame, who mind earthly things.) [Phil. 3:17-19].

Whoever these individuals were, the Apostle concluded them to be *"enemies of the Cross of Christ."* He didn't say *"enemies of Christ,"* but rather *"enemies of the Cross of Christ."* He was speaking of the Judaizers, whom he mentioned at the beginning of this Third Chapter of Philippians.

The Judaizers were Jews who had accepted Christ as the Messiah, but who also insisted that all Believers, both Jews and Gentiles, had to keep the Law. As such, their emphasis was on the law, and not at all on the Cross of Christ. Regrettably, the problem didn't die with the Judaizers. In fact, it is <u>the</u> problem which plagues the Church even unto this hour.

Anyone who purposely makes something other than

734

the Cross of Christ the Object of his Faith, no matter who that person might be, can be concluded to be none other than an *"enemy of the Cross of Christ."* All Salvation is found in the Cross; all Victory is found in the Cross; all Power is found in the Cross; all overcoming Glory is found in the Cross; all healing is found in the Cross; all Life is found in the Cross. Anything and everything that we receive from the Lord actually comes to us exclusively from Christ as the Source and the Cross as the means, with the Holy Spirit superintending all that is done.

How much of the modern Church would have to be concluded to be *"enemies of the Cross of Christ"*? I'm afraid that almost all would fall into that category. Through the Apostle, the Holy Spirit says four things about such Preachers and people, which are:

1. *"Whose end is destruction"*: If the Cross of Christ is rejected, ignored, or given a secondary position, then destruction is the only conclusion, inasmuch as the Cross Christ alone stands between men and Hell. If we reject the Cross, we have, at the same time, rejected Christ.

2. *"Whose God is their belly"*: This refers to the fact that they are concerned about material things, and material things alone.

3. *"Whose glory is in their shame"*: The material things they seek, God labels as *"shame."*

4. *"Who mind Earthly things"*: This means they have no interest in Heavenly things; they are merely using the Lord for their own personal gain.

Let us say it again:

If anyone rejects the Cross, they have, at the same time, rejected Christ!

NOVEMBER

6

*r*ejoice in the Lord always: and again I say, Rejoice (Phil. 4:4).

Paul here gives his teaching on emotional well-being. It is:

1. *"Rejoice in the Lord always"*: This means that in our heart of hearts there is to be a continuous praise to the Lord, because He has done so much for us. He didn't say here that we should rejoice only when things go well, but *"always."* That means we should rejoice, even when we don't feel like rejoicing.

2. *"Let your moderation be known unto all men. The Lord is at hand"*: The idea is, we aren't greedily grasping after things. Why not? The Rapture will soon take place. In the light of eternity, that is literally true.

3. *"Be careful for nothing"*: This simply means, *"Don't worry about anything."*

4. *"But in everything by prayer and supplication with thanksgiving let your requests be made known unto God"*:

736

The cure for worry is believing prayer. *"Supplication"* refers to telling the Lord what we need and then *"thanking Him"* for all He has done for us. When we make our requests known to the Lord, we are talking to Someone Who is able to do all things. When we seek the help that men can give, we then get the help that they can give, which is mostly nothing. When we seek the help that God can give, He can do all things.

5. *"The Peace of God shall keep us"*: This is *"Sanctifying Peace,"* which can come to the Believer only as the Believer places his faith exclusively in Christ and the Cross. We then have a peace which *"passes all understanding,"* which means that it is *"beyond the pale of human comprehension."* If we do this which the Holy Spirit here through the Apostle is telling us to do, it will *"keep our hearts and minds through Christ Jesus."* As we constantly state, Christ is the Source, while the Cross is the means.

6. Finally, he tells us that we should think on things which are *"true, honest, just, pure, lovely, of a good report, virtue, and if there be any praise, think on these things."*

All of these things can be done, providing the Cross is the Object of our Faith, which then gives the Holy Spirit latitude to help us, without Whose help nothing can be done.

These exhortations are God's prescription, as stated, for emotional well-being.

NOVEMBER

7

n *ot because I desire a gift: but I desire fruit that may* *abound to your account. But I have all, and abound: I am* *full, having received of Epaphroditus the things which were* *sent from you, an odor of a sweet smell, a Sacrifice acceptable,* *well-pleasing to God. But my God shall supply all your need* *according to His riches in Glory by Christ Jesus* (Phil. 4:17-19).

The Holy Spirit through Paul here gives us a tremendous truth that is overlooked much of the time.

Paul is in prison in Rome. A man by the name of Epaphroditus had come all the way from Philippi to bring him an offering from the Philippians, a Church founded by Paul. From his terminology, it seems the gift was generous. The Holy Spirit likens this gift as *"an odor of a sweet smell,"* which had to do with the Levitical Offerings of the Old Testament. When the smoke would go up from those Sacrifices, it was said to be *"a sweet savor unto the LORD"* (Lev. 1:9).

How could greasy smoke going up from the burning

of the carcass of a lamb on an Altar be a *"sweet savor unto the LORD"*?

It was this to God because that animal sacrifice represented His Only Son, Who would ultimately come to this world, Who would die on a Cross, which would redeem the fallen sons of Adam's lost race.

Remember, Paul is likening this offering sent by the Philippians to the Cross of Christ. Then he says, *"A Sacrifice acceptable, well-pleasing to God,"* which refers, first of all, to the Cross being *"well-pleasing to God,"* and now this monetary offering. The great truth here presented is this:

When we give of our resources to help take this Message of the Cross to a hurting world, the Holy Spirit through Paul tells us that the Lord places such a gift in the same category as His Cross, because for everyone who doesn't know what Jesus did on the Cross, Jesus' Death, as it regards that person, was in vain. When we give to help take this Message to a hurting world, we are making it possible for people to hear the greatest story ever told.

That tells us several things:

First of all: If we support any Ministry that is not of the Cross, whatever it is we are supporting, it is <u>not</u> well-pleasing to God. In other words, and to be blunt, you are wasting your money.

Second: The next great truth presented here is that if we support that which truly is of God, and I continue to speak of the Cross, then we have the Promise of the Lord that *"He shall supply our need according to His riches in Glory by Christ Jesus."* Otherwise, He won't!

NOVEMBER
8

*b*lotting out the handwriting of Ordinances that was against us, which was contrary to us, and took it out of the way, nailing it to His Cross (Col. 2:14).

The *"Ordinances"* of which Paul speaks here concern the Law of Moses and all its wide concepts, whether ceremonial, civil, or moral.

The Law was against us and contrary to us in the sense that man, due to the Fall, simply was unable to keep its precepts. The Law could show a man what he was, i.e., incapable, but it gave him no power to change the situation. It was like looking into a mirror and seeing what you are, but understanding that the mirror cannot change your appearance.

When Jesus died on the Cross, He satisfied every demand of the broken law, of which every human being was guilty, with the Sacrifice of Himself paying the debt that man owed to God, which man could not pay.

The term, *"nailing it to His Cross,"* means that it was

the Cross and what there transpired which settled the account. Everyone who believes Christ and what He did at the Cross is thereby redeemed from the curse of the Law and given Eternal Life (Jn. 3:16).

There was an old Jewish custom called *"possessing the double,"* which Paul may have had in mind when he wrote this Verse. The custom pertained to an individual who had gone bankrupt. As such, the individual was required to take a dried animal skin and write on it every debt he owed and to whom it was owed. The skin was then nailed in a public place by the gate of the city, so it could be seen by all.

One can well imagine the humiliation of such proceedings.

Every once in a while, a wealthy benefactor, someone with a charitable heart, would observe these skins of animals nailed to the wall. For whatever reason, the wealthy man might take one down, fold it double, write his name on the back, and then nail it back to the wall. This meant that all the people to whom this particular individual owed money could come see the man whose name was on the doubled over animal skin. All the creditors would be paid in full. This was, as stated, referred to as *"possessing the double."*

One can imagine the joy of a person who would be lifted out of bankruptcy by such an action.

Two thousand years ago, when Jesus Christ died on the Cross, He took all of our sins, our terrible indebtedness (and, to be sure, we were completely bankrupt), and doubled over the account so that it no longer could be seen (thus making unseen also the humiliation), and wrote His Name on it, the Lord Jesus Christ, meaning that the debt has now been paid. Then it was nailed to His Cross for all to see.

That's why the Cross is so important! It was there that the debt was paid, paid by such a price that no one in eternity future will ever be able to say that the price was insufficient.

NOVEMBER
9

*a*nd having spoiled principalities and powers, He made a show of them openly, triumphing over them in it (Col. 2:15).

We are told in this Passage that Jesus totally and completely defeated Satan and all of his minions of darkness at the Cross.

Just exactly how was this done?

Sin is the legal means by which Satan can hold men in bondage. It's called *"the Law of sin and death"* (Rom. 8:2). Satan has a legal right, a right given to him by God, to do what he is doing, as it regards holding men captive, because man has sinned.

What is sin?

"Sin is the transgression of the Law" (I Jn. 3:4).

The Law of God, as given to Moses, was God's Standard of Righteousness. Morally, it is summed up in the Ten Commandments. So, in some way, sin is the transgression of those Commandments. Regrettably, every human being who has ever lived, other than Jesus Christ, has transgressed the Law, thereby incurring its penalty. That penalty is death (Rom. 6:23).

When Jesus died on the Cross, He atoned for all sin, past, present, and future, at least for all who will believe (Jn. 3:16; Heb. 10:12). When He atoned for all sin, this removed Satan's legal right to hold man in bondage. Satan's *"right"* was sin; with that gone, i.e., the Law of God was satisfied, Satan's legal right was gone, as well.

If men presently are held in Satanic bondage, it's because they haven't availed themselves of what Jesus has done for them at the Cross. They can do so by simply exhibiting Faith in Christ and His Finished Work, which guarantees Eternal Life and Victory in every capacity.

When Jesus atoned for all sin, He not only atoned for acts of sin, but He also addressed the very cause of sin, which is Satan. Sin, with its cause and effect, was, therefore, totally defeated at the Cross. Furthermore, this Victory was heralded all over the spirit world, which means that Satan, every fallen angel, and every demon spirit knows what Jesus did at the Cross, and knows that it spelled their death knell.

Not only did Jesus defeat Satan and his hordes, but also *"made a show of them openly, triumphing over them in it."* This carries the idea of a Roman General who had won a great victory. If the victory was great enough, he was given a parade through the middle of Rome. As the cheering crowds thronged the sides of the road, the General rode in a gilded chariot pulled by prancing steeds. Behind the chariot were the kings and military leaders he had defeated in battle, attached to the chariot by a noose around their necks. In humiliation, they stumbled as

744

defeated foes while the people of Rome cheered.

This same connotation is meant to apply to Satan and all his cohorts of darkness. As stated, when Jesus died on the Cross, the entirety of the spirit world knew, beyond the shadow of a doubt, that Satan was totally and completely defeated. His defeat was totally humiliating, meaning that he was defeated in every capacity. All sin was atoned, leaving him with no legal right to hold one single person in bondage.

The answer is in the Cross, even as the Word of God says. Israel of old was told to look at the brazen serpent on the pole and thereby live. Poor, sinful, wicked man is likewise told to simply look at Christ and what He did at the Cross. If they will believe in their hearts, they are instantly and wondrously saved (Rom. 10:9-10).

NOVEMBER

10

Set your affection on things above, not on things on the Earth. For you are dead, and your life is hid with Christ in God (Col. 3:2-3).

"*Dead with Christ*" (3:3) — Peace.
"*Risen with Christ*" (3:1) — Power.
"*Hidden with Christ*" (3:3) — Preservation.

A dead man is beyond judgment, for Christ is beyond judgment. Hence, the Believer has a peace that nothing can destroy. Resurrection means power and victory.

Paul's arguments in these Passages are:

"*What have Ordinances to do with people who died with Christ?*" and,

"*How can they possibly find a place in the realm into which those are brought who are risen with Christ?*"

Those who believe the great fact of the union of the members with the Head, and the perfection and nourishment furnished them by the Head, do not set their affections on things on the Earth, i.e., on Ordinances,

746

Sacraments, and all the religious rites of man's invention, but they set their affections on things above where none of these things have any meaning, and where they could not exist or be practiced.

Those who died with Christ are justified in Him, and, consequently, need no Ordinances to add to that Justification, for it is Divine, infinite, and complete; and those who are risen with Christ are sanctified in Him, and they need no Ordinances to perfect their Sanctification. It also is Divine, infinite, and perfect, in fact made possible by the Cross.

The short phrase, *"For you are dead,"* characterizes the Christian experience possibly better than anything that could be said. The Lord does not rehabilitate people, does not try to improve the old man, does not engage in moral evolution, etc. In Christ, and we speak of His Crucifixion, the Believer has died. Concerning this very thing, Paul also stated, *"For he who is dead is freed from sin,"* i.e., from domination by the Sin Nature (Rom. 6:7).

Now that a person is dead to the old life, which means he is not what he once was, old things have passed away, and all things have become new (II Cor. 5:17). The Apostle also said, *"Now if we be dead with Christ, we believe that we shall also live with Him"* (Rom. 6:8). We died with Christ in order that we might live with Christ, which speaks of the *"newness of life"* (Rom. 6:4).

All of this was done at the Cross. The Believer gains all the Victory there won by Christ by simply exhibiting Faith in Christ and the Atonement. This is the only way that the individual can have perpetual victory over sin, meaning that the Sin Nature no longer dominates the individual (Rom. 6:14). He has to trust what Christ did at the Cross, and continue to trust what Christ did at the Cross, which the Holy Spirit demands (Rom. 6:1-14).

The Believer's ignorance is the source of Satan's successful operation in the Believer's heart and life. In other words, if the Believer doesn't know and understand how Sanctification is brought about, which refers to the Cross, Satan, to be sure, takes advantage of that.

At this moment, the far greater majority of Believers, and we speak of the entirety of the world, are not walking in Victory, but rather in defeat. However, each and every one of these Believers can walk in total and complete victory. But first they must know and understand how victory is obtained, which can only be done by and through the Cross.

NOVEMBER

11

*f*or the Lord Himself shall descend from Heaven with a shout, with the voice of the Archangel, and with the Trump of God: and the dead in Christ shall rise first: Then we which are alive and remain shall be caught up together with them in the clouds, to meet the Lord in the air: and so shall we ever be with the Lord. Wherefore comfort one another with these words (I Thess. 4:16-18).

I Thessalonians 4:13-18 portrays the Rapture of the Church.

The two words, *"Rapture"* and *"Resurrection,"* both mean the same thing. In this Passage, Paul gives us the fact of the Rapture, or the Resurrection, whichever term one desires to use. In the Fifteenth Chapter of I Corinthians, he gives us the details.

The people in the Church at Thessalonica were not clear on the subject regarding the state of Believers who had recently died in Christ.

Where were they? Because they had died, would they

miss out on some of the things the Lord would do?

Paul answers these and other questions.

First of all, he tells them that those who have died in Christ are actually now with the Lord, and they will not miss anything because of their death. As Paul more perfectly explains in the Fifteenth Chapter of I Corinthians, the soul and the spirit of every Believer who has died is now with Jesus in Heaven.

When the Lord comes back, He will bring all of these people with Him (4:14), where they will be given, and instantly, a Glorified Body. As stated, the Fifteenth Chapter of I Corinthians explains this clearly. The dead in Christ shall rise immediately upon the sound of the Trump of God, and those who are alive when the Lord comes will follow immediately after.

The Scripture says that *"the Lord Himself shall descend from Heaven with a shout."* This is the Victory Shout, which will signal the Resurrection, and which will be the greatest *"Shout"* the spiritual world has ever known. The *"Shout"* will be accompanied by *"the Voice of the Archangel,"* who, incidentally, is Michael. The Lord Himself will *"Shout,"* but we aren't told exactly what the *"Voice of the Archangel"* will be.

Why the Archangel at this time?

Michael is the only Archangel, so-named, in Scripture. This means he might be the highest ranked Angel, but Gabriel is a possible exception. Michael's sphere of operation is the protection and guidance of Israel (Dan. 10:21). A possible reason for Michael is that the Dispensation of the Church is now over. Events are beginning to transpire which will bring Israel to Christ, hence,

Michael's involvement.

Finally, we have *"the Trump of God."* From the way the Scripture reads, it seems that God the Father will actually be the One Who blows this *"Trump."* In Israel of old, trumpets were used at several occasions, whether for celebration or the advent of war. This *"Trump"* will signal both: a celebration of the Church going to be with Christ, and the advent of war against the Antichrist.

Paul also stated, *"Then we which are alive and remain shall be caught up together with them in the clouds"* (4:17). This is not speaking of clouds in the sky, as we normally think of such, but rather *"clouds of Saints,"* all joined together to *"meet the Lord in the air."*

Incidentally, the Greek word here used for *"air"* is *"aer,"* which refers to anything below 6,000 feet, which is the height of Mount Olympus. For everything above that height, the Greeks used another word. So, according to Paul, when Christ returns to take the Church away, both those who have died and those who are alive, while He will not set His feet on the Earth, He will come at least within a mile of the Earth, possibly even closer.

For those who claim there will be no Rapture of the Church, they need to be asked, *"Do you believe in the Resurrection?"* I'm sure they do! They need to be told that the *"Rapture"* and the *"Resurrection"* are one and the same. So if one believes in the Resurrection, which one has to do if one is saved, then, whether they understand it or not, they are believing in the Rapture.

NOVEMBER

12

*n*ow we beseech you, Brethren, by the coming of our Lord Jesus Christ, and by our gathering together unto Him, That you be not soon shaken in mind, or be troubled, neither by spirit, nor by word, nor by letter, as from us, as that the Day of Christ is at hand. Let no man deceive you by any means: for that day shall not come, except there come a falling away first, and that man of sin be revealed, the son of perdition (II Thess. 2:1-3).

The people in the Church in Thessalonica were still confused about some Endtime issues. Some believed, erroneously, that Christ was about to come back then, or else had already come. Paul answers all of this in this Second Chapter of II Thessalonians.

The phrase, *"The Day of Christ,"* should have been translated, *"the Day of the Lord,"* because this is how the best manuscripts read; the *"Day of the Lord"* refers to all events after the Rapture; even in Paul's day, some were claiming that the Second Coming was about to take place, which, of course, was wrong.

Paul answers these claims by saying that Believers should not be shaken in mind or be troubled. He then said, *"neither by spirit"* (this referred to messages in tongues and interpretations, which purported to be of the Lord, but really were not), *"nor by word"* (this pertained to those who claimed to have a word from the Lord, but really didn't), *"nor by letter as from us"* (someone had written a letter claiming certain prophetic things, and had evidently signed Paul's name to it, which means it was a forgery).

The Apostle then tells them that the Second Coming cannot take place *"except there come a falling away first."* Some of the very best Greek Scholars state that this phrase, *"a falling away first,"* should have been translated, *"For that day shall not come, except there come a departure first"*; this speaks of the Rapture, which says that Second Coming cannot take place until certain things happen.

"And that man of sin be revealed, the son of perdition." This speaks of the Antichrist, who must come upon the world scene before the Second Coming. So Paul tells the Thessalonians that the Second Coming has not taken place, and it will not take place even in the near future, at least speaking of Paul's day.

However, we are presently living in the time of which Paul spoke. The Rapture of the Church should take place very soon. Sometime after the Rapture, the Antichrist will make his debut, ultimately plunging the world into Great Tribulation, a time which will conclude with the Battle of Armageddon, which will then signal the Second Coming of the Lord.

But none of these things can take place until the Church is first taken out of this world.

To further state this Doctrine, the Apostle also said, *"And now you know what withholds* (speaks of the Church) *that he might be revealed in his time* (the pronoun *'he'* speaks of the Antichrist, who will be revealed or made known after the Rapture of the Church).

"For the mystery of iniquity does already work (concerns false teaching by false teachers): *only he* (the Church) *who now lets* (who now hinders evil) *will let* (will continue to hinder), *until he* (the Church) *be taken out of the way.* (The pronoun *'he'* confuses some people. In Verses 4 and 6, it refers to the Antichrist, while in Verse 7, *'he'* refers to the Church.)

"And then (after the Rapture of the Church) *shall that Wicked* (the Antichrist) *be revealed* (proving conclusively that the Rapture must take place before the Great Tribulation [Mat. 24:21]), *whom the Lord shall consume with the spirit of His Mouth* (should have been translated *'the breath of His Mouth'* [Isa. 11:4]), *and shall destroy with the brightness of His Coming."* (Both phrases refer to the Second Coming, which will actually take place in the midst of the Battle of Armageddon.)

As stated, these events are presently very close upon us. This should make us want to draw closer to the Lord.

NOVEMBER

13

*n*ow the Spirit speaks expressly, that in the latter times some shall depart from the Faith, giving heed to seducing spirits, and doctrines of Devils *(I Tim. 4:1).*

This Word, given by the Holy Spirit through Paul, proclaims the Spirit speaking pointedly. In other words, He minces no words.

He says, *"In the latter times some shall depart from the Faith."* The *"latter times"* are the times in which we now live, the close of the Dispensation of the Church.

The *"departure from the Faith"* deals more with Believers who are misled than it does with the heretical teachers who do the misleading, although it refers, in some measure, to both.

The word *"depart"* in the Greek is *"aphistemi,"* which actually means *"to apostatize."*

The definite article before the word *"faith"* marks it out as speaking, not of faith as an act, but of *"the Faith,"* that body of Doctrine which forms the basis of what we, as Christians, believe. To sum it up, the bedrock of meaning refers to the fact that these particular individuals, whoever they may be, no longer believe in Christ and Him Crucified, or else they have divorced Christ from the Cross, placing no emphasis on the Cross.

The word *"seducing"* is *"planos,"* and means *"wandering, roving, misleading, leading into error."*

The word *"spirits"* refers to evil spirits, moving upon human beings with the spirit of error, namely, that which is of Satan (I Jn. 4:1-6).

The word *"doctrines"* is, in the Greek, *"didaskalia,"* which means *"teaching, instruction which is actuated by demons."* This, in fact, tells us that all false doctrine is instigated, in some way, by demon spirits, who then move upon certain individuals to proclaim such false doctrine.

When one looks to the root of false doctrine, one will trace it, as stated here, to demon spirits; however, the manner in which these seducing spirits carry out this false doctrine is always, and without exception, connected in some way with the Cross of Christ being misinterpreted, ignored, ridiculed, misunderstood, or denied. This is what is meant by a departure from *"the Faith."*

In the last several decades, there has been less preaching about the Cross than possibly any time since the Reformation. As a result, the modern Church is Cross-illiterate. Having lost its foundation and moorings, the modern Church hardly knows where it has been, where it is, or where it's going. It is extremely susceptible to false doctrine. As usual, Satan presents his wares in a very religious light, actually as an *"angel of light."*

In 1997, after some six years of almost constant prayer

meetings, the Lord began to open up to me the Revelation of the Cross. Yet what He gave me was not at all new, but rather that which had already been given to the Apostle Paul. Along with the giving of this Revelation, He has instructed us to use our resources, such as the Telecast, the SonLife Radio Network, and all of our writings, to preach and teach the Cross.

The Lord meant we are to do exactly as the Apostle Paul, when he said, *"We preach Christ crucified."* And that's exactly what we have done, and are doing.

I believe I can say that when the Cross is properly preached and taught, the Holy Spirit always will then begin to work, and work greatly, which we are now beginning to see, which I believe is going to spearhead a Move of God such as this world has never seen. I do not believe that the Lord is coming back after a weak, emaciated Church. But for the Church to be what it ought to be, it has to come back to the Cross!

NOVEMBER
14

*f*ight the good fight of Faith, lay hold on Eternal Life, whereunto you are also Called, and have professed a good profession before many witnesses (I Tim. 6:12).

First of all, the original Text reads, *"Fight the good fight of The Faith."* Reference is not here being made to *"faith"* in general, as exercised by the Christian, but to *"The Faith,"* which consists of a body of Doctrine with its corresponding ethical responsibilities, namely, Christianity and the Christian Life. It can be summed up in the words, *"Jesus Christ and Him Crucified"* (I Cor. 1:23).

Many Believers hear the Message of the Cross, it bears witness with their spirit, they embrace it, and do so with joy. They soon find, however, that Satan does not break and run, so to speak. In fact, he presses even harder, trying to make the Believer turn loose of this Truth of all Truths. Regrettably, he oftentimes succeeds.

The only fight the Christian is called upon to engage is this *"good fight of Faith."* We are not called upon to fight the Devil. Jesus has already done that at the Cross, and Satan is a defeated being. So if we pursue a fight with the Devil, we are fighting a battle that has already been fought and won, and one which we are never intended to fight.

Moreover, the Believer is not actually called upon to fight against sin, not as such, at least. Sin also was defeated at Calvary, where Jesus atoned for all sin. So if we are fighting against sin, this, once again, is a battle that has already been fought and won.

We are called upon to *"fight the good fight of Faith,"* and that is the only fight we are to engage. If we are engaging in other fights, we are, pure and simple, out of bounds. The results will not be good.

What did Paul mean by *"fighting the good fight of Faith"*?

As stated, it is actually *"The Faith,"* which refers to many things, but most of all to the Cross of Christ. *"The Cross"* and *"The Faith"* could, in fact, be said to be one and the same. So, Satan will endeavor to push us away from the Cross, thereby doing everything to discourage us.

And yet, it is a *"good fight,"* simply because it is the *"right fight."* The wonderful thing about this fight, as difficult as it may at times be, is that this is a fight in which we steadily grow stronger while the Evil One steadily grows weaker. For any other type of fight in which the Christian engages, the opposite is true.

Finally, this is a fight that will not conclude until the Trump sounds. The Lord allows Satan this latitude in order to strengthen our faith, which it most definitely does. Satan continues to push because there are some who will get discouraged and quit. That is sad and regrettable, but it is true.

Engaging in this fight demands that we adhere to the Cross so strongly that we actually take it up *"daily"* (Lk. 9:23). If we do this, we don't have to worry about losing our way. We will get stronger and stronger, in fact, which is all by faith, *"The Faith,"* i.e., *"The Cross"*!

NOVEMBER

15

*t*his know also, that in the last days perilous times shall come. For men shall be lovers of their own selves, covetous, boasters, proud, blasphemers, disobedient to parents, unthankful, unholy, Without natural affection, trucebreakers, false accusers, incontinent, fierce, despisers of those that are good, Traitors, heady, highminded, lovers of pleasures more than lovers of God; Having a form of Godliness, but denying the power thereof: from such turn away (II Tim. 3:1-5).

The Holy Spirit through the Apostle Paul tells us in these Passages what the condition of the world will be in the *"last days,"* actually in the days in which we presently live. These are the last days of the Church, meaning that its Dispensation is about over, with the righteous soon to be raptured. The world will then be plunged into a cataclysmic judgment such as it has never known before. Jesus said so! (Mat. 24:21). The Second Coming will then usher in the Kingdom Age, and the Restoration of Israel. So we are presently living in the last of the last days of the Church Age.

Paul's statements here completely eliminate the fallacious thinking of some who claim that the world is getting better and better, and that Christianity is going to come to terms with the other religions of the world and usher in the Kingdom Age, which will then bring Jesus back. Such thinking completely disavows the coming Great Tribulation, the rise of the Antichrist, the Battle of Armageddon, etc.

The Bible doesn't teach that the situation is going to get better and better, but, as stated here, worse and worse.

It also teaches, as we see from Verse 5, that the Church will go into total apostasy. It will have, and presently has, *"a form of Godliness, but denies the power thereof."*

What does *"denying the power thereof"* mean?

Paul said, *"For the preaching of the Cross is to them who perish foolishness; but unto us which are saved, it is the Power of God"* (I Cor. 1:18).

How is the preaching of the Cross the Power of God?

In truth, there is no power in the Cross, per se, and there certainly isn't any power in the fact of death. The Power is actually in the Holy Spirit; however, He works exclusively within the parameters of the Finished Work of Christ, and, in fact, will work no other way (Rom. 8:2). When the Believer expresses Faith in Christ and what Christ did at the Cross, the Holy Spirit will then manifest His Almighty Power on behalf of such an individual. The Holy Spirit's Work on behalf of the Believer is the Power of which Paul speaks.

However, the modern Church, at least as a whole, is denying the Cross. And when the Cross is denied, ignored, ridiculed, or set aside, then the Holy Spirit refuses to work in such an atmosphere. So the Power is denied as well!

How many Churches presently are preaching the Cross? The answer is simple: precious few!

Why aren't they preaching the Cross?

There are many reasons, but the greatest reason of all, sadly, is *"unbelief."*

Let me, however, quickly add:

Even though the situation isn't good, and, as far as the general direction of the Church is concerned, it's not going to get any better, still, the Lord, I believe, in these last days, is going to do a great thing, something so great that it will eclipse anything done in the past. While most of the Church will continue to go deeper into apostasy, still, even as Daniel prophesied:

"And they that be wise shall shine as the brightness of the firmament; and they who turn many to righteousness as the stars forever and ever."

"Many shall be purified, and made white, and tried; but the wicked shall do wickedly: and none of the wicked shall understand; but the wise shall understand" (Dan. 12:3, 10).

NOVEMBER
16

*f*or I am now ready to be offered, and the time of my departure is at hand. I have fought a good fight, I have finished my course, I have kept the Faith: Henceforth there is laid up for me a Crown of Righteousness, which the Lord, the Righteous Judge, shall give me at that day: and not to me only, but unto all them also who love His appearing (II Tim. 4:6-8).

Paul wrote this last Epistle to Timothy, entrusting him with the greatest Message on Earth, *"Jesus Christ and Him Crucified,"* and all which that means, which is, in fact, the entirety of the New Covenant. This Epistle was written from the Mammertine Prison in Rome. During Paul's day, this was merely a cell beneath a cell. In other words, it had no outside entrance; everything had to be let down through a trap door in the ceiling. It had been carved out of solid rock.

This cell stills exists today, and I have been in it. As I stood there that day, along with others, I cannot even begin to tell you how I felt, knowing that the great Apostle had spent his last months of life in this cell, and knowing that he had written his last Epistle (II Timothy) from this very place. I began to read Verses 6, 7, and 8, but I could not finish.

One might say, *"The Apostle Paul is possibly the greatest example of Righteousness produced by Christ."* There never has been anyone else quite like the little Jew from Tarsus.

When Paul said, *"I am now ready to be offered,"* he knew, no doubt by the Holy Spirit, that his work was finished. The word *"offered"* in the Greek is *"spendomai,"* which refers to a Drink Offering poured out. Paul uses the same word in Philippians 2:17. He looks upon himself as the libation poured out upon the sacrifice. The libation refers to the lesser part of the sacrifice poured out onto the more important part, i.e., the Drink Offering poured out upon the sacrifice of the lamb. Only one who considered himself less than the least of all Saints could write with such deep humility.

The phrase, *"And the time of my departure is at hand,"* proclaims the fact that Paul's work is over; otherwise, Nero could not have taken his life. The servant of the Lord is immortal until his life's work is done.

The phrase, *"I have fought a good fight,"* should have been translated, *"I have fought the good fight,"* because this is the way it is written in the original Greek. Paul wasn't speaking of himself as fighting a good fight, but rather that he had fought the correct fight. It speaks of an action completed in the past with present results. Paul fought his fight with sin to a finish, and was resting in a complete victory.

The phrase, *"I have finished my course,"* has reference

to a race course. The words, *"have finished,"* is a like a Greek runner who has crossed the finish line and is now resting at the goal. Paul's life's work is over.

The phrase, *"I have kept the Faith,"* refers to that to which the Lord had entrusted him. He had been given the meaning of the New Covenant; he also had been called upon to plant (or found) the Church. He was the Masterbuilder of the Church. Paul had defended the great truth of the New Covenant, which is the truth of the Cross, in every way. He had defended it against the attacks of the Gnostics, the Judaizers, and others. He never allowed it to be compromised, perverted, polluted, or hindered in any way.

We have what we have today because, against all odds, Paul *"kept the Faith."*

The *"crown"* to which he refers is, in the Greek, *"stephanos,"* and refers to the *"victor's crown."* The victor's crown of righteousness is the crown which belongs to, or is the due reward of, Righteousness. The One Who will grant that is *"The Righteous Judge,"* Who is the just Judge, the Umpire Who makes no mistakes, and Who is always fair. This *"crown"* will be given to all *"who love His appearing."*

We might say that Paul, the spiritual athlete, his victory won, is resting at the goal post, awaiting the award which the Judge's stand will give him (Wuest).

NOVEMBER

17

*b**ut you speak the things which become sound Doctrine: Exhort servants to be obedient to their own masters, and to please them well in all things; not answering again; Not purloining, but showing all good fidelity; that they may adorn the Doctrine of God our Saviour in all things* (Titus 2:1, 9-10).

"*Sound Doctrine*" pertains to the great Message of the Word of God, "*Jesus Christ and Him Crucified*" (I Cor. 1:23).

The word "*servants,*" as used by Paul, is "*doulos,*" which means "*slaves.*" These to whom Paul wrote were Christian slaves serving, for the most part, in pagan households.

The freedom of the Gospel and its brotherhood conflicted with the institution of slavery, and ultimately abolished it; but meanwhile slaves were commanded to be subject to those who owned them; for in no rank of society was there more danger of the equality of Christians being misunderstood than in that of slaves. Hence, the large legislation given by the Holy Spirit affecting them (I Cor. 7:20, 24; Eph. 6:5; Col. 3:22; I Tim. 6:1; I Pet. 2:18, etc.).

So great a portion of inspired Scripture being given to slaves ennobles them, and reveals how warmly God loved them, and how largely they engaged His thoughts. The most amazing revelations from God before which great kings and mighty scientists stand dumb and stupid are in the Scriptures connected with slaves and revealed to them.

The best testimony to the doctrines of the Gospel is to adorn them by a Christlike life. Some few carnal men might be ready to die for the Gospel, but only spiritual men can live it. God would have His Truth adorned even by slaves, whom the world at that time regarded as no better than beasts of burden.

True liberty and true equality must reign in a Divinely governed and consistent Church. Its moral order secures both. Satan's aim is to introduce disorder and thus, disrupt the fellowship and destroy its testimony. But if the precious proprieties ordained by God are not maintained, liberty perishes and carnal tyranny replaces Christian freedom.

The Holy Spirit recognizes, even as is dealt with in this very Chapter, every relationship which God has formed. Age and youth, husband and wife, child and parent, servant and master, all have their own proprieties and ministries to maintain toward each other in the sweetness and power of the Grace that at its appearing brings health and healing to all men.

So the conduct of Christian people among themselves in the Church, and their conduct among their fellow citizens in the State, are both based upon the great doctrines of Christianity.

Grace appeared — not to a particular people — but to all men — and it did not bring them nutriment for their passions, but nourishment for their souls. It did not demand righteousness from men, but brought righteousness to them. They needed Righteousness. So Grace overleaped every obstacle in order to reach every man and to discipline him so that in relation to himself he should be sober; in relation to his neighbor, righteous; and in relation to God, pious (Williams).

NOVEMBER
18

*P*ut them in mind to be subject to principalities and powers, to obey Magistrates, to be ready to every good work,
To speak evil of no man, to be no brawlers, but gentle, showing
all meekness unto all men (Titus 3:1-2).

The conduct of the Christian as a subject of the State
is governed by the same principle as motivates our conduct as a member of the Church. We are to be obedient to
the government, and to show to our fellow citizens, however hostile, immoral, debased, or degraded they may be,
the same Grace that God showed to us, remembering that
we possess the same corrupt nature as they, and that in
that nature the seeds of all vile passions are also present.

The governing principle of public conduct is foreign
to, and opposed to, human nature. Self-interest, ambi-
tion, and love of ease, of money, or of position animate
the ordinary members of society. The Christian's conduct
is regulated by his relationship to God as the Saviour. We
recognize that that which makes us different from others

is not any merit in ourselves, or any personal or moral superiority. In a sense, we are even as they. Grace makes the difference, and it teaches us to be as kind and merciful to others as God is to us.

The sense of what we once were, and of the evil of the nature which dwells in us, and of the graceful action of our Lord toward us, all of this combines, or should do so, to govern our conduct toward others.

The Christian is to cheerfully obey the government and to willingly volunteer to support it in *"every good work,"* unless something is done personally to us which violates our conscience. This is our duty, for the Magistrate is a Divinely appointed officer (Rom., Chpt. 13) to punish evildoers and protect society.

In our own private lives and in our relationship to all men, however hostile and abominable they may be, the Christian is to be gentle toward those who attack us, and generally to pursue a course of peace and benevolence, because the principle of Grace excludes all violence of thought, language, or action.

Some time back, a Television reporter did everything he could do to hurt us, even to destroy us. His last effort was over CNN, which went into some 157 countries. Every effort was made to besmirch, sully, hinder, hurt, and even destroy. In our prayer meeting the morning after the CNN program aired, I endeavored to pray for the reporter. The Scripture says that we should *"pray for those who despitefully use us."* But, to be frank, I couldn't pray. In my heart, I wanted something very bad to happen to him. His efforts actually had gone on for many years, with the CNN program only being the latest.

Finally, I asked the Lord to help me. I knew my feelings were not pleasing to the Lord, and I knew that I needed His help to be able to handle this thing correctly. The Lord spoke to my heart and said, *"You show him the same mercy that I have shown you."* That was all there was, and that was enough! All of a sudden, the entire complexion changed. I honestly could pray for the man. To this day, I don't have a single thing in my heart against him.

I realize how much Mercy and Grace the Lord has shown me. As such, how could I do less regarding him?

NOVEMBER
19

l et us therefore fear, lest, a Promise being left us of entering into His rest, any of you should seem to come short of it. For unto us was the Gospel preached, as well as unto them: but the Word preached did not profit them, not being mixed with faith in them who heard it. Seeing therefore it remains that some must enter therein, and they to whom it was first preached entered not in because of unbelief (Heb. 4:1-2, 6).

It is my belief that Paul wrote the Book of Hebrews. Whoever wrote it had to have a profound knowledge of the Law, the New Covenant, and the Cross. Concerning these subjects, no one had such knowledge as did Paul.

The Book of Hebrews concerns Christian Jews, who, through discouragement or whatever reason, were turning their backs on Christ, so to speak, and going back into Judaism. In effect, the entirety of this most important Epistle is written as a warning that the Cross of Christ must not be abandoned. If it is, spiritual tragedy is the conclusion!

There is only one way that a person can *"enter into His*

rest," and that is by accepting Christ and what Christ did at the Cross. When this is done, and the Believer maintains his Faith in Christ and the Cross, the Believer enters into a *"spiritual rest"* that Jesus described as *"more abundant life"* (Jn. 10:10). In fact, this *"rest"* was symbolized during the time of Law by the *"Sabbath."* Of course, when Jesus came, the Sabbath was totally fulfilled. One does not need the symbol when one has the Substance! As one now properly follows Christ, it is the same thing as keeping the Sabbath once was, which, incidentally, was Saturday.

The pronoun *"us"* in Verse 2 refers to those alive in Paul's day, which continues even unto the present. The pronoun *"them"* refers to Israel in the wilderness. The Word was preached to those in the wilderness, but *"not being mixed with faith in them who heard it,"* it did not *"profit them."* Carrying forth the same thought, Paul also stated to the Galatians, *"If you be Circumcised, Christ shall profit you nothing"* (Gal. 5:2). The principle is the same!

One must have Faith in Christ and what Christ did at the Cross in order for the *"Word"* to be of profit. People can study the Word, memorize the Word, and quote the Word; however, if their faith doesn't make Christ and the Cross its sole Object, then again there is no profit. Regrettably, that's the place and position in which the modern Church, for the most part, now finds itself.

As Verse 6 proclaims, the major problem is *"unbelief."*

At a given point in my life and Ministry, it seemed like total wreckage would be the end result. I simply did not know what to do! How is it possible for the Believer to live a victorious, overcoming Christian life, and do so on a consistent basis, guaranteeing the defeat of Satan and all evil spirits?

I well remember the day I laid my Bible on the table and stated, *"I do not presently know the answer to that, but I know the answer is in the Bible, and, by the Grace of God, I'm going to find it."* That was the best decision I've ever made. I did find it, and in a capacity that I never dreamed possible. In 1997, the Lord began to open up to me the Revelation of the Cross. It was not something new, actually that which He had already given to the Apostle Paul. But, regrettably, it is new to most of the present Church world. In fact, most Christians have no idea whatsoever as to the part the Cross plays in their Sanctification.

I watched the Denomination with which I had been associated for many years reject the Word of God and embrace humanistic psychology. I turned to the Bible, while they turned to the world.

Why did they do this?

For the same reason that Paul addresses in this Fourth Chapter of Hebrews. The reason was, and is, unbelief! They simply do not believe that what Jesus did at the Cross, and one's Faith in that Finished Work, can guarantee victory in every capacity. But it most definitely can!

There is no bondage, perversion, sin, transgression, or problem that Jesus didn't address at the Cross. As a result, total and complete victory, and in every capacity, can belong to the Child of God. In fact, it is meant to belong to the Child of God.

Our Lord paid a great price for this victory, and it certainly should be understood that He desires that we have all for which He paid such a price! (Rom. 6:1-14; I Cor. 1:17-18, 23; 2:2; Gal. 6:14).

NOVEMBER

20

f or we have not an High Priest which cannot be touched with the feeling of our infirmities; but was in all points tempted like as we are, yet without sin. Let us therefore come boldly unto the Throne of Grace, that we may obtain Mercy, and find Grace to help in time of need (Heb. 4:15-16).

Jesus Christ is our Great High Priest. The heart of that Priest is not insensible to the sorrows, needs, infirmities, and temptations of those for whom He acts, for He Personally, as Man, suffered the worst form of temptation, but never sinned. To come timidly to the Throne of Grace is to disobey God, for He commands His People to come boldly. Man, unfortunately, condemns this boldness and applauds his own faithless fearfulness.

The true Christian does not wish for sympathy with the sin that is in him. He detests it, and desires that it be slain with the two-edged sword of Hebrews 4:12, and to have no mercy shown to it. This is the purpose and action of the sword, i.e., the Word of God.

But the Believer does desire sympathy for his weakness and difficulties in temptation, and this sympathy he finds in all perfection in the Great High Priest, Who wields the sword of the Word. These Divine provisions of the sword and the Priest encourage him to hold fast his confession despite the difficulties that beset his path.

The type of temptations that Jesus experienced is actually the root of all temptation. Jesus wasn't tempted to steal money, commit adultery, to lie, etc., as some think. His temptation came in the form of Him stepping outside the Will of God. An excellent example would be His temptation to turn the stones into bread while in the wilderness (Mat. 4:3-4). He had the power to do such, but it would not have been the Will of the Father for Him to use His Power in such a manner.

Satan does the same thing with Believers – tempting us to step outside the Will of God, i.e., *"the Word of God."* When the Believer comes to the place that he is tempted to steal, to lie, or to engage in some type of immorality, etc., this is a position that he shouldn't be in. If our Faith is correct concerning Christ and the Cross, we will definitely be tempted to step outside of the Will of God; but, if Victory is won there, there will be no problem with the other types of temptations. They simply won't happen!

Sadly, when temptation gets to the place that we are tempted to commit particular acts of sin, we will, at some point, probably yield, because we have been maneuvered by Satan into this place.

One might say the temptation comes in two steps:

The first step, as stated, pertains to the Believer getting out of the Will of God, actually into the flesh.

The second step pertains to committing acts of sin.

No Believer should get past the first step; we won't, in fact, if our faith is properly placed. If we do drop down to the second step, then the situation becomes critical, because, as we've also already stated, failure will be, more than likely, the result.

Jesus knows exactly the types of temptation that Satan brings against us, and He empathizes greatly with us, because, as the Man Jesus Christ, He has been there, at least as it regards the temptation to step outside of the Will of God — a temptation, of course, to which He never succumbed. Because He never sinned by stepping out of the Will of God, He never experienced the lower form of temptation, but He does understand it. He understands it not by experimentation, but by the fact that He is God, and knows all things.

The position of safety is Faith in Christ and the Cross, and it is the only position of safety (Phil. 3:1; Ps. 91:1-7).

NOVEMBER
21

*t*herefore leaving the Principles of the Doctrine of Christ, let us go on unto perfection; not laying again the foundation of Repentance from dead works, and of Faith toward God, Of the Doctrine of baptisms, and of laying on of hands, and of Resurrection of the dead, and of Eternal Judgment (Heb. 6:1-2).

The above quoted Scriptures are those used by individuals who claim that the Cross, although proper for Salvation, has no meaning thereafter, and that the Believer should go beyond the Cross.

There is, however, nothing beyond the Cross, as there needs to be nothing beyond the Cross. These individuals are basing their belief system on a gross misinterpretation of the Scriptures, which we will address here.

We must, first of all, understand that the entirety of the Bible points to Christ, both Old and New Testaments. The Old Testament points to Christ Who was to come, while the New Testament points to Christ Who has come. Christ and the Cross are ever before the Reader in the entirety of the Word of God (Jn. 1:1).

When Paul said, *"Therefore leaving the Principles of the Doctrine of Christ,"* he was speaking of the first principles (Heb. 5:12), which pertained to the Law of the Moses. The entirety of the Law of Moses, and in every capacity, pointed to Christ, which it was meant to do. With Christ now having come, it is not proper, Paul tells these Christian Jews, to try to cling to the old Law. It has already been fulfilled in Christ. Consequently, we should leave those first principles of the Law.

The phrase, *"Let us go on unto perfection,"* should have been translated, *"maturity."* The Apostle is saying that it's not possible for the Believer to mature when he is improperly addressing Christ, i.e., when he is going back to the Law.

The phrase, *"Not laying again the foundation of Repentance from dead works,"* had to do with repentance as it regarded the animal sacrifices. Due to the fact that Christ has come and has gone to the Cross, thereby atoning for all sin, the Sacrificial System of old is now adjudged to be *"dead works."* Repentance must be on the basis of what Christ has done at the Cross, and not on the Sacrificial System of old (I Jn. 1:7).

The short phrase, *"And of faith toward God,"* refers, as here stated, to improper faith. It is faith toward God based on the old Sacrificial System, which the Lord now will not accept. Our faith must be in Christ and what Christ has done at the Cross (Rom. 6:1-14).

The phrase, *"Of the Doctrine of baptisms,"* should have been translated *"of the Doctrine of Washings,"* which is what the original Greek actually says. The *"washings"* mentioned here had to do, once again, with the animal sacrifices, which required washings before they were offered up on the Altar. It also referred to the Priests, who had to wash in the Brazen Laver, both hands and feet, every time they entered into the Holy Place of the Tabernacle or Temple.

The phrase, *"And of laying on of hands,"* is not pertaining to the custom of laying on of hands to bless people, or to pray for their healing, etc., but rather of the sinner who had brought the lamb for sacrifice. Just before the lamb was killed, the sinner laid his hands on the lamb's head and confessed his sins. That is no longer needed, as should be obvious, inasmuch as Jesus has gone to the Cross. Now, we pray to God the Father in the Name of Jesus, confessing our sins (Jn. 16:23; I Jn. 1:9).

The phrase, *"And of Resurrection of the dead,"* simply means that before the Resurrection of Christ, the fact of the Resurrection was known only in shadow. Now, since the Resurrection of Christ, there is a far greater understanding.

The phrase, *"And of Eternal Judgment,"* was, in Old Testament times, also known only with very little knowledge. In fact, during those times, God was looked at more so as a Judge than a Saviour.

So, it shows a great misunderstanding of these Passages of Scripture for Believers to use them to claim that Believers are to leave the Cross after getting saved and go on to other things. I hope this is, by now, overly obvious. It is impossible to go beyond the Cross, because every single thing the Lord does is based on the foundation of the Cross, and in totality.

That's why Paul said, *"We preach Christ Crucified"* (I Cor. 1:23). In fact, the Cross of Christ is an Everlasting Covenant (Heb. 13:20).

NOVEMBER

22

*f*or it is impossible for those who were once enlightened, and have tasted of the Heavenly Gift, and were made partakers of the Holy Spirit, And have tasted of the good Word of God, and the powers of the world to come, If they shall fall away, to renew them again unto Repentance; seeing they crucify to themselves the Son of God afresh, and put Him to an open shame (Heb. 6:4-6).

These Passages, as should be overly obvious, completely refute the unscriptural doctrine of Unconditional Eternal Security.

The people to whom Paul was writing were Christian Jews. They had grown discouraged for one reason or the other, and some of them went back into Temple worship, actually the old Mosaic Law. The Apostle here warns them that if they fall away from Faith in Christ and what Christ did at the Cross, they have then repudiated the Plan of Salvation, which means there is no way for true Repentance to be enjoined.

The manner of Salvation is faith; however, it is Faith in the correct Object, which is Christ and Him Crucified. As long as one maintains Faith in Christ and what He did at the Cross, Salvation is maintained. If one loses faith in Christ and the Cross, thereby placing faith in something else (and it really doesn't matter what the something else is), if they continue on that path, they will ultimately lose their soul.

Please note carefully:

These individuals to whom Paul was writing were not people who had merely heard the Gospel and now had decided not to accept it. They were people who had wondrously and gloriously accepted the Gospel, had been thereby *"enlightened,"* which is impossible for an unsaved person, and they had also *"tasted of the Heavenly Gift, and were made partakers of the Holy Spirit."*

(The Greek word for *"partaker"* is *"metochos,"* which means *"a sharer, a partaker,"* which no unbeliever could be.)

No! These were individuals who had accepted Christ, which means they had been Born-Again. But now they are ceasing to believe in Christ; by doing what they did, they were making a mockery of Christ, actually *"crucifying to themselves the Son of God afresh, and putting Him to an open shame."*

Because it is so important, let us say it again:

Faith is the key to Salvation (Rom. 5:1). If that, in fact, is the case, and it most definitely is, if faith ceases to be, at least in the correct Object, which is Christ and the Cross, then Salvation is forfeited. This is what the Apostle is saying, which means that what these Christian Jews were doing was serious indeed!

The same thing holds true presently. If Satan can get the Believer to subscribe to something which is not Christ and the Cross, the possibility definitely exists that the soul of such a person can be lost. Our Faith must ever have Christ and the Cross as its Object. Further, this means it cannot be Christ and the Cross plus. . . !

NOVEMBER
23

*W*herefore *He is able also to save them to the uttermost who come unto God by Him, seeing He ever lives to make intercession for them. For such an High Priest became us, Who is Holy, harmless, undefiled, separate from sinners, and made higher than the heavens; Who needs not daily, as those High Priests, to offer up sacrifice, first for His Own sins, and then for the people's: for this He did once, when He offered up Himself* (Heb. 7:25-27).

The *"intercession"* made by Christ for us, which He does continually, is intercession for sin. Several things are said here. They are:

1. Sin is of far greater magnitude than most Believers know or understand. Without the intercession of Christ on our behalf, and on a constant basis, the best of us, whoever that might be, wouldn't last one hour.

2. His *"intercession"* for us is not something that He does; it's actually something He has already done. The very fact of His Presence at the Throne (Heb. 1:3) proclaims

the fact that God the Father has accepted what Christ has done for us regarding Atonement; therefore, His Presence is all that is needed. Intercession is thereby guaranteed.

3. Every last Believer needs intercession, and continually. If someone thinks they don't, this means they do not really understand themselves, what sin actually is, and what Christ has actually done for us at the Cross.

4. Jesus Christ is our Great High Priest; as such, He intercedes for us on the basis of a Finished Work, which means there is no danger that the intercession will not be accepted.

5. The reason for the total acceptance by God the Father of such intercession is because it is all in Christ and not at all in those for whom He is interceding. All of this means that we have a perfect High Priest, *"Who is Holy, harmless, undefiled, separate from sinners, and made higher than the heavens."*

NOVEMBER

24

*b*ut now has He obtained a more excellent Ministry, by how much also He is the Mediator of a Better Covenant, which was established upon better Promises (Heb. 8:6).

"The Better Covenant" is that of Hebrews 8:10; "The Better Promises" are those of Hebrews 8:10-12.

Concerning this statement made by Paul, Wuest says, "The Book of Hebrews was written to prove the following proposition: The New Testament in Jesus' Blood is superior to, and takes the place of, the First Covenant in animal blood. The writer has proved this to be true on the basis of pure logic and the Old Testament Scriptures. Using the logical argument that a superior workman turns out a superior product, he has shown that Messiah, the Founder of the New Testament, is better than the founders of the First Testament, who were the Prophets, Angels, Moses, Joshua, and Aaron. Therefore, the Testament He brought in is superior to, and takes the place of, theirs."

"The Better Covenant," which was established upon

"Better Promises," was made possible totally and entirely by the Cross. Even as the Scripture says (Heb. 8:7), the First Covenant was never meant to solve the human problem, since animal blood was woefully insufficient to do that. So, for a *"Better Covenant,"* based on *"Better Promises,"* to be brought about, God would have to become Man, live a perfect Life, never fail, not even once, thereby keeping the Law of Moses in every respect, and then go to the Cross in order to address the broken Law, which Christ did, and atone for all sin, which God the Father accepted totally and completely as full payment. The Law was, therefore, satisfied in every respect.

The Believer must understand the following:

All of this was done for you and me. It was not at all done for Heaven, for the Throne of God, for Angels, or for Himself, only for sinners. It was done so perfectly and so completely that everyone who evidences Faith in Christ and His Finished Work becomes the recipient of this *"Better Covenant,"* based on *"Better Promises."* This is what Jesus was talking about when He said that the least Believer in the Kingdom of God was, and is, greater than John the Baptist, all because of the privileges afforded under the New Covenant (Lk. 7:28).

What a privilege we have! All because of the Cross of Christ!

NOVEMBER

25

*h*ow much more shall the Blood of Christ, Who through the Eternal Spirit offered Himself without spot to God, purge your conscience from dead works to serve the Living God? (Heb. 9:14).

There are some who claim that *"The Eternal Spirit"* here specified is not the Holy Spirit, but rather the personal Spirit of Christ. They conclude this because, as they say, there is no definite article, *"the,"* in front of *"Spirit"*; however, the definite article does precede *"Eternal Spirit,"* signifying the Holy Spirit. God the Father is referred to as *"The Eternal God"* (Deut. 33:27), and the Lord Jesus is also referred to as *"The King Eternal"* (I Tim. 1:17). We also have here *"The Eternal Spirit,"* so-called.

The idea is this:

The Holy Spirit superintended Christ in every facet of His Life and living. It was the Holy Spirit Who decreed the Conception (Mat. 1:20). The Holy Spirit also superintended His Birth (Lk. 2:26-27) and His Childhood (Lk.

2:40). At His Water Baptism, *"the Holy Spirit descended in a bodily shape like a Dove upon Him"* (Lk. 3:22). Just before beginning His public Ministry, the Scripture says that He *"was led by the Spirit into the wilderness"* (Lk. 4:1).

At the beginning of His Ministry, and continuing throughout His Ministry, He said, *"The Spirit of the Lord is upon Me, because He has anointed Me . . ."* (Lk. 4:18). So now when it is time to die, the very purpose and reason for which He came, He would breathe out His Life only when *"The Eternal Spirit"* told Him to do so. He was guided, helped, strengthened, empowered, and led by the Holy Spirit in every facet of His Life and living, even at His Death.

But it didn't stop there:

"The Spirit . . . raised up Jesus from the dead" (Rom. 8:11).

Moreover, concerning His Disciples and all His followers, and for all time, just before He ascended back to Heaven, *"being assembled together with them, Commanded them that they should not depart from Jerusalem, but wait for the Promise of the Father . . . For John truly baptized with water; but you shall be baptized with the Holy Spirit not many days hence"* (Acts 1:4-5).

The Lord is telling them, and us, that since the Cross, which has made it all possible, the Holy Spirit can abide in the hearts and lives of all Believers, and will, in fact, do so, exactly as He abode in the heart and life of Jesus in His earthly Ministry.

What a privilege!

Exactly as He promised, He sent the Holy Spirit back, and did so in a completely new dimension. It is recorded in the Second Chapter of Acts.

If there is any great mistake the Church makes, it is undervaluing the Holy Spirit. Without the Holy Spirit, the Church is no more than any other earthly club or gathering. But with the Holy Spirit, the Church becomes a living dynamo.

There is nothing more dangerous than a Church which can function without the Holy Spirit. While there might be great religious activity, there is nothing truly done for the Lord. Sadly, that's the state of the far greater majority of the modern Church.

If Jesus needed the Holy Spirit, and the evidence is overwhelming that He did, then we, most definitely, also need the Holy Spirit!

NOVEMBER
26

*b*ut this Man, after He had offered One Sacrifice for sins forever, sat down on the Right Hand of God; From henceforth expecting till His enemies be made His footstool. For by one Offering He has perfected forever them who are Sanctified *(Heb. 10:12-14).*

Sin is the problem, whether it's an unbeliever or a Believer. The Cross is the only answer for sin. There is no other!

When Jesus died on the Cross, He atoned for all sin and all sins, past, present, and future, at least for those who will believe (Jn. 3:16). In other words, He addressed not only the effect of sin, but also its cause. To be sure, the *"One Sacrifice,"* which spoke of Christ offering Himself, was enough. It will never have to be repeated, because it was totally sufficient to accomplish the task.

That Christ presently has *"sat down on the Right Hand of God"* tells us that the work was complete, absolute, total, will never need to be repeated, and was accepted fully by God the Father. In other words, the effect was perfect because the Sacrifice was Perfect; the Sacrifice was Christ.

There is only one way that a proper Sanctification can take place in the heart and life of the Believer and have an ongoing positive effect. That way is by the Believer placing his Faith and trust exclusively in the *"One Offering of Christ,"* even as Hebrews 10:14 proclaims. As stated, the Cross is the only Sacrifice for sins.

When the Holy Spirit through the Apostle Paul gave instructions as to how this Sanctification was to be carried out, i.e., how the Believer could have perpetual victory over the world, the flesh, and the Devil, He took the Believer straight to the Cross (Rom. 6:3-5). There He tells the Believer that the same way he got in (was converted) is the same way he stays in. It is by making the Cross of Christ the Object of one's Faith, and maintaining one's Faith in the Cross of Christ. This, and this alone, is the manner of Sanctification.

Unfortunately, the modern Church has accepted, and is accepting, almost anything and everything that one might think or suggest in place of the Cross. But no matter how religious these other efforts might be, and no matter that the far greater majority of the modern Church accepts them, there will be no positive effect regarding Sanctification.

There is nothing more miserable than a Christian living a life that falls short of victory. That's not the way it ought to be. There should be victory, and on a perpetual basis. If the Believer will look exclusively to Christ and His Finished Work, and continue to do so, to be certain, the Holy Spirit will get it done (Rom. 6:1-14).

Concerning this, the Scripture boldly says: *"Whereof the Holy Spirit also is a witness to us"* (Heb. 10:15).

To have the witness of man is one thing, but to have the witness of the Holy Spirit is something else altogether. The Holy Spirit has just put His seal of approval on the things we have just taught.

There is victory in the Cross of Christ, and there is victory only in the Cross of Christ!

NOVEMBER
27

n *ow Faith is the substance of things hoped for, the evidence of things not seen. For by it the Elders obtained a good report* (Heb. 11:1-2).

Having proved from the Scriptures that the *"rest"* and *"the good things"* of the New Covenant are secured and held by faith, the Holy Spirit now illustrates the activities of faith. Verse 1 is not a definition of faith, but a declaration of its action. It makes Promises present and real and unseen things visible.

So the Promises respecting Canaan were real to Abraham and to Isaac, Jacob, and Joseph, though they were wanderers, and all died without getting them. Similarly, Abel saw the Lamb of God Who takes away the sin of the world; Enoch saw his Divine companion; Noah saw the coming Flood; Abraham saw the city which has foundations; Moses saw Him Who is invisible; women saw *"a better resurrection,"* and they all saw the *"better thing"* which God provided for them.

795

By faith Abel — by faith Enoch — by faith Noah. These three Patriarchs illustrate Worship, Walk, and Witness; and, Salvation, Consecration, and Condemnation. This is faith in action upon the path of Faith. Verse 4 proclaims Abel offering to God *"a more excellent Sacrifice than Cain."* It was a lamb. Here was a lamb for one man; in Exodus 12, a lamb for a family; in Leviticus 16, a lamb for a nation; and in John 1:29, a lamb for the whole world.

Going to Verse 7, the human race, we find, owes its existence to the fact that one man, Noah, was *"moved with fear."* As a factor in Salvation, fear is decried at the present day, and only love is declared to be the true Gospel. Enoch predicted the Wrath of God, i.e., the Flood (Jude, Vs. 14). Society laughed; Noah trembled.

Looking at Verses 25 through 27, we find that Moses chose the slave driver's lash rather than Egypt's crown. Thus, he forsook the throne of Egypt, and, in so doing, braved the anger of the king, who must have been much incensed that a royal prince should degrade the imperial throne and family by such a decision.

The Scripture says that Moses, *"Through Faith he kept the Passover, and the sprinkling of the Blood, lest He Who destroyed the firstborn should touch them"* (Heb. 11:28).

The Blood of Christ, we find here, is precious to Faith, but the Doctrine of the Atonement is offensive to the self-righteous moralist. While Providence placed Moses in the court of Pharaoh, faith caused him to forsake it. Thus, faith as a motive produced the effect which Providence prepared. Providence governs circumstances; faith governs conduct.

The faith that did not fear the wrath of Pharaoh feared

the Wrath of God. By the sprinkling of the Blood, Moses acknowledged that he was as much the object of the just judgment of God as was Pharaoh himself. There was no moral difference between them. Both were sinners. Neither of them was innocent. Both stood under the sentence of death; and, being guilty, both merited it. However, the faith that sprinkled the blood, and the unbelief that refused its shelter in the form of Pharaoh, fixed this great gulf between the two men.

Moses balanced the best of the world with the shame of Christ, and deliberately chose the latter. He saw its future wealth. However, he could see it only in Christ and the Cross, of which the Passover was a symbol!

The Cross helps one to see one's self, to see this world as it really is, and, above all, to see the Promises of God as they really are!

NOVEMBER

28

f or whom the Lord loves He chastens, and scourges every son whom He receives. If you endure chastening, God deals with you as with sons; for what son is he whom the father chastens not? But if you be without chastisement, whereof all are partakers, then are you bastards, and not sons (Heb. 12:6-8).

In these extremely informative Passages, several things are here seen:

1. The words, *"chasten"* and *"chastisement,"* do not carry the idea of punishment, but rather of corrective measures, which drive the person to the Lord, with the Holy Spirit then correcting the situation, which He Alone can do.

2. The problem is sin, even as the problem always is sin (Heb. 12:4). To be sure, the Holy Spirit will not rest until the problem is solved, ever how long it takes, and ever how severe the chastening has to be.

3. The Believer is not to despise *"the chastening of the Lord,"* but rather understand its necessity.

4. Every single true Believer is loved by the Lord. That

means that every single true Believer experiences chastening from the Lord. There has never been one, and never will be one, who doesn't need such chastening.

5. In the chastening process, which will never end until either we die or the Lord comes, we may be assured that the Lord is dealing with us, not as sinners, but as *"sons."* So that means that the chastening is always guarded by love.

6. If one claims the Lord, and there never seems to be any chastisement, that's a perfect sign that the person is really not saved. The Holy Spirit is blunt in his assessments. These people are *"bastards, and not sons."*

7. All of this is being done *"for our profit, that we might be partakers of His Holiness"* (Heb. 12:10).

8. Admittedly, chastening is not joyous, but rather grievous; however, we can rest assured that it will ultimately *"yield the peaceable fruit of Righteousness unto them which are exercised thereby"* (Heb. 12:11).

NOVEMBER
29

*n*ow the God of Peace, Who brought again from the dead
our Lord Jesus, that Great Shepherd of the sheep, through the
Blood of the Everlasting Covenant, Make you perfect in every
good work to do His Will, working in you that which is
wellpleasing in His sight, through Jesus Christ; to Whom be
glory forever and ever. Amen (Heb. 13:20-21).

By virtue of Christ's Blood, i.e., His Atoning Sacrifice
as the Good Shepherd, He is the Great Shepherd of the
sheep. He could not be such had He not, as the Good
Shepherd, shed His Blood for the sheep and so established
the Everlasting Covenant.

The Twentieth Verse of this Thirteenth Chapter presents the only time in the entirety of the Book of Hebrews
that Paul mentions the Resurrection. Even then, it is in
connection with the Cross, evidenced by the phrase, *"The
Blood of the Everlasting Covenant,"* proclaiming the fact
that it was the Cross that established that Covenant.

Unfortunately, all too many modern Christians place

the emphasis of strength in the Resurrection, and not in the Cross. When they do that, they are doing the same thing that Israel did with the Abrahamic Covenant.

The Abrahamic Covenant was meant to be the theme of Israel's relationship with God, the only way, in fact, that such relationship could be established. It had to be by faith (Gen. 15:6). However, when the Law was given, Israel inverted the process. They made the Law the primary objective instead of the Abrahamic Covenant; thereby, they lost their way.

In a sense, the modern Church does the same, when it places the emphasis of the Atonement on the Resurrection instead of on the Cross. To be sure, the Resurrection is a product of the Cross, and not the other way around. The Resurrection, even as the Law, was, and is, of extreme significance, as should be overly obvious, but the Resurrection is not the central theme of the Gospel, but rather the Cross.

If the Resurrection was the central theme, wouldn't it stand to reason that Paul would have done more than mention it just one time in this great Book of Hebrews? The answer to that is obvious.

The Covenant that Jesus established at the Cross was so perfect, so complete, so total, that the Holy Spirit referred to it as *"The Everlasting Covenant."* This means that this Covenant will never have to be amended, will never lose its power and be discarded, and nothing will ever have to be substituted for it. It is Everlasting, which means Eternal.

It is so Eternal, in fact, that in the last two Chapters of the Book of Revelation, the word *"Lamb"* is used some seven times, which always denotes the Cross. This is remarkable when one considers that Satan and all of his cohorts are then in the Lake of Fire, where they will remain forever (Rev. 20:10).

In the New Heavens and the New Earth, there is no more sin, no more failure, no more transgression, no more disobedience, no more pain, sickness, suffering, or death, all caused by sin. It will be a perfect eternity. And yet, some seven times, the Holy Spirit then refers to Christ as *"the Lamb."*

This is to let us know that all of these beautiful things described in the last two Chapters of Revelation are all made possible, and exclusively so, by the Cross, hence *"the Lamb."* Not only is the Cross an Everlasting Covenant regarding the coming perfect day which will never end, but it is that, and that alone, which brings the Saint to maturity, *"perfect in every good work to do His Will."*

It is ever the Cross! Ever the Cross! Ever the Cross!

NOVEMBER

30

*d*o you think that the Scripture says in vain, The Spirit Who dwells in us lusts to envy? But He gives more Grace. Wherefore He said, God resists the proud, but gives Grace unto the humble. Submit yourselves therefore to God. Resist the Devil, and he will flee from you. Draw near to God, and He will draw near to you. Cleanse your hands, you sinners; and purify your hearts, you double minded (James 4:5-8).

The phrase of Verse 5, "The Spirit Who dwells in us lusts to envy," speaks of the Holy Spirit. The two words connected with Him, "lusts" and "envy," seem strange to the ear.

As we presently understand the word "lusts," it virtually always denotes something bad; however, the real meaning of the word is "to earnestly or passionately desire." Of what is the Holy Spirit envious? What does He passionately desire?

The Holy Spirit is envious of any control the fallen nature might have over the Believer, and is passionately desirous that He control all our thoughts, words, and deeds. He is desirous of having the Believer depend on Him for His Ministry to him, so that He might discharge His responsibility to the One Who sent Him, namely God the Father.

The pronoun *"He"* in Verse 6 refers to the Holy Spirit, and that He is the Dispenser of Grace. Providing the Believer ever makes the Cross the Object of his Faith, Grace will continue to come in an uninterrupted flow.

Concerning *"pride"* and *"humility,"* God resists those who look to something other than the Cross, and blesses those who humble themselves by looking strictly to Christ and the Cross, which alone develops humility.

When James said, *"Submit yourselves therefore to God,"* this means that the Holy Spirit desires that we submit ourselves to the Plan which God has provided, which is *"Jesus Christ and Him Crucified."*

Millions of Believers have read the phrase, *"Resist the Devil, and he will flee from you,"* and have wondered, deep in their hearts, *"What does this mean?"* They have tried to resist Satan, and have had little success.

The way to resist the Devil, and the only way, is to strictly look to Christ and what He has done for us at the Cross, where Satan was totally defeated (Col. 2:14-15). When we do this, we have the help of the Holy Spirit, with Whom Satan has no desire to tangle. However, far too many Christians attempt to resist the Devil in all the wrong ways. He can only be resisted in one way — that which we have given — which is Christ and the Cross and our Faith in that Finished Work.

Every Believer must have a desire to *"draw near to God."*

If this is done, He will draw near to us. We have here His Promise. Once again, this is ever done by Faith which ever makes the Cross of Christ its Object.

Last of all, the Holy Spirit through James told us to *"cleanse our hands,"* which refers to that which we do, and to *"purify our hearts,"* which can only be done by making Christ and the Cross the Object of our Faith. This is the Sanctification of the Saint. It is impossible otherwise for the Believer to live a victorious, Christian life.

DECEMBER
1

Is any sick among you? let him call for the Elders of the Church; and let them pray over him, anointing him with oil in the Name of the Lord: And the prayer of Faith shall save the sick, and the Lord shall raise him up; and if he has committed sins, they shall be forgiven him (James 5:14-15).

Divine Healing is part and parcel of the great Gospel of Faith. While the Lord does not heal all of the time, He most definitely still heals.

I was wondrously healed when I was about ten years old. My parents took me to the doctor several times, but nothing could be found. I stayed nauseous constantly, and, at times, would go unconscious. Actually, I passed out several times at school, and the last time this happened, the Principal told my parents, *"If something is not done, you are going to have to take Jimmy out of school. We don't want him dying on our hands."* That's how critical the situation was.

My family belonged to the tiny Assembly of God

Church in our little town of Ferriday, Louisiana. Our Pastor, although young, was a Godly Brother, who definitely believed that the Lord healed the sick. I was prayed for any number of times by him and others, but seemingly to no avail. The problem not only did not get better, it grew worse.

I will never forget the day that healing came. It was Sunday. The Church Service had ended, and my parents were taking the Pastor and his wife out to lunch. But first they had to go by the home of a parishioner who was ill and pray for him.

I remember us walking into the humble dwelling, praying for the dear Brother, and then coming back out to the front room, ready to leave. Suddenly, my Dad spoke up and said, *"Brother Culbreth, anoint Jimmy, and pray for him. If the Lord doesn't do something for him, we're going to have to take him out of school."*

This dear man, as stated, had prayed for me many times, but to no avail. Other Godly people had also prayed for me, but still there was no healing. Most of the time we have little clue as to exactly why the Lord does things in the manner in which He does them. Whatever He does, however, is always for purpose.

In my mind's eye, I can see Brother Culbreth as he walked across the floor with a bottle of oil in his hand, which he had just used to anoint the dear Brother for whom we had all just prayed.

Brother Culbreth put some oil on the tip of his finger, anointed my head, and, all of a sudden, it happened. Without warning, the Spirit of God came down in that room. I felt something like a ball of fire start at the top of my head and slowly go down through my body and out my feet. I was only about ten years old, but I knew the Lord had healed me. I knew it beyond the shadow of a doubt. And that's exactly what happened.

Whatever the problem was, it went and has never returned. In fact, I've had almost perfect health from that day until this, which is just a few days before my 70th Birthday.

Why did the Lord do it this way?

Why wasn't I healed at the other times the Pastor prayed for me?

I don't have the answers to those questions. However, for the following I am very thankful:

I'm glad we attended a Church that believed in praying for the sick. Had that not been the case, I probably would not be here today.

Second, I'm glad our Pastor was a Godly Brother, and that he kept believing with us, despite the fact that healing did not come immediately.

I'm glad my parents didn't get discouraged and quit seeking the Lord concerning my healing. They kept believing and the Lord rewarded our faith.

When I say the Lord heals, I'm saying it on the authority of His Word; however, I'm also saying it on the authority that Word has had in my life in effecting healing for me.

The husbandman must be first partaker of the fruit. And by the Grace of God, I have been a partaker of that fruit (II Tim. 2:6).

DECEMBER
2

*e*lect according to the foreknowledge of God the Father, through Sanctification of the Spirit, unto obedience and sprinkling of the Blood of Jesus Christ: Grace unto you, and peace, be multiplied (I Pet. 1:2).

There are three steps, one might say, which pertain to the sinner coming to Christ:

1. God the Father chooses you for Salvation.
2. God the Spirit brings you to the act of faith.
3. God the Son cleanses you from your sin.

The two terms, *"elect"* and *"foreknowledge of God,"* need to be explained.

First of all, the *"elect"* are those who elect to favorably respond to the Call of the Holy Spirit.

The *"foreknowledge of God the Father"* pertains to the Omniscience of God, i.e., that He knows all things, past, present, and future. Through foreknowledge, He knew that He would have to send a Saviour to redeem man from the Fall; all who accept the Saviour are the *"elect."*

809

The words, *"elect,"* *"foreknowledge,"* and *"predestina-tion,"* do not mean, as some teach, that God has selected some to go to Heaven and some to go to Hell, and there is nothing they can do about the selected destination. These words refer to the Plan of God; it is the Plan of God which has been foreordained, elected, or predestinated. How-ever, who will be in that Plan is determined by *"whosoever will"* (Jn. 3:16; Rev. 22:17).

So the first step in the Salvation process is God the Father, through Christ and by the Holy Spirit, presenting the Plan of Salvation, by whatever means, to the lost soul. That person has the privilege of responding with either *"Yes"* or *"No"*! Regrettably, most, it seems, reject.

The second step pertains to Sanctification of the sin-ner coming to Christ, which is carried out strictly by the Holy Spirit. The Greek word used here for *"sanctify"* means *"to be set apart unto God."* Actually, when the sinner comes to Christ, the very thing that happens is that a *"washing and sanctifying"* takes place (I Cor. 6:11). Before the believing sinner can be *"declared"* clean, which is *"Justification,"* he must first of all be *"made"* clean, which is Sanctification.

All of this is done under the covering of the shed Blood of Jesus Christ, which could be constituted as the third step, in which God the Son cleanses the believing sinner in His Own Precious Blood. This is given to us in the words, *"sprinkling of the Blood of Jesus Christ"*; Peter uses the phraseology and typology of the Levitical ritual where the Priest sprinkled the people with the sacrificial blood (Heb. 9:19).

All of this is a legal work, carried out by the Lord,

which constitutes one being *"born again."* All the believing sinner has to do is to exhibit Faith in Christ, which then sets all of this in motion, and which is, in fact, carried out instantly.

Actually, all of this which we have just mentioned, and I refer to the Salvation process, has already been done. It just awaits the faith of the sinner. When the Holy Spirit deals with the lost soul, the person has the choice of accepting or rejecting. If he accepts, and does so by faith, Salvation instantly is accomplished, because the Work has already been accomplished at the Cross and accepted by the Father.

DECEMBER

3

*f*orasmuch as you know that you were not Redeemed with
corruptible things, as silver and gold, from your vain conversation (lifestyle) received by tradition from your fathers;
But with the Precious Blood of Christ, as of a Lamb without
blemish and without spot: Who verily was foreordained before
the foundation of the world, but was manifest in these last
times for you (I Pet. 1:18-20).

These three Verses of Scripture proclaim to us the fact
that the Doctrine or principal of the Cross of Christ is the
oldest doctrine known to man. Through foreknowledge,
God knew, in eternity past, that He would make man, and
that man would fall. So it was deemed necessary by the
Godhead that man would be redeemed by God becoming
Man, going to the Cross, and thereby atoning for all sin,
actually serving as man's Substitute. All of this was decided before the foundation of the world.

"Foreordained," in the Greek Text, means "to designate
beforehand" to a position or function. In the councils of

the Triune God, the Lord Jesus was the Lamb marked out for Sacrifice. Before this Universe was created, the Lord Jesus had been foreordained to be the Saviour of lost sinners, and the Saints had been foreordained to become recipients of the Salvation He would procure for lost sinners at the Cross (Eph. 1:4; Rom. 8:29).

Considering that the Cross of Christ was foreordained from before the foundation of the world to be the essential core principal of Salvation, this means that every other doctrine must be built squarely on the basis of the Cross of Christ. If it is not, at least in some manner or way, it will be specious. That, in fact, has been the problem from the very beginning. It began with Cain and Abel, even at the dawn of time.

After the Fall, the First Family was given instructions by the Lord as to how sins could be forgiven and fellowship restored. It was by virtue of the slain lamb, which would be a symbol of the Coming Redeemer. Abel carried out the instructions of the Lord to the letter, but Cain substituted something else. The "something else" has been the problem from then until now.

All false doctrine has its beginning through a misinterpretation, a lack of understanding, or a denial of the Cross of Christ. When the Church gets off track, or even the individual Believer, the Church or the Believer has to come back to the Cross before things can be made right.

Even though the Cross of Christ was foreordained before the foundation of the world, still, it has been "manifest in these last times for me and you." If we ignore what the Lord has done, there is no way we can go in the right direction. The foundation is the Cross of Christ, and it will always be the foundation. Paul labeled it "The Everlasting Covenant" (Heb. 13:20).

813

DECEMBER

4

*f*or even hereunto were ye called: because Christ also suffered for us, leaving us an example, that we should follow
His steps: Who did no sin, neither was guile found in His
mouth: Who, when He was reviled, reviled not again; when
He suffered, He threatened not; but committed Himself to
Him Who Judges Righteously: Who His Own Self bore our
sins in His Own Body on the tree, that we, being dead to sins,
should live unto Righteousness: by Whose stripes you were
healed (I Pet. 2:21-24).

Men can only believe in God by believing in the Lamb
of God. It is not by means of the Creation that they believe, for that can not give rest to the conscience; nor by
means of Providence, for that leaves the way of God upon
Earth in profound darkness; nor by means of the Law, for
that fills the conscience with terror. It is only by the means
of Jesus, the Lamb of God Who redeemed them to God.

Just as a child, with painstaking effort and close application, follows the shape of the letters of his teacher

814

and thus learns to write, so Saints should, with like pains-taking effort and by close application, endeavor to be like the Lord Jesus in their own personal lives. Or, as a small child endeavors to walk in the footprints made by his father's feet in the snow, so we are to follow in the path which our Lord took.

The Greek word for *"follow"* literally means *"to take the same road"* as someone else takes. We should walk the same road that Jesus walked — in short, be Christlike.

However, the only way we truly can follow in Christ's footsteps is that we ever look to the Cross. Without the help of the Holy Spirit, we certainly cannot do it, and the Holy Spirit will help us only if we ever look to the Cross. That is the pattern we ought always to follow!

The word *"bore,"* used in the 24th Verse, is the trans-lation of a word used of the Priests carrying the Sacrifice up to the Altar. The Brazen Altar was 4 1/2 feet high, and was approached by an incline up which the Priest bore the Sacrifice.

Alford says that this word belongs to the idea of Sacri-fice, and is not to be disassociated from it. The Greek word translated *"tree"* does not refer to a literal tree, but to an object fashioned out of wood, in this case the Cross. Thus our Lord, Himself the High Priest and the Sacrifice, carried our sins as a burden of guilt up to the Cross.

The phrase, *"Being dead to sins,"* is literally *"having be-come off with respect to sins."* It speaks of the action of God in breaking the power of the sinful nature in the believing sinner when he puts his faith in the Lord Jesus as Saviour. Henceforth he need not be a slave to sin.

Concerning the *"stripes"* which Jesus suffered on our

behalf, Wuest says:

"The Greek presents a picture of our Lord's lacerated back after the scourging He endured at the hands of the Roman soldiers. The Romans used a scourge of cords or thongs to which were attached pieces of lead, brass, or small sharp-pointed bones. Criminals condemned to crucifixion were ordinarily scourged before being executed. The victim was stripped to the waist and bound in a stooping position, with his hands behind the back, to a post or pillar. The suffering under the lash was intense. The body was frightfully lacerated. The Christian martyrs at Smyrna about A.D. 155 were so torn by the scourges that their veins were laid bare, and the inner muscles and sinews, even the bowels, were exposed.

"The Greek word translated 'stripes' refers to a bloody wale trickling with blood that arises under a blow. The word is singular, not plural. Peter remembered the Body of our Lord after the scourging, the flesh so dreadfully mangled that the disfigured form appeared in his eyes as one single bruise.

"Thus we have the portrait of the suffering Servant of Jehovah, His Blessed Face so pummeled by the hard fists of the mob that it did not look like a human face any more, His back lacerated by the Roman scourge so that it was one mass of open, raw, quivering flesh trickling with blood, His Heart torn with anguish because of the bitter, caustic, malevolent words hurled at Him. On that bleeding, lacerated back was laid the Cross.

"Unsaved Reader, this was all for you, just as if you were the only lost person in the universe. The Lord Jesus died for you, in your stead, took your place on the Cross, paid your penalty, so that God could offer a Salvation from sin based upon justice satisfied.

"Will you not right now appropriate the Lord Jesus as your own personal Saviour, trust Him to save you?

"And Saint, does not all this make you love the Lord Jesus more, soften and make more tender your heart? The Blood of Christ heals our sin in that He, by One Offering, put away sin forever."

It is ever the Cross! The Cross! The Cross!

DECEMBER
5

*b*eloved, think it not strange concerning the fiery trial which is to try you, as though some strange thing happened unto you: But rejoice, inasmuch as you are partakers of Christ's sufferings; that, when His Glory shall be revealed, you may be glad also with exceeding joy (I Pet. 4:12-13).

Some Christians have the erroneous idea that if they embrace Christ and the Cross, making that the sole Object of their Faith, then they will never again be tempted, never have another problem, etc., etc. Bluntly and plainly, the Holy Spirit through Simon Peter here tells us that that's not the case at all. In fact, we are not to even think it out of the ordinary, or *"strange,"* concerning the *"fiery trial which is to try you."* The words, *"fiery trial,"* carry the connotation of *"furnace,"* referring to a smelting furnace where gold is refined.

The words, *"strange thing,"* are the translation of a Greek word referring to something alien or foreign in nature. The word *"happened,"* is, in the Greek, literally *"to go together,"* i.e., *"to happen."* But nothing just happens in the life of a Christian. Even this suffering for Righteousness' sake is all within God's Plan. It is used by the Lord as part of the process, to cause us to run to Christ.

Instead of thinking it a strange thing, we are exhorted not only to expect such suffering, but to rejoice in the fact that we can be partakers of Christ's sufferings. However, the Christian has no cause for rejoicing because of suffering that is brought on because of our own misdoing. But insofar as suffering is the result of doing well, we have cause for rejoicing. Our rejoicing arises from the fact that we share in common with Christ suffering for Righteousness' sake.

We should, however, be reminded that these sufferings of Christ, which we share in common with Him, are not His expiatory sufferings on the Cross, but His sufferings for Righteousness' sake while enduring the opposition of the religious establishment previous to the Cross.

Whenever a person accepts Christ and the Cross, making that the sole Object of his Faith, which will automatically cause him to throw aside all false doctrine, many times the opposition from the religious sector will be fierce. Sometimes our own family will oppose us. I know of no other avenue which will attract such opposition as when one places one's total Faith in Christ and the Cross. The opposition will come from the world of religion, even as it did with Christ.

But instead of feeling sorry for ourselves, the Holy Spirit through Peter here plainly tells us, *"Rather rejoice"*!

DECEMBER

6

*f*or the time is come that judgment must begin at the House of God: and if it first begin at us, what shall the end be of them who obey not the Gospel of God? And if the Righteous scarcely be saved, where shall the ungodly and the sinner appear? (I Pet. 4:17-18).

After the horror of 9/11/01, when the lives of some 4,000 Americans were snuffed out due to Muslim terrorism, two Preachers of my acquaintance were interviewed over Network Television. They were asked why the Lord allowed this to happen to America.

Their answer was most interesting! Both agreed, *"It is because of the homosexuals and the abortionists in this nation!"*

That is basely incorrect!

While the two sins mentioned definitely are abominable, as should be overly obvious, that is not the problem in this country. According to the Word of God, the problem is the *"House of God."* The Church in America has failed, and failed miserably! The Gospel is little preached from behind fashionable pulpits. The Cross of Christ, the very heartbeat of Christianity, has been relegated to the dustbin of antiquated doctrines, no longer applicable, or so it is said, for this modern age.

What I have just said is, in effect, the same as what Jesus said: *"Verily I say unto you, that the Publicans and the harlots go into the Kingdom of God before you"* (Mat. 21:31). Jesus certainly wasn't condoning the sins of thievery and harlotry. What He was saying was that while the publicans and the harlots would repent, or at least some of them would, the religious leaders of Israel would not repent (Mat. 21:32).

Judgment always begins with Believers, and pertains to their Faith, whether in the Cross or otherwise; the Cross alone is spared judgment, for there Jesus was judged in our place.

If God will judge His Own, how much more will He judge the unredeemed? The Cross alone stays the Judgment of God. That must ever be understood.

The modern Church in this country is little preaching the Gospel. If it was preaching the Gospel, i.e., *"the Cross,"* which, as stated, alone stays the Judgment of God, then this nation would escape much punishment, and could very well have escaped the horror of 9/11/01.

Because it is so important, let us say it again:

If the Church faithfully preaches the Cross, most Judgment can be spared, for there Jesus was judged in our place. If the Cross is little preached, the nation is opened up for Judgment, and that's exactly what is happening!

The Cross of Christ alone stands between man and eternal Hell. We must never forget that (Eph. 2:13-18; Gal. 6:14).

821

DECEMBER

7

*b**ut there were false prophets also among the people, even
as there shall be false teachers among you, who privily shall
bring in damnable heresies, even denying the Lord Who bought
them, and bring upon themselves swift destruction. And many
shall follow their pernicious ways; by reason of whom the way
of Truth shall be evil spoken of. And through covetousness
shall they with feigned words make merchandise of you: whose
judgment now of a long time lingers not, and their damnation
slumbers not* (II Pet. 2:1-3).

In some ways, Simon Peter preached the Cross just as
strongly as did the Apostle Paul.

The *"damnable heresies"* here mentioned would be better rendered *"heresies of destruction."* Peter is dealing with
that which is the most serious of the heretical teachings,
either denying the substitutionary death of our Lord, or
failing to give it its full due. The word *"bought"* in the
Greek is *"agorazo,"* one of three words translated *"redeemed"*
in the New Testament. In classical use, the word meant

"*to purchase in the marketplace,*" and was used of the purchase of slaves in the slave market. Our Lord's Precious Outpoured Blood was the ransom paid to redeem slaves of sin from that slavery. His Death satisfied the just demands of the High Court of Heaven, paying the penalty for the sinner, and making a way whereby a righteous God could be just and, at the same time, the Justifier of the believing sinner.

The denial seems to have consisted of an inadequate view of the Person and Work of Christ in our relation to the problem of human sin. Sadly and regrettably, that is the sin of the modern Church.

As we have said in other daily devotionals, the Cross of Christ, for it is this of which Peter speaks, has been so little preached in the last several decades that the modern Church attempts to serve a "*Cross-less*" Christ. For the most part, the Cross is ignored, misunderstood, or outright rejected.

Incidentally, the word "*heresies*" constitutes one of the "*works of the flesh,*" which characterize themselves in the lives of Believers who have made something other than the Cross of Christ the Object of their Faith.

Paul said, "*Now the works of the flesh are manifest, which are these* (if one attempts to function by means of Law of any nature, the '*works of the flesh*' will be manifested in one's life); *adultery, fornication, uncleanness, lasciviousness,*

"*Idolatry, witchcraft, hatred, variance, emulations, wrath, strife, seditions, heresies,*

"*Envyings, murders, drunkenness, revellings, and such like* (if one is walking after the flesh [Rom. 8:1], one or more of these sins will manifest themselves in one's life; the only way, and I mean the only way, one can walk in perpetual victory is to understand that everything we receive from God comes to us by the means of the Cross; consequently, the Cross must ever be the Object of our Faith; this being the case, the Holy Spirit, Who works exclusively within the confines of the Sacrifice of Christ, will exert His mighty Power on our behalf, which will enable us to live a Holy life): *of which I tell you before, as I have also told you in time past* (refers to the fact that the Apostle was not afraid to name specific sins), *that they which do such things shall not inherit the Kingdom of God.* (This tells us in no uncertain terms that if our Faith is not everlastingly in Christ and the Cross, we simply won't make it. God doesn't have two ways of Salvation and Victory, only one, and that is *'Jesus Christ and Him Crucified'''* [Gal. 5:19-21].)

Now, let us exegete what Peter said:

"But there were false prophets also among the people (refers to the false prophets who plagued Israel of old), *even as there shall be false teachers among you* (the false teacher is one who presents a way of Salvation, or a way of Sanctification, other than the Cross), *who privily shall bring in damnable heresies* (the idea is that these false teachers would teach some true Doctrine and then cleverly include false teaching with it; it is the introduction of false teaching alongside the Truth that makes it very subtle, and which abrogates the True), *even denying the Lord Who bought them* (refers to denying the Cross), *and bring upon themselves swift destruction* (upon themselves and upon those who follow them, which refers to the ultimate loss of the soul).

"And many shall follow their pernicious ways (actually most!); *by reason of whom the way of Truth shall be evil*

spoken of (proclaims the fact that not only is the Truth castigated, but the bearer of Truth, as well; in short, it is a denigration of the Cross).

"*And through covetousness shall they with feigned words make merchandise of you* (the people are exploited instead of developed; the underlying cause is *'money'*): *whose judgment now of a long time lingers not, and their damnation slumbers not* (the Judgment seems to be delayed, but it definitely is not idle; sooner or later, all who travel the path of *'damnable heresies,'* which refer to any way other than the Cross, will ultimately face *'utter ruin and destruction'*)."

DECEMBER

8

*f*or if after they have escaped the pollutions of the world
through the knowledge of the Lord and Saviour Jesus Christ,
they are again entangled again therein, and overcome, the
latter end is worse with them than the beginning. For it had
been better for them not to have known the way of Righteousness, than, after they had known it, to turn from the Holy
Commandment delivered unto them. But it is happened unto
them according to the true Proverb, The dog is turned to his
own vomit again; and the sow that was washed to her wallowing in the mire (II Pet. 2:20-22).

Peter is saying the same thing here that Paul said in
Hebrews 6:4-6 and 10:26-29. He is speaking of Believers,
that is, people who have truly been Born-Again, who have
now ceased to believe Christ and what He did at the Cross.
While they may claim to believe Christ, they have actually
divorced Him from the Cross, hence the Apostle saying
that they are *"denying the Lord Who bought them,"* i.e., denying what Christ did for them at the Cross (2:1).

These are not individuals, as some claim, who have merely heard about the Lord, and who have refused to accept Him. These are people who have *"known the way of Righteousness,"* which means that they once accepted the Righteousness of Christ and were Born-Again. Actually, no unsaved person can *"know the way of Righteousness."* These individuals knew that way, but turned to something else, which Peter likens to a *"dog turning to his own vomit again, and a hog that was washed going back to her wallowing in the mire."* This completely refutes the unscriptural doctrine of Unconditional Eternal Security.

We teach Conditional Eternal Security. As long as the Faith of a person remains in Christ and what He did at the Cross, that person is eternally secure. If the person moves his faith to something else, and it doesn't really matter what the *"something else"* is, he loses his way. The correct ingredient of Salvation is Faith in Christ and what Christ did at the Cross. If that is denied, they have *"crucified to themselves the Son of God afresh, and put Him to an open shame"* (Heb. 6:6). And if a person stays in that condition, and we speak of continuing to deny the Cross, such a person will be eternally lost, despite the fact that they once were saved.

As previously stated, this is the sin of the modern Church. It professes Christ loudly, but it denies the Cross.

How do I know that?

I know that because of the many and varied schemes offered which claim to be the way. I speak of the *"Purpose Driven Life"* doctrine, the *"Government of Twelve"* doctrine, the *"Word of Faith"* doctrine, *"Denominationalism,"* *"works righteousness,"* etc. If one accepts these doctrines, and a host which we haven't named, one is *"denying the Lord Who bought them"* (2:1).

If there ever was a time that Believers should renew their Faith in Christ, it is now!

DECEMBER

9

*k*nowing this first, that there shall come in the last days scoffers, walking after their own lusts, And saying, where is the Promise of His Coming? for since the fathers fell asleep, all things continue as they were from the beginning of the Creation. The Lord is not slack concerning His Promise, as some men count slackness; but is longsuffering to us-ward, not willing that any should perish, but that all should come to Repentance (II Pet. 3:3-4, 9).

In the Second Chapter of his Second Epistle, Peter speaks of false teachers who had denied the Atonement and now are denying what the Bible teaches about Endtime events.

What *"Coming"* is Peter addressing?

Actually, he is addressing the Second Coming, which incorporates a number of events, namely, the rise of the Antichrist, the Great Tribulation, the Battle of Armageddon, and the Kingdom Age. In Scripture, there are four *"days"* listed as such. They are:

    1. The day of man (I Cor. 4:3): This *"day"* started

with Adam's Fall, and will last until the Second Advent of Christ.

2. The day of Christ (Phil. 1:6): This refers to Christ catching away the Church, i.e., *"the true Church,"* at the Rapture.

3. The day of the Lord (Isa. 13:9; Rev., Chpts. 6-20): This pertains to the seven-year Great Tribulation, and then the Millennium, which will last for 1,000 years.

4. The day of God (II Pet. 3:12): This pertains to the time beginning with the close of the Millennium, which will incorporate the Great White Throne Judgment (Rev. 20:11-15), and the restoration of the Earth and its planetary heavens to their pristine glory. This is the Eternal Forever (Rev., Chpts. 21-22).

Exactly as the Holy Spirit said through the Apostle Peter, many Preachers in the modern Church are claiming that there is no such thing as a coming Rapture, and no such thing as a coming Great Tribulation, Antichrist, or Battle of Armageddon. They deny these things, claiming that if they happened at all, it was in the past. They claim that the world is getting better and better, and that Christianity is more and more gaining an upper hand, which will ultimately bring Christ back.

Some of these modern prognostications, such as the *"Purpose Driven Life"* doctrine and the *"Government of Twelve"* doctrine, claim they are going to completely revolutionize the world, making it better and better. Now, we know that the Saints of God definitely are the *"salt"* and *"light"* of the world (Mat. 5:13-14), but the Bible does not teach that the world in the last days will get better and better, but rather that it will get worse and worse (I Tim. 4:1; II Tim. 3:1-7).

Furthermore, many are denying a coming Judgment. The world and the Church have become so psychologized that they actually deny personal responsibility — hence, no Judgment!

The reason for all of this is because of a denial of the Cross. As previously stated, *"Jesus Christ and Him Crucified"* must be the foundation Doctrine of all that we believe and teach (I Pet. 1:18-20). This means that every doctrine must be built upon that foundation. If the Cross is denied, whatever doctrine is presented is going to be, in some way, specious and spurious, hence, the denial of Biblical Endtime events.

If there ever was a time that Believers should huddle around Christ and the Cross, it is now!

DECEMBER
10

*b*ut the Day of the Lord will come as a thief in the night; in the which the heavens shall pass away with a great noise, and the elements shall melt with fervent heat, the Earth also and the works that are therein shall be burned up. Seeing then that all these things shall be dissolved, what manner of persons ought you to be in all Holy conversation (lifestyle) and Godliness. Looking for and hasting unto the Coming of the Day of God, wherein the heavens being on fire shall be dissolved, and the elements shall melt with fervent heat? Nevertheless we, according to His Promise, look for new heavens and a new Earth, wherein dwells Righteousness (II Pet. 3:10-13).

The Church presently is in the last days of its time, better described as the *"Laodicean"* period (Rev. 3:14-19). The next prophetic event will be the Day of Christ, or the Rapture of the Church. Following that will come the Great Tribulation, a period of seven years, called *"the seventieth week of Daniel"* (Dan. 9:24-27). That is to be followed by the 1,000 year world empire of the Lord Jesus

(Rev. 20:1-7); at its conclusion, the Great White Throne Judgment will occur, and the wicked dead will be judged. This is what Peter is speaking of in 3:7 when he speaks of *"the day of judgment and perdition of ungodly men."*

Immediately after this, the renovation of the Earth and its planetary heavens will occur (3:7, 10, 12). As stated, the Day of the Lord comprises the Great Tribulation and the Millennium. The Millennium merging into eternity is the *"Day of God,"* which will be eternal (3:12).

Peter also speaks of the *"new heavens"* and the *"new Earth."* Both the heavens and the Earth have been marred by sin: the heavens by Lucifer's revolution against God, which took place in eternity past; the Earth, by Adam's Fall.

When Peter speaks of both the heavens and the Earth *"burning up,"* he is not speaking of annihilation, but rather *"passing from one condition to another."* As stated, this will take place at the conclusion of the Millennial Reign. Exactly how the Lord will do this, we aren't told; however, it should be obvious that the Creator of the universe, and all that is therein, can easily bring forth this which He proclaims He will do.

In the Twenty-first and Twenty-second Chapters of Revelation, however, we are told exactly what this new Heaven and new Earth will be like, and more so the new Earth.

Peter's phrase, *"Wherein dwells Righteousness,"* also tells us that there will be nothing in this new Earth that will cause sorrow and heartache. In fact, John the Beloved said that the Lord will *"make all things new"* (Rev. 21:5).

Concerning this, Paul said, *"But as it is written (Isa. 64:4), Eye has not seen, nor ear heard, neither have entered into the heart of man, the things which God has prepared for them who love Him.*

"But God has revealed them unto us by His Spirit (through the Word of God) . . ." [I Cor. 2:9-10].

DECEMBER
11

*b*ut if we walk in the Light, as He is in the Light, we have fellowship one with another, and the Blood of Jesus Christ His Son cleanses us from all sin (I Jn. 1:7).

The word *"walk,"* as John uses it here, even as Paul, refers to the manner in which we live this life for the Lord, i.e., our walk with God.

The *"fellowship"* of which John speaks here is not fellowship with other Christians, as most think, but rather us fellowshipping God and God fellowshipping us. In other words, this Passage takes the Believer to a far higher place and position than mere fellowship with other Believers, as wonderful and necessary as is the latter.

In Verse 6, John tells us that we cannot have *"fellowship with Him"* and, at the same time, *"walk in darkness"* and *"do not the truth."*

First of all, what is the *"Light"*? What is the *"Truth"*?

Christ is the *"Life"* (1:1-2); He is, therefore, the *"Light"*!

He Who is the Light and the Life reveals God. This

knowledge is of priceless value, for it searches the heart. It also declares the Deity of Christ, for only Deity could reveal Deity. That Light judges everything, and is the rule of Faith to those who walk in it. The moral rule of the Christian's will is God Himself, as revealed in Christ and the Scriptures.

So, Christ and Him Crucified, even as John will say (1:7), is both *"Light"* and *"Truth."*

As the Believer places his Faith exclusively in Christ and the Cross, we then continually have *"fellowship with the Father, and with His Son Jesus Christ"* (I Jn. 1:3). As well, while we are continually having fellowship with Them, the Blood of Jesus, God's Son, keeps constantly cleansing us from sins of omission, sins of ignorance, and sins in our lives of which we are unaware (for the reason that we have not grown enough in Grace to see that they are sin).

Please understand that these sins are not rare; they are prevalent! If the Blood of the Lord Jesus Christ did not make Divine provision for the constant cleansing away of the defilement of sin in our lives, these sins would prevent our fellowship with God.

Actually, each and every Believer, even the Godliest, is constantly *"coming short of the Glory of God"* (Rom. 3:23). (The Greek Text indicates a continuing action.) However, even as we are continually coming short of that glory, we are continually being cleansed by the Blood.

This does not pertain to willful sin, which demands confession to the Lord, as is evidenced in 1:9. In fact, 1:7 proclaims the intercession that Christ constantly makes for all Believer, guaranteeing that there is a constant cleansing (Heb. 7:25), and thereby a constant fellowship.

DECEMBER

12

*i*f we say that we have no sin, we deceive ourselves, and the Truth is not in us (I Jn. 1:8).

The Apostle John here emphatically states that the Christian continues to have the sin nature. Paul explains this in Romans, Chapter 6, proclaiming the fact that while the Believer is to be dead to the sin nature, the sin nature itself is not dead in the Believer, and will not be taken out completely until the First Resurrection of Life (Rom. 6:11; 8:23).

In this Passage, John addresses the heresy then being proclaimed by some, which presently is being proclaimed by many, that the Christian doesn't have a sin nature.

"*Sin,*" as John uses it here, is singular in number. Despite the fact that it is used without the definite article (i.e., "*sin*" rather than "*the sin*"), it points to the fact that the nature is referred to, not acts of sin. Here we have the denial of the indwelling and totally depraved nature, which is passed down through the race from Adam. John says, therefore, as rendered in the literal Greek, "*If we say that sin we are not having, ourselves we are deceiving."* Notice, if you will, the emphatic position of the pronoun *"ourselves."*

The Christian who believes he has no sin nature, that it is completely eradicated, is deceiving himself, nobody else. All others can see sin stick out all over his experience. To be sure, that sin must come from the indwelling sinful nature. When John says, *"The truth is not in us,"* he is not meaning that the person is not saved, but rather that the truth of the sin nature is not in that person.

The first thing regarding the meaning of the New Covenant (which is the meaning of the Cross) which the Lord taught the Apostle Paul was the fact of the sin nature, which Paul gave us in Romans, Chapter 6. The Lord then told Paul what the answer to the sin nature was, in fact the only answer, which is the Cross of Christ (Rom. 6:3-5). There is only one answer for sin and that is the Cross.

To be sure, the only thing standing between the Christian and eternal Hell is the Cross. We must never forget that (Jn. 3:16).

DECEMBER
13

i f we confess our sins, He is faithful and just to forgive us our sins, and to cleanse us from all unrighteousness (I Jn. 1:9).

When the Believer sins, and we speak of a sin that he knows he has committed, he is to take that sin to the Lord and confess it before Him. The Lord has promised to forgive, and that He will do. His faithfulness is involved because He promised to forgive; and His Righteousness is in question, for it would be unjust to punish sin a second time — the penalty of the Believer's sins having been already borne at Calvary.

There is also no limit to the number of times that the Lord will forgive; however, no true Believer habitually sins, unless his faith is in something other than the Cross of Christ. If that is the case, the sin nature will begin to dominate such a Believer, who will then constantly carry out habitual acts of sin, despite trying to do otherwise (Rom. 7:15).

The Believer must first of all learn to place his Faith exclusively in Christ and the Cross, which will then give the Holy Spirit latitude to work in his life, which guarantees that sin will no longer have dominion over such a Believer (Rom. 6:14). This does not mean sinless perfection, for the Bible does not teach such; but it does teach that sin is not to have dominion over the Believer.

If sin, however, is committed, confession first of all should be made, in fact, must be made, to God. Confession of sin on the part of the Saint means to say the same thing that God says about that sin, to agree with God as to all the implications of that sin: those which relate to the Christian who commits it and to a Holy God against Whom it is committed. That includes the Saint's hatred of that sin, his sense of guilt because of it, his contrition because of it, and his determination to put it out of his life and never to do that thing again. This is what confession of sin here means.

The English word *"confess"* means *"to admit the truth of an accusation, to own up to the fact that one is guilty of having committed the sin."* But the Greek word means far more than that, as we here see. The Greek teaches that the constant attitude of the Saint toward sin should be one of a contrite heart, ever eager to have any sin in the life discovered for him by the Holy Spirit, and ever eager to confess it and put it out of the life by the Power of the Holy Spirit, which is the only way it can be done.

Let it ever be understood:

When the Lord forgives sin, which He always will do upon proper confession, then the sin is completely, totally, and absolutely forgiven. Not only does God forgive the Believer, but He cleanses him from the defilement which is incurred in committing the act of sin.

A true Christian hates sin. As we have repeatedly stated, the only answer for sin is the Cross!

DECEMBER

14

*M*y little children, these things write I unto you, that you sin not. And if any man sin, we have an Advocate with the Father, Jesus Christ the Righteous: And He is the propitiation for our sins: and not for ours only, but also for the sins of the whole world (I Jn. 2:1-2).

The Apostle John is not here revealing these great truths in order that we may sin and keep sinning, but rather that we stop sinning. But if the Believer does sin, we have an Advocate, Who is the Righteous One, and, at the same time, the Mercy Seat, so to speak. His Work, His Person, and His Action all unite in maintaining the Believer in the enjoyment of conscious fellowship with God. As a Priest, He deals with the guilt of sins; as an Advocate, with the restoration of the soul. Sin interrupts communion; the Advocate restores it.

The efficacy (effectiveness) of His action is guaranteed by the Righteousness of His Person and the value of His Propitiation, and these are unchangeable. Before Peter sinned, Christ prayed for him; when he sinned, He looked on him; and when he repented, He restored him — and so effectually restored him that Peter was able to strengthen his Brother Apostles. So effective is that Mercy Seat as a Propitiation for sins that if all men would approach Him for forgiveness of sin, then all men would be pardoned. The atoning Sacrifice of Christ furnishes an ample provision for the Redemption of all men, but its benefit is only appropriated by those who believe (Jn. 3:16).

Jesus Christ is our *"Advocate with the Father."* He is always in fellowship with the Father. Thus, if the Saint loses fellowship with Him through sin, and if the Believer properly confesses that sin, the Lord, in a sense, pleads our cause on the basis of His Precious Blood, and thereby brings us back into fellowship again. However, when we say *"plead,"* we are not really meaning that Jesus says anything or does anything. His very Presence before the Father guarantees that the intercession will be accepted, at least for those who will believe (Heb. 7:25-27; 10:12-14).

The word *"Propitiation,"* in its short form, means *"to make satisfaction."* However, while that does explain the word, it does not give the true meaning. The Scriptural conception of the word is not that of merely appeasing one who is angry with a personal feeling against the offender, but of altering the character of that which, from without, occasions a necessary alienation, and interposes an inevitable obstacle to fellowship.

That from without which occasioned the alienation between God and man was, and is, sin. It was the guilt of sin that separated man from his Creator. On the Cross, our Lord assumed that guilt and paid the penalty in His

Own Blood, and thus removed the cause of alienation. Now a Holy and Righteous God can bestow Mercy upon a believing sinner on the basis of justice satisfied. Our Lord provided a satisfaction for the demands of the broken Law. That satisfaction is the *"Propitiation."* The Greek rendition is: *"He Himself is a satisfaction."* The point is that the Old Testament Priest offered an animal sacrifice, but not himself as the sacrifice. This wonderful New Testament Priest, the Lord Jesus Christ, is both the Priest and the Sacrifice.

That Propitiation is as wide as the sin. We must never forget that! If men do not experience its benefit, the fault is not in the effectiveness of the Propitiation, but in the man himself. That fault, if there is a fault, is *"unbelief."*

If men believe in Christ and the Cross, they will obtain the benefits of all that Christ has accomplished.

DECEMBER

15

*b*eloved, now are we the sons of God, and it does not yet appear what we shall be: but we know that, when He shall appear, we shall be like Him; for we shall see Him as He is. And every man who has this hope in Him purifies himself, even as He is pure. Whosoever commits sin transgresses also the Law: for sin is the transgression of the Law. And you know that He was manifested to take away our sins; and in Him is no sin (I Jn. 3:2-5).

Here John states that Believers are *"now"* sons of God, meaning that it's not something future, but present. The world neither recognizes nor acknowledges Believers as sons of God; just as they neither recognized nor acknowledged Christ to be The Son of God.

The term *"manifested"* occurs three times in the Greek Text (Vss. 2, 5, 8), and responds to three cries of the heart:

1. The cry for liberation from sins and their eternal doom. The answer to that is: He was manifested to take away sins, and as He could not possibly fail in what He

came to do, the Believer learns with wonder and joy that his sins are taken away forever (Vs. 5).

2. The second manifestation concerns the cry of the renewed heart to be sinless. This cry will be satisfied when we shall be manifested, for His People shall be like Him (Vs. 2).

3. This third cry is that of anguish and perplexity of the heart awakened to the misery, injustice, cruelty and suffering in the world. The answer is found in Verse 8. They are *"the works of the Devil"*; the Son of God was manifested to destroy them, and so will He do.

The *"likeness,"* as John introduces the statement referring to the similarity with Christ, presents a physical likeness, and not a spiritual one. Saints are already spiritually like the Lord Jesus in a relative sense; through the sanctifying work of the Holy Spirit, we are being conformed more and more to His spiritual likeness. Actually, here John is speaking of the Rapture and the change that will take place in the physical body upon that great event. It refers to all Saints at that time having a Glorified Body, exactly as Jesus did when He was resurrected. The change, at least that which John addresses here, which comes at the Rapture, is, therefore, a physical one. We shall be like our Lord as to His physical, glorified Body.

The phrase, *"Be fashioned alike,"* in the Greek is *"summorphon,"* which means *"the outer enswathement of glory that now covers the Body of the Lord Jesus, and which will, at the Rapture, cover ours."* Only at the Rapture will we be able to see our Lord as He is now, for physical eyes and a mortal body could not look on that glory, only eyes in a glorified body. And that is the reason we shall be like

Him, for only in that state can we see Him just as He is.

As to the expression, *"purifies himself,"* this is not to be taken in the sense that man can purify himself, for he cannot. *"Apart from Me,"* says our Lord, *"you can do nothing"* (Jn. 15:5). The statement implies a will to purify oneself, not out of, nor independent of, this hope, but ever stirred up by and accompanying it.

So this will is really not our own, but the result of the Christian state, in which the Lord also ministers to us the power to carry out that will in self-purification. It is done only by the Believer placing his Faith exclusively in Christ and the Cross, which then gives the Holy Spirit latitude to do this necessary work within our lives, which He most definitely will do. Thus, in dependence upon the Holy Spirit, the Saint can put sin out of his life and keep it out (Rom. 8:1-2, 11).

DECEMBER
16

*b**ut the Anointing which you have received of Him abides
in you, and you need not that any man teach you: but as the
same Anointing teaches you of all things, and is Truth, and is
no lie, and even as it has taught you, you shall abide in Him*
(I Jn. 2:27).

There are two Divine safeguards which preserve from
error. They are the Holy Spirit and the Holy Scriptures.
These teach young converts, actually all Believers, to recognize and reject false teaching.

The Roman Catholic plea of *"Development,"* which
refers, as they claim, to the Word of God being developed
in the Church, is overthrown by the words of Verse 24,
which says, *"That which is from the beginning. . . ."* This is
the safeguard of the Word of God, which pertains to that
and only that which was heard from the beginning, meaning that the Word of God is already fully and totally developed. Nothing must be taken from or added to it.
The sheep listen to nothing else, for they know the

Shepherd's voice.

The Holy Spirit indwells all Believers. When Believers diligently study the Word, the Holy Spirit, according to the Word, will help them to know what is Truth. They will be able to detect a lie as being opposed to the Truth. All Believers, that is, if they properly know and understand the Word, as can all who so desire, are furnished with Divine equipment capable of enabling all of us to know *"all things."* So, according to the Word of God, since the *"anointing"* abides in us and teaches us what is right and wrong, that is, if we will only properly heed, there is no excuse for Believers to accept false doctrine.

A proper understanding of the Word refers to a proper understanding of the Cross. If one doesn't properly understand the Cross, one does not understand the Word. The story of the Bible is the story of Jesus Christ and Him Crucified. In truth, the Cross was established in the mind of the Godhead even before the world was created, which means that the Cross was an established fact even before the first words of the Bible were given (I Pet. 1:18-20).

So if one properly understands the Cross, that will go a long, long way toward the recognition of false doctrine, for this is the way the Holy Spirit works (Rom. 8:2; Gal., Chpt. 5; 6:14; Eph. 2:13-18).

DECEMBER
17

*W*hosoever is born of God does not commit sin; for His seed remains in him: and he cannot sin, because he is born of God (I Jn. 3:9).

The person who has accepted Christ now has the Divine nature (II Pet. 1:4). While he still retains the sin nature, now his human nature is guided and controlled by the Divine nature — at least that's the way it should be! If the Believer continually makes the Cross of Christ the Object of his faith, which gives the Holy Spirit latitude to work within his heart and life, then he will walk in victory, with no possibility of the sin nature having dominion over him (Rom. 6:14).

But most Christians do not have even the foggiest idea as to the part the Cross plays regarding our Sanctification; consequently, they attempt, by various ways, to sanctify themselves, which, of course, is impossible. But for the person whose Faith is exclusively in Christ and the Cross, it is impossible for that individual to live a life

849

of habitual sinning.

"*Commit*" in the Greek is "*poieo,*" which means "*a continuous action,*" at least as it is used here. The actual translation reads, "*Everyone who has been born out of God, with the present result that he is a born-one of God, does not habitually practice sin.*" The short phrase, "*His seed,*" refers to the principle of Divine Life in the Believer, i.e., "*the Divine nature.*" It is this principle of the Divine nature that makes it impossible for a Christian to live habitually in sin, for the Divine nature causes the Child of God to hate sin and love Righteousness, and gives him both the desire and the power to do God's Will.

The phrase, "*And he cannot sin, because he is born of God,*" means that the Believer "*cannot practice sin, because he is born of God.*" The Text, as it is translated in the King James Version of the Bible, does not mean, as some think, that John is teaching sinless perfection. The Bible doesn't teach that. The Holy Spirit through John is teaching that the Born-Again Believer cannot live a life of practicing sin, which should be obvious. If the Believer is practicing sin, which means that he sins with impunity, this simply means that the one so doing is not actually Born-Again.

DECEMBER

18

*n*ot as Cain, who was of that wicked one, and slew his brother. And wherefore slew he him? Because his own works were evil, and his brother's righteous. (I Jn. 3:12).

We learn from this Text that there is no such thing as a middle ground between the Children of God and the children of the Devil. In other words, one cannot be a little of both. One is either — or!

Abel was a Child of God. Cain was a child of the Devil. To "do Righteousness" is to act as Abel did. He humbled himself and accepted God's way of Righteousness. To "commit sin" is to act as Cain did. His religious works were evil. Cain was, in fact, a very religious man, but not a righteous man. His worship would have secured the admiration of "modern thought," but the Holy Spirit here says it was evil. He rejected the Divine Way of Righteousness, and thus showed that he was "out of" the Evil One.

Popular modern Preachers teach that both religions

are equally good; but God did not think so, for He accepted the one and rejected the other. He also states here that there is a Devil, that morally he has children, and that these children may be very religious.

Satan actually has two ways of Salvation: one by Sacraments, and the other by ethics. Christ's Atonement — possessing infinite moral value — condemns and destroys both these false ways of seeking acceptance with God. Christ is the measure of the Believer's acceptance; therefore, that acceptance is perfect, full, and eternal. In that Righteousness, the Righteousness of Christ, which was gained at the Cross and is given freely to believing man, no one can find a flaw; it needs neither ecclesiastical ceremonies nor human merits to add to its perfection.

The word "*slew*" in the Greek is "*sphazo*," which means "*to butcher by cutting the throat.*" The inspired writer goes out of his way to use a specialized word to describe the murder of Abel by Cain. Cain slit his brother's throat.

God said to Cain, "*What have you done? The voice of your brother's blood cries unto Me from the ground*" (Gen. 4:10). The method Cain used to kill his brother was one in which much blood would be shed. The cutting of the jugular vein would fit that description. As is overly obvious, Cain was evil, which played out to what he did to his brother.

In view of all of this, John said that we are not to "*marvel, if the world hate you*" (3:13). John's readers were astounded at the fact that people of the world should hate them because they were Children of God. The hatred of the world toward the Child of God is, however, a fact. This will not change. And yet, at the same time, we must not do things that would give the world a legitimate reason to think ill of us. No matter what the world thinks, our business is to commend Jesus to it, and to win it to the Lord.

Most of the hostility, however, will not come from the world, but rather from professing religion. I speak of that which calls itself *"the Church."* Cain was very religious. He built an altar and offered sacrifice; however, it was not the type of sacrifice that God could accept, so Cain was rejected by the Lord. In this context, he murdered his brother.

Such hostility from the religious counterpart began with Cain and has continued ever since. As proved by the saga of Cain and Abel, the greatest animosity is tendered by the Church, and the reason is the Cross. The reason always is the Cross! (Gal. 5:11).

DECEMBER

19

*b*eloved, believe not every spirit, but try the spirits whether they are of God: because many false prophets are gone out into the world. Hereby know ye the Spirit of God: Every spirit that confesses that Jesus Christ is come in the flesh is of God: And every spirit that confesses not that Jesus Christ is come in the flesh is not of God: and this is that spirit of Antichrist, whereof you have heard that it should come; and even now already is it in the world (I Jn. 4:1-3).

The idea of these Passages is that Believers are to stop believing every spirit. Paul finds the source of false doctrine in demons who actuate the false teachers who propound heresy (I Tim. 4:1). Thus, these spirits are human beings actuated either by demons or by the Holy Spirit.

The exhortation is to try these individuals, whoever they might be, to see whether they are of God or not. The word "try" in the Greek is "dokimazo," which means "to put to the test for the purpose of approving, and finding that the person put to the test meets the specifications laid down, to put *one's own approval upon him."* Thus, the Bible teacher, for instance, was not to be put to the test for the purpose of condemning him, but with the intent to approve him. The brother was not to be treated as a heretic before he had shown himself to be one.

The reason for putting visiting teachers to such a test was that many false prophets *"are gone out into the world."* In the Greek, the words speak of an action that is taking place presently. They have gone out; as a present result, they are in the world of mankind, and they have established themselves among the people.

John now gives the test which will prove that the Holy Spirit is actuating a teacher. If that teacher confesses that Jesus Christ has come in the flesh, that is proof of the fact that he is a true Believer and is actuated by the Holy Spirit. What does John mean by this?

The statement, *"Jesus Christ is come in the flesh,"* refers to the Incarnation, and what that means. The name *"Jesus"* means *"Jehovah saves."* *"Christ"* means *"The Anointed One."* It speaks to the fact that the God of the Old Testament, Who, in the Person of His Son, became incarnate in human flesh without its sin, died on the Cross to satisfy the just demands of His righteous Law, which man broke, and raised Himself from the dead in the Body in which He died, to become the Living Saviour of the sinner who places his Faith in Him in view of what He did for him on Calvary's Cross.

John says that the person who teaches that is actuated by the Holy Spirit; likewise, the teacher who does not agree with that doctrine is not of God. Such a teacher is actuated by the spirit of Antichrist, who denies and is against all that the Bible teaches regarding the Person and Work of the Lord Jesus.

(Our thanks to Kenneth Wuest for most of the above material on the Person of Christ.)

To simplify the statement, John, in essence, is saying, *"Christ and the Cross must be the Object of Faith."* If that is denied in any way, the person is not of God. That's the reason that we look askance at many of the modern schemes which claim to be of God, such as the *"Purpose Driven Life"*, doctrine, the *"Government of Twelve (G-12)"* doctrine, the *"Word of Faith"* doctrine, etc.

The last one openly repudiates the Cross. The G-12 claims to believe the Cross, but then turns to works to effect one's Sanctification, which, in effect, denies the Cross. In no way could one come to the conclusion that the *"Purpose Driven Life"* theory looks to the Cross at all. It is a religion of supposed ethics, which God can never accept.

John the Beloved, who wrote this Epistle, is saying, *"Such is not of the Lord."*

As it regards doctrine, Christ and His Cross are always the deciding factor!

DECEMBER
20

*t*here is no fear in love; but perfect love casts out fear: because fear has torment. He who fears is not made perfect in love *(I Jn. 4:18).*

If we properly love the Lord, and know that He loves us, which He most definitely does, then we know that He is working everything according to our benefit. Everything that happens to a Child of God is either *"caused"* by the Lord or *"allowed"* by the Lord. While the Lord definitely does not cause sin, He does allow it, and with consequences.

Further, the Lord is not the cause of negative situations which come our way. But He does, at times, allow them. But no matter what He does, it is always for our benefit. We must know this, understand this, and believe this. If we love Him as we ought to, we will know that He likewise loves us, and that He will allow nothing to hurt us. We have this confidence in Him.

The phrase, *"Perfect love casts out fear,"* pertains to God.

This love is not known by the poor results of its action in man, but by its perfect action in God. And here is something we must never forget: that perfection manifested itself at Calvary. This perfect love is a fact, and it manifested itself outside of man in order to effect the Salvation of man.

The Believer knows it by the Gift of God's Son, and he enjoys it by the Gift of God's Spirit. It is at Calvary that we learn what love is (4:10); and that when we had no love for God, the Lord loved us perfectly, even though we were far from Him and dead in sins. Man has no love for God; his pretension to possess it is self-deception. He cannot find it by searching within himself, but he can know it as manifested in the Atoning Sacrifice of Christ. Jesus gave the Life which loves and made propitiation for sins.

We who really possess this Divine nature love because we are loved. It is especially a fraternal love; it loves fellow-Believers more intimately than the nearest relatives who are unconverted. It binds the heart with a stronger bond to persons never seen than to the dearest companions of childhood. It is a new nature, a realm outside of natural human affection — a realm of Divine love — a fellowship with God and with all who know Him. In truth, there is no real love outside that realm.

The *"fear"* of which John here speaks, *"fear"* which *"has torment,"* is certainly not a Godly fear, a holy fear of displeasing the Father through sin (I Pet. 1:17; Heb. 12:28), but rather a slavish fear of a slave for a master, or of a criminal before a judge.

The word *"torment"* carries the thought with it of punishment. Thus, the Saint who has experienced the fullness of this Divine Love in his earthly life will have no fear of correction or penalty (loss of reward) at the Judgment Seat of Christ.

While the *"perfect love"* has its home in Christ, and is exercised at the Cross, the Saint can also have all that Christ has, which means that we can have *"perfect love,"* which is gained through our Faith in Christ and what He has done for us at the Cross. It is at the Cross that this great love was shown by God to a dying world, and it is at the Cross that the Believer takes upon himself this *"perfect love."* It can be gained at no place other than the Cross (Jn. 3:16).

DECEMBER
21

*f*or whatsoever is born of God overcomes the world: and this is the victory that overcomes the world, even our Faith (I Jn. 5:4).

We are emphatically told in this Passage that it is *"our faith"* that gives us victory over the world.

What exactly does John the Beloved mean by the phrase, *"our faith"*?

To understand the type of faith of which John speaks, i.e., the Faith that overcomes the world and guarantees victory, we must understand what the Object of this Faith must be. John tells us in Verses 6 through 8 of this same Chapter.

John says, *"This is He Who came by water and blood, even Jesus Christ* (this refers to the Living Word becoming flesh [Jn. 1:1, 4], which is symbolized by *'water,'* and then as the Lamb of God, Who took away the sin of the world, which was effected by the shedding of His Blood on the Cross of Calvary); *not by water only, but by water and blood* (testifies to the fact that the Incarnation, within itself, although absolutely necessary, was not enough; the phrase also testifies to the absolute necessity of the Atonement). *And it is the Spirit Who bears witness, because the Spirit is Truth* (the Holy Spirit bore witness to the Divine Birth of Christ and to the Divine Sacrifice of Christ [Mat. 1:18; Heb. 9:14]).

"*For there are Three Who bear record in Heaven* (the Law has ever required the Testimony of two or three witnesses [Deut. 17:6; 19:15; Mat. 18:16; II Cor. 13:1]), *the Father, the Word* (Jesus Christ is the Word [Jn. 1:1]), *and the Holy Spirit: and these Three are One* (the only sense in which Three can be One is in essence and unity, which is clear in John 17:11, 21-23).

"*And there are Three Who bear witness in Earth* (as in Heaven, so on Earth), *the Spirit, and the Water, and the Blood* (speaks of the Holy Spirit; the humanity of Christ, while never ceasing to be Deity; and the Atonement, i.e., 'the Cross'): *and these Three agree in One.* (These Three agree that Christ is Very Man, while at the same time being Very God, Who died on the Cross to redeem fallen humanity [I Jn. 5:6-8].)"

All of this tells us that our Faith must be anchored in Christ as the Source of all things which come from God to us, and the Cross is the Means by which all of this is done. *"Jesus Christ and Him Crucified"* must be the Object of our Faith. Such faith, properly registered, will guarantee victory that we overcome the world in every respect (I Cor. 1:23; 2:2).

DECEMBER

22

*b*eloved, when I gave all diligence to write unto you of the common Salvation, it was needful for me to write unto you, and exhort you that you should earnestly contend for the Faith which was once delivered unto the Saints. For there are certain men crept in unawares, who were before of old ordained to this condemnation, ungodly men, turning the Grace of our God into lasciviousness, and denying the only Lord God, and our Lord Jesus Christ (Jude, Vss. 3-4).

Jude, the half-brother of our Lord (Mat. 13:55; Mk. 6:3), was thinking of writing a letter explaining the way of Salvation, a letter similar to Paul's Epistle to the Romans; however, news reached him of such a nature to cause him to put that project aside and hasten to write this letter, urging Believers to contend earnestly for the Faith once for all entrusted to them. It was a fully revealed Faith, needing no additions, repelling all corruptions, and infallibly declared in the Apostolic writings.

The short phrase, *"It was needful,"* carries the idea of

862

being constrained. The compulsion to exhort the Saints to contend for the Faith found its source in the Holy Spirit. To be sure, it was no welcomed task: necessity was laid upon him.

The exhortation was to Preachers, and actually to all Believers, that they earnestly contend for the Faith. This Faith here is not faith as exercised by the individual, but Christianity itself in its historic doctrines and life-giving Salvation.

The short phrase, *"Earnestly contend,"* in the Greek is *"epagonizomai,"* which means *"a vigorous, intense, determined struggle to defeat the opposition."* Our word *"agony"* is the English spelling of the noun form of this word. The Greek athletes, for this is the form in which the word is given, exerted themselves to the point of agony in an effort to win the contest. Jude says that the Saints should defend the doctrines of Christianity with the same degree of intense effort, seeing that God gave the Christian doctrines to the Saints as a deposit of truth to be faithfully guarded.

In the Fourth Verse, Jude gives the reason why the Saints should contend for the Faith: False teachers were in the Church!

Wuest addresses this by saying:

"There is a Greek word in II Corinthians 11:13-15 which admirably describes the methods of those who take after their father, the Devil. The Greek word is 'metaschematizo,' which means 'to be transformed.' It refers to the act of an individual changing his outward expression by assuming an expression put on from the outside, an expression that does not come from, nor is it representative of, what he is in his inner character.

"Lucifer did that after he struck at God's Throne, and

became the fallen angel, Satan. As a fallen angel, he gave expression to his sin-darkened heart. But he knew that he could not attract the human race that way. He must impersonate God, if he expected to be worshipped as God. He therefore assumed an outward expression of light, put on from the outside, and not representative of his inner sinful being. He disguised himself as an angel of light.

"His ministers have done the same. They use the same terms that Godly Preachers use, but put their own private meanings upon them, which negate the Biblical view.

"Reader, do not trust these false teachers any farther than you would a rattlesnake. A rattlesnake will give you warning before he strikes, but not these false teachers. The eternal welfare of your soul depends upon what you believe regarding the Person and Work of our Lord on the Cross."

When Jude mentioned "The Faith," he was speaking primarily of Christ, which refers to Who He was, and is, the Son of God, and what He did on the Cross, which was to effect Salvation by the giving of Himself in Sacrifice, which He did by the pouring out of His Life's Blood.

It is not pleasant to point out false teachers and false doctrine, but it must be done. The Holy Spirit through Jude said so!

DECEMBER
23

*W*rite the things which you have seen, and the things which are, and the things which shall be hereafter (Rev. 1:19).

In this one Verse, we have an overlook of the entirety of the Book of Revelation. It is basically divided into three sections. They are:

1. *"The things which you have seen"*: This concerns the First Chapter of Revelation, and pertains to the Vision of Jesus. Even though the Apostle John had been personally chosen by Jesus as one of His closest Disciples, and had walked with Christ for some three and a half years, still, he would now see Jesus in a completely different light.

John now saw Him in all of His Glory — so much Glory that John says:

"I fell at His Feet as dead. And He laid His right Hand upon me, saying unto me, 'Fear not. I am the First and the Last:

"'I am He Who lives, and was dead: and, behold, I am alive forevermore, Amen; and have the keys of Hell and of death'" (Rev. 1:17-18).

John saw Jesus standing in the *"midst of seven golden candlesticks."* The *"candlesticks"* represent and symbolize the *"Church."* As the *"Head"* of the Church, Jesus stands in its midst. There were *"seven"* candlesticks; the number *"seven"* is God's number of perfection, totality, universality, and completion.

Despite the apostasy, Jesus will have a perfect Church, made up of those who truly trust Him and what He did at the Cross.

2. *"And the things which are"*: This constitutes Chapters 2 and 3 of Revelation, which pertain to the Church Age. Even though only two Chapters in the Book of Revelation are devoted to it, the Church Age constitutes the longest period of time of the three sections, now nearly 2,000 years.

The seven Churches named portray the entirety of the Church Age; each Church denotes a particular period of time:

The Church at *"Ephesus"* is the first Church to which Jesus spoke. It represents the Apostolic Age, which lasted for approximately the first one hundred years.

The Church at *"Smyrna"* is second, and was the Church of persecution. Its time frame was from approximately A.D. 100 to A.D. 300.

"Pergamos" is the third Church, and constitutes the State Church, so-called. In a sense, it continues unto this hour.

The Church at *"Thyatira"* is the fourth, and constitutes the Papal Church. It began approximately in A.D. 600, and continues unto this hour.

The Church at *"Sardis"* is the fifth, and it constitutes

the Reformation Church. It began about A.D. 1500, and continues unto this hour.

The Church at *"Philadelphia"* is the sixth, and it constitutes the Missionary Church. It began approximately in the 1800's, and continues unto this hour.

The *"Laodicean"* Church is the last, and it constitutes the apostatized Church. It began approximately at the turn of the Twenty-first Century. It is the age in which we now live.

3. *"The things which shall be hereafter"*: This part constitutes the greater bulk of the Book of Revelation, beginning with the Sixth Chapter and continuing through the end. It denotes the Great Tribulation, which is soon to come, which will be followed by the Millennial Reign, and then by the Perfect Age, which will have no end. The Perfect Age is described in the last two Chapters of the Book of Revelation.

The Book of Revelation is not easy to understand; but yet, all who read it and study it are promised a blessing (Rev. 1:3). As we shall see, the Book of Revelation also portrays the Cross of Christ in detail, actually mentioning Christ as *"the Lamb"* some 28 times.

DECEMBER
24

*a*nd unto the Angel of the Church of the Laodiceans write; These things saith the Amen, the faithful and true witness, the beginning of the Creation of God; I know your works, that you are neither cold nor hot: I would you were cold or hot. So then because you are lukewarm, and neither cold nor hot, I will spue you out of My mouth. Because you say, I am rich, and increased with goods, and have need of nothing; and knowest not that you are wretched, and miserable, and poor, and blind, and naked (Rev. 3:14-17).

Jesus sent a Message to each of the seven Churches of Asia; of these, Laodicea was the last. This particular Church constitutes the conclusion of the Church Age, and represents the time in which we now live. In other words, the modern Church is the Laodicean Church, and the Laodicean Church is the modern Church. Unfortunately, the Message given by Christ is not very positive.

The Laodicean Church is actually an apostatized Church, which means that it has departed from the Truth.

It is neither *"cold"* nor *"hot,"* but rather *"lukewarm."* As a result, Jesus said, *"I will vomit you out of My mouth."* And thus is the modern Church!

The Seventeenth Verse, sadly and regrettably, describes the modern Church to the proverbial *"T"*. In not only the United States, but also over the balance of the entire world, the modern Church has never been richer, at least regarding material things. It is *"increased with goods,"* which again speaks of material things, but definitely not spiritual things. In the modern Church, *"faith"* has been reduced to *"things,"* instead of what the correct object ought to be, which is the Cross of Christ. The modern Church basically claims that *"it has need of nothing."* It is lukewarm, rich, increased with goods, and sees no need for anything else.

But what did Jesus say with respect to the answer of the Laodicean Church?

He described this Church, first of all, as *"wretched."* The word in the Greek refers to a test that has been given, and the one taking the test has failed.

Second, Christ called this Church *"miserable."* It means *"to be pitied."*

Third, He referred to it as *"poor,"* meaning that it literally was, at least in His eyes, a spiritual beggar.

Fourth, He called it *"blind."* The word, as used here, actually means *"to be lifted up in pride."*

Fifth, and last of all, He described it as *"naked."* It refers to being spiritually naked.

So, as is obvious, Jesus' summation of the Laodicean Church was not very positive. Considering that this Church characterizes the modern Church, i.e., refers to what the

Church is presently, the situation is dire indeed!

At the beginning of John's Vision, Christ is pictured as standing in the midst of the seven golden candlesticks, which represent, as stated, the Church. Now, He is no longer in the midst of the Churches, but rather is standing outside, knocking at the door, and saying, *"If any man hear My voice, and open the door, I will come in to him, and will sup with him, and he with Me"* (3:20).

The essence of that particular invitation shows that the Lord is no longer dealing with the institutionalized Church as a whole, but rather is dealing with individuals. While He has always dealt with individuals, now He is dealing <u>only</u> with individuals. This shows that the Church has completely apostatized, except for the Remnant who truly love the Lord (Rom. 9:27).

DECEMBER
25

*f*or unto you is born this day in the city of David a Saviour, which is Christ the Lord. And this shall be a sign unto you; You shall find the babe wrapped in swaddling clothes, lying in a manger. And suddenly there was with the Angel a multitude of the Heavenly Host praising God, and saying, Glory to God in the highest, and on Earth peace, good will toward men (Lk. 2:11-14).

Several things happened at the birth of Christ which were literally astounding. Some of them are as follows:

1. Beginning at about the time that Jesus was born and continuing for approximately 33 years, the great war gates of Janus in Rome were closed, signifying that there was no war anywhere in the Roman Empire during this particular time. This is the only time that such a thing happened, at least for such a period of time.

While the Romans may have given the credit for this peaceful situation to many and varied things, the real reason was that the Prince of Peace had come to this

Earth in the form of a baby. While He was here, war would come to a standstill. In fact, the Angel had cried, *"On Earth peace, good will toward men."* And that's exactly what happened.

When Jesus gave the Olivet Discourse, He told His Disciples that due to Israel's rejection of Him, Who Alone is the Prince of Peace, war would then become the mainstay of the Earth, with nation rising against nation, etc. (Mat. 24:6-8). And so it has been, from then until now.

Despite the great advancement of modern technology, the world still has not learned to live in peace, with more people being killed in wars in the Twentieth Century than at any other time in history. That will end when Jesus comes back, which He most definitely will.

2. The birth of Jesus took place at a public inn, crowded with people — so possible of public verification — and not in secret. Never was there such a wondrous birth, for it was God manifest in the flesh (Isa. 9:1-7).

3. When Caesar Augustus ordered a census to be taken, which was really a taxation, he understood not at all that he was fulfilling Bible Prophecy. Probably no one at that time, including Joseph and Mary, understood that this census was ordered of God so as to fulfill not only the prediction of the Forty-ninth Chapter of Genesis, but also that of Micah 5:2, and so secure the birth of the Holy Child at Bethlehem. Thus, God manifested His Wisdom.

Bethlehem was not the home of Mary and Joseph. So they had to go there, which this taxation demanded, because they were of the Tribe of Judah. This would fulfill the Prophecy of Micah that Jesus would be born in Bethlehem.

4. Sinless Angels and not sinful men first praised Him on coming to Earth, and yet the Angels needed no forgiveness.

5. When God manifest in the flesh came to Earth, there was no room for Him there. So much the more wonderful and perfect is the Love that brought Him thither. He began His Life in a manger, ended it on a Cross, and along His ministerial way had not where to lay His Head!

6. His birth was not trumpeted forth in lordly guise to Priests and Princes and the great ones of the Earth, but first of all to obscure shepherds — the lowest caste in society at that time.

7. Jesus was not to become a King and a Saviour. He was born both. He was The Saviour; He was Christ; He was Jehovah.

8. God's glory in Creation was high; in Revelation, higher; but in Redemption, highest. His Power was seen in Creation; His Righteousness, in Law; but His highest attribute, His Love, in Atonement (Lk. 2:14).

9. His Name was called "*Jesus.*" The word means "*Saviour.*" He might have chosen a loftier title, for the highest titles are His, but He passed them all by and selected a Name which speaks of deliverance for a lost world.

10. Jesus was made of a woman under the Law (Gal. 4:4). The fact is emphasized by His circumcision. The Law is mentioned five times in the Second Chapter of Luke, more often than in the rest of the Book, and so confirms the statement in Galatians. To save man, justly doomed to death by the Law, it was necessary that Christ should be born under the Law.

11. The Virgin Mary was not sinless. This is evidenced

by Luke 2:21-23 in conjunction with Leviticus 12:1-6.

12. The poverty of Joseph and Mary appears in their lowly offering of two pigeons in sacrifice at the presentation of baby Jesus. The Law stated that they should offer a *"lamb,"* but, if they didn't have the financial resources to do such, they could offer two pigeons (Lev. 12:8).

13. When Jesus was born, wise men from the east came and worshipped Him, even though He was only a baby at the time. They also presented Him with gifts. These wise men were more than likely from what we now refer to as *"Iraq."*

14. Last of all, it is almost certain that Jesus wasn't born on December 25. Flocks were out in the pastures in Israel from April through October. Some Bible Scholars believe that Jesus may have been born in October. It doesn't really matter what day He was born. What matters is that He was, in fact, born. If the Lord had wanted us to know, we would have been told the exact day.

Again, I quote the Angels:

"Glory to God in the highest, and on Earth peace, good will toward men" (Lk. 2:14).

DECEMBER
26

*t*o him who overcomes will I grant to sit with Me in My Throne, even as I also overcame, and am sat down with My Father in His Throne *(Rev. 3:21).*

In each one of the seven Messages of Christ to the seven Churches of Asia, the demand to be an overcomer is given and the reward is specified (2:7, 11, 17, 26; 3:5, 12, 21). Considering that this admonition is given seven times, it should be obvious that the Lord demands that the Believer be an overcomer.

So, the great question is, *"How does a person come to the place that the Lord would say that he or she is an overcomer?"*

Another question looms, *"What does it mean to be an overcomer?"*

First of all, the Believer must understand that, within himself, he cannot hope to arrive at this place and position which the Lord demands. Such is absolutely beyond the reach of any person, no matter who he might be, and we speak of the effort being made by the individual himself or herself. Regrettably, there are quite a few people who actually think they can do such, and who would conclude themselves to be overcomers, even though their effort is totally unbiblical. While they might refer to themselves as overcomers, the Lord, Whose decision Alone matters, doesn't say so. The Lord will declare a person to be an overcomer only on one premise.

For a Believer to attempt to be an overcomer by his own means, he must resort to Law, because that's the only place to go. He may not look at it as Law, and he may not think of it as Law, but, if it's not Grace, it's Law.

Concerning this, Paul said: *"Christ is become of no effect unto you, whosoever of you are justified by the Law* (who seek to be justified by the Law); *you are fallen from Grace"* (Gal. 5:4).

So, as should be obvious, there is no hope for the Believer down that path.

The only way that one can be an overcomer is God's Way, which is according to the following:

The Believer must place his Faith solely and completely in Christ and the Cross; he must get his eyes off himself and completely on Christ and what Jesus did for us in the Atonement, which will then give the Holy Spirit latitude to work in such a life. That person is then an overcomer, and so judged by the Lord (Rom. 6:1-14; 8:1-2, 11; I Cor. 1:17-18, 23; 2:2; Gal. 6:14).

Most all Believers look to themselves in trying to ascertain whether they are an overcomer or not. To be sure, when one looks at oneself, one will find flaws aplenty. So one must discontinue looking at oneself, and look exclusively to Christ and the Cross.

This definitely does not mean that we ignore the flaws and faults in our person. Not at all! But it does mean that we'll never get victory over these flaws and faults by our own machinations, even as religious as those machinations might be. The victory comes by faith, but it comes only by Faith anchored squarely in Christ and the Cross. If anything else is made the object of faith, that's when the victory stops, and stops instantly! The Holy Spirit will work in our hearts and lives, Who Alone can bring about these things, strictly on the basis of the Finished Work of Christ (Rom. 8:2). In other words, the Cross of Christ is what gives the Holy Spirit the legal right to do what He does.

Therefore, to be an overcomer, one has to place his faith solely in Christ and the Cross. When one does this, one is instantly judged by the Lord as an *"overcomer."* This is not something that one works toward, or gradually comes into, but is a place and position we have solely in Christ. He Alone is the Source, and the Cross is the means.

DECEMBER
27

*h*e who has an ear, let him hear what the Spirit says unto the Churches *(Rev. 2:7)*.

The Lord addressed the *"overcomer"* seven times; likewise, seven times He demands that we *"hear what the Spirit says unto the Churches."* One time would be significant; but considering that this Command is given seven times, I should think we would realize just how important it actually is.

That which the Spirit, i.e., *"the Holy Spirit,"* is saying to the Churches is found in the Word of God. If it's not found in the Word of God, then whatever is being said, and whoever is saying it, it is not the Holy Spirit. The Spirit of God will never go beyond the Word of God; in fact, He will always adhere strictly to the Word of God.

So why did Jesus give this admonition seven times?

He gave it seven times simply because of its vast significance. The problem with the modern Church, which has been the problem with the Church from the very beginning, is that it hears what men have to say, but not what the Spirit has to say. The utter absurdities that are taking place in the modern Church presently, i.e., worship, so-called; prayer, so-called; Church growth, so-called; all type of prophecies, so-called, all type of proposed manner of deliverances, which are, in fact, no deliverances at all; all, and without exception, at least of this nature, fall into the category of being unscriptural. If they are unscriptural, then the Spirit of God is not the One Who has directed this.

For instance, even though basically the entirety of the Church world has opted for *"The Purpose Driven Life"* philosophy, it is strictly of man and by man, which means it is not by the Lord. Although *"The Purpose Driven Life"* is a catchy title for a book, it's not what the Spirit of God is saying to the Churches. Neither is the *"Government of Twelve (G-12)"* debacle from the Lord. It also is man-birthed and man-instituted, which means it's not what the Spirit is saying to the Churches. You can say the same for the *"Word of Faith"* doctrine, which actually repudiates the Cross of Christ.

What, in fact, is the Spirit of God saying to the Churches?

The Message the Spirit of the Lord is promoting at present, that, in fact, which He has ever promoted, is *"Jesus Christ and Him Crucified"* (I Cor. 1:23). The Church has left the Cross; whenever the Church leaves the Cross, it goes into spiritual declension and all type of fanaticism.

When man fell in the very beginning, the Lord took man to the Cross (Gen., Chpt. 4). When the Lord began to carry out the provision of Redemption by calling a man to do so, namely Abraham, He took him to the Cross (Gen. 12:7). When the Law of Moses was given, the central theme of that Law was the Sacrificial System, which was, in effect, the Cross of Christ in symbol (Lev., Chpts. 1-7). When Jesus finally came to this world, His goal, His destination, was the Cross (Isa., Chpt. 53). When the Church was established by the Apostle Paul under the guidance of Jesus Christ, it was established on the Foundation of the Cross (I Cor. 2:2).

The Cross of Christ is the Word of God, as the Word of God is the Cross of Christ. That's what the Spirit is saying to the Churches!

DECEMBER
28

*a*nd there came one of the seven Angels which had the *seven Vials, and talked with me, saying unto me, Come hither; and I will show unto you the judgment of the great whore who sits upon many waters: With whom the kings of the Earth have committed fornication, and the inhabitants of the Earth have been made drunk with the wine of her fornication* (Rev. 17:1-2).

Who is this *"great whore who sits upon many waters"*?

In the first place, the term *"many waters"* speaks of vast numbers of people (17:15). The *"great whore,"* which is the name given by the Holy Spirit, pertains to every false religion which has ever existed, irrespective as to what it is. It is that which has been devised by men as a substitute for *"Jesus Christ and Him Crucified."* God's Way is Christ and Him Crucified, and that alone!

The *"many waters"* are symbolic of many people and pertain to the bondage in which religion places people. In fact, all religion, in one way or the other, is filled with superstition. As a result, it always places hardship on people and provides absolutely nothing for them spiritually. So when the Holy Spirit tagged religion as the *"great whore,"* there could be no more perfect description. Religion, it might be said, sells itself to the highest bidder.

Down through the many centuries, even millennia, of the past ages, kings and leaders of nations have either developed a State Church or they have given over their nation in its entirety to various gods, so-called — something which was prevalent in Bible times. In fact, during Old Testament times, Israel was the only monotheistic nation in the world (worshipers of one God, Who is Jehovah), while all the other nations of the world were polytheistic (worshipers of many gods). Submission to these various heathenistic gods involved everything from human sacrifice to temple prostitution, etc.

In the Middle Ages, the Catholic Church, which literally was the State Church in many countries, forced individuals, upon pain of death, to work for little or nothing in the building of their giant cathedrals. Many people were used as virtual slaves.

So, when the Holy Spirit labeled these various religious systems as the *"great whore,"* it was, and is, an apt description.

Another example is the religion of Islam. Nations which are ruled by Islam are some of the most poverty stricken in the world. There are approximately 300 million Arabs in the Middle East in the nations of Islam which make up that region, but the gross national product of all of these nations combined is only $60 billion, which is less than the one nation of Spain. While a few of the

Arabs are obscenely rich, the rest are in dire poverty, and also have very few freedoms. And all because of the religion of Islam! Most of the people in that religion live in a form of virtual slavery.

A further example is India. The people from India are exceptionally bright, having the ability to do just about anything they so desire as far as technology, etc.; however, the nation is kept down because of the religion of Hinduism. The people worship rats, snakes, etc. If the truth be known, the majority of the problems in the world are caused by superstitious religion, which is of Satan. Once again, the appellative of *"great whore"* is apt.

Personally, I also think it would be proper to refer to much of what passes for *"Christianity"* as part of the *"great whore."* To be blunt, if it's not the Gospel of Jesus Christ, which is *"Christ and Him Crucified,"* then, in some way or another, it is a spurious gospel and should be labeled exactly as all the other religions. Christianity without *"Christ and Him Crucified"* is reduced to a mere philosophy. As such, it falls under the same category as all others, i.e., *"The Great Whore."*

DECEMBER
29

*a*nd after these things I saw another Angel come down from Heaven, having great power; and the Earth was lightened with his glory. And he cried mightily with a strong voice, saying, Babylon the great is fallen, is fallen, and is become the habitation of devils, and the hold of every foul spirit, and a cage of every unclean and hateful bird. For all nations have drunk of the wine of the wrath of her fornication, and the kings of the Earth have committed fornication with her, and the merchants of the Earth are waxed rich through the abundance of her delicacies. And I heard another voice from Heaven, saying, Come out of her, My people, that you be not partakers of her sins, and that you receive not of her plagues. For her sins have reached unto Heaven, and God has remembered her iniquities (Rev. 18:1-5).

There are two major cities in the Bible: Jerusalem and Babylon. The True Messiah and His City, Jerusalem, contrast with the false messiah and his city, Babylon. These two cities represent, respectively, the True Plan of God and false religion. All the idolatries, both ancient and modern, originated in Babylon.

As an example, under the ancient mysteries and in the east presently, this Satanic worship was addressed to the phallus (the man's male member). This is one of the reasons why the Scriptures so frequently speak of it as an abomination. Although it was philosophically held to honor the Creator and to promote the population of the Earth, yet its effect was to depopulate whole countries and produce desolation. This was probably the hateful form of idolatry commanded by Nebuchadnezzar described in Daniel, Chapter 3.

The first organized rebellion against God was carried forth in Babylon, in the building of the Tower of Babel, described in Genesis, Chapter 11. This Eighteenth Chapter of Revelation describes the destruction of a rebuilt Babylon. The construction to rebuild Babylon will begin soon, and the destruction will soon follow.

The United States is presently fighting a war, the war against terrorism, that I'm afraid it little understands. It has relegated the danger, that which caused the destruction of 9/11/01, to a few fanatics; however, the real cause is the religion of Islam, which our governmental leaders are loathe to admit. For instance, we are attempting to install democracy in Iraq. This may be a noble gesture, but the religion of Islam and democracy have no meeting ground whatsoever. Philosophically speaking, they are not even on the same planet.

But yet, the presence of the United States in Iraq may very well have prophetical overtones in setting the stage for the rebuilding of this system, or city, or both! Considering the times in which we live, that is probably correct. It's later than we think.

Iraq is mentioned in the Bible a great deal. It went under the names of *"Shinar," "Babylon,"* and *"Mesopotamia."* It is believed that the Garden of Eden was situated in the exact spot where ancient Babylon came to be built. If that is the case, and it probably is, this means that man was created by God in Iraq, and the first temptation, which resulted in the Fall, came in Iraq; also, the first Sacrifice was offered, by Abel, in Iraq (Gen. Chpt. 4).

It is believed that Noah lived in Iraq and that he built the Ark in Iraq. When Israel, the Northern Kingdom, was destroyed, it was by the Assyrian Empire, which was in Iraq. When Judah was destroyed some 133 years later, it also was destroyed by the Babylonian Empire.

Daniel wrote the Book in the Bible that bears his name in Iraq. Esther falls into the same category. The Tower of Babel was constructed in Iraq. The fiery furnace episode involving the three Hebrew children took place in Iraq. So did the episode of Daniel in the lions' den. It is believed that the three wise men who came to visit baby Jesus were from Iraq.

The first organized rebellion against God, the Tower of Babel, took place in Iraq. The last organized rebellion against God will take place in Babylon, as outlined in Revelation, Chapter 18. The first rebellion was confounded by God with the changing of languages; the last rebellion will be completely destroyed by God.

As we stated earlier in this devotion, the presence of the United States in present day Iraq could well be the beginning of the end. Jesus is coming soon!

DECEMBER
30

*a*nd I saw Heaven opened, and behold a white horse; and He Who sat upon him was called Faithful and True, and in Righteousness He does judge and make war. His eyes were as a flame of fire, and on His Head were many crowns; and He had a Name written that no man knew, but He Himself. And He was clothed with a vesture dipped in Blood: and His Name is called The Word of God. And the armies which were in Heaven followed Him upon white horses, clothed in fine linen, white and clean (Rev. 19:11-14).

The Scriptures just given describe the Second Coming. As someone has well said:

"When Jesus came the first time, He was ridiculed, lambasted, criticized, and greatly opposed. They plucked the beard from His Face, put a crown of thorns upon His Head, and beat Him unmercifully. They nailed Him to a Cross and mocked Him while He died — died for them!

"But when Jesus comes the second time, it will not be to be beaten, spit upon, and nailed to a tree. He rather will come in

887

such Power and Glory as the world has never known before. He will come as King of kings and Lord of lords."

That day, to be sure, will come.

His *"vesture dipped in blood"* portrays the price that He paid at Calvary's Cross in order that mankind might be saved. According to the Prophet Zechariah, Jesus will wear the marks of His Crucifixion forever and forever, the marks in His Hands and Feet (Zech. 13:6). It is the Cross which has made, and will make, the Second Coming possible.

Satan was defeated at the Cross, plus all of his minions of darkness (Col. 2:14-15). For reasons known only to the Lord, he has been allowed to continue for this last 2,000 years. But when Jesus comes the second time, Satan and all his hordes of darkness are going to be placed in the bottomless pit, unable to wreak their torture and horror any more (Rev. 20:1-3).

At the Second Coming, the world will begin a thousand years of peace and prosperity such as it has never known before (Rev. 20:4-6). Christ will rule the world at that time, and do so with a justice, fairness, and right government such as the world has never seen before (Isa. 9:1-7; 11:1-10). Because of this Perfect Government under Christ, which means there will be no more graft, bribery, stealing, etc., the world will know prosperity as it has never known before. Poverty will be no more. Sickness will be no more, because the great Healer of the ages will be present among men.

Israel will now be restored, because she will accept Christ as her Saviour, Lord, and Messiah. Then the great Promises made to the Patriarchs and Prophets of old will be brought to total fulfillment. The great question asked by His Disciples, *"Lord, will You at this time restore again the Kingdom to Israel?"*, will then be answered and the Kingdom will be restored (Acts 1:6).

With Christ, every Saint of God who has ever lived, all the way from Abel until the conclusion of the Great Tribulation (which will conclude the First Resurrection of Life), will rule and reign with Christ for that thousand years, and then finally forever (Rev. 20:4).

Israel is God's prophetic time clock. Looking at this tiny nation, we know that the *"fig tree is putting forth leaves and that summer is nigh."* Then Jesus said, *"So likewise, when you shall see all these things, know that it is near, even at the doors"* (Mat. 24:32-33).

DECEMBER
31

*a*nd he showed me a pure river of Water of Life, clear as crystal, proceeding out of the Throne of God and of the Lamb (Rev. 22:1).

The last two Chapters of Revelation portray a world that is totally free of sin of any type or description, totally free of Satan, all demon spirits, and all fallen angels, and totally free of those who will not serve the Lord. All those in that capacity are in the Lake of Fire; there they will remain forever and forever (Rev. 20:10-15). God the Father will then actually change His Headquarters from planet Heaven to planet Earth.

The Scripture says, "*Behold, the Tabernacle of God is with men, and He will dwell with them, and they shall be His People, and God Himself shall be with them, and be their God*" (Rev. 21:3).

And yet, some seven times the title "*Lamb,*" which refers to Christ, is given in the last two Chapters of Revelation.

Why would that be necessary, considering that there is

no more sin and destruction?

The very name *"Lamb"* implies the Crucifixion, the Redemption, the great price that was paid for Salvation. The Holy Spirit used the title *"Lamb,"* referring to Christ, some seven times in these last two Chapters, in order that all may know that all of this which is listed — all this glory, beauty, grandeur, and eternal life — were all made possible by the price paid at Calvary's Cross by our Lord and Saviour, Jesus Christ. This must never be forgotten!

The seven occasions of the mention of the *"Lamb"* in the last two Chapters are as follows:

1. *"And there came unto me one of the seven Angels which had the seven vials full of the seven last plagues, and talked with me, saying, Come hither, I will show you the Bride, the Lamb's wife"* (Rev. 21:9): This speaks of the New Jerusalem, which will be inhabited by every Believer, made possible by what Jesus did at the Cross.

2. *"And the wall of the city had twelve foundations, and in them the names of the Twelve Apostles of the Lamb"* (Rev. 21:14): The Twelve Apostles chosen by Christ were able to be what they were, and have what they now possess, all because of what Christ did at the Cross.

3. *"And I saw no Temple therein: for the Lord God Almighty and the Lamb are the Temple of it"* (Rev. 21:22): There will actually be a Temple in the New Jerusalem, but not one used for worship. The Presence of the Lord will be everywhere, and worship will continue uninterrupted eternally. This is all made possible by what Christ did at the Cross.

4. *"And the city had no need of the sun, neither of the moon, to shine in it: for the Glory of God did lighten it, and the*

Lamb is the light thereof" (Rev. 21:23): Jesus is the Light of the world, and now that Light can shine to such a degree that it will make the planetary bodies seem insignificant by comparison. This too is made possible by the Cross.

5. *"And there shall in no wise enter into it anything that defiles, neither whatsoever works abomination, or makes a lie: but they which are written in the Lamb's Book of Life"* (Rev. 21:27): Every Believer has his name written in this wonderful *"Lamb's Book of Life,"* all made possible by the Cross.

6. *"And He showed me a pure river of Water of Life, clear as crystal, proceeding out of the Throne of God and of the Lamb"* (Rev. 22:1): This is made possible by the Cross!

7. *"And there shall be no more curse: but the Throne of God and of the Lamb shall be in it; and His servants shall serve Him"* (Rev. 22:3): Jesus answered the curse at the Cross of Calvary (Gal. 3:13).

Our Lord being referred to as *"The Lamb"* seven times in the last two Chapters of Revelation tells us that what He did at Calvary made possible a perfect Salvation for all who will believe. It will never have to be amended in any form, hence the Apostle Paul referring to it as *"The Everlasting Covenant"* (Heb. 13:20).

"Behold the Lamb of God, Who takes away the sin of the world" (Jn. 1:29).

And so He did!